"This book is a needed addition to the fields of communication and theology for both the university and the local church. The family is the central foundation of any society but is often damaged and in need of repair. The authors share hopeful and practical solutions for all the various relationships in the family unit with a strong biblical worldview. I recommend this book for pastors, youth workers, parents, and university students."

—**Jeff Baxter, DMin**, Next Gen Pastor, Mission Hills Church

"With important assumptions about the goodness of God and the blessedness of family, Pettigrew and Badzinski provide a truly helpful book, rich with specificity and the wisdom of the ages. Its anchor in Western tradition and grounding in the living God help make this volume shine. This book will be a gift to all its readers."

—**Stephanie Bennett**, PhD, Director of Wordship, Professor of Communication and Media Ecology, Palm Beach Atlantic University

"As a pastor, I deeply appreciate the influence and impact that family communication and connection can have on a person's faith, self-image, relationships, and witness for God. This book marries biblical and scholarly principles to provide insights for pastors, parents, families, and students who seek to understand and improve their relationships and awareness of how to encourage, challenge, and reinforce familial relationships."

—**Michael Dally**, Senior Pastor, Gateway Christian Church

"At a time when family dynamics are complicated, life and work are chaotic, and research shows most people say they've never felt more exhausted, I am thrilled for students to engage with the strategies, theories, and research provided by this text."

—**Heather Thompson Day**, PhD, Author, *It's Not Your Turn*

"God designed the family to reflect the fellowship and unity of the Trinity and point to the goodness of rightly ordered relationships. In this age where confusion reigns on what the family is, the importance of family in the social order, and how families best relate, scholar-teachers Pettigrew and Badzinski explicate God's intentions for family, engage thoroughly with modern scholarship using multiple theoretical perspectives, and call

all of us to more effective (and loving) engagement in the most important relationships in our lives."

—**Ryan T. Hartwig**, PhD, Provost & Vice President for Academic Affairs, Vanguard University

"This book promises to deal with the 'messy realities of family communication,' and as a professor, husband, and father of four sons, I can say that the authors deliver. They also introduce the hope of the redeeming nature of God's design for our life journey together with family. With a helpful balance of diverse theories, research findings, and practical applications, the authors allow those of us using this book to fully engage the mind, the spirit, and our own experiences. They provide a vast array of secular and sacred sources to bring a complete and thorough picture of the essential role of communication in the important context of the family. In the end, we are given the gift of helping us clarify our imperfect relationships and communication to make our families a better reflection of what God has intended. This book finds itself successfully at the intersection of faith integration and the scholarship of family communication to the benefit of us all."

—**Chris M. Leland**, PhD, Professor and Chair of Communication, Azusa Pacific University

"Family communication has never been more challenging. Thankfully, Pettigrew and Badzinski have written this book to help family professionals and students understand the landscape of theory and practical application. Integrating social science theory and biblical perspectives into a myriad of topics, this resource covers different approaches to building stronger families through communication. This is an appropriate choice for psychologists, social workers, upper-level college students, and laypeople who help families through conflict, forgiveness, and resilience in light of current research and biblical approaches."

—**Elizabeth W. McLaughlin**, PhD, Professor of Communication, Bethel University, Indiana

"The greatest compliment I can give is that I've already adopted this text for my advanced class on family communication. Like you, I look forward to learning and putting their ideas into practice." (from the Foreword)

—**Tim Muehlhoff**, PhD, Professor of Communication, Biola University

"Understanding and doing family is a struggle. Pettigrew and Badzinski recognize that family has changed drastically, creating confusion and uncertainty that add to the struggle. However, the authors combine factual data, biblical truth, and practical communication principles to provide a clear picture of what God intended the family to be and do. God bless you for reasserting the importance, design, and value of family in American culture!"

—**William L. Mullen**, PhD, Chair and Professor of Communication Studies, Shorter University

"This excellent text arrives on the scene at a time when many families are in a downward spiral, offering hope for redemptive communication in one of the most challenging contexts. As both an educator and a coach, I'm grateful for the authors' theoretical depth and research-based recommendations, all grounded in the life-giving truth of Scripture. Bravo!"

—**Heidi Petak**, PhD, Communication Strategies, SpeakEagle.com

"This book marvelously shows how important families have always been for the flourishing of human beings. It also reveals how familial relationships can become broken and be repaired. By focusing on family communication from a biblical perspective, the authors make a major contribution to the literature. Engagingly written for college students, pastors, and parents alike."

—**Quentin Schultze**, PhD, Professor of Communication Emeritus, Calvin University

"With Scripture, social science, and family theory, Pettigrew and Badzinski offer a robust blend of sources to develop a nuanced understanding of family communication. The authors rely on troubled families depicted in Scripture to show patterns of struggle and redemption and offer practical tips for contemporary couples and kids. The authors present no white-picket-fence, *Father-Knows-Best* idealism but remain true to an evangelical posture towards marriage and family. Suitable for upper level undergraduate and graduate students in communication, sociology, and psychology at Christ-centered liberal arts institutions."

—**Bill Strom**, PhD, Professor of Media + Communication, Trinity Western University

"Pettigrew and Badzinski's text fills a large gap in the available texts discussing family communication, performing an important service for students and professors. For students, the diverse number of theories discussed provide a solid foundation for further inquiry. For professors, the text offers a high-quality survey of the literature to encourage discussion in their classes. Deftly pulling together several threads of thought that are frequently in tension, Pettigrew and Badzinski gently demonstrate how the practical biblical wisdom found in the Christian Bible can enrich and texture our study and practice of communication within families."

—**Joel S. Ward**, PhD, Associate Professor of Communication, Geneva College

Family Communication
and the Christian Faith

Family Communication and the Christian Faith

An Introduction and Exploration

JONATHAN PETTIGREW AND
DIANE M. BADZINSKI

Integratio Press
Pasco, Washington

FAMILY COMMUNICATION AND THE CHRISTIAN FAITH
An Introduction and Exploration

Integratio Press
An Imprint of Christianity and Communication Studies Network
11503 Easton Dr.
Pasco, WA 99301

www.theccsn.com

Cover design: caroloc.com
Interior design: caroloc.com
Image: Depositphotos

PAPERBACK ISBN: 978-1-959685-00-5
EBOOK ISBN: 978-1-959685-01-2

Library of Congress Control Number: 2022950127

Dedication

To all who strive for godly families; to those awakened by the
Holy Spirit to care about God's intentions and his heart for family.

JP
DMB

Instructor's Resources available at:

https://www.theccsn.com/
integratio-press-family-communication-instructor-resources/

Table of Contents

List of Figures

List of Points to Ponder

List of Application Activities

Acknowledgements

WE PRINCIPALLY ACKNOWLEDGE OUR GOD, who shares with us his amazing capacity for relationships, families, and communication—*soli Deo gloria*.

We also recognize our own families who have given us plenty of experiences—good and bad, but mostly good—to better relate to the scholarship we have covered about family communication. Our experiences have shaped our understandings of what makes families work. Our families also have given us the raw material from which to derive our own models and theories of family interaction. To Toviah, Talya, Eliora, Azariah, and Lizanne, I (Jonathan) continue to enjoy and experience more of both parenting and childhood from each of you, experiencing love in fuller measure each day. To my dearest wife, Breanne, I can only say that life with you is full and fun! Thanks for all you mean to me. To Jon, and our children Alyssa, Luke, and Hannah, I (Diane) am grateful beyond words for the love and beauty you bring to my life. To my parents and siblings, thank you for the many ways you show me what it means to be family.

This book project also has benefited from several who have offered helpful feedback and wise council along the way. Though we cannot list them all, we are especially grateful to Douglas Kelley, Arielle Leonard, Tim Muehlhoff, Quentin Schultze, Greg Smalley, Bill Strom, and Robert H. Woods Jr., as well as anonymous reviewers. Your suggestions and comments made this text better. We feel that you exemplify the Scripture that "two are better than one" (Eccl. 4:1) and that "the first to speak seems right, until someone comes forward and cross-examines" (Prov. 18:17). We sincerely appreciate the refinement that your contributions have achieved.

Additionally, we owe gratitude to Colorado Christian University (CCU) students Paige Lier, for her work on the instructor's manual, and Sierra Peissner, for her careful and gracious review of the text. A special note of appreciation is also extended to CCU's library staff for their research support throughout the project.

Finally, we are grateful for Robert H. Woods Jr. and his team at Integratio Press. Thank you for publishing our book and for your editorial oversight throughout the process. In a society that increasingly cancels orthodox voices in favor of political expedience, we are grateful for your foresight to develop a press that supports quality scholarly materials from a Christian faith-integration perspective. May this book, and others in your press, serve the next generation of Christian educators!

Foreword

IF YOU COULD REQUIRE only *one* course that every college student should take, what would it be? A class on philosophy, ethics, art, world history, or government? I have no doubt that scholars from each field of study could offer powerful arguments. People need to learn to think correctly, asserts the philosopher, while a historian offers a paraphrase of George Santayana, *those who don't learn from history are doomed to repeat it.*

Perry L. Glanzer—professor of Educational Foundations and a resident scholar with Baylor Institute for Studies of Religion—offers an interesting option: a mandatory course on marriage and family. Perry argues that if polled, college students worldwide would list marriage and family as a crucial aspect of living a good life and the key to personal happiness! Sadly, a mandatory course on marriage and family is not required. Thus, graduates from colleges and universities across the world never learn how to form a healthy marriage or family. "The lack of a required course on romantic friendships, marriage, and family," asserts Perry, "is likely one of the reasons that contemporary students' knowledge about what contributes to a successful marriage and family is so pathetic."[1]

According to Perry, what students most need is knowledge about marriage and family and practical tools for implementing what they learn.

When I first moved to southern California, I wanted to put up a basketball hoop on our garage so that my three sons could practice. The problem was, I did not have the foggiest idea how to do it. I called a friend to help. "Grab your tools and get it done," my friend suggested. I sheepishly walked out of my house with the only thing I had—my wife's *Do It Herself Tool Kit* that contained a mini-hammer, screwdriver, tape measure, plyers, and scissors. That's it! I'll never forget my friend's response, "We can't do this job with those tools."

Constructing a healthy marriage and family is vastly more complex that putting up a basketball hoop. Yet, most who try it will have equally inadequate knowledge or relational tools. What most excites me about the book you are about to read is that authors Jonathan Pettigrew and Diane Badzinski provide what educators call *praxis*—the combining of theory and practice. Each warrants a quick word.

The information you'll encounter comes from the fields of communication theory, psychology, marriage and family therapy, and spiritual formation. You'll encounter thinkers and practitioners both within and outside the Christian tradition. The authors hold to the idea that—via common grace—God has saturated our world with information that helps us navigate a fallen world often filled with broken relationships (Ps. 145). Common grace means that God gives this information to everyone—including scholars who don't hold to our faith. The great traveling preacher John Wesley rightly notes that "to imagine no one can teach you but those who are themselves saved from sin is a very great and dangerous mistake. Give not place to it for a moment."[2] The authors don't fall prey to this mistake, and you'll read the best experts and up-to-date research on marriage and family from both a religious and non-religious perspective. If what you read is true and doesn't contradict Scripture, then we know that gift of knowledge comes from the Giver of Gifts himself (James. 1:17).

The authors don't just stop with theory, but also augment it with tools that readers can use in their own relationships. For example, in the chapter on conflict, you'll learn signs of conflict—harsh start-ups, defensiveness, flooding, failed repair attempts, negative body language—but also, most importantly, how to address conflict through time-tested tools like the speaker-listener technique. What makes this text unique is that the authors are not afraid to address an area that many fail to consider—spiritual battle. Almost 20% of everything Jesus said had to do with spiritual battle. The Apostle John goes so far as to assert that the entire world has been deeply influenced by the evil one (1 Jn. 5:19). Yet, most Christian books on conflict or relationships merely give it a perfunctory nod, if not neglecting it entirely. Not so with the text you are about to read. While the authors understand that all conflict cannot be blamed on evil forces, they equally recognize that if anger is not properly addressed, it can give the devil a foothold in your life and relationships (Eph. 4:26–27). No doubt, sections like this will challenge you intellectually and spiritually. Don't shy away from these parts, but rather lean in through study and prayer.

For the past few years, I've not only taught communication courses, but also have served as the co-director of the Winsome Conviction Project, which seeks to reintroduce compassion, empathy, and civility into our disagreements. In today's argument culture—a term coined by Georgetown linguist Deborah Tannen[3]—we approach each other as adversaries. Sadly, this attitude has crept into relationships with those closest to us. I'm sure many of you can resonate with family relationships strained, or even fractured, by disagreements over politics, religion, and other pressing social issues. What gives me hope is that scholars like Pettigrew and Badzinski not only take their faith seriously, but also have spent a lifetime studying this complex issue and offer solutions rooted in both research and the Scriptures.

The greatest compliment I can give is that I've already adopted this text for my advanced class on family communication. Like you, I look forward to learning and putting Pettigrew and Badzinski's ideas into practice.

Tim Muehlhoff, PhD
Professor of Communication, Biola University
Author, *Defending Your Marriage: The Reality of Spiritual Battle*
Co-director, Winsome Conviction Project

Authors' Note: What Do We Mean by "Christian Faith"?

IN A RELIGION THAT HAS HUNDREDS of denominations and thousands of viewpoints, how can we even hope to write something that rings true for the "Christian Faith"? As doctoral-level social scientists, we acknowledge the pluralism of forms and interpretations that comprise Christianity in America. Yet, as those who have spent a lifetime studying the Bible, learning from Christian authors, digesting and analyzing sermons, and experiencing a personal and developing relationship with God through Christ and the Holy Spirit, we are convinced that for mature Christians there is grace to accept others and glean from their teachings. Even when we disagree with someone's conclusions, we can learn from their perspectives and reasoning. We invite you to do the same. We believe that some of the variations in Christian practice are minor, preferential, or historical. For those that are more substantial, we believe that there is room for hearing out others' arguments, evaluating their evidence, and considering their conclusions by reconciling them with Scripture under the guidance of the Holy Spirit. Such maturity, in essence, discerns and tests the truth (see 1 Thess. 5:19–22). In that spirit, we offer this textbook. To further clarify our perspective, we share our fundamental assumptions about what it means to be Christian and what we believe about the Bible.

Without offering a theological statement of beliefs, we simply strive to represent what could be considered "mere Christianity," with a nod to the influential book of that title by C. S. Lewis.[1] By this we mean that our views accord with Christianity's most basic tenets: God created the world; sin came through human disobedience to God's command, generating both a universal and an intrinsic need for a Savior; Jesus Christ, a real, historic figure, came as God's only begotten Son to redeem mankind from sin and its curse. Like the ancient Apostles' Creed, we affirm Jesus Christ was "born of the virgin Mary, suffered under Pontius Pilate, was crucified, died, and was buried; he descended to hell and, the third day he rose again from the dead; he ascended to heaven and is seated at the right hand of God the Father almighty. From there he will come to judge the living and the dead."[2] This basis forms our fundamental Christian theology. While we assume these to be true, other resources lay out an apology for the reasonableness of these beliefs. For example, *Cold-Case Christianity* by J. Warner Wallace and *The Case for Christ* by Lee Strobel both share autobiographical investigations of atheists-turned-Christians along with the evidence that persuaded them to convert.[3] For us, presenting a Christian perspective on family communication is grounded in this confession.

We also aim to integrate biblical wisdom. The Bible is an incredible book that shares history, philosophy, poetry, prophecy, and much more. We believe that the Bible is God's inspired Word and we aim to interpret it faithfully. Our own views on biblical hermeneutics are informed by works like Howard G. and William D. Hendricks's *Living by the Book* or Kay Arthur's text *How to Study Your Bible*, which lays out an inductive Bible study method.[4] Interpreting text is one skill that was reinforced by our doctoral training, although not from a Christian standpoint. While we include many examples from scientific studies, theological reflections, and our own ideas and experiences, we also incorporate passages from the Bible and our analysis of it for several reasons. First, the Bible is God's primary revelation to us. It shares who God is, who we are as members of humanity, how we relate to God, and his plan of redemption. It is true. Every word is tested. It is flawless (Prov. 30:5). Second, the word of God is also divinely powerful (Heb. 4:12; 2 Cor. 4:10; Rom. 1:16; Eph. 6:17). Our words and thoughts—all the books and philosophies in the world—will pass away, but what God says is timeless. Plus, the Holy Spirit of God enlivens the word of God for all people and situations. As expressed in Isaiah 40:8, "Grasses wither and flowers fade, but the word of the Lord stands forever." Another reason is that drawing on Scripture gives us all a common reference point. You can examine the passages we quote and our exegeses of them. You can decide if what we say rings true for your understanding of the Bible. If you think differently (and we are sure there are many faithful Christians from various denominations and backgrounds who do), then you can take that to God in your own reading of his word to process it with him. You can juxtapose our interpretations with doctrinal or theological literature. We believe God will make himself clear and teach you himself from his word (Phil. 3:15). Thus, by pointing you to the Bible, we are inviting you to learn directly from God and surpass us as teachers. Here is how the Psalmist put it: "I have more insight than all my teachers, for I meditate on your statutes" (Ps. 119:99).

These attributes of the Bible—its veracity, persistence, and power—are not exclusively demonstrated in the Bible's testimony about itself, but they are witnessed throughout generations by countless martyrs who staked their lives on this claim. Most had nothing to gain and everything to lose by their confession. Since the days of Jesus, millions have been tortured and killed, all the while confidently holding to their belief in God and his word. Classic and contemporary testimonies of martyrs are catalogued in books like *Jesus Freaks: Stories of Those Who Stood for Jesus* by D. C. Talk in collaboration with Voice of the Martyrs.[5] To represent a Christian perspective throughout this text, we draw from the Bible and share our own and others' interpretations of it.

Our approach, then, seeks to integrate contemporary scholarship with timeless biblical wisdom that aligns with the fundamental tenets of Christianity. We recognize that some of the positions we affirm in this book are debated, both within society as well as within Christianity. Our goal is not necessarily to debunk or discredit other views, but to present our perspective with supporting evidence from Scripture and scholarship. At different points in this book we acknowledge a diversity of perspectives while simultaneously presenting our own views on the topics.

A central theme, or assumption, that runs throughout the text and helps capture our perspective is this: God's design for society, family, and individuals is good. Yet, the reality we observe and experience is riddled with selfishness, trauma, and pain that diverge from God's good design. We explain this divergence simply as a result of "the Fall"—the introduction of sin into the world and human systems (see Gen. 3). Nevertheless, we live in hope that we can attain the ideals of God's good design through his enabling grace and redemption. We attempt to hold in tension the reality and the ideal, under grace. We invite you to do the same across the variety of human and family communication experiences.

Why Write This Textbook?

With our assumptions about Christianity and the Bible clear, the aim of this book is to integrate our expertise in communication, knowledge of the social sciences (e.g., sociology, psychology, human development, family studies), and our understanding of the Bible and theological reflections.

This text is designed to introduce relevant theories and research, to encourage thoughtful, integrative Christianity, and especially to improve family communication for readers. We strive to weave together concepts that are just as relevant to the church pulpit as they are to the university pupil. We hope that this book will help you to develop informed attitudes and habits that will sustain godly and rewarding family experiences throughout your lives.

One common misconception about the Christian family is that it should be perfect, look perfect, and act perfectly. Unfortunately, this misses the point of Christianity. Consider this: God created everything, and everything God created was good (Gen. 1:1, 31). All things were created to live together in harmony with God, nature, and each other—including the family. We were placed in a perfect world. So what happened? Sin entered the world when humans disobeyed God. From that point on, the world was no longer perfect. We struggle now. We realize that life is not perfect, and neither are our relationships. This makes it totally irrational, even harmful, to expect perfection from ourselves and from others. Families are not perfect, and the ways in which we communicate with each other are not perfect either.

We recognize this relational imperfection. At the same time, we know that the theories and research in family communication and in Christian Scripture and theology have identified ways for creating and maintaining strong and vibrant (albeit imperfect) family relationships. This text was birthed from our desire to share this work with our readers. We offer practical, theologically-sound, research-based strategies for building great family relationships. We know that God designed the family and that the family is fundamental to our understanding of theology and relationships. Family life blesses the young through positive, loving socialization, but it also encompasses elder care, brings individual mental and emotional benefits, and creates a place for developing identity and meaning, sharing culture and values. Family—imperfect as it is—matters.

Structure of the Book

Our book is primarily informed by academic sources and our own experiences that examine families in the United States. Most of the empirical studies and reviews that we use were conducted in the United States. Similarly, our views on theology and Christianity are largely shaped by Western thought. Even though Christianity originated in the Eastern, Jewish culture (see, for example, Marvin R. Wilson's *Our Father Abraham: Jewish Roots of the Christian Faith*), and we believe it is universal in the sense that it is for all people and all times, our own experiences with it are culturally grounded.[6] Many of the sources and theological reflections from which we draw are also based in Western thought. While some of the topics, theories, and philosophies we share may apply in other contexts, the scope of our work is most relevant to the United States. *Family Communication and the Christian Faith* is divided into three parts.

Part I: Definitions and Perspectives

Definitions and Perspectives provides foundational information that frames our exploration of family. We want our readers to understand what it looks like to take a Christian perspective to the study of family communication, and why it matters. We start with a brief chapter including four primary assumptions that construct a framework for understanding family communication from a Christian perspective. In Chapter 2, we examine definitions of family, arguing that the way we choose to define family is important. Next, we address the role of family in society. Chapter 3 presents a model of social organization for understanding family communication in context and identifies societal trends related to family. Finally, Chapter 4 introduces the notion of theory, demonstrating how theory is an interpretive lens for understanding family dynamics. Four broad perspectives on family (systems, narrative, relational dialectics, and developmental), alongside Christian models that frame our understanding of all human interaction, are presented.

Part II: Functional Family Communication

Functional Family Communication presents five major categories of communication tasks that all families face. We present practical ways for connecting with one another (Chapter 5), managing conflicts (Chapter 6), offering and receiving forgiveness (Chapter 7), building resilience (Chapter 8), and taking care of the business side of family life (Chapter 9). This section begins with looking at rituals for connection and covers topics such as making listening a lifestyle, employing relationship maintenance behaviors, and communicating in one another's love language. After exploring ways of creating rituals for growing family relationships, we move into rules for conflict in families and discuss topics including the causes of conflict, types of conflict, signs of conflict, and ways for handling conflict that honor God. We recognize that hurt and misunderstanding are unavoidable, and thus we address research on types of hurtful messages and responses to them with emphasis on relational repair and forgiveness. We then turn to discuss strategies for coping with family stress and building resilience. Olson's Circumplex Model of Effective Family Function and theories of stress provide a framework for how communication works in managing adversity and creating resilience. This section ends with a chapter devoted to everyday tasks associated with doing life together, including budgeting, household chores, and managing technology in families.

Part III: Communication through Different Family Stages

Communication through Different Family Stages approaches specific time frames of family experience. It begins with three chapters devoted to courtship and marital interaction. Chapter 10 explores pathways to marriage. It includes the psychological, biological, and sociological forces that impact how people enter romantic relationships, and it considers how communication is involved in different relationship stages. Next, Chapter 11 explores marriage as a covenant, with a focus on sexual communication in marriage. Chapter 12 then looks at marital communication dynamics, including topics such as relational violence and divorce. This chapter concludes by listing practical strategies for developing strong marriages. The next two chapters center on parent-child interaction. No doubt, the introduction of children into family impacts the system in complex and wonderful ways. Chapters 13 and 14 cover various theories and models related to parenting and offer a biblical case for disciplining in ways that reflect and honor God. Finally, we conclude the book by presenting the topic of family legacy and review ways in which families leave behind financial, spiritual, and relational blessings.

Who Wrote This Textbook?

We thought you might like to know a little bit about us, the authors of *Family Communication and the Christian Faith*.

Jonathan Pettigrew

I studied psychology for my bachelor's degree at a small state school in Texas. After college I moved across country and worked as a Christian campus minister for two years. I loved the university community and decided to pursue graduate degrees. I attended Indiana University where I earned a Master's in Applied Communication. From there, I went to Pennsylvania State University where I earned a PhD in Communication Arts and Sciences. I have published books on family (*Stepfamily Worlds*)[7] and faith integration within public universities (*Professing Christ*)[8] and several peer-reviewed scholarly articles in journals like *Health Education*, *Journal of Adolescent Research*, and *Journal of Family Communication*.

At the time of publication, I have been married about 15 years and my wife Breanne and I have five kids (three girls and two boys, from 8 to 14 years of age). Three were born in four years, all while I was earning my PhD. The younger two were born during my first few years as a professor. I know it is kind of cheating, but based on our kids ages and how many there are, my wife and I each already have 56 years of parenting experience. I have lived in eight states and visited over a dozen countries. We have even traveled as a family of seven to four different countries on mission trips with our church! We always have a lot of life in the house, which I have come to love. I enjoy backpacking and indoor rowing. When not working, you can find me hanging out with my kids, reading some fiction book aloud, catching up with my wife, playing games, or exploring somewhere in the back country.

Diane M. Badzinski

I studied communication and criminal justice for my bachelor's degree at St. Cloud State University. From there, I earned my MA in Communication at the University of California-Santa Barbara and my PhD in Communication at the University of Wisconsin-Madison. As I reflect back, it should be no surprise to me that I am now a professor at a Christian university, Colorado Christian University, studying interpersonal and family communication. As a doctoral student at the University of Wisconsin-Madison, I had the privilege of learning from one of the most well-known and well-respected scholars in family communication, Dr. Mary Anne Fitzpatrick. My first publication was a co-authored chapter with Mary Anne titled "All in the Family: Interpersonal Communication in Kin

Relationships" in the *Handbook of Interpersonal Communication*.[9] About 30 years later, I had the privilege of co-authoring a book titled *An Essential Guide to Interpersonal Communication: Building Great Relationships with Faith, Skill, and Virtue in the Age of Social Media*, with one of the most well-known and well-respected scholars in Christian communication, Dr. Quentin Schultze.[10] I am so grateful for the opportunity to learn from these two amazing scholars, and many others, as I continue to study, write, and teach in the areas of interpersonal and family communication.

Growing up, my parents—my father one of nine children and my mother the youngest of 12 children—placed a high priority on family, emphasizing the importance of faith, hard work, and education. My husband Jon and I, married over thirty years, have worked hard (along with much prayer, time, and money) to instill these values in our three children, Alyssa, Luke, and Hannah, all of whom are now bright young adults figuring out what it means to live out their faith in this world. As a family, we enjoy spending our vacations together, and they all know that I am especially happy when we play board games.

PART I
Definitions and Perspectives

Do not skip Part I. Chapters 1–4 provide important foundations for the book. We want to set the stage for an exploration of family communication from a biblically informed perspective. To do this, Chapter 1 briefly presents four assumptions of *Family Communication and the Christian Faith*: We assert that (1) God communicates; (2) God designed family purposefully and full of purpose; (3) the social reality of family diverges from God's ideal, which creates tension; and (4) communication helps families mediate the tension between God's good design and social experiences. We move to review definitions of family in Chapter 2, offering a working definition of the family as natural and fundamental to society. Then, in Chapter 3 we present the Truth Project's model of social organization to understand how family fits alongside other social institutions and in context with broader structures. Finally, we turn to theory and theology in Chapter 4. We offer a broad set of considerations for understanding family interaction. These chapters tend toward the abstract. But mastering the basics will better prepare you to study and evaluate family communication from a Christian perspective.

Let's begin with addressing the question, "What does a model of Christianity and family look like?"

Chapter 1

Modeling Family Communication and the Christian Faith

Chapter Summary: Chapter 1 briefly describes four fundamental assumptions woven throughout the textbook and presents a heuristic model that illustrates them. First is the assumption that God communicates. Second, God designed family purposefully, that is, on purpose and full of purpose. This includes the belief that families are woven into the fabric of society, and that they are natural and fundamental to the social order. The third assumption admits that neither families nor communication are perfect—a divergence from God's good design that creates a tension between the ideal and the reality for all families, and all communicators for that matter. Finally, as the model presents, communication serves as a mediator between God's design and social reality—a mediation represented most profoundly through the cross of Jesus Christ (Eph. 2:16; 2 Cor. 5:18; 1 Tim. 2:5).

Introduction

IN THIS FIRST CHAPTER, we present four fundamental assumptions about Christianity and family communication that weave through all the chapters of this book. These are themes that relate to God, Christianity, family, and communication. Figure 1.1 presents a heuristic model of these assumptions.

God Communicates

One of our first assumptions is that God exists and that he reveals himself. In other words, God communicates. Many theologians consider

3

Figure 1.1: Family Communication and the Christian Faith.

God's revelation to be Scripture and creation, termed primary (specific) and secondary (general) revelation, respectively. As Paul writes, "[S]ince the creation of the world God's invisible qualities—his eternal power and divine nature—have been clearly seen, being understood from what has been made, so that people are without excuse" (Rom. 1:20). This is secondary revelation. Scripture itself is considered primary revelation, God's holy word (2 Tim. 3:16).

Further, we believe God communicates to people today. We are not left to deduce from science or interpret from Scripture, but God sent his Holy Spirit to convict the hearts of those who do not know him and to indwell and empower his people. God is as active a communication agent today as he was when he spoke to Noah, discussed the fate of Sodom and Gomorrah with Abraham, presented the Torah to Moses, predicted the future through the prophets, or walked with the disciples. God communicates. He speaks. He listens. We can actually converse with God. This is a fundamental assumption for our text.

God Designed Family Purposefully

Our second assumption is that God created and fashioned family. There is an aim and an ordering to family life. Family is not an accident. It is not just a convenient or expedient social form. Family, and all of the individuals and relationships that comprise it, was instituted by God. It reflects his nature and purpose and was blessed in the first chapters of the Bible and the first hours of human history.

Genesis 1:27 records, "So God created mankind in his own image, in the image of God he created them; male and female he created them." Family is the first social institution recorded in the pages of Scripture. Before government or any religious ceremonies are prescribed, God made relationships and family. We, therefore, are relational, familial, and social beings. This reflects God's own nature as a social entity—Triune God comprised of equal but different personalities of Father, Son, Spirit.

Further, the Genesis account shows that God made two sexes as complementary, co-equals. Both are made in the image of God, yet they are distinct. Although contemporary scholarship separates biological sex from a person's gender, the Bible assumes throughout that gender and biological sex are synonymous. God also designed one man and one woman to live together in matrimony for all of life. Even though Adam lived over 900 years, he and Eve never divorced! As Jesus interpreted the creation story, he said, "What therefore God hath joined together, let not man put asunder" (Mark 10:9, KJV).

The nature of sexual union in relation to marriage is also evident from these first pages of Scripture. Genesis records that for woman, a man will leave his father and mother to be "united to his wife, and they become one flesh" (Gen. 2:24). This pictures God's design for sex as exclusive within marriage. Other passages of Scripture elaborate and confirm this design, instructing that there should be complete sexual abstinence outside the context of marriage. That is, there should be total celibacy either before marriage or in cases of divorce or separation. This feature of marriage seems to reflect that God designed marriage to portray Christ's relationship with his Bride on earth, as we cover in Chapters 2 and 11.

In addition to designing family on purpose, God designed family with purpose. "God blessed them [Adam and Eve] and said to them, 'Be fruitful and increase in number; fill the earth and subdue it'" (Gen. 1:28). Family is designed to reproduce. It is also designed to be a blessing to the world. God blessed the first family and commanded them: "Rule over the fish in the sea and the birds in the sky and over every living creature that moves on the ground" (Gen. 1:28). This commandment is not given to governments, businesses, or churches. It is given to families. One of our assumptions about the nature and purpose of family is that it is different from other spheres of society. Each social sphere has a role with rights and responsibilities. Family is charged with reproducing after their own kind, transmitting blessings to the next generation, as we review in Chapter 15.

The global mandate God gave the first family ("be fruitful, and multiply," Gen. 1:28, KJV) is reflected in the global mandate Jesus gave to his disciples, the family of God, after his resurrection ("go and make disciples of all nations," Matt. 28:19). These commands represent the purpose and plan for the original family as well as the redeemed purpose and plan of God's family on earth. Humanity's mission is to reproduce the life of God into every generation and all the earth. As Isaiah prophesized, "[T]he government will be upon his [Christ's] shoulders. . . . Of the increase of his government and peace there shall be no end" (Isa. 9:6–7, KJV). Just as the natural family is to be fruitful and multiply, the fulfillment of Isaiah's prophecy is brimming over with purpose for God's family. Christians are to bring the restoration of God's government to all parts of the planet and to all people.

Families and Communication Are Imperfect

A third assumption and theme in this book is that there exists a tension between the way God designed things to be and the realities of our social experience. While a Christian ideal admits that God never intended divorce, for example, it does not deny the reality that divorce has been an aspect of family life for millennia. Neither does a Christian perspective deny that people can divorce and subsequently live fulfilled, happy lives. Many do. Even Father Abraham had two wives and sent one away, picturing divorce. God did not reject Abraham because of this, nor should Christians today reject those who have been divorced. Similarly, a large proportion of people engage in sex outside of marriage, or cohabit. These realities diverge from God's design, but they are prevalent. Another way of stating our assumption is that the manifestations of sin are evident in all societies and cause unintended complexities in human relations across a variety of domains. Yet the grace of God can cover it all. Love can and will continue to cover a multitude of sins (1 Peter 4:8) across all types of family relationships. This tension between God's design and our lived experience is at the crux of a Christian perspective—literally, the cross of Jesus is the embodiment of living the tension between the ramifications of sin and reconciliation to God's design.

Families are not perfect, and neither is communication. The Fall of humanity created barriers in all relationships. Pictured by the infamous fig leaves in the Garden of Eden that covered the nakedness of Adam and Eve, sin introduced barriers into all human relationships. The classic literary conflicts of God versus humanity, humanity versus nature, person versus person, and humanity versus itself all were introduced at the Fall. Communication would never be the same as it was prior to that defining moment in human history.

These imperfections in family and communication make family communication forever imperfect. But that does not make family or communication any less valuable than before the Fall. The innate value of God's good design for family and for communication make them worthy of redemption. As Christianity teaches, this is why Christ died for humanity—to restore us into relationship with God and each other, to remove the fig leaves that blocked our relating, to make us once again naked and unashamed (Gen. 2:25). Humans are broken and beautiful. We are imperfect but being perfected. We make mistakes, yet as we continue to grow and develop, our thoughts, actions, and habits can become more and more godly. God does not work in spite of us; he works with and through us. No one communicates perfectly. None of us come from a perfect family. Yet, in the midst of our mess, Christ makes us beautiful and initiates us into God's family.

Our book admits the messy realities of family communication (e.g., divorce, conflict, violence) but also tries to shed light on ideals, pointing toward God's design for practices that breed beautiful family dynamics. Families are a gift from God. Communication is a gift, too.

Families Communicate to Live the Tension

A final theme of our perspective on family communication is that individuals and families reflect the nature of God by communicating. If God reveals himself, his ways, and his deeds on the earth (Ps. 103:7–8), we also reveal ourselves. Communication is a gift from God. It allows us intimate connection with others and with God himself. Communication is the first act we see of God: he speaks creation. And without God revealing himself to us, we would not know him. So, too, we reveal ourselves through our communication.

It is through communication that we mediate the tension between God's ideal and our social reality. As we present throughout the book, our communication facilitates connection with others (Chapter 5). It facilitates connection with God, too. It is through our communication that we misunderstand one another and stoke conflicts (Chapter 6). But it is also through our communication that we extend forgiveness and receive it (Chapter 7). These examples illustrate ways that communication reflects God's design for humanity.

Figuring centrally in our model is the cross of Christ, which is situated between God's design and our imperfect families and communication. As 2 Corinthians 5:17–19 puts it, "[I]f anyone is in Christ, the new creation has come: The old has gone, the new is here! All this is from God, who reconciled us to himself through Christ and gave us the ministry of reconciliation: that God was reconciling the world to himself in Christ, not counting people's sins against them." This incredible message of reconciliation through Christ bridges the imperfect and the ideal (cf. Heb. 9:15). The death and resurrection of Christ brings together (*communis*) imperfect humanity and God's good design.

Conclusion

Truly, communication is both the vessel and the navigation for those sailing through both the calm and the storms of life. Learning to communicate well, and gaining insight into family realities and theories, equips us to journey well through the different family stages from courtship to marriage to parenthood and beyond. We encourage you to join the journey as you study *Family Communication and the Christian Faith*.

Chapter 2

Understanding Family

Chapter Summary: Definitions of family are fundamental to policy and research. This chapter describes three approaches communication scholars use to define family (structural, functional, and transactional) and looks at how family relationships are both voluntary and involuntary. It then considers how the Bible might approach the task of defining family. The chapter concludes with a working definition that comes from the United Nation's Universal Declaration of Human Rights and argues that the family is natural and fundamental to society.

Introduction

ARE YOU FAMILIAR WITH ESTHER'S STORY from the Old Testament? Esther's father and mother died when she was young, and Esther's cousin Mordecai took "her as his own daughter" (Esther 2:7). Based on an order from King Xerxes, Esther was taken along with other "beautiful young virgins" (2:2) as a sex slave to the king's palace—Esther had no choice but to enter the king's harem. "Now the king was attracted to Esther more than to any of the other women, and she won his favor and approval more than any of the other virgins. So he set a royal crown on her head and made her queen" (2:17). The story unfolds with Esther playing a significant role in delivering the Jewish people from a plot to destroy them.

In this remarkable story, who is Esther's family? Her biological parents are not around, but are they still her family? Are Esther and Mordecai a family? Esther and King Xerxes? How about all three of them, or would King Xerxes consider Mordecai as family?

These questions show that the answers to who is and who is not

Esther's family are not easy. Neither are the answers to questions about contemporary family situations. Is a Greek pledge class really a brotherhood or sisterhood? Are there really "dog moms"? How about at church—is there a family of God? These questions all turn on the definition of family and show that defining family is not always clear cut.

IIIIIII ▶   **Application Activity 2.1:**
                  Who Is Family?

- **Make a list of everyone who is in your family. After you write out names, go back and write out how they are related to you.**

- **Without looking at your list, now write a definition of the word family.**

- **Compare the two. Did your list of who is in your family differ from your definition?**

- **To what extent is your definition of family colored by your experience? By the broader culture you experience? By the Bible? The church?**

Because our aim in this book is to learn about family communication theory and research, we need a common vocabulary. Definitions set boundaries and help us to decide what to include and exclude in our exploration of families and family communication. This chapter considers three approaches that communication scholars typically use to define family (structural, functional, and transactional) and describes family relationships as either voluntary or involuntary. It then explores the question, "How might the Bible define family?" We conclude the chapter with a working definition that comes from the United Nation's Universal Declaration of Human Rights: Family is "the natural and fundamental group unit of society."[1]

Categories of Definitions

In the communication discipline, family scholars[2] often categorize definitions of families into three types: structural, functional, and transactional.[3] These ways of defining family move from rigid to flexible to fluid. Structural definitions are most rigid. They apply more uniformly than others and allow clearer understanding of who is and is not considered family.

Functional definitions also apply uniformly but leave room for argument about who does or does not fulfill a certain function. There is more room for both error and inclusion. A transactional definition is fluid. On a moment's notice who is in or out of the family can change. Let's look at each category more closely.

A *structural* definition is one that clearly defines who is and is not a family. It answers the question, "Who makes up a family?" and gives clear-cut criteria for inclusion/exclusion. Traditionally, structural definitions come down to biological and legal relationships. Children, aunts, and grandparents are all related by blood, so they are family. A husband and wife or adopted children are family because they are united by law. But foster children, pets, and close family friends are not considered family by a structural definition; they are related neither legally nor by blood. Structural definitions are not swayed by emotion or experience. They are not dynamic, but provide logical classifications that apply uniformly to everyone.

A *functional* definition answers the question, "What do families do?" These definitions look at the social tasks accomplished by the family unit. Any group that accomplishes those tasks are classified as family. Douglas Kelley used a functional definition in his book *Marital Communication* to capture a variety of relationships that are marriage-like. He enumerates some functional characteristics of these relationships as "long-term, publicly-committed, romantic, partners."[4] Thus, any relationships that fit these criteria (e.g., long-term cohabitations) are included in his examination of marital communication. Another example of a functional definition may be households that take primary responsibility for socializing the young. Focusing on socialization as the definitional criteria includes foster households as families. It also adds aunts, uncles, and grandparents who have residential care for young. It excludes, however, childless married couples—they do not socialize the young. If the function becomes primary, any group that does not accomplish that function is not defined as family. Functional definitions allow for some ambiguity and change.

Finally, a *transactional* definition is the most ambiguous and dynamic definitional category. Transactional definitions presume that how people view themselves and how they communicate with one another should be privileged in defining family. For example, defining a family as "a self-defined group of intimates" allows for family to be almost anything—roommates, fraternity brothers, adoptive parents, pets, and dating partners.[5] It also allows for contradiction. While one person may see himself or herself

11

as part of a family, the other may not. A person may also consider herself part of a family one day and then, after experiencing some unexpected hurt, decide to disassociate with that family. Transactional definitions are often used by communication scholars because they feature communication as essential.

Voluntary and Involuntary

We can also understand family by classifying relationships as voluntary or involuntary. Marriage is a committed yet voluntary relationship. Couples agree to be in a relationship. Friendships, teams, and other kinds of clubs are all voluntary. No one requires these affiliations or activities, and they can be ended at any time. Sonship, however, is involuntary. Biological kin are not chosen. There is nothing you can do to change your paternity.

Life is full of both voluntary and involuntary relationships. So how do we classify family? Can we not cut off relationships whenever we want, regardless of our ancestry? In a sense, we can. In another sense, we cannot. We can change how we communicate with others, and that is consequential. If someone ceases all interaction with a father or never sees him after a divorce (statistics show that only about 40% of youth consistently see their biological father after a divorce), then it is hard to say that there is a relationship, certainly not one that is involuntary.[6] Or if a child does not know she was adopted, it would be hard to say she has a voluntary relationship with her biological parents. But if you go to a doctor and are asked to fill out a medical history form, the doctors do not really care if your stepdad or your mom's friend whom you call "uncle" have a history of heart disease or diabetes. Voluntary relationships do not put you at more or less risk for cardiac events. But if your biological father or your paternal grandfather had high blood pressure or high cholesterol, then you could be predisposed to have these health issues.

Reasons for Defining

Asking which classification of definition is "right" misses the point; there is room for multiple types of definitions. Instead, we want you to see that definitions serve various purposes.

For social scientific research, definitions need to be precise. We need to draw lines clearly between inclusion and exclusion. For this reason, structural definitions are often used for research. Structural features that are privileged change from study to study, but having clear-cut criteria for sampling and research is important. The same holds for policy. When crafting national, state, or local law, who it applies to is important to know. Legal definitions also must be consistent, applying the same in every circumstance.

In other settings, the precision and immutability of the definition is not as important. For example, in everyday conversations we are not usually worried if our statements would hold up in a court of law. We might call a family friend "Uncle Josh"; in fact, many Asian cultures say "Auntie" or "Uncle" as a term of respect and intimacy that does not necessarily denote a formal biological relationship. The point is that definitions of families can serve different purposes at different times.

**||||||||▶ Application Activity 2.2:
Organizational Definitions for Family**

- Locate a definition of family produced by a well-known company, nonprofit, or other organization.
- Discuss: Who is included (uncles, teammates, marrieds without kids, pets)? Who is excluded?
- Read the definition with a classmate, and classify it as structural, functional, or transactional.
- Discuss: How easily does the definition fit into one of these categories? What are the pros and cons of the definition?
- What purposes do the definition serve for the organization?

God's Definition of Family?

Having seen that there are different categories of definitions and that they serve various functions, what are Christian perspectives on family? Does God define family, and if so, could it be classified as structural, functional, or transactional? To answer these types of questions, we look to the Bible—God's specific revelation to humanity.

Reflecting the Trinity

We start in Genesis to reflect on the nature of God as Father, Son, and Holy Spirit. Examining the first chapters of the Bible with an eye toward social interaction shows that it began with God and is reflected in the created order. In other words, God is social. The social nature of humans is a manifestation of God's essence. As Pastor Adam Reed puts it,

> Before the beginning of time, before humans walked the earth, before the birds of the sky and the beasts of the fields, before the stars were resting in the cosmos, God was. He was, completely. He lacked nothing. The Father, Son, and Holy Spirit were content in their perfect unity and relational rapport of preferring one another. There wasn't a human sized hole inside God's heart that forced him to make mankind.[7]

Let's look at Scripture. First we read, "In the beginning God created . . . and the Spirit of God was hovering over the waters" (Gen. 1:1–2). Then, "Let us make man in our image" (Gen. 1:26). The Genesis account begs the question of what plural entity ("us") was referenced in creation. The answer is found in the doctrine of the Trinity. For example, the "Spirit of God" is mentioned as creator in Genesis 1:2 and confirmed in the Psalms (e.g., Ps. 33:6; 104:30). John's Gospel begins with striking similarities to the Genesis account and clearly indicates that Jesus was part of the creative force: "In the beginning was the Word [Jesus Christ] and the Word was with God, and the Word was God" (John 1:1). Paul reinforces this in Colossians 1:16 when he writes, "For by him [Jesus Christ] all things were created." These Bible passages demonstrate that an inherently social God created men and women in his image as relational, social beings.

The First Institution

Genesis 2 shares the story that establishes Adam and Eve's relationship with one another. God created the woman and brought her to be with the man. Thus, marriage is the first human social institution. "For this reason a man shall leave his father and his mother, and be joined to his wife; and they shall become one flesh" (Gen. 2:24, NASB). There was no government document that sealed or defined their marriage, and it was not accompanied by a religious service or minister's blessing; instead, the biblical account says that the "two shall become one flesh."

The consummation of marriage was central to the institution that was initiated and blessed by God. Understanding family from a Christian perspective, then, starts with the understanding that it was God's idea and reflected his relational character.

Let's consider it another way. In the first two chapters of Genesis, there are at least three primary relationships. We see the relationship between God and humanity (1:27), between nature and humanity (1:29), and between man and woman (2:22–25). In Genesis 3 we see two new relationships, between Satan and humanity and between humanity and sin. Sin impacted these other relationships in particular ways. It redefined humanity's relationship with God (3:8, 22), with nature (3:17), with evil spirits (3:15), and with each other (3:7, 12). Fig leaves became a barrier erected between humanity and God and between men and women. God cursed the ground, so humanity's relationship with nature also changed, instituting a new kind of dependence on labor. God also "put enmity" between the demonic and humanity (Gen. 3:15). We also see a new relationship between God and people, where God makes a sacrifice to clothe Adam and Eve with animal skins.

The next scene in Genesis 4 reveals parent-child relationships and sibling interaction, but they are far from ideal. These new relationships display the family God ordained when he commanded in Genesis 1:28, "Be fruitful and increase in number." We have the first murder recorded as Cain kills his brother Abel. We then watch humanity devolve into evil as the generations pass (Gen. 6:5). Clearly, the first family in human history was dysfunctional!

But even so, God does not seem to give up on the family unit. He created it and blessed it in Genesis, and throughout the Bible we see his concern for family. For example, in the limited space that makes up the Bible, God takes time to include genealogies. God seems to care who is birthed to whom (e.g., Gen. 5, Num. 26). One of the Ten Commandments is to "[h]onor your father and mother" (Exod. 20:12). He even goes so far as to say that when family relationships are not right, a nation or region would be punished. One of the minor prophets predicted that before the coming of the Messiah, a prophet would come to "turn the hearts of the fathers to their children, and the hearts of the children to their fathers; or else I will come to strike the land with a curse" (Mal. 4:6).

The Bible also records promises given to families. God could have called a community, nation, or people intact as a unit, but instead he opted to grow a people for "his treasured possession" (Exod. 19:5; Deut. 7:6) from a single family. God selected the Jewish nation first as a childless couple, Abraham and Sarah. From this couple, he reproduced a family through Isaac, Jacob, and Jacob's twelve sons. We see blessings prayed over this family-nation, like the blessings Jacob bestowed on his sons (Gen. 49) or those that Moses prayed for the tribes of Israel (Deut. 33). We also see promises given to the Jewish people, like God's covenant with Abraham (Gen. 22:17) and his assurance to David (2 Sam. 7:12–16). God is clearly concerned with families.

This review of the Scriptures gives some grounding for saying that family is defined structurally, based on biological relations, but that God is not bound by rigid structural practices. Think about this. Ishmael and Isaac were both biological offspring of Abraham, both sons. But the Bible differentiates the son of the "slave woman" and the "son of the free woman" (Gen. 21:10). Isaac fulfilled the function of miraculous promise (Gen. 18), but Ishmael did not. Paul argues that Abraham's "son by the slave woman [Ishmael] was born in the ordinary way; but his son by the free woman [Isaac] was born as the result of a promise" (Gal. 4:23). This is one example of how God uses a functional definition of family. Other examples include that Jacob, the youngest, was blessed over his older brother Esau (Gen. 25:19–34). Ruth, a foreigner, married into a Jewish family and became the great-grandmother of the most famous king in Israel, King David (Ruth 1:16–2:23). These departures from cultural practice prevent us from adopting an overly simplistic definition of family. Both biological structures and functions of families matter as does family communication.

IIIIIIII ▶ **Application Activity 2.3:
Families of the Bible**

There are a variety of definitions of what is or is not family across society, including in various denominations and Christian traditions. Take a minute and think about your faith tradition and its doctrines about family. How would someone in that denomination or tradition define family? What Scriptures can help you understand family and marriage?

Family of God

Perhaps, like many things in the Old Testament, family is a picture of how God wants us to relate with others. Once Jesus was asked about his biological family. He responded in an unusual way that both clarifies and confuses God's definition of family. Here is the account from Matthew 12:46–50 from the Passion Translation of the Bible.

> While Jesus was still speaking to the crowds, his mother and brothers came and stood outside, asking for him to come out and speak with them. Then someone said, "Look, your mother and brothers are standing outside, wanting to have a word with you." But Jesus just looked at him and said, "Let me introduce you to my true mother and brothers." Then gesturing to the disciples gathered around him, he said, "Look closely, for this is my true family. When you obey my heavenly Father that makes you a part of my true family."

Authors Jack and Judith Balswick, who wrote *The Family: A Christian Perspective on the Contemporary Home,* go so far as to say that "a case could be made that Jesus actually undermined the family" in choosing the single life and teaching "a radical discipleship that sets people at odds with their family."[8] However, they contend that this understanding would fall short of God's teaching. Rather than see this story as a disposal of structural definitions of family, we can view it as an expansion of who we are to consider family. Jesus employed a functional definition: Anyone who obeys God the Father is part of the family. Like the famous story of the Good Samaritan (Luke 10:29–37), which challenged contemporary understandings of who counts as a "neighbor," Jesus's teaching here expanded definitions of who counts as family.

Father God. The obedience-based definition Jesus gave moves away from structural definitions and common understandings of family as those related by birth and marriage. The Gospel of John helps explain this difference. John writes that as many as received Jesus, "to those who believed in his name, he gave the right to become children of God—children born not of natural descent, nor of human decision or a husband's will, but born of God" (John 1:12–13). Later in the same Gospel, Jesus instructs the religious leader Nicodemus that only those who are "born again" can see the kingdom of God. "[N]o one can enter the kingdom of God unless he is born of water and the Spirit. Flesh gives birth to flesh, but the Spirit gives birth to spirit" (John 3: 5–6). Pictured a different way, the religious rite of baptism symbolizes death and new birth. Romans 6:4 is sometimes quoted along with a baptism ritual. It reads "We were therefore buried with him through baptism into death in order that, just as Christ was raised from the dead through the glory of the Father, we too may live a new life." This indicates that the family of God is marked by a spiritual birth into it.

Taking up a different parental metaphor, Paul writes that we are adopted into God's family. In Ephesians 1:4–5, Paul claims, "In love he predestined us to be adopted as his sons through Jesus Christ, in accordance with his pleasure and will." Paul mirrors this language elsewhere, as well, saying, "For you did not receive the spirit of slavery to fall back into fear, but you have received the Spirit of adoption as sons, by whom we cry, 'Abba! Father!' The Spirit himself bears witness with our spirit that we are children of God" (Rom. 8:15–16, ESV). Jesus also taught that we are to pray to "[o]ur Father in heaven" (Matt. 6:9). Whether born or adopted, this biblical language relates us to God as Father-Child.

Christ's Bride. In other places, the Bible indicates that the church collectively is the bride of Christ Jesus. In 2 Corinthians 11:2, Paul reminds the church that they are pledged in marriage to Christ. This imagery is also taken up in Revelation 19:7–8. It is a picture of Jesus's wedding to the church, his bride. While we are portrayed individually as children of God, the church's relationship to Jesus is pictured as that of a husband and wife.

Indeed, marriage is a picture. Paul compares marriage to the relationship between Christ and his church. Ephesians 5:21–23 in the Passion Translation portrays the relationship in this way:

> And out of your reverence for Christ be supportive of each other in love.
>
> For wives, this means being supportive to your husbands like you are tenderly devoted to our Lord, for the husband provides leadership for the wife, just as Christ provides leadership for his church, as the Savior and Reviver of the body. In the same way the church is devoted to Christ, let the wives be devoted to their husbands in everything.
>
> And to the husbands, you are to demonstrate love for your wives with the same tender devotion that Christ demonstrated to us, his bride. For he died for us, sacrificing himself to make us holy

and pure, cleansing us through the showering of the pure water of the Word of God. All that he does in us is designed to make us a mature church for his pleasure, until we become a source of praise to him—glorious and radiant, beautiful and holy, without fault or flaw.

Husbands have the obligation of loving and caring for their wives the same way they love and care for their own bodies, for to love your wife is to love your own self. No one abuses his own body, but pampers it—serving and satisfying its needs. That's exactly what Christ does for his church. He serves and satisfies us as members of his body.

For this reason a man is to leave his father and his mother and lovingly hold to his wife, since the two have become joined as one flesh. Marriage is the beautiful design of the Almighty, a great and sacred mystery—meant to be a vivid example of Christ and his church.

This passage in Ephesians clearly demonstrates that a marital relationship pictures the relationship between the church and Jesus Christ.

Relating to "One Another" as Family. It is obvious that the New Testament writers encourage readers to view their union with God the Father and Jesus Christ as something that mirrors family relationships. So how should Christians view their relationships with each other? What language describes how the church operates? The answer here is also family relations.

Interestingly, when Ananias, the church leader from Damascus, goes to heal the blindness of the then well-known church persecutor, he addresses him as "Brother Saul" (Acts 22:13). Can you imagine calling someone who planned to arrest or kill you "brother"? After his conversion, though, Saul, who became known as Paul, used similar language. He refers to Timothy as "my dear son" (2 Tim. 1:2) and Titus as "my true son in our common faith" (Titus 1:4). To Timothy, Paul instructs that he should appeal to older women as mothers, older men as fathers, and younger women as sisters (1 Tim. 5:1–2). He also reminds the church that his team came to them "like a nursing mother cares for her children" and as a "father deals with his own children" (1 Thess. 2:7, 11). James instructs his "[b]rothers and sisters" on how to live (James 4:11). These familial terms of address show how close-knit the church is expected to be.

The church is instructed to live like family. Francis Chan's book *Letters to the Church* compares a church to a gang.[9] He scoffs at the ridiculous idea of saying something like, "How was gang this week?" "I could not make it to gang because of little Timmy's soccer game." Just the idea of a gang being only a 90-minute meeting once a week is laughable. That we could miss "gang" in favor of other activities also seems a bit odd. There is a more demanding level of commitment and devotion that accompanies gang involvement. So, too, Chan argues, there should be a different, family-like level of commitment and devotion that goes with being part of a church.

Family Is Natural and Fundamental

Given our review of scholarly categories of definitions and several Biblical considerations for defining family, we close this chapter with a historic definition that seems to capture much of the essence of the biblical perspective. The newly formed United Nations drafted the Universal Declaration of Human Rights in 1948. The context was on the heels of World War II, and the collective consciousness was global. Amid recent recognition of forced marriages, child betrothals, honor killings, and grievous inequity in male and female relations, the UN included an article on family:

> 1) Men and women of full age, without any limitation due to race, nationality or religion, have the right to marry and to found a family. They are entitled to equal rights as to marriage, during marriage and at its dissolution.
>
> 2) Marriage shall be entered into only with the free and full consent of the intending spouses.
>
> 3) The family is the natural and fundamental group unit of society and is entitled to protection by society and the State.[10]

This definition certainly prizes family, even if it does not acknowledge that God ordained it as the first social institution. The UN definition labels the family as "natural" and admits that it is "fundamental" to social organization (something we take up in Chapter 3). Indeed, the UN's definition presumes that family is the basis on which society forms and therefore is worthy of state and social protection. Its understanding also puts men and women as equals in the formation, duration, and ending of marriage. This definition aligns well with our own understanding and builds on a philosophy called "natural law."[11] While family may be more than this, it is not any less.

Some of the most explicit arguments in favor of defining family in terms of natural law were presented by Allan Carlson and Paul Mero in a manifesto.[12] Their manifesto represents a set of five doctrines of the "natural family," including that it is:

- part of the created order.

- imprinted on our natures.

- the source of bountiful joy.

- the fountain of new life.

- the bulwark of ordered liberty.

These bedrock principles undergird their vision of a "natural" family. They argue that "the story of the family, [is] at once an ideal vision and a universal reality."[13] To Carlson and Mero, the family is clearly the natural and fundamental group unit of society. They also argue that natural families begin as the union between one man and one woman. As you reflect on defining family from a natural law perspective, how well do you think it aligns with a Biblical perspective? Who is included and excluded by this definition?

In our view, the weight of thousands of years of human history and the logic of natural law are on the side of the natural family, which also fits with God's design. However, holding such a view too strictly misses the importance of the family of God, a family defined by creed and practice, function and interaction. Defining family is complex, and any single definition omits important facets of other definitions.

Conclusion

Looking back over this chapter suggests both a natural and a spiritual family. Taking a simplistic look at family through any one of the categories of definitions has pros and cons. God ordained family as the first social institution, and it symbolizes and embodies the relationship God designed for how he relates to his church and how church members should relate with one another.

In the New Testament there are about 50 commands to the followers of Jesus about how to treat "one another." They are commandments for interaction, family communication. These provide a blueprint for how God planned for people to live in community. There is a wealth of knowledge in the Scriptures and from experience studying social interactions that show

how families best operate. We believe that by learning more about how God instructed communities to relate, we can be better family members. And by studying how we communicate in families, we can learn more about how to relate to one another within the spiritual family of God.

Chapter 3

Family, Faith, and Society

Chapter Summary: Families do not exist in a vacuum. They are interwoven into the very fabric of society and interface with other social institutions like churches, schools, government, media/technology, and workplaces. Communication within and outside the family is the mechanism for these interfaces, and communication is fundamental to how these larger social systems interact with one another. This chapter presents a biblically informed model for understanding family in context and reviews societal trends related to family that demonstrate a pluralistic array of family types.

Introduction

THINK ABOUT THESE biblical illustrations of family:

Jacob married two sisters and had two concubines. Together these unions produced twelve sons, who became the nation of Israel. Israel organized as a theocracy and engaged in domestic and foreign affairs, informed by their commitments to God and beliefs about his leading (Gen. 29–50).

The Bible records that King Solomon had 700 wives and 300 concubines, which created conflicts of interest for the nation (1 Kings 11:3). Theology, politics, and family relations intermixed, leading the nation into idolatry.

The prophet Hosea married a prostitute and lived faithfully with this one woman, even after her affair with another lover. His marriage became a living portrayal of God's faithfulness to the adulterous nation of Israel (Hos. 1, 3).

John the Baptist was imprisoned, and eventually executed, because he spoke against the king's immoral marital relationship (Matt. 14).

These biblical vignettes of diverse family experiences and how they corresponded with social issues of their day illustrate some of the interplay between family, faith, and society. They introduce questions about the roles of prophet, priest, and king; which forms of government Scripture endorses; responsibilities and rights of families toward society and vice versa; and liaisons between private and public. While we cannot address all these important topics, in this chapter we do two things. First, we present a biblically informed model for understanding the role of family in society. Family is integral to society because it is the "natural and fundamental group unit of society."[1] Second, we survey family trends in the United States, illuminating how the policies and practices of social institutions (e.g., courts, companies, churches) influence family forms and functions (e.g., marriage and divorce rates, fertility) in society.

Theological Models of Society

Around the turn of the millennium, Del Tackett led a team to develop the Truth Project, a video series of lectures on topics related to truth, theology, philosophy, anthropology, sociology, politics, ethics, and law.[2] One aim of the Truth Project was to illustrate that at the foundation of any social system questions like, "Who is God?," "Who is mankind?," and "What is Truth?" need answers.

Atop this foundation, the Truth Project presented a comprehensive model of social systems in which pillars of philosophy, science, history, and ethics uphold the social order comprised of distinct social spheres. In this model, the church, family, relations between God and humankind, the state, labor, and community are separate spheres of society, while law, politics, economics, art, media, music, and literature also form part of the social order (see Figure 3.1). This comprehensive system has many elements, so let's break it down.

First, the foundation for the social order depends on how we answer theological ("Who is God?") and anthropological ("What is mankind?") questions and what we consider truth ("What is really real?"). If we assume that God exists and that God created humanity in his image, then it follows that all who bear God's image are important, regardless of age, sex, race, creed, or any other category. Furthermore, what is real goes beyond the natural, visible world and includes the supernatural realm of God, demons, and angels. In other words, how we answer these foundational questions

Figure 3.1: Truth Project Model of Society. Image from Focus on the Family's The Truth Project. © 2006 Focus on the Family. All rights reserved. Used with permission.

informs our ontology (beliefs about the nature of our being), epistemology (beliefs about the nature and origin of knowledge), and axiology (beliefs about the nature of value and what is valuable).

The Truth Project's model goes on to show that our beliefs about ourselves and our world play out in the arena of social structures and relationships. Family, from a Christian perspective, is made up of God's image-bearers, and children are a blessing from God, who authors all of life. Family is part of the social fabric as the first institution God ordained (see Chapters 1 and 2). Human labor is good and fulfills God's commandment to exercise stewardship over the whole earth (Gen. 1:28). Laws that define acceptable and unacceptable behavior emanate from the nature of God (for example, many times in the Book of Leviticus, God provides a commandment and then states "I am the Lord God"), and governments should be subject to the authority of God (Matt. 15:1–9). The model illustrates that the fundamental beliefs people hold will impact structures, policies, and practices in society and in individuals' lives. Stated in the words of Tim Hansel, author and founder of Ignite!, "All of our theology must eventually become biography."[3]

|||||||| ▶   **Application Activity 3.1:**
          Answering Foundational Questions

- Take a moment and reflect on the following question: Who is God? Of course, you do not have to answer the question comprehensively, but think about how you would answer a friend who asked your perspective about who God is. Jot down a few ideas.

- Now, reflect on your answers. Where did your ideas come from? Did you draw from a sermon or lecture? The Bible? Observations of the natural world? Spiritual experiences you have had? Prayer? A book? A movie? The point is that there are assumptions you make or ideas you believe to be true based on authority or experience. This epistemological starting point (i.e., your belief about God) is really a presupposition—an assumption held to be true upon which other beliefs or actions rest.

- Share with a partner what you discovered about your own beliefs and listen to what she learned about her beliefs about God.

If we start with different assumptions, then our understanding of how society should be ordered will look different. For example, if our theology is atheism, then we arrive at different conclusions about social order and family. One assumption about anthropology (the nature of humanity) for many atheists comes from evolutionary teaching that humanity is shaped primarily by a motivation to survive and continue its existence. From this, it follows that life matters most if it promotes our own self-interests or those of our offspring. Many have interpreted social organization and political affiliations as expedient for inclusive fitness (a term used by proponents of macroevolution to describe the continuation of the human species). But with these starting assumptions, there is no ultimate meaning or purpose to existence. Humanity is the result of cosmic accidents occurring over millions of years. People create meaning through relationships, philanthropy, family, and other avenues, but existence itself has no ultimate meaning. Life is all there is, so we need to maximize our benefit and enjoyment of it. The state and the legal system exist to prevent catastrophe or social collapse, and to maintain social order, but the state has no transcendent basis or axis. Morality becomes mutable and socially constructed, not fixed on a divine *ethos* that anchors it. Family becomes a useful, pragmatic social organization system that cares for the young but ceases to have value over social systems that can be equally efficient.

The Truth Project's model of social organization reminds us that the fundamental beliefs a society holds will influence how it is organized. As these beliefs change in a population or national leadership, the resulting order changes. If different members or groups within a society have contradicting answers to the fundamental questions, they will come to different conclusions about how society should be structured. Think about the two-party political system in the United States. The Republican and Democratic parties share some common values but also have fundamental differences (i.e., different answers to these basic questions) that often result in radically oppositional policy decisions.

With an understanding of how our fundamental beliefs about God, humanity, and reality influence our structuring of society, it becomes clear why different societies around the world place different values on the family. Think about the example of the Hebrews in Egypt. The book of Exodus relates that a shrewd Egyptian Pharaoh realized that his country was vulnerable because of a large subpopulation of Hebrews. He determined to force them into slavery and to kill all the male children—thinning the herd, so to speak. Pharaoh's actions placed the State at the center of determining what was right and wrong, acceptable and unacceptable. Not all life was viewed the same. Hebrew slaves could be killed because there was no intrinsic value to their lives. This tragic episode in history has been repeated (recall the Nazi campaign against the Jewish people or the displacement of First Nations people in the Americas), and it consistently stems from pervasive social thought that elevates some at the expense of others. How a society views family will impact the role, form, rights, and responsibilities of family in that society.

Romanian Orphan Crisis

An example that illustrates how ideas about family have consequences played out in recent history during the Romanian Orphan Crisis. As the story goes, a former Romanian ruler thought that the pathway to power was a large population. He encouraged families to have babies and promised that the State would care for all the children. Mass infant orphan wards were established to nurture children of the baby boom, which effectively dismantled family units. Unfortunately, these children were deprived of affection, physical touch, interaction, stimulation, and even nutrition. Many died. Others developed very slowly or experienced blunted growth, cognitive deficits, and other results of malnourishment and neglect. The international community became interested in the situation and offered adoption, which placed infants in parent-headed households around the globe. Many recovered in their adopted families, but for a substantial minority of these orphans, deficits persisted for years and even into adulthood (e.g., the height and weight of these children never reached normal levels).[4] Some researchers examined the effects of adoption and found that the younger infants were when placed in homes, the better the long-term outcomes for these children.[5] Lessons from the Romanian Orphan Crisis include the absolute necessity of physical affection and touch for normal development. It also demonstrates the benefits of beliefs about family and children, which can shape society, and that other social institutions, like the State, can influence family forms and trends.

Another concept from the Truth Project's model is that society consists of different types of institutions. Family is one social institution, but the state, religion, labor market, and community are also social institutions. How these institutions relate to one another is another defining feature for societies that has implications for families. Which institution is the most important? Which gets the most resources? Who decides what social institutions are responsible for which social tasks?

With this framework in mind, recognizing that family is one societal sphere and that beliefs about family and family trends are greatly impacted by society, let's examine how researchers look at family forms and trends.

Points to Ponder 3.2:
Whose Job Is It Anyway?

Jurisdiction is the official power to make legal decisions or execute justice. United States marshals have jurisdiction across the entire nation, whereas sheriffs and their deputies have jurisdiction within a particular county. So, who has jurisdiction over children, and when does that jurisdiction change? Children face contexts within family but also in school, church, neighborhoods, sports teams, and more. When a child interacts across multiple locations and social groups, who is responsible? We believe the answer is parents. Too

Points to Ponder 3.2 *continued*:
Whose Job Is It Anyway?

often Christian families have abdicated jurisdiction over their children in various areas. Let's consider education and religion.

Family, not the state, market, or church, is responsible for training children. Parents may take a supervisory or a direct role, but ultimately education is within their purview. This responsibility is comprehensive. It spans important life decisions as well as academics. Think of it as a general contractor. Even if a contractor hires a plumber or an electrician to do work on a project, the contractor is ultimately responsible for the building. Parents, too, may subcontract aspects of education, but they are the ones ultimately responsible for training their children toward adulthood. If a parent sends his child to a public or a private school, it reflects a decision to subcontract training to the state or the private school and its academic curriculum. It may also mean exposing children to the school's lifestyle curriculum (e.g., sex education or philosophical viewpoints). Subcontracting, like when a general contractor hires a plumber, requires oversight and inspection of the work done by the subcontractor. For schooling, this may look like participating in parent-teacher associations or serving on the schoolboard. Helping with homework, debriefing school experiences, and monitoring educational goals are other ways to be involved. Homeschooling is another option, where parents do not subcontract education but take a more active and directive role.

Family is also ultimately responsible for training children in religious matters. Churches and professional ordained ministers can be viewed as experts with more authority to train children than families, but the Bible clearly puts the responsibility for religious education on families (see Deut. 6). Like with schooling, parents may subcontract some religious or spiritual training, but they maintain the ultimate responsibility over their children. Religious education begins in the family.

Because the family is the first institution of Scripture, and it is the most fundamental organizational unit in society, there are responsibilities that fall within the jurisdiction of the family.

Demographic Trends of Family

When demographers examine family in society, they often track key indicators to paint a picture of family forms and trends. Some examples of family forms that are tracked include single-parent families, stepfamilies, same-sex unions, and cohabiting couples. They also track trends such as age of first marriage, marriage rate, divorce rate, and fertility rate. Demographers often look at how these key indicators change across subgroups of the population, like comparing those with a college degree against those who obtain a high school diploma or looking at how racial groups differ on these indicators. They also examine new social forms as they emerge. We look more closely at some of these trends in Part III of the text, but for now let's consider how trends help paint a picture of the current state of family.

To better understand changes and trends, demographers often theorize about them. Their explanations most often originate from an intellectual framework that does not acknowledge spiritual forces or motivations. This does not mean that the explanations are wrong or should be discounted completely, but it does imply that Christian readers and thinkers need to consider the data and trends alongside the truth revealed in Scripture. Consider the historic legalization of homosexual marriage in the United States (see Box 3.3). In this case, a principle can be seen: Even though something is normative or legal within a particular culture does not mean it aligns with biblical teachings (cf. Lev. 18:22; Lev 20:13; Rom. 1:18–32; 1 Cor. 6:9–11). Our view does not deny the reality of same-sex marriage or homosexuality, but it does maintain that a biblical understanding of marriage is premised on heterosexual union. Another example of social definitions that change and require a thoughtful integration of faith revolves around the often-politicized issue of abortion. How viable is the claim that abortion of a fetus is different than killing a human? If people become convinced that what grows inside a uterus is not human, then ending the life of the unborn is different from infanticide. A society's definition of when human life begins will influence public perceptions and policy decisions on abortion. How the church answers the question is interdependent with other spheres of society. If church and state diverge, whose belief wins the day? Who is silenced? How are biblical perspectives and definitions about life reconciled with popular or political perspectives? Truly, the interplay of societal spheres has life and death consequences.

Points to Ponder 3.3:
A Historical Look at Homosexual Marriage

In 1948, when the United Nations published its Universal Declaration of Human Rights and its definition of marriage as a fundamental unit of society, debates about lesbian, gay, bisexual, transgender, and queer marriages were not public, if they existed at all. Certainly, there were same-sex relationships; however, at that time they were considered deviant. This perspective on same-sex attraction and relationships remained intact for the next several decades. In fact, until the 1987 edition of the Diagnostic and Statistical Manual (DSM) of the American Psychological Association (APA), homosexuality was included as a disorder of some kind, and until 1992, the World Health Organization (WHO) also included it as a disorder.[6]

Globally, according to Pew Research, same-sex unions started gaining traction in the 1990s with a few countries granting civil union and domestic partnership status to gay and lesbian couples.[7] In the 2000s and 2010s, about 26 countries had legalized gay marriages. The Netherlands was the first in 2000 with an additional six countries joining in that decade (Belgium, Canada, Norway, Spain, South Africa, and Sweden). Considering that there are 195 countries in the world, the number of countries where homosexual marriage is recognized was a minority.

In the United States, based on a timeline compiled by the news outlet CNN, the legal status of same-sex couples became a national issue in September 1996 when President Bill Clinton signed the Defense of Marriage Act, which defined marriage as "a legal union between one man and one woman as husband and wife."[8] In December of that same year, Hawaii was the first state to recognize same-sex couples as legal equals to heterosexual couples, although the court ruling was overturned the next day. A few years later in 1999, a case in Vermont came to the same ruling. In 2003, the Massachusetts Supreme Court deemed the Defense of Marriage Act's effectual ban on same-sex marriage as unconstitutional.

Over the next several years there were political moves in the courts and in congress both to support and to oppose legal status of same-sex marriages. The society and the courts wavered back and forth between allowing and disallowing marriage for same-sex partners.

Points to Ponder 3.3 *continued*:
A Historical Look at Homosexual Marriage

In 2004, a court in Massachusetts legalized homosexual marriages, becoming the first state to do so. In several other states, popular votes ratified bans on same-sex marriages. These political battles continued over the next several years. In 2009, President Barack Obama granted benefits to same-sex partners of federal employees by executive order, and in 2011 the Department of Defense allowed military chaplains to perform same-sex unions. In 2013, the U.S. Treasury Department recognized legally married same-sex couples for federal tax purposes. These shifts indicated that regardless of the legal standing of same-sex couples, there was increasing multi-sector support for such partnerships.

In 2014, more courts ruled in favor of same-sex marriages and overturned individual state's decisions to ban them. The case that finally made it to the Federal Supreme Court led to a 5–4 ruling that states could not legally ban same-sex marriages. The ruling made same-sex marriage legal in all 50 states in June 2015. One of the dissenting (minority) opinions offers thoughtful critique of the court (majority) decision. Chief Justice Roberts articulated his concern:

> There is no serious dispute that, under our precedents, the Constitution protects a right to marry and requires States to apply their marriage laws equally. The real question in these cases is what constitutes "marriage," or—more precisely—who decides what constitutes "marriage"? . . .

> As the majority acknowledges, marriage "has existed for millennia and across civilizations." For all those millennia, across all those civilizations, "marriage" referred to only one relationship: the union of a man and a woman. . . . This universal definition of marriage as the union of a man and a woman is no historical coincidence. Marriage did not come about as a result of a political movement, discovery, disease, war, religious doctrine, or any other moving force of world history—and certainly not as a result of a prehistoric decision to exclude gays and lesbians.[9]

Indeed, questioning that marriage is between anyone other than one man and one woman is a recent turn in the United States.

Points to Ponder 3.3 *continued*:
A Historical Look at Homosexual Marriage

The debate on defining family and gay and lesbian marriage took place not only in the public sphere but also among academics. Books like *The Meaning of Marriage: Family, State, Market, and Morals*,[10] *The Natural Family: A Manifesto*,[11] *The Future of Marriage*,[12] and *Defending Marriage: Twelve Arguments for Sanity*[13] all predated the Supreme Court decision and supplied evidence and logic for maintaining the status quo definition of marriage. David Blankenhorn, for example, noted that proponents of gay marriage left two key ideas out of their definitions: sex and kids.[14] Contrasting anthropological literature on marriage and contemporary definitions of it, Blankenhorn reported that many of the modern definitions centered on love, personal fulfillment, companionship, and social success. Many of the anthropological practices from around the world and across time, however, centered on nurturing the young and regulating sexual liaisons. This disparity was important, and at that time Blankenhorn argued that it did not merit a legal redefinition of marriage.

Marriage historian Stephanie Coontz reported that varied sexual practices, including both heterosexuality and homosexuality, have been enacted for much of known history.[15] But the more radical shift in social understandings of marriage really occurred as the result of prizing love as the basis of marriage. Through much of history, Coontz argues, marriage was a societal practice as much as it was an interpersonal one: "Until the late eighteenth century, most societies around the world saw marriage as far too vital an economic and political institution to be left entirely to the free choice of the two individuals involved, especially if they were going to base their decision on something as unreasoning and transitory as love."[16]

When "love conquered marriage," it created a space for any number of new forms that diverged from one man and one woman.[17] If marriage is about personal fulfillment, then why not be able to divorce your spouse when your "soulmate" comes along years later? Why not let two men who love each other marry? On what grounds could they be denied? Coontz summarized demographic trends, stating that "everywhere marriage is becoming more optional and

> ### Points to Ponder 3.3 *continued*:
> ### Historical Look at Homosexual Marriage
>
> fragile. Everywhere the once-predictable link between marriage and child rearing is fraying."[18] This "world historical transformation of marriage"[19] was a slow-moving evolution that eventually cascaded into the social landscape. The same-sex marriage movement was just one logical implication of this fundamental alteration that moved marriage from a social, normative good to a personal, individualized choice.

Contemporary Landscape of the American Family

Each ten years, the *Journal of Marriage and Family* publishes a "decade in review" article that updates trends on family. The most recent review is from 2020 and reports findings from studies about family in the United States.[20] The Pew Research Center also conducts studies looking at the demographic trends on family. Drawing on these sources and others, let's sketch the landscape of the American family.

A word of caution before we begin. To interpret demographic data, you must realize that it presents a sociological, population-level picture of family. For example, you will see that we present data showing that about 45% of marriages fail, but this data does not mean that any given marriage has a 45 to 55% chance of failing or surviving. The data show the landscape, but there are many reasons that make any *particular* marriage end or continue. Statistics, as a field, is based on aggregating data—looking for trends and patterns across samples and populations. We have had too many conversations with students who say something like, "Wow, if the divorce rate is almost 50%, why bother getting married? There is just as much of a chance of getting divorced as there is sticking together." Unfortunately, this kind of conclusion misunderstands what the data shows. The data does not say that *your* marriage has a 45% chance of dissolving but rather that there is about 45% probability in aggregate that first time marriages end. This is an important distinction.

Marriage

There is a consistent age gap between men and women, where men are about two years older than women when they marry. By 2020, the average age for first marriage was 29.8 years for men and 27.8 for women.[21] Additionally, marriage rates—the total proportion of the population that is married—have been steadily falling: 70% of adults lived with a spouse in 1967 compared to 51% of adults in 2018.[22] It is important to note that many trends in marriage and other demographic variables are different for groups based on their race/ethnicity and education attainment. A total of 63% of Asian, 57% of White, 48% of Hispanic, and 33% of Black adults are married.[23] Those who earn a bachelor's degree tend to marry more, marry later, and cohabit less than those who earn a high school diploma or equivalent.

Why the decline in marriage rates? Economics may account for part of the decline as individuals decide to wait to get married until they have a comfortable income, little debt, and a secure job. Increases in cohabitation rates also partly explain the delay in marriage; it is not that young people are waiting to partner, but that cohabiting with one or more partners in their early 20s delays marriage. Some interpret these trends as a social retreat from marriage, but about 75% of youth report that it is a primary lifegoal to get married.[24]

Remarriage

Rates for remarriage are also declining, with a drop by one half between 1950 and 2017.[25] The increase in cohabitation for divorcees may account for some of this decline.[26] Divergence by race and education is also evident. Black and Latina women take longer to remarry than White women, for example. Remarriage is more likely for individuals with some college or a bachelor's degree than for those without a high school diploma.

Divorce

Divorce rates remain high but have been declining since 1980, with about 45% of marriages dissolving. Divorce rates are decreasing in young adults (partially due to increased cohabitation and an increase in age at first marriage) but increasing in older adults—a shift which has been labeled the "gray divorce revolution."[27] Marital dissolution rates diverge by race/

ethnicity and education. The proportion of groups whose first marriage ended within 20 years are as follows: Black 63%, Hispanic 47%, White 46%, and Asian 31%. Those with higher levels of education also report more stable marriages than their less educated counterparts.[28] In general, those who finish college have better marital outcomes than those who do not.[29] For college graduates, only about 22% ended their marriages within 20 years, compared to 51% of those with some college education, 59% of high school graduates, and 61% of those without a high school diploma.[30]

Cohabitation

Cohabitation rates have increased since cohabitation measurements began, with the growth plateauing in the past decade.[31] In 2019, Pew Research reported that 59% of adults ages 18 to 44 have lived with an unmarried partner at some point in their lives. Cohabitation has increased for all age groups: 12% of adults younger than 30 are living with an unmarried partner (up from 5% in 1995); 9% of adults ages 30 to 49 are cohabiting (up from 3% in 1995); and 4% of adults over the age of 50 are cohabiting (up from 1% in 1995). As with other demographic patterns, rates differ based on race and ethnicity (62% of White adults, 59% Black adults, and 56% Hispanic adults have cohabited) and education attainment (74% of adults with less than a bachelor's degree compared to 59% of adults with a bachelor's degree or more education have cohabited).[32]

Fertility Rates

With a few exceptions, the fertility rate (number of babies born) in the United States has declined over the past century. Recently, births have increased in women 40 years and older, but at a lower rate than the decrease in births to women in their teens and 20s, with a particularly sharp decrease in teen birth rates. The decrease in fertility rates holds for many race-ethnic groups, including Black, White, Asian, and Hispanic, with most notable decline for Hispanic women.[33] Women with more education have lower fertility rates than women with less education and often only begin having children in their 30s when their less educated counterparts are completing their childbearing years. Declines in fertility have happened alongside major social movements in the U.S., such as legalization of birth control pills, the sexual revolution, women's suffrage, changes in family economic structures, and shifting cultural views on the value of children. Fertility declines in the U.S. have matched global shifts in fertility as well, particularly among higher-income and developed nations.[34]

Family Structure

The trends we have reviewed so far (marriage, remarriage, divorce, cohabitation, and fertility rates), among others, shape the structure of the American family. Many contemporary married couples do not have children. Some experience infertility, while many others today are "voluntarily childless," choosing to avoid pregnancy and child-rearing. Today about 71% of adults are living without children compared to 52% in 1967.[35] Households that include children can be classified in terms of children's living arrangements. The majority of children (60%) live with their married, biological parents, while an additional 3% live with biological parents who cohabit. Another 24% live in a single-parent home (21% with mothers, 3% with fathers). Stepfamilies account for 9% of children's living arrangements.[36] Some children (2%) also live with grandparents.[37]

IIIIIIII ▶ **Application Activity 3.4:**
Shaping the Family in the United States

- **Think about how government policies such as paid parental leave, subsidized childcare, and work schedule flexibility might impact a couple's decision to have children.**

- **How have/might policies and attitudes in other social spheres (e.g., church, education) shape the landscape of the American family?**

One of the most dramatic changes has been children living in single-parent households, with about 12% of all children in 1970 living in a single-parent household to about 25% of all children living in a single-parent household in 2018, which is a number higher than any other developed nation. The volatility of children's living arrangements is also surprisingly high in the U.S. compared to other countries.[39]

Family life in the United States involves more transitions than anywhere else. There is more marriage but also more divorce. There are more lone parents but also more repartnering. Cohabiting relationships are shorter. Over the course of people's adult lives, there is more movement into and out of marriages and cohabitating relationships than in other countries.[40]

Family structure in the United States is diverse and ever-changing.

Conclusion

The Bible clearly teaches the importance of marriage and family, yet the way the biblical characters practiced it—from King Solomon's 700 wives and 300 concubines to the prophet Hosea, who lived faithfully with one wife—varied, as it does today.[41] Such diversity illuminates how family impacts and is impacted by what happens in other societal spheres. This chapter presented theologically based models for understanding family in social context and reviewed societal trends to paint a portrait of the American family. Throughout the chapter, we showed how the family is a social structure—"a creative, pulsing, changing, adapting system"—knitted into the very fabric of society.[42]

Chapter 4

Theory and Theology

Chapter Summary: This chapter introduces readers to fundamental theological understandings of social reality and to some of the widely cited theories of family interaction. The biblical grand narrative is presented as a framework for understanding Christian thought about humanity and relationships. Theoretical paradigms and four theories—systems, narrative, dialectic, and developmental—for studying family are reviewed, along with ways that theological ideas integrate with these theoretical perspectives.

Introduction

To BEGIN, LET'S REFLECT ON A PARABLE, one that you are likely familiar with: the Good Samaritan (Luke 10:30–36).

> A man was going down from Jerusalem to Jericho, when he was attacked by robbers. They stripped him of his clothes, beat him and went away, leaving him half dead. A priest happened to be going down the same road, and when he saw the man, he passed by on the other side. So too, a Levite, when he came to the place and saw him, passed by on the other side. But a Samaritan, as he traveled, came where the man was; and when he saw him, he took pity on him. He went to him and bandaged his wounds, pouring on oil and wine. Then he put the man on his own donkey, brought him to an inn and took care of him. The next day he took out two denarii and gave them to the innkeeper. "Look after him," he said, "and when I return, I will reimburse you for any extra expense you may have." Which

of these three do you think was a neighbor to the man who fell into the hands of robbers?

How do we interpret this parable? Do we interpret it literally as an exhortation to treat all people as our neighbors? Can this parable be a condemnation against those who know God's law but do not love others well? What about an allegorical interpretation? Saint Augustine suggests that the man left to die represents fallen humanity and the Samaritan represents Christ.[1]

Which interpretation is correct? All of them? None of them? Our point is that this parable, as all human activity, can be interpreted in different ways using different lenses. The lens impacts the interpretation. Theories are lenses for helping us understand different aspects of reality, including different aspects of family. Communication professor and author Em Griffin and his co-authors say it this way: "Theories shape our perception by focusing attention on some features of communication while ignoring other features, or at least pushing them into the background."[2] In this chapter, we show how theory is an interpretive lens for understanding the family.

To begin, we present a common view of human history as presented in the Bible. This narrative arc encompassing creation, the Fall, redemption, and restoration provides the basis for understanding Christian thought about humanity and relationships. We then overview the predominant philosophies that guide family communication theorists. After reviewing these philosophical paradigms, four widely used theoretical perspectives on family communication—systems, narrative, dialectic, and lifespan—are reviewed, along with ways that theological ideas integrate with these theoretical perspectives. One theory is not sufficient to understand something as universal and complex as family communication, so we present several. We hope that you will understand that theories are developed based on certain assumptions about how the world and people work and that you will have a grasp of some fundamental theological understandings of social reality as well as some of the predominant theories of family interaction.

Biblical Grand Narrative

Western theologians have suggested that Scripture has a grand narrative that includes four acts: creation, fall, redemption, and restoration. This narrative arc provides an analytical framework for understanding family from a Christian perspective.

Creation is the ordered way things were intended to be, offering us life-giving connections with God, nature, and others. Humans were created in the image of God (Gen. 1:26–28) and given the ability to communicate with him and others. God created all things to live in wholeness and harmony (captured in the Hebrew *shalom*) with each other. There was peace and the physical presence of God. Mutual flourishing was a reality for humans and all of creation, including family.

The Fall is the disruption to that order. When Eve believed the serpent's lie (see Gen. 3:1–7) that she surely would "not die from eating from the tree that is in the middle of the garden," sin entered the world. This choice separated humanity from God, which broke intimacy and union with God, others, and nature. It forced us into a system of evaluating good and evil.[3] The results of sin subjected all of creation to its effects (Rom. 8:20–22). From the Fall onward, Adam, Eve, and all their descendants, struggled "to restore relational unity with the Creator" and with each other.[4] Alienation from God, as communication scholar Quentin Schultze points out, corrupts our ability to communicate well.[5] Family communication was forever made imperfect, partial.

Redemption is God's reconciliation with humankind through the life, death, and resurrection of Jesus Christ. While intimacy with God and others was marred by the Fall, God made a right relationship with him possible only through the blood sacrifice of his son, Jesus, on the cross. Through this sacrifice, "we have been given direct access to God and we can re-establish communication with him" and "restore God's original intention for communication for all humanity."[6] Living within God's redemptive narrative makes relational flourishing with God and others possible. So even though we exist in a time when all communication is marked by the Fall, we can still experience connection and unity within family because of common grace and God's redemption of humanity through Christ.

Finally, *restoration* is a future act in the narrative arc of the Bible. It is the establishment of a new creation when death will be abolished and all the dead will be raised in Christ: "He will wipe every tear from their eyes. There will be no more death or mourning or crying or pain, for the old order of things has passed away" (Rev. 21:4). The hope of new creation is the confidence that one day God will restore his relationship with all of creation for all eternity. It is only then that our ability to communicate with God and others and to live in right relationships will be fully realized.

This biblical narrative provides a comprehensive explanation for human social experiences, including family experiences. Humans are basically selfish (sinful) and that selfishness has pervaded society. Evil in the world results from this selfishness. Yet, God in his mercy has provided grace even amid judgment. God cursed the ground and the serpent, not humankind. And he foreshadowed his plan of redemption that the seed of woman (Christ) would crush the head of the serpent (Satan). Exile from the Garden of Eden was the most lovingly just option God could take. Now we all live under both the effects of the Fall and common grace. The narrative arc depicts a wide gap between God's design for relationships and humanity's experience. Yet, there is hope: relationships can be redeemed and repaired. And one day, all things will be made new.

The biblical grand narrative is part of a worldview that guides much of Christian thinking and scholarship. It shapes our views of humanity and human history. But other philosophies are also present in the Academy. Theorists draw on their own worldviews (for an excellent resource on various worldviews, see James Sire's *The Universe Next Door*) and assumptions about God, humanity, and the nature of reality and knowledge.[7] That means that no scholarship is intellectually neutral. It all is informed by a perspective—a set of assumptions about how reality works. In the next section, we review three main theoretical perspectives for understanding family and then consider another option.

Theoretical Paradigms

Theories about family communication develop according to worldviews. A Christian worldview starts with the theological assumption that God exists and that he communicates with us. Phenomena are explained by natural and supernatural causes. Most of the dominant worldviews in contemporary Western scholarship start with the assumption that God is not (i.e., that matter is all that is) and that phenomena can be explained entirely by events and experiences within the natural world. These worldviews are typically divided into three broad paradigms: naturalism (positivism), interpretivism, and critical.

Naturalism is a modern-era research paradigm. It became popular during the Enlightenment and is considered responsible for advancing the scientific method, which has been adopted in social science. This approach focuses on understanding what exists in nature and manipulating it to our benefit. Much of the creative development of communication technologies like cell phones and computers grew out of a naturalistic framework. Naturalism holds that there is an objective reality that exists, is governed by logic and universal constants, and can be discovered through observation. Scholars who take this approach believe that communication processes are patterned, predictable, and explanatory. They are committed to discovering and understanding those patterns. While many scientists hold a theistic worldview, the dominant view of scientific naturalism does not. It believes that only the "natural" exists.

Naturalism aligns with a biblical perspective in the study of God's invisible attributes and divine qualities (Rom. 1–2) but diverges from a biblical stance in rejecting his special revelation (the Bible) and the Transcendent God who created nature and holds everything together by the word of his power (Heb. 1:3). Because naturalists are objectivists and base their decisions on what is documented, Christians taking an objectivist position may hold a literal interpretation of Scripture.[8] For example, with Scripture as its authority, objectivists outline the roles of husbands and wives. There is little room for debate.

The *interpretive* paradigm rejects the idea of a single, objective, discoverable reality and advocates for multiple subjective views of reality. Reality is not discovered but constructed. Interpretivists are committed to learn how particular realities are produced, maintained, and changed through the everyday practices of family members interacting within and outside various social systems, including the family. Interpretivism tackles research by trying to reflect participants' truths. It generally denies that there is anything absolute, without reconciling the self-refuting nature of such a claim (i.e., saying there is no truth is a universal truth claim). Interpretivist research could be used to promote positive change or simply to describe the experiences and perceptions of individuals and groups.

This perspective aligns with a biblical perspective in understanding that we each hold unique perspectives and experiences. For example, while the four Gospels all describe the life of Christ, each emphasizes different aspects of Christ and includes a somewhat different account of events. Interpretivism diverges from a biblical perspective in denying that God is the author of all Truth. In other words, because interpretivism holds all "truths" equal, it does not submit to God's revelation of creation, sin, or redemption through Christ alone. Christians taking this view may believe in absolute truth but claim that in our limited capacities as humans, knowing absolute truth is difficult if not impossible. Referencing 1 Corinthians 13:12, Strom

43

and Agodzo put it this way: "In faith, they [subjectivists] believe that the entire creation is a certain way . . . but in humility they acknowledge that humans still see through a glass darkly while attempting to understand and describe God's created, social, and spiritual order."[9]

The *critical* paradigm focuses on social change. Scholars who take a critical perspective are activist-scholars, focusing on power dynamics within society and how institutions of power impact social realities. In contrast to those who hold to the naturalism and interpretivism positions, critical theorists are not concerned with discovering or constructing social realities but focus their attention on the "contradictions, dissension, or inequalities" that exist within social institutions.[10] Critical theorists focus on the inherent inequality within systems and then maneuver politically to advocate change. Critical theorists are often concerned with social justice and reforming institutions of power. From a critical perspective, the individual or a particular family can never be completely at fault for any grievance because it is impacted by external discourses and forces.

A critical paradigm aligns with a biblical perspective in seeking to right injustice and recognizing that broader forces impact individuals and families. It can also align by seeking harmony or *shalom* for families and society. A critical perspective diverges from a biblical perspective by using individuals or groups as the standard for what is just and unjust, right and wrong, good and bad. Like all paradigms, it is limited and tainted by sin within the human heart. Because critical theorists focus on power and are advocates of change, Christians looking at family through this lens are concerned with how power is disseminated in families and how institutions of power impact the family. Critical theorists may be quick to question Scripture that talks about, for example, different roles of husbands and wives (e.g., Eph. 5), favoring their own or particular cultural interpretations of these verses. They may also be opposed to any other institution, including the church, sharing guidelines for how families or family members should act.

Following communication professor and scholar Ryan Bisel, we want to take yet another approach in this book. Writing about the Apostle Paul on Athens's Mars Hill, Bisel reports:

> On the one hand, Stoics argued that heaven is mostly identical to earth; no need for the gods, since god is in all and all is god. On the other hand, Epicureans argued that while the gods made the earth, their heavenly dwelling is far away and they almost never

get involved in its functioning. What other possibility from experience and reasoning could a thinking person propose?[11]

As Bisel explains, Paul offered an alternative option: an option that endorsed the good and eschewed the bad from both theoretical perspectives. We, too, try to present this option throughout this text. Let's clarify this view.

Data and theories about family are not "neutral," and how researchers interpret data is subjective and limited by their paradigms and theories. Nevertheless, there is generally something we can learn from any data. If nothing else, we learn that there are people who view aspects of family in a variety of ways. These insights are useful for moving us into the position of humble learners. From naturalism, we gain a focus on the created order and learn from it. From interpretivism, we gain an appreciation for the individual, for the experiences and perspectives that guide personal behavior. From the critical paradigm, we gain a perspective on the systemic influences that can limit and enable various people and a recognition of the injustices in the world. The Christian perspective transcends these research worldviews and adheres to a comprehensive set of beliefs that are *supernatural*—by definition, beyond nature. It provides an opportunity to "hold on to what is good" (1 Thess. 5:20). For individuals from multiple Christian backgrounds and various paradigms, this approach encourages listening and learning without compromising your own position.

Theories

Paradigms offer a wide-angle view of reality, offering principles for interpreting that reality. In practice, we often need to narrow our view, zooming into a specific aspect of reality in order to understand it from different angles. Theories do just that. A theory is "a set of systematic, informed hunches,"[12] "an explanation of a fact pattern,"[13] and "any systematic summary about the nature of the communication process."[14] Simply put, a family communication theory is an informed set of propositions that illuminates some aspect of family to understand it more clearly. Theories are important. They help us describe, explain, and predict family structures, patterns, and interactions. They help us make sense of the complexity of family communication.

The theories we cover in this chapter have played a prominent role in understanding family interaction. Other theories are also useful, and communication scholars have published catalogues of family theories, such as *Engaging Theories in Family Communication*.[15] Theories hypothesize how things work, and as studies of human behavior that increase our knowledge, they are often expanded or modified. With this in mind, we turn to highlighting major tenets of four theoretical approaches: systems, narrative, dialectical, and developmental.

Systems Theory

A systems approach to family life focuses on how the actions of individuals within the family impact the family unit and vice versa. This theory proposes that the family is a system: a "series of interactive, interdependent parts that operate in patterned ways to create a synergistic whole."[16] A systems perspective is a broad theory with several important characteristics.[17]

Interdependence refers to the interconnectedness of the family members. Actions of one family member affect all family members and their communication patterns. You have likely witnessed this characteristic of system in your own family. Your mother receives a job offer out of state, requiring changes for everyone. Your brother is charged with the distribution of drugs, and the entire family is devastated.

Hierarchy means that the family is organized in various systems and subsystems (e.g., siblings, parents), with each grouping viewed as its own system and as part of the larger family system. A child whose parents divorced could experience very different family hierarchies with her mother-stepfather family, which includes half-siblings, and with her single-father family, which just includes her and her father.

Wholeness is the idea that the family unit is greater than the sum of the individual members that make up the family. The family as a whole becomes the primary unit of analysis for understanding communication, and the interaction patterns of subsystems become secondary. For instance, a therapist might apply systems thinking and explain that a child's depressive symptoms are caused by arguments between his parents. Wholeness links effects on one member to interaction patterns of others and rejects simplistic, individualistic explanations.

Patterns arise from the rules and regulations for operating within the family. A family may have developed bedtime or Sunday morning rituals. These patterns contribute to the stability of the family. Relatedly, *interactive complexity* is the idea that it is impossible, or at least impractical, to look for singular, mechanistic explanations for human behavior. A single cause-effect relationship is too simplistic. Instead, a systems theory approach proposes that interaction patterns better explain behaviors.

Openness acknowledges that the family is influenced by conditions outside the family. The family is not insulated from broader societal forces. School sporting events may put pressure on family schedules and finances. Movies may give families ideas about how adolescents typically behave. Families are open systems, but they can erect *boundaries* to help control the influence of outside sources. A family, for example, may place strict limits on social media use in order to curb its influence.

Feedback refers to the ways in which families achieve some level of *equilibrium* or balance. There are different types of feedback loops that can maintain the status quo or lead to changes in the family. If a family system is operating well, it is said to be *homeostatic*, balanced. Operating according to established rules and regulations makes families functional. A *morphogenic* change comes from a disruptive feedback loop, one that changes the form or nature of the family. The birth of a new baby is morphogenic. Different from "feedback" that you might get after giving a speech, feedback loops in a systems theory approach have to do with how families are regulated or altered as a unit.

Equifinality refers to the idea that there are different ways to accomplish a goal. Systems theory proposes that we are goal-oriented beings and that the same outcome—for example, family satisfaction—can be reached via different paths.

Systems thinking originally aimed to provide a general framework for integrating knowledge from all disciplines of study, from molecular chemistry to geopolitical cycles, from particle physics to personality psychology.[18] In your view, how well does systems thinking apply to Christian theology?

Trinitarian Perspective

One way to view God, the Trinity, is as a system. The Nicene Creed, a fourth-century declaration of the Christian faith, proclaims: "We believe in one God, the Father the Almighty . . . We believe in one Lord Jesus Christ, the only Son of God . . . We believe in the Holy Spirit, the Lord and giver of life."[19] The Trinity is one God in three persons: the Father, Son, and Holy Spirit. They are all part of one broader system yet also complete and unique. Each person of the Trinity is fully God, mutually interdependent, and dwelling in each other in love.

The Trinity is a model for family flourishing. Families are called to create relationships in which each person, made in the image of God, is interdependent with each other and bound together in love. "Our love of each other should thus reflect the truth of our human existence—that we are all interconnected and interdependent. We discover our deepest selves only through our relationships with each other."[20] This implies that no one is truly self-sufficient. Each family member, with his or her own distinct gifts and personalities, fulfills a unique and valuable role. A Trinitarian perspective is grounded in relationality, mutuality, diversity, equality, and community.[21]

**IIIIIIII ▶ Application Activity 4.1:
The Divine Trinity as a System**

- In what ways do the characteristics of the Trinitarian perspective mirror key elements of a systems perspective? How do the two differ? Would you argue that the Trinity is an example of a system? Why or why not?

- A system is a metaphor for understanding family. How does this metaphor help or hinder your understanding of family communication? Is a system too mechanical of a metaphor to capture the heart of family interaction? Why or why not? What metaphor might you offer that better captures the dynamics of family?

Narrative Theory

Tell me a family story. Stories. Who does not like a good story? We all love them. Stories captivate and illuminate. They serve to create, maintain, and understand family. God is quite a storyteller, too. As we reviewed earlier, the grand narrative of the Bible preserves a story of human history. It weaves together a compelling, convoluted, and complex story of the Hebrew family, from Abraham and the Patriarchs, through their Egyptian slavery and exodus, and through judges, prophets, and kings. God's redemption of all of humanity through the Messiah, Jesus Christ, is a theme that laces throughout the Hebrew family story.

Narrative Theory, advanced by communication theorist Walter Fisher, argues that we are storytelling beings, enacting human experiences.[22] Stories give meaning to experiences, and it is our shared stories that build communities. According to Fisher, narratives must be both coherent, that is, have *narrative probability*, and "ring true," or have *narrative fidelity*. As scholars critique Fisher's narrative paradigm, they expand upon his ideas. William Kirkwood persuasively argues that Fisher's criteria for judging a story needs to include its ability to stir the imagination and open new possibilities.[23] *Narrative empathy* was proposed to encourage us to consider the story from multiple perspectives.[24]

Communicated narrative sense-making, proposed by Jody Kellas and Haley Horstman, encourages narrative empathy.[25] Family stories often present multiple views of an event, which can affect both individual and relational well-being within the family. Narrative sense-making includes four processes: engagement, turn-taking, perspective-taking, and coherence.

Engagement is the verbal and nonverbal telling of family stories, warmly inviting members to participate. *Turn-taking* is the volleying back and forth as the tale is told. *Perspective-taking* is integrating others' perspectives and experiences in the telling of the narrative, and *coherence* is negotiating the story happenings, creating a tale that makes sense.

Imagine your family gathered to share a story. Would you be invited to share? Who would dominate the storytelling? Would multiple perspectives be entertained? Would the story make sense to you, or would something not quite fit together? As you reflect on these questions, you are engaging in communicated narrative sense-making.

Why tell family stories? Stories "both *affect* and *reflect* family" in countless ways.[26] Stories serve many incredibly important functions for families. We focus on three broad functions: identity formation, sense-making, and socialization.[27]

Identity formation. Stories frame our identities. As we tell and retell stories, we often choose to emphasize experiences that reinforce how we wish to portray ourselves and our families.[28] These retrospective stories take a "looking-back approach" to mark events and experiences in time and are often marked by "inconsistent memories, exaggerations, and denials."[29] The accuracy of the story is not the point; rather, what is significant is how the family chooses to remember the story as a reflection of their identity.

This identity formation function is central to faith conversion narratives. Christian evangelism often utilizes personal conversion stories to exemplify how a person's identity has changed. This "testimony" follows a typical pattern that shares what life was like before Christ, narrates the spiritual experience of conversion, and then describes what difference being Christian has made in a convert's life. Sharing and re-sharing this testimony reinforces a sense of identity as a Christ-follower.

Sense-making. Stories also help us to make sense of experiences, whether pleasant or traumatic life events. Storytelling offers us an avenue for gaining a sense of control over an event and provides a way to process and express feelings about it.

Here is one of Diane's family stories that highlights the complexity of sense-making: My father was one of nine children growing up in a small Polish town in Wisconsin. During the harsh winters, when temperatures often reached -10 to -20 degrees Fahrenheit, my grandmother would send each of her children walking to school with one "hot potato." The children would clutch the potato to keep their hands warm as they made their way. Upon arrival at school, the children placed the potato on the classroom heater. You probably guessed it: the potato doubled as their lunch entree. I love this story. It shows the resourcefulness of my grandmother. At the same time, it reveals the painful reality that my grandmother struggled to feed and clothe her nine children; she struggled to protect and provide for them. In a memorable way, the story helps make sense of the complexity of family history.

Socialization. Stories socialize us to the rules and norms of everyday life within our family, creating a culture of what to expect and what is expected of us. These rules and norms are mnemonic devices that help us to recall and enact values. Many of Jesus's vivid parables are memorable and help guide Christian living. The parable of the Good Samaritan teaches that race and class do not preclude loving others. An important function of

IIIIIIII ▶   **Application Activity 4.2:**
A Family Story

- Take a few minutes and write down a family story, providing as much detail as possible.
- Reflecting on that story, consider the following questions: What is the significance of this story to you? Your family? How is this story a reflection of your family identity? How does this story help you make sense of some aspect of family? In what ways does this story help in understanding family values, rules, or patterns?

stories is to pass important values and lessons down from one generation to another, with the expectation that we will embrace those values and learn from those lessons.

Dialectical Theory

Relational Dialectics Theory is another prominent approach to understanding family communication. The lens of this theory focuses our attention on inherent contradictions in human relating. "At the heart of dialectical theory is that contradictions or tensions are inevitable and necessary"; meaning is constituted from the "interpenetration of opposing discourses."[30] As family members struggle with and navigate through these competing discourses, relationships can flourish or disintegrate. Meaning is jointly constructed through dialogue, and it is through family talk that a family constructs its identity and that family members come to understand their roles and responsibilities. It is also through dialogue that families begin to understand how outside influences, cultural and social discourses, affect them.

The three dominant contradictions identified through dialectical theory are autonomy-connectedness, openness-closedness, and certainty-uncertainty. We struggle with and navigate through a desire for both aspects of these sets of tensions.

Autonomy-connectedness is expressed in a variety of ways, including time spent alone or together and one's rights and obligations to self and others. It can be framed in terms of "I" identities and "we" identities. This can be reflected in activities enjoyed jointly as a family that lead to a shared "we" identity and activities enjoyed individually that privilege an "I" identity.

Openness-closedness contrasts candid disclosure with discretion and privacy. It can be framed in terms of the right to privacy and a right to freedom of expression. On one hand, we might want to be open and vulnerable with each other, but at times we choose not to share.

Novelty-predictability pits the need or desire for consistency and routine against spontaneity and change. That is, sometimes predictability is prized above spontaneity, and sometimes it is not. Of course, tensions not only exist between the family members but can also exist between the family and outside networks, referred to as external contradictions. The three parallel external contradictions are labeled *inclusion-seclusion, conventionality-uniqueness,* and *revelation-concealment.*

It is easy to view relational dialectics/contradictions as negative—struggles, oppositions, tensions—or to see relating to others as strained. This view aligns with the theological view of the Fall—no relationship is perfect. However, an intriguing study by Melissa Framer Black shows how tensions can strengthen relationships.[31] The study examined dialectics experienced by women who practiced the Orthodox Jewish family purity laws, where a man and woman are forbidden from all forms of touch during the wife's menstruation and the seven days following. The study investigated marital maintenance strategies alongside the dialectics that couples faced. Findings identified ways in which women experienced these tensions and also identified a new tension in married couples—the friend-lover dialectic. For example, when couples were in a prescribed hiatus from touch, they went for walks or played games that encouraged their friendship, all the while recognizing that they were intentionally avoiding engaging as lovers. The study found that rituals surrounding family purity punctuated marital dialectics with specific maintenance behaviors and that the prescribed, intentional abstinence created dialectics that enlivened marital relations.

It is also easy to view contradictions as forces to be eliminated. However, even if such was ideal, dialectical theorists argue that it is impossible. Relationships in this perspective are an ongoing process of contradictions in creating and co-creating family interaction. Moreover, based on the grand narrative arc of Scripture, we live in tension of already experiencing redemption but not yet experiencing restoration. This *already-not yet* reality is a

---

|||||||| ▶ Application Activity 4.3:
Identifying Relational Dialectics

- Interview a classmate, friend, or family member, and ask them to think about a specific relationship and to describe an event or situation that resulted in a change in that relationship, either pulling the relationship further apart or drawing it closer together. Analyze the response in terms of dialectical tensions.

- What dialectical tension was most prevalent? Could you classify the tension in terms of one of the three primary dialectics, or did you uncover another dialectic?

- To what extent did the tension draw the people together or push them apart?

dialectic that we must learn to navigate successfully. As the eminent scholar Parker Palmer notes, "Our first need is not to release the tension but to live the contradictions, fully and painfully aware of the poles between which our lives are stretched. As we do so, we will be plunged into paradox, at whose heart we find transcendence and new life."[32] Recognizing ways in which we live the tension awakens our senses to the biblical narrative arc, the reality of the God-Man Christ who is Redeemer and soon-coming Restorer.

Family Development

Developmental theories of family communication focus on changes experienced by families over time. Some have looked at families progressing through different life stages, like when a couple first marries, when they have kids, or after their kids move out of the home. These researchers examine family communication within each particular life stage. Others have taken a lifespan developmental approach, which looks at the changes that occur within individuals and families as they age. For example, taking a lifespan approach might look at how communication develops for infants, toddlers, and children and how older people loose memory or experience decreased vocabularies. These researchers do not examine a particular life stage but look at development more generally. Development does not stop in childhood but occurs across the lifespan.[33] We adopt a developmental approach in Part III of our book to zoom in on communication in marriage, parenting, and end of life. Here we review four major assertions of a lifespan developmental approach,[34] which is a lens that focuses our attention on the continuous changes that individuals and families experience throughout their existence.

First, adopting a lifespan development approach recognizes that *positive development occurs throughout life*. Lifespan theorists reject a widely held view that positive development declines as one ages. Viewing only physiological changes (e.g., weakened body, dimmed eyesight) across the lifespan is myopic, so lifespan theorists encourage us to acknowledge other aspects of growth. For example, conflict resolution skills and wisdom to know when to engage in an argument can increase over years of marriage. Knowing God's character and his ways, not just his deeds (Ps. 103:7), might be an aspect of spiritual maturity that changes over a lifetime. Recognizing positive development across the lifespan broadens our outlook beyond purely physical development.

A second assertion is that *diversity and pluralism occur in the changes throughout life.* Development is a complex process. It is not linear nor do individuals move through life cycles in the same way or at the same rate. In addition, different developmental capabilities often do not move at the same pace. The systems concept of equifinality applies here. Even though many people reach the age of 50, they will almost all have different capabilities and wisdom. An inspiration for us is Moses, who lived 120 years, yet his eyesight did not dim nor did his strength diminish (Deut. 34:7). It is unlikely that this will be true of us (after all, Jonathan and Diane have both worn glasses since childhood), but it does demonstrate the diversity and pluralism of development across a lifespan.

Third, *development is best viewed as a gain-loss dynamic.* This is one of the most important teachings of a developmental perspective. Throughout the life cycle, we gain some capabilities, and we lose others. We learn over time to accentuate our gains and find ways to compensate successfully for our losses. For example, teenagers have faster reaction times than those who have been driving for 15 to 20 years. Yet, older drivers are safer (just ask any insurance salesperson). Why? Because the accumulation of driving experience accrues driving skills that outweigh reaction time. This gain-loss dynamic plays out across a wide array of domains. We learn to listen well to mitigate conflicts. We adapt to decreased memory abilities with technological solutions like birthday reminders. The list goes on.

A fourth assertion is that *inter- and intra-individual diversity exists as we progress throughout the lifespan.* This means that any particular individual may develop at different rates on different attributes (intra-individual diversity). A person may be a prodigy on piano but slow to learn guitar. It also means that different individuals develop at different rates on the same ability (inter-individual diversity). You may be faster at picking up piano than some but slower than a prodigy. Another implication of the fourth assertion is that differences in thinking and behaving between people at different life stages might be explained by factors other than age, such as education or life experiences. In other words, chronological age may not be a strong predictor of someone's ability, which would result in large amounts of variability among individuals within a particular developmental stage. Spiritual maturity, for instance, is not just a function of how many years a person has been a Christian. As the saying goes, you can be a 5-year-old Christian or someone who has been a 1-year-old Christian for five years. Time alone does not equate with spiritual depth or maturity (see Matt. 7:24–27; James 1:22; Heb. 5:12).

Communication scholar Jon Nussbaum and his colleagues apply the lifespan developmental perspective to our understanding of how communication develops, changes, and functions at different life stages (e.g., infancy, early childhood, emerging adulthood, older adulthood).[35] This lifespan communication perspective is interdisciplinary—drawing on work in developmental psychology (e.g., changes in language and cognition) and sociology (e.g., impact of demography and social policy on life stages)—to understanding communication at different life stages.

IIIIIIII ▶ **Application Activity 4.4:**
Gain-loss Framework

- Reflect on 1 Timothy 4:15: "[G]ive yourself wholly to them, so that everyone may see your progress." In what ways does 1 Timothy 4:15 embody the lifespan development approach?

- How do you communicate with others now (e.g., language, mode of communication, topics)? Compare this to the way in which you communicated at an early life stage. What are some differences?

Conclusion

Collectively, paradigms and theories deepen our understanding of family communication by offering multiple ways of viewing reality. Studying family through the biblical arc—creation, fall, redemption, and restoration—centers our concern on God's design and purpose for humanity, including how communication is a means for redeeming and restoring family relationships. A Trinitarian perspective focuses attention on how each family member, made in the image of God, is independent yet also interdependent. Systems, narrative, dialectical, and developmental theories of family give broad frameworks for understanding family communication. Individually, each theory provides a closer inspection of specific aspects of the family. No theory completely covers all aspects of family interaction, and there are good and bad aspects of each theory. Our goal is to focus on what we can learn from each without compromising on what is presented in the Bible. Just as there are multiple ways to interpret the parable of the

Good Samaritan, there are different lenses for looking at communication, with each lens offering unique views and advancing our understanding of the family.

PART II
Functional Family Communication

There are at least five major communication functions that all families need to accomplish. They include (1) connecting with one another, (2) handling inevitable conflicts, (3) finding ways to seek and extend forgiveness, (4) handling stress, and (5) taking care of the business side of life. In the following five chapters, we look at each of these in turn. We consider them as family communication tasks. These are applicable for newlywed couples as much as for families with kids, within immediate and extended families. In other words, connection is an important function of family, no matter how long a couple has been married or how old siblings are. Conflict does not end after the first year of marriage nor after going through "terrible twos," meaning that forgiveness must continue throughout our lives. As we address these functions, we weave applicable theory and examples from Scripture and Christian thought into each chapter.

Let's start with one of these fundamental family functions, connection.

Chapter 5

Rituals for Connection: Creating Rhythms for Healthy Relationships

Chapter Summary: Rituals are often associated with religious practice, like taking communion, but they are also important for conveying meaning and significance in families. This chapter discusses ways to build family connection by establishing general and idiosyncratic rituals, as God commanded families to remember his work and promises. It overviews topics like how to make listening a lifestyle for connecting, employing relationship maintenance behaviors, and communicating in one another's love languages. The chapter concludes with a helpful mnemonic for offering encouragement as a practical strategy for communicating connection.

Introduction

ONE OF THE MOST FAMOUS and practiced Christian rituals is communion. Luke 22:7–20 records:

> Then came the first day of Unleavened Bread on which the Passover lamb had to be sacrificed. . . . And [Jesus] said to [his disciples], "I have earnestly desired to eat this Passover with you before I suffer; for I say to you, I shall never again eat it until it is fulfilled in the kingdom of God." And when he had taken some bread and given thanks, he broke it and gave it to them, saying, "This is my body which is given for you; do this in remembrance of me." And in the same way he took the cup after they had eaten, saying, "This cup which is poured out for you is the new covenant in my blood."

Jesus established communion, a rite of the church, as a reinterpretation of the Jewish Passover Seder (the Jewish feast Jesus celebrated with his disciples the day before his crucifixion, see Mark 14:12–26). It has become the quintessential ritual of Christian faith, celebrated across various traditions in many ways.

Rituals convey meaning and significance in patterned ways and are important not only for religious practice but also for family communication. This chapter discusses ways to build family connection by establishing rituals, making listening a lifestyle for connecting, employing relationship maintenance behaviors, and lavishing others with a hefty dose of love and encouragement.

Family Rituals

While there are lots of metaphors and organizing schemata we could use to describe connection, perhaps one of the best is the idea of ritual. A ritual is a set of "recurring behaviors and routines that hold positive symbolic meaning."[1] Important to the definition is that rituals are positive and meaningful. Steven Wolin and Linda Bennett emphasize this by saying that ritual is "a symbolic form of communication that, owing to the satisfaction that family members experience through its repetition, is acted out in a systematic fashion over time."[2] Through everyday encounters, families enact rituals that promote relational connection. Children feel loved and appreciated with the predictability of packing a lunch and being walked to the school bus. Husbands and wives enjoy the process of grinding coffee, boiling water, and brewing the perfect cup to share each morning. These routine encounters, over time, create rituals for connecting.

The act of creating and enacting rituals forms shared experiences and memories, serving important functions in relationships. Rituals can help generate and sustain identities—they make people feel like they belong to something bigger than themselves.[3] They can also transmit history and, in the process, "socialize children within their cultural context."[4] As an example, think about the Passover Seder. Passover is a ritualized celebration of God's deliverance of the Hebrews from slavery in Egypt. It encourages families to communicate the story of the exodus from Egypt to the next generation and annually offers a reminder of God's promises to sanctify, deliver, and redeem his people, eventually bringing them to the Promised Land.

God often commands families to remember his work and promises.

Psalm 145 states that one generation will commend God's kingdom to the next. Deuteronomy 6:7–10 encourages families to pass on the commandments of God:

> These commandments that I give you today are to be on your hearts. Impress them on your children. Talk about them when you sit at home and when you walk along the road, when you lie down and when you get up. Tie them as symbols on your hands and bind them on your foreheads. Write them on the doorframes of your houses and on your gates.

Rituals can also serve to stabilize and entertain families. In turbulent and uncertain times, rituals can provide an anchor of expectation that mitigates waves of uncertainty and stress. Rituals like weddings and funerals also offer a way to navigate the stress of normative family transitions like gaining or losing a family member.[5] Other rituals can promote intimacy and camaraderie. By participating in joint activities surrounding rituals, families build and sustain unity, cohesion, and intimacy.[6] Plus, rituals can be a lot of fun! They can become sources of entertainment for family members, like playing capture the flag each year on a family vacation or having a couple's game night once a week.[7]

Categories of Rituals

Rituals can be formal or informal. Wolin and Bennett identify three categories of family rituals: *celebrations, family traditions,* and *patterned interactions.*[8] A wedding is an example of a formal family celebration ritual. It is symbolic of joining two family cultures, and it is (usually) a positive experience.[9] It is important to note that a ritual "is not just the ceremony or actual performance but the whole process of preparing for it, experiencing it, and reintegration back into everyday life."[10] Wedding planning, including things like picking a venue, determining details about the ceremony, generating a guest list, selecting decorations, and coordinating a reception, is as much a part of the ritual as is the "big day." Other celebration rituals that are more formal and socially scripted might include Thanksgiving, Easter, funerals, and rites of passage (like a baby shower, Quinceañera, or Senior Prom).

Not all rituals are widely recognized across society. Some just exist within particular families. These idiosyncratic *family traditions* can create powerful positive memories for those involved. Whereas Christmas is a common celebration ritual, different families have different traditions associated with the ritual. Perhaps reading about Jesus's nativity from the Bible or watching certain movies mark the holiday. Some families follow an advent calendar or light advent candles. Not all families put up Christmas lights, but for some it is a tradition. In Jonathan's family, we make hot chocolate from raw cacao beans at Christmas time. It is an hour-long process of roasting the beans, husking and grinding them, and then mixing in other ingredients to enjoy a gritty, rich, chocolatey mug. Family traditions might include annual hunts, shopping excursions, certain meals on special days, periods of family fasting or prayer, and others.

A final category of rituals is *patterned interactions*. These are the most common kind of family ritual and include things like greetings and goodbyes. Such informal patterned interactions can happen every day. An example is a bedtime routine. The ritual can symbolize love, care, and stability for parents and children. The predictability of the routine makes kids feel safe and parents feel needed. The ritual might include all the preparation, such as washing faces, brushing teeth, showering, and changing into pajamas. It might then move into reading a chapter out of *The Lord of the Rings* or *Winnie the Pooh* or a picture book like *Goodnight Moon*. Then the children might reflect on something that day for which they are grateful and offer prayers of thankfulness. Connecting with God through a meditation, Bible reading, or regular prayer is another kind of daily ritual that can bring peace and direction to life. As family members attribute positive meanings to these daily routines, they can be transformed into meaningful rituals for connecting.

|||||||► **Application Activity 5.1:**
Family Rituals

- Share some family rituals and their significance to you.
- Classify them in terms of the three main categories of family rituals: celebrations, family traditions, and patterned interactions.

A study that examined marital rituals focused on different types of patterned interactions. Based on interviews and open-ended surveys, Carol

Bruess and Judy Pearson describe five types of patterned interactions in married couples.[11] First, everyday talk involves individualized language (e.g., honeybun) and having routine times to talk (e.g., over coffee each morning, after kids are in bed each evening). A second ritual includes routines for completing day-to-day tasks, such as preparing and sharing meals, washing dishes, shopping, and doing laundry. Third, couple time includes rituals associated with time spent together engaging in leisure activities. This could be something like a couple date night. There are also rituals of patterned interaction that are unique to couples, such as idiosyncratic traditions and celebrating special events in the relationship (e.g., anniversaries, first date celebrations). Finally, couples enjoy rituals related to sexual intimacy, including intimate displays of affection, patterns of frequency, and when they engage in sexual intercourse. While rituals can encompass a wide variety of cultural celebrations and family traditions, rituals of patterned interactions are probably some of the most important for sustaining connection in families.

Rituals are a good framework for understanding connection because they remind us of the rhythm of meaning that is needed to create family. This framework adopts a perspective that the daily joy and the hard work of relationships should be endowed with significance. We turn now to look at several ways in which significance and ritual are communicated in family life. We start with a fundamental bedrock to all types of family relationships—listening. We then turn to look at behaviors that help maintain marital and sibling relationships. We close by examining how to develop rituals for showing love and encouraging one another.

Listening as a Lifestyle for Connection

Proverbs 18:13 says it is folly and shame to answer before listening. James 1:19 says everyone should be quick to listen and slow to speak. Another Proverb (10:19) conveys that when there are many words, transgression is unavoidable, but whoever remains silent is prudent. Psalm 141:3 says, "set a guard, O Lord, over my mouth; keep watch over the door of my lips!" Obviously, these verses put a premium on listening and understanding. Most agree that listening is important, but we want to focus on the process of listening.

Proverbs 20:5 (NASB) says, "A plan in the heart of a person is like deep water, but a person of understanding draws it out." Have you ever drawn water from a well? Most people in places with running water have not. So, imagine you have a bucket attached to a rope as you stand before a hole in the ground. The rope is prickly and thick, long and heavy. It just fills your hand when you wrap your fingers around it. The rope is coiled but is about 300 feet long. That is taller than a 24-story building. There is no pulley system or hand crank on this well, just a circumference of stones around a two-foot opening. You lower a heavy wooden bucket down the 275 feet into the water below. You let the bucket sink into the water and then draw it up. It fills two gallons of water, about 16 pounds. Then you start to pull. If you want the maximum amount of water, you cannot exactly let the rope pull against the top edge of the well because the bucket will bounce along the well as you draw it up, losing water—the very thing you are trying to draw out. Instead, you have to reach out over the well and hand-over-hand pull the rope up. You must be slow, patient, methodical, and consistent.

Drawing water from a well may be closer to the Proverb writer's imagination than a pump or water faucet. The passage claims that someone of understanding can draw out deep thoughts from another person's heart. Think through the analogy. The proverb puts a premium on slow, patient, methodical, and consistent practices for connecting. These will reach the deep plans, thoughts, feelings, and motivations of another person to draw them out. Often, in conversation, this takes form in questions. As Christian minister Steve Shadrach advises, "Never tell anyone something when you could ask them a question that would help them discover it themselves."[12] Some open-ended questions Shadrach and others suggest are: Have you ever had any spiritual experiences? Could you tell me about them? What terms would you use to describe your prayer life? What brings you complete fulfillment? When was the last time you did something and felt as though God was in it? Asking such open-ended questions is a conversational move that draws out the plans of another person's heart.

If you want to connect regularly with another person in a relationship, then it takes intentionality and effort common to good listeners. A useful acronym for remembering good listening is to become an "ACE" listener. First, "A" stands for *attention*. It means you should listen with your whole body. Put down any distractions like a phone or book. Turn away from your computer or tablet screen. Make eye contact and lean into the conversation. Maintain an open posture, and avoid crossing your arms. Face your conversation partner, and do not try to talk over your shoulder.

The second role of an ACE listener is to *clarify*. You can think of it as listening with your heart. If you do not understand something, then ask! "What do you mean when you say. . . ?" "I've never heard something described that way. Can you give me an example?" An easy phrase to remember and practice is simply, "Tell me more." All of these give opportunity for your child, friend, classmate, or spouse to keep the floor and keep sharing. It also signals that you are paying attention and want more detail. You can also simply repeat a phrase that you want to be explained. Or you can paraphrase what someone has said, trying to see if you have rightly interpreted the emotional subtext of their message.

Finally, ACE listeners *encourage* continued conversation and intimate disclosure. The idea is that you are the person of understanding drawing plans from the deep well of another. Create a safe environment while being mindful of your physical and social surroundings. Some things are best said in private. Other topics need tact when in mixed company. To make a safe environment you can invite stories, offer positive feedback, and seek to truly know the other person. Beyond the setting, you can become a safe person. Give safe touches (hugs, fist bumps, high fives, pats on the shoulder). Be non-judgmental. Let others know that they can share anything—successes and mistakes—with you. It is also paramount to maintain confidentiality. Gossip is a quick way to kill depth in any relationship.

||||||||▶   **Application Activity 5.2:**
Drawing from the Well

- **Think of a time when you were able to draw someone else out. Without sharing the details about the conversation, what communication tools did you use to draw them out?**
- **Partner up with someone to share and compare lists. What is similar? What is different?**
- **What specific ways did you engage in ACE listening?**

Employing Relationship Maintenance Behaviors as Rituals for Connecting

Relationship maintenance refers to a set of communication behaviors designed to keep a valued relationship in a desired state.[13] Relationships are created and sustained in interaction; therefore, relationship maintenance behaviors are the things we say or do intentionally to maintain our relationship with another individual, often involving mundane or routine aspects of day-to-day life but also including planned, strategic behaviors.[14] Laura Stafford and Daniel Canary developed the most recognized relationship maintenance typology.[15] The typology, as originally presented, consists of five categories:

- **Positivity**: communicating in an upbeat, cheerful, optimistic way.

- **Openness**: communicating directly and honestly about the nature of the relationship.

- **Assurance**: communicating one's affection and commitment to the relationship.

- **Networks**: including friends and family members in couple activities.

- **Tasks**: sharing in joint activities and household chores.

Decades of research confirm that these relationship maintenance strategies are essential for the stability and satisfaction of relationships.

Connection, however, is not one-sided. It takes two to form and maintain a relationship. Equity Theory is used as a theoretical framework for making predictions about relationship maintenance behaviors. The theory proposes that we want to sustain a dynamic equilibrium in a given relationship that keeps things balanced. Therefore, we engage in maintenance behaviors if we see the relationship as fair or equitable. An equitable relationship is one in which the benefits and rewards for each person are equal to the contributions or the costs of being in the relationship. Inequity takes one of two forms: Underbenefitted is when one's ratio of benefits to contributions is lower than one's partner, while overbenefitted is when one's benefits/contributions ratio is higher than one's partner. It is easy to see why a person would be dissatisfied if she feels underbenefitted. Based on the theory, maintenance behaviors ebb and flow with this cost-benefit analysis, investing more in a relationship when overbenefitted and less when underbenefitted. The ideal relationship is one in which there is an equal exchange of benefits so that it is mutually and equally beneficial. Put another way, relational satisfaction is based on a "mental balance sheet" that monitors relational cost and rewards and adjusts maintenance behaviors accordingly.[16]

Another theory that helps to explain why we engage in positivity, openness, assurances, networks, and shared tasks is the theory of "inclusion of the other in the self" (IOS) developed by Arthur Aron, Debra Mashek, and Elaine Aron.[17] IOS proposes that in close relationships, a person's partner (i.e., "the other") is part of a person (i.e., "the self").[18] By definition, closeness requires including the other in the self. Within this framework, relationship maintenance behaviors "are communicative acts that foster perception of shared resources, identities, and perspectives."[19] Here are some definitions for each of these areas of inclusion.

- **Shared resources**: access to shared resources, including tangible resources, knowledge, and tasks.

- **Shared identities**: activities that foster shared memories and identities, including physical contact, direct expression of affection, discussion pertaining to relationship management, nicknames, and private codes.

- **Shared perspectives**: behaviors that construct shared perspectives, often developed from shared experiences, including casual talk, humor, deep talk, "hanging out," and shared entertainment.

Engaging in these sets of behaviors can help maintain a relationship and is not limited to married couples. Siblings can develop shared identities as "the Joneses" or "sisters." And over time, as the other in a relationship develops, learns new things, or changes, their gains can be incorporated into the self, which keeps the relationship dynamic fresh and motivates more relationship maintenance.

From a Christian perspective, IOS is appealing as it emphasizes the "we," the interconnectedness between individuals, while equity theory centers on "I," what is in the best interest of the individual. We also can see how being "born again" (see John 3) includes God's Spirit in us. Like the Apostle Paul wrote, "[I]f anyone is in Christ, he is a new creature" (2 Cor. 5:17, NASB). There is an inclusion of God (other) in self. As Andrew Ledbetter and his colleagues note, the self-other inclusion approach captures Martin Buber's conceptualization of interpersonal communication "as located in the essence between two people."[20] On the other hand, there is a vast overbenefitting for humans in the exchange that God offers. "God was reconciling the world to himself in Christ, not counting people's sins against them. . . . God made him [Christ] who had no sin to be sin for us, so that in him we might become the righteousness of God" (2 Cor. 5:19–21). That God forgave sin by condemning sin in his son, Jesus Christ, is an unfair exchange, but one that models love and a total commitment toward relating with us.

Siblings' Relationship Maintenance Behaviors

How do you maintain relationships with your family members? Research has shown that most of us prefer to use positivity and shared tasks to maintain familial bonds, with openness almost always being the least frequently used behavior.[21] Why? Positivity may suggest that we enjoy communicating with one another, and shared tasks speak to our obligation to support each other in very practical ways. Why is openness the least preferred? In contrast to romantic relationships, where self-disclosure creates deeper intimacy, self-disclosure within family relationships is a means of conveying or receiving information without deep intimate sharing.

What are the expectations for maintaining sibling relationships in your family? How do those expectations impact your actual relationship maintenance behaviors? What happens to family satisfaction when those expectations are not met? Elizabeth Hall and Jenna McNallie examined siblings' perceptions and expectations of siblings' relationship maintenance behaviors and how these perceptions and expectations were associated with satisfaction. Survey results revealed that higher perceptions of relational maintenance behaviors with siblings were associated with higher relationship satisfaction.[22] Participants expected brothers and sisters to engage in relationship maintenance behaviors and were more satisfied when they did. Findings also showed that upbringing often sets those expectations.

How would you classify your relationship with one of your siblings—intimate, congenial, loyal, apathetic, hostile? How does the quality of your relationship impact how the two of you maintain the relationship? Not surprisingly, relationship quality matters. For instance, if you see your relationship with your sibling as intimate, then you are more likely to use assurances, openness, and networks to maintain that relationship than if you perceived your relationship as congenial or loyal.[23] If you classify that sibling relationship as either intimate or congenial, then you likely perceive that your sibling uses more relational maintenance behaviors with you than if you classified that relationship as either loyal, apathetic, or hostile.[24]

Love and Encouragement

Regardless of the type of relationship one is in, listening creates a foundation for connection. More fundamental, however, is love. Love originates with God, for it emanates from his character. God always initiates with love, for he is love. Christ's death is a demonstration of that love. We can consider Christ as God's communication (the Word made flesh) and the perfect expression of the love of the Father. Our communication also should express our love, which is the focus of this next section. We discuss "love languages" and an acronym for communicating encouragement.

Speaking One's Love Language as a Ritual for Connecting

Over three decades ago, Gary Chapman was a pastor who did marriage counseling for parishioners. In talking with dozens of couples, he began to see that couples who genuinely loved each other were having difficulty connecting because they did not feel loved. Borrowing a psychological concept that we all have a "love tank" that needs to be filled, Chapman began to understand that couples were not filling each other's love tanks because they did not understand when their partner was expressing love. Even though they spoke the same verbal language, it was as if they communicated love in two different languages. To play out the metaphor, it is like a wife is screaming "I love you" in Italian to a husband who only understands Chinese. The urgency of a message may come through, but it could easily be misinterpreted as anger or frustration. Chapman eventually developed a typology of five "love languages" that represent the dominant ways of expressing and receiving love in marriage, friendships, and parenting.[25] The five languages include:

- **Words of Affirmation**: a preference for others to communicate affection regularly via verbal compliments and other words of appreciation and encouragement.

- **Quality Time**: a preference for others to provide focused attention, marked by empathetic, reflective listening and self-disclosure, and engagement in mutually enjoyable activities.

- **Receiving Gifts**: a preference for others to give visual symbols of affection; these gifts are received regularly but need not be expensive.

- **Acts of Service**: a preference for others to perform practical actions to express affection (i.e., partners doing everyday tasks for them).

- **Physical Touch**: a preference for tactile expressions of love from others, including both sexual touch for couples and nonsexual touch in other relationships.

Chapman suggests that each of us has a primary love language, and some people are bilingual or even trilingual. To be effective communicators of love, we have to recognize that what makes us feel loved "is not always the thing that makes another person feel loved emotionally."[26] We must learn the primary (and secondary) love languages of our family members and choose to speak them in order to fill their love tanks.

Speaking each other's love language improves relational satisfaction. Nichole Egbert and Denise Polk[27] tested Chapman's love language framework against Stafford, Dainton, and Haas's well-established relationship maintenance typology (assurances, social networks, openness, positivity, and shared tasks)[28] and found parallels between the two models. People who scored highly on communicating the love languages of others also scored highly on relational maintenance. Coupled with research that shows relationship maintenance is correlated with relational satisfaction,[29] Egbert and Polk's work suggests that expressing a partner's primary love language is a relational maintenance strategy that increases relationship satisfaction. More recent research, questioning the link between love languages and relational satisfaction, found that mere knowledge of a partner's love language does not correspond with relational satisfaction, but the researchers acknowledged that "it is plausible that willingness and capability to express

||||||| ▶ **Application Activity 5.3:**
Discover Your Love Language

- **Take Chapman's love language quiz:**
  https://www.5lovelanguages.com/quizzes/couples-quiz
- **Partner up and share the results. Does the test accurately identify your love language(s)? What are specific ways others can fill your "love tank"?**
- **Think of someone close to you and brainstorm two specific ways you can fill that person's "love tank."**

relevant behaviors do."[30] In other words, better relationships come not only from knowing a partner's love language but also communicating in it.

What would it look like to develop a ritual of communicating love? One idea is to take one week and find a creative way to express affection through a different love language each day of the week. On Monday, work to show love through gifts, Tuesday through touch, Wednesday through words, and so forth. Or find a way to show love through each language on one day. Rituals like a goodbye hug express love through touch. A note in a lunchbox shows love through words. There are countless rituals that might express love and promote connection.

Encouragement

In addition to expressing love, we all need encouragement. There are many Bible verses in the New Testament that instruct us to encourage (e.g., 1 Thess. 5:11; Heb. 10:24; Gal. 6:2). Unfortunately, hearing encouragement is not as common as it should be. John and Julie Gottman, the foremost marriage researchers in the country, suggest that people need five encouraging or affirming comments for each discouraging message. This "magic ratio" of 5 to 1 helps to balance our perspectives.[31] We hear a barrage of negativity, so communicating positivity allows us to come back toward a neutral place in our relationships.

Communicating positivity can feel kind of weird at first. It feels unnatural because most of us are not trained to speak every encouraging thing that comes to mind.[32] It can feel fake, cheesy, or even shallow to make positive comments to our friends, siblings, or romantic partners. I (Jonathan) have practiced this for some time now, and I find that it is less and less shallow the more I try it. It really helps to give voice to some of the thoughts that run through my head. None of us can read minds, so unless we say something, our siblings, co-workers, spouses, and friends will not hear our positive thoughts. Communication matters! Sharing compliments gives a sense of stability and nurtures fondness in a relationship. Far from being shallow or fake, it creates a much-needed balance in a relationship. In turn, offering lots of positivity also creates a safe space to vent frustrations, make suggestions, give advice, or discuss serious areas of disagreement in a relationship. Without the balanced positivity in the day-to-day ebbs and flows of conversation, these harder topics can lead to dissociation, disenfranchisement, or disgust in relationships.

A memorable acronym to help guide encouragement is CPA. Usually this means Certified Public Accountant, but for us it stands for Character, Performance, and Appearance. The three areas for affirmation encompass a wide swath of human experience. We can share compliments, encouragements, and affirmations about almost anything. Also, the areas are ordered intentionally. They move from areas in which we have the most control to areas where we have the least control. The order also corresponds to the most important aspects of who we are (e.g., our character, identity, core values) toward less important areas like our hair styles.

The CPA model of encouragement is important for all types of relationships, but we illustrate it with an example from parenting. Let's imagine a nine-year-old boy gets a base hit in little league baseball. After the game when the child and his parents are reliving the experience, the parents might say, "You looked good out there!" or "Nice hit!" These praises corresponding to appearance and performance will certainly cheer the boy. The parents might also say something like, "I'm proud of your hit today. I really love how you worked hard at practices to work on your swing!" This encouragement is also about performance, but at a deeper level than "Nice hit!" This comment links hard work with desired performance, which can be a powerful motivator for continued hard work. Going a step further, parents might affirm, "You did great at the game today! I'm proud that you're a hard worker and that all your practice paid off today! Nice hit!" This encouragement gets to the level of character. It affirms that the boy is a hard worker. By framing an encouragement in terms of character, the parents affirm values they hold, like hard work or persistence. When we affirm someone's character, it creates a deep reservoir of confidence that drives positive action across an array of fields, not just baseball. A biblical example is when Jesus encourages Peter: "I tell you that you are Peter, and on this rock I will build my church, and the gates of Hades will not overcome it" (Matt. 16:18). Jesus did not mince words. He did not focus on Peter's appearance or performance. He cut straight to the core identity—his character.

Another dimension that can affect the meaning of communication, particularly encouragement, is whether it is public or private. Both settings for encouragement are needed and important. But the setting can really impact the weight a message carries. Public declarations generally add value. It may embarrass someone to hear public praise, but it also adds recognition. The Academy Awards or Miss America Pageant would not be the same without an audience. In fact, the audience is a key motivator for many. Similarly, making praise public can make it more meaningful. Even God made his family praise public: "This is my beloved son, listen to him" (Matt. 3:17). Parents should do the same from time to time.

Spouses, too, should take opportunities to "brag" on each other in public. "Wow, honey, you're one of the best joke tellers I know!" "I'm always impressed by how kind you are!" "What a generous act! Thanks for leading the way in giving!" While praise can also take place in private, we also need to express our affection and admiration publicly. A wedding ceremony is a good example of a public declaration, but it should not stop there.

Conclusion

Finding ways to connect with one another is one of the most prominent tasks families face throughout their existence. Along with handling conflict, seeking and extending forgiveness, building resilience, and doing life together, creating meaningful connections is one of the blessings of family life. However, knowing that you can innovate, maintain, or develop rituals for connecting does not necessarily translate into practicing rituals with shared significance. In fact, Leslie Baxter theorized that families approach rituals in six different ways.[33] *Under-ritualized* families practice family routines rarely, often ignoring important milestones. *Rigidly ritualized* families have strict rules for enacting rituals. *Skewed ritualization* occurs when ritual practices are linked to one member of the family or one aspect of family life. Family members can practice *hollow rituals*, patterned communication events that lack meaningful significance. *Interrupted rituals* refer to changes in ritual practices due to sudden change in the family such as death or illness. *Flexible ritualized families* maintain the significance of family rituals and are able to adapt the practices across lifespan. We encourage that you move toward flexible (not rigid), meaningful (not hollow), shared (not skewed) family rituals for connecting.

Chapter 6

Rules for Conflict: Establishing Parameters for Hard Conversations

Chapter Summary: Conflicts are an inevitable part of family life, and navigating them well is important not only for the emotional, physical, and spiritual health of the family but also because Christ said that love for one another is how everyone will know his disciples. This makes handling conflict in ways that honor God a core value for Christians. This chapter begins with a discussion about the causes of conflict in families. It then defines conflict, identifies types and signs of conflict, and presents a typology of conflict management styles. The last section of the chapter shares ways that researchers and therapists have found to engage successfully in conflict and offers strategies for handling conflict in ways that honor God.

Introduction

AN INFAMOUS BIBLICAL FAMILY FEUD was between the twins Esau and Jacob. These brothers got into a spat over the cultural practice of granting a double portion of the inheritance and governance of the family estate to the first-born. Jacob "purchased" the birthright for a bowl of red lentil soup, which earned him one angry older brother. Then, with his mother colluding, Jacob deceived his nearly-blind father by clothing himself in Esau's garments, putting animal hair over his arms, and roasting meat. When approaching his father's death, Esau vowed: "The days of mourning for my father are near; then I will kill my brother Jacob" (Gen. 27:41). It was not until decades later that Esau and Jacob reconciled. Esau forgave and "ran to meet Jacob and embraced him; he threw his arms around his neck and kissed him. And they wept" (Gen. 33:4). In terms of family favoritism and conflict, this sibling pair and their parents are a case study. You can take some time to think through the geopolitical and theological implications of Jacob and Esau's conflict, but our purpose is to examine how this relates to family communication.

Conflict is an inevitable part of social life. During early years, conflict is perhaps even more prevalent in family settings than others because many of us, especially young children, spend the majority of time in family set-tings.[1] Take sibling rivalry. As the joke goes, Cain hated his brother as long as he was Abel. This chapter begins with a discussion about the causes of conflict in families. We then define conflict, identify types of conflict, and review research showing that handling conflict is important for the emo-tional, physical, and spiritual health of families. Our goal with this text is not just to teach you about issues in families, but also how to navigate them successfully. The last section of the chapter shares ways that researchers and therapists have found to manage conflict successfully.

What Causes Conflict in Families?

Think of your family or a family you know well. What causes conflict in that family? Is it money? Household chores? In-laws? Entertainment? These are all common topics of argument along with sex, (future) children, religion, careers, and friends.[2] What topics are "hot button" issues for you? Most items that make these kinds of lists boil down to external factors that dis-rupt family harmony. Couples feel limited by not having enough money to cover all their goals. Children feel that the household rules are too strict or too lenient. Too much screen time breeds family discord.

The Bible is replete with examples as well as instruction about the roots of conflict. For example, James 4:1–2: "What causes quarrels and what causes fights among you? Is it not this that your passions are at war within you? You desire and do not have, so you murder. You covet and cannot obtain, so you fight and quarrel." The book of Proverbs also has a lot to say about the causes of conflict.

- Hatred stirs up conflict. (Prov. 10:12a)

- Pride leads to conflict. (Prov. 13:10a)

- The greedy stir up conflict. (Prov. 28:25a)

- An angry person stirs up conflict. (Prov. 29:22a)

Christian writer and founder of Peacemaker and Relational Wisdom Ministries Ken Sande argues that unmet desires in our hearts are the root causes of destructive conflict. He writes, "When we feel we cannot be satisfied unless we have something we want or think we need, the desire turns into a demand. If someone fails to meet that desire, we condemn him in our heart and quarrel and fight to get our way. In short, conflict arises when our desires grow into demands and we judge and punish anyone who gets in our way."[3] The progression is undeniable, asserts Sande: I desire. I demand. I punish.[4]

While there is plenty of room for conflict to arise because of our own selfishness, there can also be spiritual dimensions to it. Conflict is a battle, and it may be a spiritual battle. Satan's forces are in the business of tearing down and destroying relationships, and this dark power cannot be ignored.[5] There are likely other examples, but one clear expression of the spiritual dimension of conflict is when the disciple Peter tried to persuade Jesus to take a different course of action. Jesus said, "Get behind me Satan" (Matt. 16:23). While we are not recommending that you use this phrase with your brother, girlfriend, or parent, it does illustrate that spiritual forces can play into our conversations and relationships.

The famous Oxford professor C. S. Lewis wrote a book from the perspective of a demon. *Screwtape Letters* is a collection of correspondence between a novice demon tempter named Wormwood and his more experienced uncle, a demonic principality named Screwtape. Here is a selection of imagined demonic wisdom in which Screwtape instructs Wormwood about family communication.

> When two humans have lived together for many years it usually happens that each has tones of voice and expressions of face which are almost unendurably irritating to the other. Work on that. Bring fully into the consciousness of your patient that particular lift of his mother's eyebrows which he learned to dislike in the nursery, and let him think how much he dislikes it. Let him assume that she knows how annoying it is and does it to annoy—if you know your job he will not notice the immense improbability of the assumption. And, of course, never let him suspect that he has tones and looks which similarly annoy her. As he cannot see or hear himself, this is easily managed.[6]

While an imagination, Lewis's portrayal of how the spiritual realm interjects into human consciousness may not be far from reality. If we can believe that God is an active speech-agent and that people have heard from angels (e.g., Elijah, Daniel, Mary, Joseph), then it is equally probable that demons can speak, distort, or mute interactions.[7] Afterall, Eve and Jesus both had conversations with Satan (see Gen. 3 and Matt. 4). Advises Screwtape, "It is funny how mortals always picture us as putting things into their minds: in reality our best work is done by keeping things out."[8] If the demonic realm had no influence over our interactions with others, why would we need the armor of God? If the flaming darts of the enemy had no effect or could have no effect, the Apostle Paul's instruction in Ephesians 6 would be nonsense. Related to conflict, Paul even urges Christians, "Do not let the sun go down while you are still angry, and do not give the devil a foothold" (Eph. 4:26–27). Allowing conflict to fester creates a spiritual opening, a vulnerability.

From our perspective, conflict is a result of the Fall and spurred on by spiritual forces. Before Satan tempted Eve and sin entered the world, Adam and Eve lived in harmony—*shalom*—with God, one another, and nature. Now, conflict is inevitable. It is caused by our fundamental belief that it is within our prerogative to assert our own way. Humans believe and act as if they know better than God. The lust of the eye, the lust of the flesh, and the pride of life wooed us into a persistent and fundamental contest against God (see 1 John 2:16). We gained knowledge of good and evil (nakedness, shame, deception, and masking) and lost *shalom*.

What Is Conflict?

Scholars often define conflict as when two people vie for limited resources and one person does not get what she or he wants. For example, Joyce Hocker and William Wilmot define it this way: "[C]onflict is an expressed struggle between at least two independent parties who perceive incompatible goals, scarce resources, and interference from others in achieving their goals."[9] Within the family context, conflict is a "process whereby family members perceive a disagreement about goals, rules, roles, culture, and/or patterns of communication."[10] The two key elements in this definition are that conflict is a *process* that develops over time and that conflict depends on *perception*, whether families are actually at odds or whether they think they disagree when they actually do not.

While there is merit to these definitions, conflict is more than a process and perception. In fact, only looking at conflict as a type of disagreement obscures the true nature of conflict. Conflict comes from two Latin words: "together" and "to strike."[11] Conflict is more analogous to a fist fight than a disagreement. It is a battle in which individuals "strike" each other with silence, words, or actions. There are key differences between disagreement and conflict. Disagreement is simply holding different opinions about questions of fact, policy, or value. Conflict is rooted in personal differences of value, emotionally charged and long-standing. It affects the quality of life and damages our credibility as followers of Jesus Christ.[12] Because of its nature, conflict always gives opportunity for the ministry of reconciliation (2 Cor. 5).

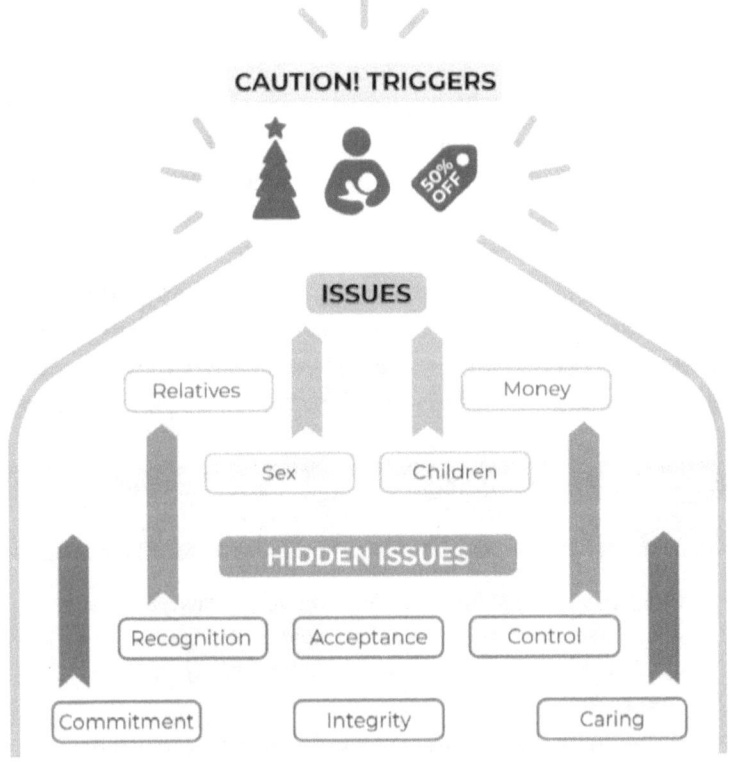

Figure 6.1: Triggers, Issues, and Hidden Issues, based on Howard J. Markman, Scott M. Stanley, and Susan L. Blumberg, *Fighting for Your Marriage: Positive Steps for Preventing Divorce and Preserving a Lasting Love* (San Francisco, CA: Jossey-Bass Publishers, 1994).

A helpful model for understanding how conflict occurs in families is included in one of the first evidence-based premarital counseling programs, the Prevention and Relationship Education Program (PREP). Howard Markman and colleagues present a model that shows how relational conflict results from triggers about issues that are fueled by other hidden issues (see Figure 6.1).[13] They imagine these interrelated aspects of human experience as geysers (like Old Faithful in Yellowstone National Park). On the surface, there are sometimes eruptions about trigger events, but these eruptions result from increasing levels of pressure underneath the surface. Pressure can build in pockets of common experiences, which become topics of conflict (e.g., money, jobs, in-laws, sex). These topics by themselves do not have enough pressure to erupt, but they are fueled by more fundamental human needs, desires, and motivations.

Imagine you overhear a conversation between a married couple about where to spend the Christmas holiday. The calendar serves as the trigger. A few days of paid time off create an opportunity for conversation about whether the couple should spend time alone or with their extended families. They talk about if they should create new traditions or carry forward traditions from the wife's, husband's, or both families. The conversation brings up issues of how to honor predecessors and what imbues holiday rituals with meaning. It brings up hidden issues like recognition and respect. The wife may get angry because she feels helpless to celebrate how she wants if they go to his parent's house. The husband may feel rejected because she does not want to eat salmon on Christmas Eve, which is his family's

---

**|||||||| ▶   Application Activity 6.1:
Scripting Conflict Issues**

- Pick a common conflict topic (e.g., money, in-laws, chores). Identify some trigger events that could lead to conflict. Now consider how two or three of the hidden issues might fuel the conflict.

- Write a potential movie script that illustrates a conflict. Be realistic. In your script, begin by having family members encounter a "trigger" event or conversation. In the dialogue about the trigger, be sure to include one of the "issues" and at least two different "hidden issues."

tradition. The hidden issues of control and respect feed into conflict about family and tradition, all triggered by December 25th. This is one example based on a common event, but there are thousands of triggers. Some are normative stressors like marriage, childbirth, and holidays while others are more idiosyncratic—specific to individuals, couples, and families.

Conflict in Family Systems

In families, conflict is not isolated between individuals. It happens within a system. Two noteworthy ways in which systems conflict happens include the spillover and compensatory effects. The *spillover effect* happens when patterns within one subsystem of a family are repeated in other subsystems. For example, perpetual conflict between husband and wife, modeling dysfunctional relationship behavior, may spillover into parent-child or child-child relationships, leading to destructive conflict patterns. Equally damaging is the *compensatory effect* in which one subsystem of a family tries to compensate in unhealthy ways for the destructive behaviors of another subsystem. Parents in distressed marital relationships may be overly involved, excessively indulgent, or too lenient in their interactions with their children as a way to atone for their negative behaviors.[14]

Conflict Types

It is simple and useful to categorize conflict into topics that are *solvable* and *unsolvable*.[15] Unsolvable problems are perpetual or repeated relational conflicts that may never lead to perfect consensus. These conflicts are often rooted in personality, roles, and value differences. It is estimated that 69% of marital conflicts fall in this unsolvable category.[16] Couples in stable, happy marriages often simply "agree to disagree" or find other ways to deal with these problems. With less stable relationships, perpetual conflicts tend toward gridlock. Couples rehash the problem over and over which leads to hurt, frustration, and/or distrust. In contrast, solvable conflicts, as the name implies, represent topics where couples come to an agreement. It is important to keep in mind, too, that just because agreement is possible does not mean that these conflicts are resolved.[17] Effective conflict resolution strategies help individuals navigate solvable conflict successfully.

Another way to understand conflict is to see ways it can occur at *content* and *relational* levels. The content level is the "what," or the subject about which individuals are disagreeing. It might be, for example, whether to attend a private or public university, buy a new car, or where to vacation. The relational level is the "how" of a conflict. The relational level is expressed primarily through nonverbal communication, such as tone of voice, facial expressions, and eye behavior. It focuses on what these behaviors communicate about the relationship between the individuals. A father and his teenage daughter's disagreement about curfew (the content of conflict) is followed by the teenager rolling her eyes and walking away (the relational conflict), which signals the teenager's disrespect for her father.

Finally, family conflict can be *constructive* or *destructive*. Some conflict is damaging, but not all conflict is bad. Nor is it always best for families to avoid conflict. If conflict means to strike, then we may do well to heed the proverb that the wounds of a friend can be trusted (Prov. 27:6). We all have blind spots, and community is a mirror to help us see them. Conflict can alert us to ways we are thinking or acting that are hurtful, destructive, or ignorant. Others help us identify and address behaviors and attitudes that need to change. Jesus's teaching comes to mind, that conflict can help us realize the plank in our own eye as we look to remove the speck of sawdust from our brother's eye (Matt. 7:3–5).

Benefits to conflict are several. Conflict teaches us to listen and to empathize with the perceptions and positions of others. We learn new things about family members. We also come to recognize that there may be many viable solutions to any given problem. Conflict can prevent groupthink because it encourages creativity to see situations differently and work out several viable solutions, often arriving at mutually beneficial ones. We can also come to see through conflict how our perspective may be overly narrow or unconsciously steeped in habit or tradition. If we allow it, conflict can promote humility, love, empathy, and patience. We learn self-control. We learn to prize unity and find resolutions that benefit the entire family. In short, conflict with others, especially within family, creates an incubator for the passages of Scripture that tell us how to treat one another. This applies both to our natural and spiritual families. We are to love, honor, build-up, accept, admonish, care for, forgive, be patient with, serve, and submit to one another.

Signs of Conflict

Observing thousands of couples and learning from relationship "masters" and "disasters," John Gottman and Nan Silver distill *Seven Principles for Making Marriage Work*.[18] In their book, they first review signs of conflict in relationships.[19] They offer six signs of impending relationship destruction.

Harsh start-ups refer to the negativity and accusatory remarks that can plague the first few minutes of a conversation. Gottman and Silver argue that they can predict with 96% accuracy the outcome of a conversation within the first three minutes. The lesson here is clear: start softly. Proverbs 15:1 reminds us that "[a] gentle answer turns away wrath, but a harsh word stirs up anger."

Four horsemen identify communication behaviors that signal the impending destruction of a relationship. The four horsemen are criticism, contempt, defensiveness, and stonewalling. While we present them in an order, they do not necessarily happen in any particular order. It is also useful to know that even healthy relationships sometimes exhibit these signs from time to time. But when they ride together and occur frequently and habitually, it can signal relationship problems.

The first horseman is *criticism*. Criticism is analogous to the logical fallacy *ad hominem* (literally, "against person"). A criticism expresses a negative opinion about an individual's character or personality. It goes a step beyond a complaint, which is a statement about a specific behavior or event. The complaint "I do not like eating dinner so late" turns to criticism by adding "just because you care more about your friends than me." The complaint "I don't think it's fair that I always have to mow the lawn" turns to criticism by adding "just because you're so lazy." Complaints commonly have three parts: a statement of how one feels (e.g., I am hurt), an identification of a specific situation or action (e.g., because you forgot our anniversary), and a resolution (e.g., could we celebrate our anniversary next weekend?). Expressing a complaint is part of normal interaction; it can even be healthy in relationships. Insulting your sibling, spouse, child, or parent with criticism is not.

The second horseman is *defensiveness*. Defensiveness is self-protection through justifying one's actions while shifting the blame to someone else. Some examples of defensive statements: "I may have spent too much money shopping, but that's because you're always traveling and don't spend time with me." "You're right, I don't want to go to your family reunion because you never want to do anything with my family." When a person feels attacked, some form of defense is a natural response. For most of us, it takes some un-learning to adopt a non-defensive posture—one that listens and seeks to understand rather than justifying our own position and derogating the other.

The third horseman is *contempt*. Contempt signals disrespect and expresses superiority over another. It is persistent disrespect. Some expressions of contempt include sarcasm, name-calling, eye-rolling, and hostile humor. Gottman and Silver put it this way: "In whatever form, contempt is poisonous to a relationship because it conveys disgust," making it nearly impossible to resolve the problem.[20]

The fourth horseman is *stonewalling*. Stonewalling is physically and/or psychologically tuning out another person. A stonewaller is non-responsive and may physically leave or simply ignore any attempts to communicate. The stonewaller may act like he is not at all interested in you or what you are saying. She may enact the silent treatment, escape into a phone or book, and will convey the message that there is no room for any further communication.

Flooding is the sensation of feeling physically and emotionally exhausted from the duration and intensity of the negativity. A conflict is so overwhelming that we disengage from the relationship. We give up and check out.

Body language signals relational troubles. Gottman and Silver are referring specifically to physiological responses to tense discussion, including increased heart rate, blood pressure, and secretion of adrenaline. Such physiological reactions lead to a reduced capacity to process information. We may fight, freeze, or flee, but our ability to deal productively with the conflict is severely diminished. These physiological reactions severely impair our ability to think clearly and reason through decisions. It is as if our more sophisticated brain functions (in the prefrontal cortex) are suspended and we are left only with the basic functions (regulated by the brain stem). It can take 20 minutes or more for the body to recuperate from high alert.[21]

Failed repair attempts are another indication of distress. Repair attempts are strategies used to de-escalate relational tension and can range from simple actions (e.g., a quirky wink) to more complex ones (e.g., a formal apology). Successful repair attempts decrease emotional tension and lower stress levels. Whether a repair strategy is successful depends on the state of the relationship at the time of the repair. The stronger the relationship, the more successful the repair regardless of the quality of the repair strategy itself. That is right: You can fumble through an apology, for example, and that repair strategy works if the relationship is in a good state at the time. On the other hand, if the relationship is already rocky, you could execute an apology flawlessly and still fail to repair the relationship.

Bad memories reflect an unhappy relationship. As Gottman and Silver note, when a relationship is in trouble, "history gets rewritten—for the worse."[22] Couples that have bad memories may recall their honeymoon with sparse detail or only remember that the food at the restaurant was served cold and that it rained. A happy couple with the same experiences might remember laughing together that their food was served cold and how funny they felt with soaking wet clothes. It is not that the happy couples are simply trying to focus on the positive, but that they really do have "rose colored" glasses, whereas the unhappy couples have reinterpreted their experiences and memories in light of their current relationship status, a condition described as Negative Sentiment Override.[23]

Applying this descriptive information into a prescription for healthy relating, we should focus on developing a strong relationship before conflict arises. "After tracking the lives of happily married couples for as long as twenty years, I now know that the key to reviving or divorce-proofing a relationship is not simply how you handle your disagreements but how you engage with each other when you're not fighting,"[24] claim Gottman and Silver. When in conflict, start softly rather than harshly; avoid criticizing, contemptuous, defensive, and stonewalling behaviors; monitor your physiology for warning signs of flooding; learn and use effective repair techniques; and focus on what has gone "right" in the relationship by recalling relational histories fondly. But most importantly, focusing daily on your relationship and contributing toward it can help weather conflict when it does storm.

Addressing Family Conflict

There are numerous ways in which you can address conflict in your family relationships. Most recommendations center on gaining knowledge, enhancing skills, and using appropriate tools. It can be very helpful to reflect on your dispositions. But just recognizing how you tend to deal with conflict is not enough. It is paramount that you develop some skills in relating well. It can also help to engage pastoral or professional counselors when conflict is intense, repetitive, or cyclical. Within the family, high-pressured conflicts may call for formal tools for dealing with conflict. Markman and colleagues give the analogy of a nuclear reactor: when conflicts are high

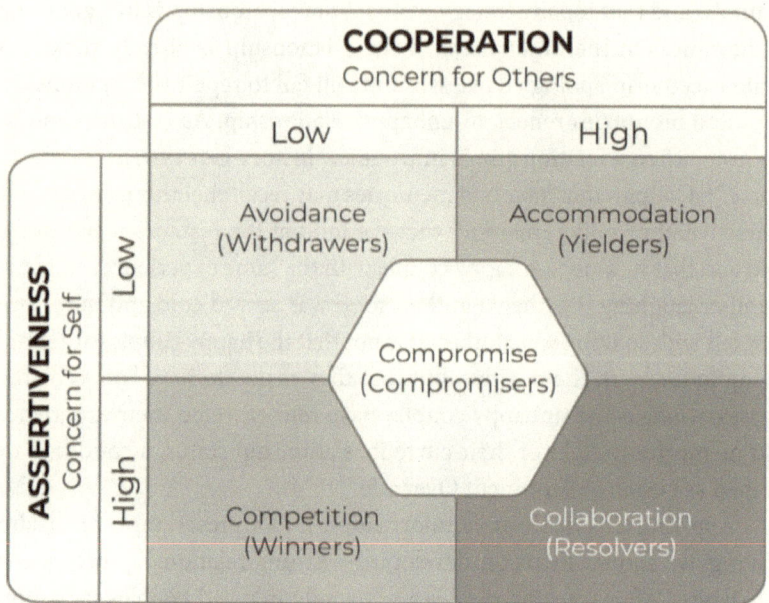

Figure 6.2: Identifying Conflict Management Styles, based on Jack O. Balswick and Judith K. Balswick, *The Family: A Christian Perspective on the Contemporary Home*, 3rd ed. (Grand Rapids, MI: Baker Academic, 2007), 262.

pressure, it is important to add structure. When they are less pressured, less structure is needed.[25] Tools, skills, and knowledge, then, can help you handle conflict in ways that honor each other and God.

Types of Conflict Management Styles

How do you handle conflict in your relationships? Do you tend to prepare for the battle, determined to "win at all costs"? Do you flee from conflict? Or perhaps you are quick to give in, not wanting to add fuel to the fire. One popular conflict management model is based on two dimensions: concern for self/personal goals (assertiveness) and concern for others/relationships (cooperation).[26] From these two dimensions, five styles are identified (see Figure 6.2).

The Winner, or the aggressor, is competitive and aggressive, demonstrating high concern for self and low concern for others. There may be times when we need to "fight" for what we believe is right, realizing that we may win the argument but damage family relationships in the process.

The Withdrawer, or the avoider, cocoons rather than engaging in conflict, with low concern for self and low concern for others. While it is acceptable to take a break and withdraw for a time (to clear our heads or calm down), withdrawing for an extended period may signal to family members that we do not care enough about them to work out conflicts.

The Resolver, or the collaborator, is solution-oriented, having high concern for self and high concern for others. Collaboration takes time, effort, and energy but often results in maximum satisfaction for all family members.

The Yielder, or the accommodator, forgoes his or her wishes and puts the wishes of other family members above his or her own, demonstrating low concern for self and high concern for others. We may assent to the wishes of others when we know that the issue is far more important to them than it is to us. While yielding out of love for others is commendable, yielding out of fear, including fear of rejection, is not.

The Compromiser settles, with balanced concern for self and others. All parties concede what they believe to be the best or the ideal solution for what is acceptable to all. Although this style may be appropriate for trivial or minor disputes and useful for decisions that need to be made quickly, it often results in all parties feeling less than satisfied.

Looking at the model, the *Compromiser* and the *Resolver* typically exhibit the best balance between a concern for self, others, and the relationship. However, family scholars Jack O. Balswick and Judith K. Balswick are quick to point out that it is counterproductive to argue for the superiority of one style over another.[27] They contend that there is Scripture support for each of the five styles. Each has its advantages and disadvantages, so the most effective style depends on the situation and the relational goal. You may have an inclination toward one strategy over another, but the more you can adjust your concern for self and others, the more flexible you will be in dealing appropriately with conflicts as they arise.

||||||| ▶ **Application Activity 6.2:**
Identifying Conflict Management Styles

- **What is your default type of conflict management?**
- **Think about a married couple you know. What conflict management style does each person exhibit? When have you seen them change/differ from their default?**

Tools for Addressing Family Conflict

Several researchers have suggested various relational and psychological methods for addressing conflict. We review three different models, all of which help families work through conflicts, though offering slightly different advice. However, because some conflicts are instigated, or at least fueled by evil spiritual forces, we first turn to identifying signs of spiritual warfare at work in our relationships and offer tools that can effectively thwart demonic influence.

Signs and Spiritual Tools for Conflict. How can we recognize spiritual battle occurring in our relationships? Communication scholar and professor Tim Muehlhoff has identified some tell-tale signs of spiritual opposition: inappropriate anger, sense of impending doom, violent dreams, and no longer believing the best about God or our self.[28] Chronic anger and bitterness triggered by even the smallest provocation and a relentless "deep-rooted sense of dread" are signs of demonic opposition.[29] Violent, fear-inducing dreams that feel real also suggest the possibility that Satan has established a foothold in a person's life and mind. The last two signs of demonic opposition pertain to Satan's cunning influence in our thinking. We can believe lies about God and about ourselves (e.g., "God has abandoned me," "God no longer cares," "I am unworthy of love") because the devil's native language is lies (John 8:44). Recognizing that the demonic agenda is always actively to steal, kill, or destroy (John 10:10) will better prepare and equip us to combat the devil's control and power in our lives.

Scripture teaches that we can submit to God and then resist the devil, causing him to flee (James 4:7). The Bible also instructs that God provides spiritual armor to protect against spiritual forces that would assail us (Eph. 6) and that there are angelic armies that support God's people (2 Kings 6:8–18). Once, Jonathan and his wife were traveling through a new area. Rather suddenly, we realized we were bickering and criticizing each other, showing little respect to one another. Simultaneously, I began thinking that my wife did not do enough for me or our family. My wife shared later that she began hearing a voice in her head that said she was not good enough and needed to be more put-together. This all happened within about two minutes while we were on a road trip and while we were bickering and picking at each other with our words. One of us realized that this type of communication was a bit out of character and said so. We paused and took a moment to pray that God would remove any spiritual forces working against us or our marriage. Immediately, the thoughts/voices stopped. The pause to pray also made us stop bickering, too. While we were left with a weird feeling, there is no way to prove that the conflict was spiritual. But it certainly could have been one of the "flaming arrows of the evil one" (Eph. 6:16), aimed at our marriage. Using spiritual weapons, we can engage spirits in battle and "take captive every thought to make it obedient to Christ" (2 Cor. 10:5). Prayer is bedrock to thwarting spiritual opposition; however, not every conflict can be addressed completely through prayer. So, we also present three excellent models for addressing conflict in families.

Getting to the Heart of Conflict. Ken Sande was trained as a lawyer and has written extensively about conflict and conflict resolution. He offers his view of how the Bible teaches about conflict and peace-making. In Sande's model, conflict begins in the heart, and he recommends four steps for resolving conflict: glorify God, get the log out of your own eye, gently restore, and go and be reconciled.[30] (The four principles have also been referred to as *go higher, get real, gently engage,* and *get together*).[31] Taking this perspective is not easy. It probably requires forced reflection to go through these steps during a conflict. But repeating the process a few times can make it routine. It can become a natural part of how you approach situations and conflicts.

Glorify God. The first step is to acknowledge that a goal should be to glorify God. As Colossians 3:17 reminds, "And whatever you do, whether in word or deed, do it all in the name of the Lord Jesus, giving thanks to God the Father through him." Even in the midst of conflict we are to bring God praise by depending on him and walking in obedience. We are to ask ourselves, "How can I please and honor the Lord in this situation?"

Get the log out of your own eye. The second step is to identify how we have contributed to the conflict. It is easy to be defensive and blame others. We must stop this knee-jerk reaction and ask, "How can I show Jesus's work in me by taking responsibility for my contribution to this conflict?" Matthew 7:4–5 pictures our need: "How can you say to your brother, 'Let me take the speck out of your eye,' when all the time there is a plank in your own eye? You hypocrite, first take the plank out of your own eye, and then you will see clearly to remove the speck from your brother's eye." It is only after taking responsibility for our own attitudes and actions that contributed to the conflict that we can begin the process of restoration and reconciliation.

Gently restore. The third step in Sande's model is to develop a strategy for when and how we should go talk privately with another person about the grievance. Sande is quick to point out that Scripture offers many ways to begin the restoration process, and that confrontation is only one possibility. We need to seek God's wisdom as we wrestle with the question, "How can I lovingly serve others by helping them take responsibility for their contributions to this conflict?" If the offense is not serious, then it may be best to overlook it. Proverbs 19:11 (NASB) says, "A person's discretion makes him slow to anger, and it is his glory to overlook a transgression." If the offense is serious, then we probably do need to talk with the offender, but we need to "adjust the intensity of our communication to fit the other person's position and the urgency of the situation."[32] There is a time for rebuke and admonition, but we are also called to instruct and encourage, all with great patience (2 Tim. 4:2).

Go and be reconciled. The fourth step is genuinely desiring and actively pursuing a right relationship with the other person. Reconciliation, according to Sande, "requires that you give the repentant person an opportunity to demonstrate repentance and regain your trust."[33] This often involves forgiving the person for the ways his actions caused harm. We must ask, "How can I demonstrate the forgiveness of God and encourage a reasonable solution to this conflict?" Addressing conflict is not easy, but peace is worth our effort: "Make every effort to keep the unity of the Spirit through the bond of peace" (Eph. 4:3). For some conflicts, reconciliation may not be possible. But we believe it should be a mark of Christian families.

|||||||| ▶ Application Activity 6.3: Family Conflict

- Describe an actual or hypothetical conflict with a family member.
- Analyze the conflict strategy/strategies used by the participants to address the conflict.
- Rewrite the conflict scene, demonstrating an understanding of Sande's model of biblical peacemaking.

The Speaker-Listener Technique. The speaker-listening technique is a second tool that can help facilitate communication around conflict topics. This is a highly formulaic way of interacting that is designed to give maximum structure to protect the relationship from blow-ups during or after conflict discussions. Using the metaphor of a nuclear reactor, Markman and colleagues advise that structure helps control heated discussions.[34]

The speaker-listener technique is a turn-based model for sharing and listening. It works when both parties agree to follow the rules and take on specific roles. Here are the rules for how the discussion goes. First, the couple agrees that the speaker has the floor. Markman and colleagues suggest that the floor is a physical object. They recommend a small swatch of carpet, but a pen or watch or paperclip will do. Second, the couple agrees to share the floor. One person will take a turn being the speaker while the other is the listener. Then they will switch roles. Lastly, when using the speaker-listener technique, the couple agrees to separate their problem discussion from problem solving. Doing so shifts the focus away from rushing to resolution or applying a relational band-aid without fixing the core issue. Instead, the focus of problem discussion becomes really understanding a situation from each person's perspective.

In addition to the rules for how to engage in the speaker-listener technique, there are rules for each role. Speaker rules include speaking for yourself (no mind reading), keeping it short and simple (no filibusters), and pausing for paraphrasing. The speaker rules force self-expression about specific topics. Listener rules require focusing on the speaker's message, paraphrasing it, and refraining from rebuttals. Effectively, these rules encourage active listening and move away from Gottman's four horsemen. Working within these roles and following these rules adds lots of structure and formality to a problem discussion. It is not natural and does not correspond to the ways we engage in everyday talk. It does slow down the interaction and engenders more understanding of each person's experience.

Here is an example of how a speaker-listener conversation sounds. John and Luke are teenage siblings sharing the same bedroom.

> **John** (holding a swatch of carpet): I get frustrated when you set the alarm for 6:00 AM and then hit the snooze button until 7:00 AM.
>
> **Luke** (holding the swatch of carpet): So, it frustrates you that my alarm rings several times. Is that what you're so upset about?
>
> **John** (holding the swatch of carpet): That's right. The constant alarm makes it impossible for me to go back to sleep. I need more sleep!
>
> **Luke** (holding the swatch of carpet): What I am hearing you say is that you want to get more sleep, and that a good night's sleep is

important for you to function throughout the day. You think that if the alarm rang only once you could fall back to sleep. Is that it?

John (holding the swatch of carpet): Exactly. Thanks for listening. I just don't understand why you can't just set the alarm for 7:00 AM. It's not necessary for you to set the alarm an hour before you actually get up.

Luke (holding the swatch of carpet): I feel bad that my hitting the snooze alarm is keeping you from falling back asleep.

John (holding the swatch of carpet): Thanks for talking about this.

There are several positive aspects of this formulaic interaction. It is important to realize that the level of structure needed should correlate with the intensity of the emotions around the conflict topic.

Four Questions for Navigating Conflict. Muehlhoff offers yet another tool for navigating conflict.[35] He proposes that amid intense disagreements we ask ourselves four questions:

- What does this person believe?
- Why does this person hold this belief?
- Where do we agree?
- Based on all that I have learned, how should I proceed?

After answering each question, we must decide on one specific course of action. That is, Muehlhoff argues, we need to make a specific plan: "With this person, at this time, under these circumstances, what is the next thing I should say?"[36] If we can isolate points in common, that is where we begin

||||||||▶   **Application Activity 6.4:**
Paul's Defense to King Agrippa

- **Read Paul's defense to King Agrippa in Acts 26:1–29.**
- **Analyze Paul's strategies for addressing this situation. Did he address each of the questions outlined by Muehlhoff?**
- **Based on your analysis, what would your model look like for addressing a conflict?**

before proceeding to address disagreements. In order to establish common ground, we need to understand both what this person believes and why he holds these beliefs.

Conclusion

Even with the most knowledge, highest skill, and best tools, conflict remains inevitable. Relational transgression will occur. Feelings will get hurt. Being Christian does not inoculate anyone from these experiences, either. As John observes (1 John 1:8), if we do not recognize our sin, then we are deceived. In this chapter we defined conflict and discussed causes of conflict, types of conflict, and different conflict management styles. Most importantly we offered strategies for handling conflict in ways that honor God. From here we need to move forward to forgiveness and reconciliation, recognizing that the leap from conflict to forgiveness is often a process that takes a great deal of time, as it did for Esau and Jacob. As we faithfully continue to follow a God who shows us mercy—"Who is a God like you, who pardons sin and forgives the transgression of the remnant of his inheritance? You do not stay angry forever but delight to show mercy" (Micah 7:18)—we, too, must extend mercy to others.

Chapter 7

Repairing Relationships: Offering and Receiving Forgiveness

Chapter Summary: Hurt and misunderstanding are unavoidable. They are ramifications of selfishness and brokenness in our relationships, but forgiveness redeems relationships. This chapter is grounded in research on types of hurtful messages and responses to them, with emphasis placed on relational repair and forgiveness. In addition to highlighting the biblical story of Joseph as a way to introduce forgiveness, this chapter reviews research from psychologists and communication scholars. It differentiates what forgiveness is and is not, and it covers the process of forgiving and its effects. In the end, the chapter presents forgiveness as a biblical command that people must choose to enact. Engaging in the process of forgiveness creates space for family relationships to flourish.

Introduction

"FATHER, FORGIVE THEM, for they know not what they do" (Luke 23:34). In his last moments on earth, Jesus asked his Father to forgive those who mercilessly beat and crucified him. Forgiveness, as Jesus modeled, is a necessary and fundamental aspect of Christian living. It is not just a nice sentiment or optional path for Christians. As Jesus taught, we pray daily: "[F]orgive us our debts, as we forgive our debtors" (Matt. 6:12, KJV). Forgiveness, paradoxically, remains a choice we make—something we offer to others—but it is also commanded and integral to the Christian family. Let's start by considering one of the oldest, most detailed stories of sibling rivalry and forgiveness.

Joseph was one of 12 brothers, who became the 12 tribes of Israel. Joseph's brothers despised him so much that "they hated him and could not speak a kind word to him" (Gen. 37:4). Joseph's brothers conspired to kill him, but instead opted to sell him into slavery "for twenty shekels of silver to the Ishmaelites, who took him to Egypt" (Gen. 37:28). God promoted Joseph while he was in slavery to an Egyptian official and continued to watch over Joseph when he was unjustly incarcerated. After years went by, Joseph eventually was elevated by God. Joseph gained the audience of the king, interpreted a prophetic dream, and advised the court on how to avoid certain calamity. He was then appointed by Pharaoh to oversee the "whole land of Egypt" (Gen. 41:41). It is an incredible rags-to-riches story, but it continues.

As a severe famine hit the entire geographic region, Joseph's brothers traveled to Egypt to purchase grain. Joseph recognized his brothers, but they did not recognize him. Joseph tested his brothers to see if they had matured and changed their hearts toward him. Finally, he decided to reveal his identity to them in a dramatic scene.

> Then Joseph said to his brothers, "Come close to me." When they had done so, he said, "I am your brother Joseph, the one you sold into Egypt! And now, do not be distressed and do not be angry with yourselves for selling me here, because it was to save lives that God sent me ahead of you. For two years now there has been famine in the land, and for the next five years there will be no plowing and reaping. But God sent me ahead of you to preserve for you a remnant on earth and to save your lives by a great deliverance." (Gen. 45:4–7)

Joseph forgave his brothers, relocated them to the land of Egypt, and provided for them and their families from that time forward.

This chapter provides hope for family relationships by offering communication practices for dealing with the inevitable friction that results from interaction. As discussed in the previous chapter, conflict is unavoidable. So are hurtful messages and actions. Our relationships with one another create opportunities for the "ministry of reconciliation" (2 Cor. 5:18) and for love to "cover a multitude of sins" (1 Peter 4:8). We all need to seek and extend forgiveness and we need it continually. It is a command from God, and it is our choice. The magnitude of hurtful events can range from a minor infraction to a large, seemingly impossible-to-forgive offense. Is an apology an acceptable response to a hurtful action? What is the difference between an apology and forgiveness? Must we forgive the one who inflicted pain? This chapter addresses these questions and then concludes by identifying themes of forgiveness based on the story of Joseph and his brothers.

Family Members' Hurtful Messages

Our words and actions will hurt family members from time to time, and their words and actions will hurt us. How do we respond to hurtful messages? Your brother questions your ability to make the basketball team. Your mother criticizes your haircut. Your father hurls snide remarks about your choice of a major. Scripture says that "[t]he tongue has the power of life and death" (Prov. 18:21) and that "[a] gentle answer turns away wrath, but a harsh word stirs up anger" (Prov. 15:1). Words are powerful. Which messages do you find particularly hurtful—messages of rejection, criticism, betrayal, teasing, or feeling ignored or unappreciated?

The family represents a unique context for the study of hurtful messages for two reasons.[1] First, the family bond is often involuntary. We are connected as a family despite destructive messages or irreconcilable differences. We cannot easily "walk away" and sever these ties. This sense of permanence is unlike most other forms of relationships. Second, the history shared by family members may affect their reactions to hurtful messages, as these remarks are only a small part of their shared experiences. It is one thing to deal with a few, isolated instances of injurious messages, but it is quite another to deal with a long history of hurtful events.

Types of Hurtful Messages

While we all could probably come up with our own lists, Anita Vangelisti collected and categorized messages from university students to propose a typology of hurtful messages.[2] These include:

- **Accusing**: blaming someone of failure or fault (e.g., "You're the reason mom and dad are angry.")
- **Evaluating**: describing value or worth (e.g., "You're the black sheep of the family.")
- **Informing**: disclosing information (e.g., "I don't love you anymore.")

97

- **Directing**: ordering or commanding (e.g., "You have to work harder.")

- **Advising**: offering a course of action (e.g., "If only you'd study more, then you would gain your father's respect.")

- **Expressing desire**: stating a preference (e.g., "I wish you'd not discuss this topic at dinner.")

- **Questioning**: inquiring or interrogating (e.g., "Do you think you could manage to help your little brother?")

- **Threatening**: intending to inflict punishment (e.g., "You'll be grounded if you don't change that attitude.")

- **Joking**: sharing a prank or witticism (e.g., "Act like a tree and just leaf.")

- **Lying**: deceiving (e.g., "You're not really part of our family, you're adopted.")

According to Vangelisti's work, the most common types of hurtful messages are accusations, evaluations, and informative messages. Her work also shows that informative messages, specifically straightforward declarations of fact, are perceived as the most hurtful.[3] No doubt, hurtful messages can crush our spirit and damage relationships. They discourage and tear down rather than encourage and build up.

Reactions to Hurtful Messages

How do you react when someone says something that hurts you deeply? Researchers have studied the ways in which undergraduate students typically respond to hurt.[4] We have grouped these responses into passive, aggressive, and assertive strategies.

Passive responses include denying hurt, what scholars call becoming *invulnerable* ("ignoring the message, laughing, and being silent").[5] Another passive strategy is what Laura Guerrero and colleagues label *avoidance/denial*, which is becoming quiet and denying negative feelings. They also identify *negative affect expression* (e.g., nonverbal behaviors indicative of emotions such as frustration, insecurity, and depression). Finally, *acquiescence* ("crying, conceding, and apologizing") reaction is another type of passive response.[6]

Aggressive strategies include *active verbal* (attacking other, defending self, reacting sarcastically, and asking for/providing an explanation)[7] and *violent communication* (threatening or harming the other physically).[8] *Distributive communication* is defined by verbally aggressive responses, such as being rude, accusing, arguing, and cursing. Finally, *active distancing* is characterized by behaviors like pulling away physically or giving the other the silent treatment.[9] While it may seem like silence is non-aggressive, actively shutting off a relationship (like Gottman's stonewalling) is an aggressive strategy.

Assertive communication is the final type of response. We advocate communicating in ways that are assertive and avoiding the pitfalls of either passive or aggressive responses. However, of all the response strategies that researchers have identified, only one is assertive. Guerrero and colleagues label it *integrative communication*.[10] It involves direct, nonaggressive communicative responses, such as calmly discussing the problem. The fact that only one out of nine response categories is assertive tells us that, unfortunately, it is not a common response. It must be learned and practiced, and odds are, it has not been modeled well in families.

A final assertive response to hurtful messages that we can see in the Bible is love. This response is one that does not deny or ignore hurt (like passive strategies) but chooses to entrust ourselves, our hurt, the hurtful messenger, and the outcome to God. Listen to Peter's testimony about the crucifixion of Jesus:

> When they hurled their insults at him, he did not retaliate; when he suffered, he made no threats. Instead, he entrusted himself to him who judges justly. "He himself bore our sins" in his body on the cross, so that we might die to sins and live for righteousness. (1 Peter 2:23)

Peter's teaching matches the encouragement of the author of Hebrews for us to fix our "eyes on Jesus, the pioneer and perfecter of faith. For the joy set before him he endured the cross, scorning its shame, and sat down at the right hand of the throne of God. Consider him who endured such opposition from sinners, so that you will not grow weary and lose heart" (Heb. 12:2–3). Christian author James Jordon says that "when you are living in the love of God, it is just impossible to be offended."[11] This does not mean that we do not feel upset or hurt sometimes, but that we are unoffendable when we take our concerns to God, determining not to be anxious about what we experience (Phil. 4:6–7), and when we intentionally and supernaturally determine to love others, because love "is not easily angered, [and] it keeps no record of wrongs" (1 Cor. 13:5). When we do this, the promise from Scripture is that the "peace of God, which transcends all understanding, will guard your hearts and your minds in Christ Jesus" (Phil. 4:7). Being filled with God the Father's love enables us to respond assertively like Jesus Christ and say, "Father forgive them."

In the remainder of the chapter, we continue to focus on positive and productive ways of addressing hurt. We start by overviewing research on relational repair attempts and then discuss forgiveness.

IIIIIII▶ **Application Activity 7.1:**
Responding to Hurtful Messages

- **Think of a memorable instance when a family member said something to you that hurt your feelings. Write a script of the conversation. What was the situation? What happened that led up to the hurtful statement? What was the hurtful message? How did you respond?**

- **Can you classify the type of hurtful message? Can you classify your response in terms of one of the types of responses to hurtful messages? To what extent did this hurtful message affect your relationship with the family member that hurt your feelings?[12]**

Relational Repair Messages

When we have broken trust or injured a relationship, we need to repair it. Janet Meyer and Kyra Rothenberg isolated eight possible relational repair strategies.[13] These include:

- **Apology**: apologize for saying it (e.g., "I'm sorry for . . .")

- **Excuse**: offer an excuse for why I said it (e.g., "I'm very short on sleep.")

- **Justification**: try to justify or defend what I said in order to minimize its offensiveness (e.g., "You told me to be honest.")

- **Denial of offense**: deny or take back what I had said (e.g., "Just kidding." or "I didn't mean that.")

- **Silence**: just act like nothing had happened (e.g., I don't say a word.)

- **Nonverbal reaction**: employ a nonverbal behavior to indicate I regret saying it (e.g., I cover my mouth, shut my eyes.)

- **Change of subject**: try to change the subject (e.g., "How about the weather we've been having lately?")

- **Offset harm**: try to say something to offset the harm done (e.g., I offer the hearer a compliment.)

Review this list of repair strategies. How likely are you to use each of these strategies in an attempt to restore a relationship after a hurtful, regrettable message? Would you classify any of these as passive? Aggressive? Assertive? Have any of these strategies ever backfired? Which strategy do you think is most effective in your efforts to repair damage to a relationship?

Forgiveness

Another repair strategy that allows relationships to continue is forgiveness. Consider what it might have been like to unexpectedly receive the following email: "You don't know me, but I am no longer dating your husband . . . I'm sorry for any pain I caused your family."[14] What would you feel? How would you respond? Christy, the email recipient, decided to confront her husband. She recalls, "Adrian was defensive at first, said it never happened, and even hung up on me. But a minute later he called back, crying, admitted it was true, and begged me to forgive him." She had a decision to make: "I could either fight for my marriage or let this event change everything." Christy made a conscious and extremely difficult decision to forgive.

Sometimes a hurt causes so much pain that an apology is hardly sufficient. Such deep, gut-wrenching hurt might come from adultery, physical abuse, abandonment, or neglect. Without extending forgiveness, we are trapped in cycles of bitterness, resentment, and retribution. Forgiveness has the power to free us from the past and enables us to move forward. In the Bible, forgiveness is simultaneously a command, a choice, and a coping skill. It allowed Christy to continue in her relationship with Adrian. It has been shown to bring about positive effects for individuals, families, and even societies.

What Is Forgiveness?

The New Testament Greek includes two words for "forgive." *Aphiemi* means letting go or releasing; *charizomai* means bestowing favor freely or unconditionally.[15] Forgiveness is a process—a process of letting go of our hurt and desire for revenge and eventually holding no ill-will against the wrongdoer. At its best, forgiveness "is abandoning the negative and *fostering* the positive."[16]

Forgiveness may seem to some like a religious idea. Indeed, almost all world religions teach about and advocate forgiveness, but it is also the subject of social research.[17] Researchers have differentiated the construct into self, Divine, and partner forgiveness. These types of forgiveness work together to aid in better understanding how people and relationships repair and function best. *Self-forgiveness* is a way to remove ill-will, guilt, or resentment that we feel toward our own personal failures or from our own relational transgressions.[18]

Divine forgiveness is forgiveness by a Supreme Being.[19] From a Christian perspective, God forgives people from sin, transgression, and iniquity (all different Hebrew words) because of Christ. The Moody Bible Institute teaches the orthodox Christian perspective:

> According to the Scriptures, sin must be paid for (Rom. 6:23; 1 Peter 1:18, 19). When Jesus Christ died, he suffered as a substitute in the place of and on behalf of fallen humanity. Christ's death made it possible for men and women to be declared righteous, based on their faith in Him (Matt. 20:28; Rom. 3:21; 2 Cor. 5:21). Christ's death was not merely a statement against evil or an expression of love, but a payment that satisfied God's demand.[20]

Divine forgiveness was purchased. Christ's substitutionary death enables us to experience the Father's forgiveness, blessing, and adoption into his Divine family (Rom. 8:15).

Partner forgiveness, or interpersonal forgiveness, is when we forgive others. Communication scholars Vincent Waldron and Douglas Kelley define it this way:

> Forgiveness is a relational process whereby harmful conduct is acknowledged by one or both partners; the harmed partner extends underserved mercy to the perceived transgressor; one or both partners experience a transformation from negative to positive

psychological states, and the meaning of the relationship is renegotiated, with the possibility of reconciliation."[21]

Notice that there are five parts to this definition: forgiveness (1) is a relational process, (2) recognizes a harm, (3) involves extending mercy, (4) leads to transformation, and (5) prompts relationship renegotiation, including reconciling or dissolving the relationship.

A helpful acronym to remember the steps involved in forgiveness is REACH. Articulated by psychologist Everett Worthington, this sequential model involves these five steps:

R: Recall the hurt.

E: Empathize with the wrongdoer.

A: Altruistically offer forgiveness.

C: Commit to forgive.

H: Hold on to forgiveness.[22]

Taking a slightly different view, rather than detailing a process, attorney and pastor Ken Sande argues that when we say that we forgive someone we make four promises.[23] We promise not to (1) dwell on the offense, (2) use the offense to bring harm to others, (3) gossip about it, or (4) let the incident keep us from moving forward in our relationship. These are four tough promises to make, but they bring a freedom that you may never have expected. Even though we cannot control the amount or severity of hurt we experience, we can control the level of forgiveness we are willing to extend.

Busting Myths about Forgiveness

In addressing the question "What is forgiveness?" it is important to keep in mind what forgiveness is not.[24] What are some myths you hold about forgiveness? Let's look at some of the most common ones.

Myth 1: Forgive and forget.

Myth 2: I do not have to forgive until they say they are sorry.

Myth 3: Forgiveness means I have to be friends with them.

Myth 4: Forgiveness is for the other person.

Myth 5: Forgiveness means becoming a doormat.

While commonly believed, these myths obscure what forgiveness really is.

Busting these myths, we learn that forgiving is not forgetting. In fact, it may not even be possible to forget a painful memory. The case could be made that we should not forget every offense, as remembering can help ensure that an offense does not reoccur. It is part of our experiences, and it may serve as a catalyst for healing and growth for ourselves and for others.

Forgiveness is also something that can happen independently of any communication with an offender. It should not be given because of external rewards, expectations, or pressure from others. A person must willingly and freely choose forgiveness. It can be given without ever speaking or interacting with another person.

It is also not the same as reconciliation. We might truly forgive someone who has hurt us deeply, but that relationship may never be restored. Forgiveness is an internal change of heart toward a person who was unfair. The offender may reject the gift of love and compassion, but the gift-giver can still decide whether or not to give it.

It has been said, "Not forgiving is like drinking poison and hoping the other person gets sick." Forgiveness not only extends the grace we have been extended, but it also frees us. Holding onto bitterness will, in the end, only hurt you and those around you. Conversely, we gain freedom from extending forgiveness. Forgiveness is even included as one of the "Seven Steps toward Freedom" developed by Neil Anderson.[25] For a more detailed inventory that can help flush out areas of unforgiveness in your own life, there are accessible guides you can follow, such as Anderson's *Bondage Breaker* or *Victory over Darkness*, both of which include biblical arguments for how forgiveness is part of unlocking personal freedom. Forgiveness often results in improved relationships (both with the offender and others), reduced anger and sadness, and increased hopefulness.[26]

Finally, forgiving is not excusing, denying, or tolerating the offense. In fact, when we forgive, it explicitly defines the other person's actions as wrong or offensive. Forgiveness requires courage and strength, not passivity. Indeed, Douglas Kelley uses the acronym TUF to remind us of the courage forgiveness requires.[27] The letter "T" refers to truth—the courage to claim truth about what has happened to us and about ourselves and our situation. TUF forgiveness claims the truth that something wrong or bad has happened to us, but also confesses that we have failed others and are prone to disappoint and hurt others at times. It also claims the truth that "we can survive what we are currently going through, we can heal our pain, and we can create a better life for ourselves and others."[28] The letter "U" refers to understanding—the courage to seek to understand ourselves and the one who offended us. The letter "F" refers to freedom—the courage to choose to be free from the hurt and extend forgiveness.

When Should We Forgive?

Forgiveness remains, fundamentally, a choice we make. It could be framed not as a choice to forgive or withhold forgiveness but as a choice to obey or disobey the Lord Jesus's command. Box 7.2 includes some Scriptures about forgiveness. A strong biblical case can be made that we should forgive from a pure motive of love for others, even our enemies (Matt. 5:44).[29] Consider the parable of the unmerciful servant (recorded in all four Gospels). The account of this story in Matthew begins with Peter asking Jesus, "Lord, how many times shall I forgive my brother when he sins against me?" (Matt. 18:21). Jesus answers seventy times seven and then explains the severe consequences of failing to forgive by telling a parable in which a servant's master canceled the servant's large debt and set him free. Afterwards, the servant went away and refused to forgive a co-worker who owed a much smaller debt, so the servant had the co-worker thrown into

---

Points to Ponder 7.2:
Scriptures on Forgiveness

- For if you forgive men when they sin against you, your heavenly Father will also forgive you. But if you do not forgive men their sins, your Father will not forgive your sins. (Matt. 6:14–15)

- And when you stand praying, if you hold anything against anyone, forgive him, so that your Father in heaven may forgive you your sins. (Mark 11:25)

- So watch yourselves. If your brother sins, rebuke him, and if he repents, forgive him. If he sins against you seven times in a day, and seven times comes back to you and says, "I repent," forgive him. (Luke 17:3–4)

- Be kind and compassionate to one another, forgiving each other, just as in Christ God forgave you. (Eph. 4:32)

- Bear with each other and forgive whatever grievances you may have against one another. Forgive as the Lord forgave you. (Col. 3:13)

---

prison until he could repay. This action angered the master: "'You wicked servant,' he said, 'I canceled all that debt of yours because you begged me to. Shouldn't you have had mercy on your fellow servant just as I had on you?' In anger his master turned him over to the jailers to be tortured, until he should pay back all he owed" (Matt. 18:32–34). The parable ends with a harsh warning if we fail to forgive each other: "This is how my heavenly Father will treat each of you unless you forgive your brother from your heart" (Matt. 18:35). God forgives us. We are commanded to forgive others.

Levels of Forgiveness

Everett Worthington and his colleagues make a distinction between individual forgiveness and interpersonal forgiveness.[30] According to these researchers, there are two types of individual forgiveness. *Decisional forgiveness* is a "statement of one's behavioral intentions toward the offender—to eschew revenge or avoidance (if it is safe to continue interacting with the transgressor)."[31] *Emotional forgiveness* is a "process of replacing negative unforgiving emotions with positive other-oriented emotions (like empathy, sympathy, compassion, and love) which can be facilitated by other non-self-oriented emotions like gratitude, humility, contrition, and hope."[32] In contrast to individual forgiveness, *interpersonal forgiveness* occurs in the context of a committed, ongoing personal relationship. It "entails removal of all negative unforgiving emotions and the additional experience of a net positive emotional valence."[33]

A final type of forgiveness is call *imaginative forgiveness*. Imaginative forgiveness is "a transformative perspective that allows relational partners to view themselves and their relational worlds in a way that encourages and enables the co-creation of a shared, relational humanity."[34] The beauty of imaginative forgiveness is that it is a relational and transformative process that creates hope by healing past hurts and reimagining the relationship as it is hoped to be. Kelley and his colleagues outline the steps:

1. One or both parties acknowledge the harmful conduct.

2. Both partners experience an emotional response and strive to make sense of their new relational situation.

3. Offending partner imagines the harmed partner's perspective and responds with remorse, sincerity, and full apology.

4. Harmed partner imagines the offending partner's perspective,

empathizes, and responds with mercy regarding the perceived transgression.

5. Partners experience a transformation from destructive to constructive cognitive, emotional, and/or behavioral responses.

6. Understandings of self, partner, and relationship are reimagined and renegotiated, and possibly (re)enacted when safe conditions for reconciliation are created or restored.[35]

IIIIIIII▶ Application Activity 7.3: Asking for Forgiveness

- Think of an offense that you committed that requires you to ask for forgiveness. How will you ask the other for forgiveness? Write down what you would say and/or do to ask for forgiveness.

- Kelley identifies three forms of forgiveness-seeking strategies: *direct*—explicit and direct request for forgiveness ("Will you forgive me?"); *indirect*—indirect request for forgiveness, including strategies such as humor, nonverbal displays of acceptance, and third-party pleas; and *relational consequences*—seeking forgiveness but conditions may apply.[36] Which of Kelley's three forgiveness-seeking strategies did you use? Explain.

IIIIIIII▶ Application Activity 7.4: Granting Forgiveness

- Think of a time when someone asked you to forgive him/her. Write down what he/she said and how you responded. Kelley identifies five forgiveness-granting strategies: *explicit*— "I forgive you"; *discussion*— "We will talk about it"; *nonverbal displays*—body language, such as a hug; *minimizing*—"I told him it wasn't a big deal"; and *conditional*—if/then.[37]

- Which of Kelley's five forgiveness-granting strategies did you use? Explain.

Notice the progression from decisional, emotional, interpersonal, to imaginative forgiveness. First, we decide to offer forgiveness to the one that caused us harm. Second, we replace negative unforgiving emotions with positive ones toward the offender. Third, we commit to an ongoing personal relationship with the offender. Finally, we move forward together with hope for the future. The process is not easy, and in some situations, interpersonal and imaginative forgiveness are not possible. But research shows there are some positive benefits that result from forgiving.

Relational Outcomes

Research has consistently found that communication strategies to express forgiveness are related to relationship satisfaction. One study revealed that direct strategies (see Box 7.3) following transgressions decreased relational damage and increased satisfaction, but that conditional forgiveness strategies detracted from relationships, increasing relational damage, and that indirect forgiveness was unrelated to relational damage.[38] Another study found that relational satisfaction was related to forgiveness strategies (see Box 7.4): in married couples, satisfaction was associated with nonverbal displays and minimizing strategies, and in dating couples, with the explicit strategy. Also, there was a negative association between relationship satisfaction and offering conditional forgiveness in both married and dating couples.[39] Yet another study showed that individuals who are satisfied in their relationship use nonverbal, minimizing, and explicit strategies to express forgiveness.[40] Collectively, findings from these studies show that forgiveness can be communicated well through explicitly asking for forgiveness, showing forgiveness through one's nonverbal actions, and minimizing the need to ask for forgiveness. These findings also point to the importance of forgiving altruistically and unconditionally. The ultimate outcome of forgiveness is unity. "Forgiveness repairs the ties that bind a community in unity."[41] Forgiveness can bring unity to relationships and the family.

Conclusion

We opened this chapter with the story of Joseph and his brothers. Now that we have a better understanding of forgiveness, let's identify some of the themes of Joseph's journey toward forgiveness.[42]

- **Joseph forgave unconditionally.** He did not wait for his brothers to apologize before offering forgiveness.

- **Joseph's forgiveness was not easy.** He struggled to give up his anger and offer forgiveness. Forgiveness is a process that takes time.

- **Joseph's forgiveness was loving.** He did not merely accept the unfairness, pretend that he was not hurt, or become indifferent toward his brothers. He offered love to his brothers as he forgave.

- **Joseph's forgiveness was life-giving for those he forgave and for himself.**

Hopefully your story is not as extreme as Joseph's. But even if it is, his life is an incredible model of forgiveness for us.

In our world, perfect relationships are impossible and hurting each other is inevitable. Finding ways to overcome offense is a fundamental communication task all families face. Our response to hurt can create space for relationships to develop, overcome, and even thrive. In this chapter we reviewed research on hurtful messages and typical responses, and then covered methods for relational repair with a focus on forgiveness. As you consistently forgive and repair by the grace of God, and privilege your relationships above yourself, you can become "unoffendable" through radical love for others. Ultimately, these types of interactions cultivate resilient family relationships. We turn to this topic next.

Chapter 8

Cultivating Resilience: Communication Strategies for Adapting to Stress

Chapter Summary: Family interaction plays an integral role in developing resilience in the face of stress. This chapter introduces ways in which communication creates resilience. The chapter first covers normative, non-normative, and chronic family stressors. Then, it presents two models to illustrate best practices for adapting to and coping with stressors and overviews the basic propositions of the communication-focused Theory of Resilience and Relational Load. The chapter ends with practical suggestions for building family resilience through communication and faith.

Introduction

THE BIBLE IS FULL OF STORIES of individuals who faced adversity and "bounced back" because of God's goodness and faithfulness. The story of Ruth in particular stands out. Her world crashes. Her husband dies. She is penniless. She is far from home. She has a tough decision to make: go back to her people in Moab or join her mother-in-law, Naomi, to relocate to Bethlehem. Despite facing rejection as a Moabite woman, Ruth chooses her Jewish mother-in-law Naomi and Naomi's God. She gives her life to the God of Israel. With boldness she declares, "Don't urge me to leave you [Naomi] or to turn back from you. Where you go I will go, and where you stay I will stay. Your people will be my people and your God my God" (Ruth 1:16). Life is difficult for Ruth in Bethlehem, but she works and persists and works and persists some more. As the story unfolds, Naomi sends Ruth to glean the fields of a wealthy relative named Boaz, who eventually marries

Ruth and abides by the cultural custom to become her kinsman-redeemer. He covers Ruth and Naomi with protection and restores their land, inheritance, financial security, and family line. As great-grandmother of King David and ancestor of Jesus the Messiah, Ruth and her story display how God weaves his beautiful, redemptive plans through our lives (see also Jer. 29:11–13).

Ruth's story portrays common family stressors (e.g., death, financial hardship, moving away, isolation) and illustrates how to build resilience into our lives: deeply caring for others, belonging to a faith community, and boldly, actively following God while maintaining integrity.[1] We, too, can use these strategies to "bounce back" from adversities we face. Family interaction plays an integral role in developing resilience because resilience is built, shaped, and maintained through our experiences and interactions with others. In this chapter, we first cover types of family stressors. We then present two models for understanding how to adapt to and cope with stressors. Next, we lay out the basic propositions of the Theory of Resilience and Relational Load—a communication-focused theory of resilience. We end this chapter with practical suggestions for building family resilience.

Family Stress and Stressors

Stress is our physical or emotional response to any novel stimuli. This means that both positive and negative events are stressful, and everyone experiences stress. It is inevitable. Scripture reminds us that we will all face trials and tribulations (James 1:2; John 16:33). Many of life's experiences—whether expected or unexpected, desired or undesired—are stressors. Stress-inducing events can range from major life events to everyday hassles. Hassles—events and activities that one perceives as frustrating and annoying—are relatively low stress.[2] Missing or losing things, long lines at the check-out counter, and interruptions to work make up the daily hassles of life. But stress can be caused by major life-transitions as well. Death of a spouse or child, job loss, and moving are major stress-evoking events. Many theories and models consider how stress accumulates. One major event may provoke as much stress as ten minor events. To quantify the number and severity of stressors, many clinicians and researchers use the Holmes-Rahe Stress Inventory. Try it out in the Application Activity 8.1: Assess Your Stress.

**|||||||| ▶   Application Activity 8.1:
                      Assess Your Stress**

- **Think about when you started something new (e.g., university, job). How much stress did you experience during that first month of transition?**

- **To quantify stress, fill out the Holmes-Rahe Stress Inventory for the first month of your transition: https://www.stress.org/holmes-rahe-stress-inventory**

- **What are some ways that you adapted or coped with these stressors?**

Family theorists often differentiate three main categories of stress: normative, non-normative, and chronic. *Normative stressors* are part of the human development process. Birth, leaving home, marriage, and death are examples of normative stressors. They are expected changes that occur across the life of families. *Non-normative stressors* are the result of some unique set of circumstances and for which the family is relatively unprepared. These are generally unanticipated events often placing the family in a state of instability.[3] A tornado destroying a family home, a family member converting to Christianity from another religion, or receiving a terminal cancer diagnosis are examples of non-normative stressors. Normative stressors may be severe but are more patterned than non-normative stress. There are models and stories of others about how to have a baby or grieve a death. Non-normative stressors, however, can be idiosyncratic and require creative problem-solving to manage. *Chronic stressors* are atypical circumstances that last for an extended period of time and are difficult to amend. Chronic stressors can be classified as environmental effects like family poverty, a family member's unusually dangerous career (such as being a police officer or military personnel), or children exhibiting congenital birth defects or problematic behavioral patterns. These chronic situations can create a high level of sustained family stress.

Although tempting, it is important not to think of stress in a solely negative way. Adopting a child, for example, may be perceived as a positive stressor. This event matches a definition for stressors as "discrete life events or transitions that have an impact upon the family unit and produce, or have the potential to produce, change in the family social system."[4]

Disruption to normal life generates potential. Some families may struggle to cope with stress and may emerge crippled and dysfunctional. For other families, stressors can promote positive change and growth.

Take a minute to reflect on your own childhood family experience. What were some of the stressors you or your family faced? Would you classify the stressors as normative, non-normative, or chronic? Did they impact your family in negative or positive ways? Or perhaps in both ways? It is not always easy or even necessary to make these distinctions, but it is helpful to understand the role of the family, especially communication within the family, in adapting to and coping with family stress. We next present two models that illuminate best practices for handling stress.

ABC-X Process Model for Stress

Reuben Hill developed a model to understand the relationship between stressful events and family crises, arguing that stressful events, with proper resources and assessment of the situation, do not need to lead to crises.[5] This model embraces a systems perspective that includes inputs represented by ABC and an output represented by X. In the model, A stands for a specific stressor. B is a family's available resources. C represents a family's perceptions or framing of the event. These inputs work together to determine X, the amount of crisis that occurs due to the stressful event. For example, a father's unemployment (A: the specific stressor) might not be perceived as disruptive (C: perceptions of the event) if the mother's income is sufficient to maintain financial stability (B: available resources), resulting in a low intensity situation (X: the amount of crisis the stressor produced).

The specific role of communication in the ABC-X Model is unspecified. From our view, communication can be a resource to draw upon during crises and can help reframe the way one views a situation. As a resource (B), communication through conversations, counseling, or prayer can provide an outlet for emotional buildup. It can diffuse internalized stress. Communication can also shift the way we see people and circumstances, changing our perceptions of events (C). As we discuss situations, we can point out the pros and cons of experiences, helping reframe stress as opportunity.

The ABC-X Model focuses on families' responses to stress, not responses to the crisis itself.[6] Others have built on this model to help account for the ongoing cycle of stress and crisis that families experience. For example, Hamilton McCubbin and Joan Patterson extended Hill's theory and developed the Double ABC-X Model.[7] The Double ABC-X Model includes the original variables in the model plus post-crisis variables. The model includes the notion of pile-up demands, defined as previous family life events, and their impact on post-crisis strain.

The Double ABC-X Model allows analysis of underlying factors in the coping and adaptation process, resulting in an even more complete, and complex, analysis of families' responses to stressors and crises.[8] Family adaptation varies on a continuum, ranging from bad (maladaptation) to good (bonadaptation). In *maladaptation*, pile-up demands (stress) continually outpace the available resources and perceptions of stress. In *bonadaptation*, there is a minimum discrepancy between demands and resources. Maladaptation leads to a deterioration in family members' sense of well-being (e.g., physical and psychological health). In contrast, in bonadaptation, families maintain or strengthen their sense of well-being.[9] Like in the basic ABC-X Model, a key to bonadaptation is having sufficient resources to meet the pile-up demands.

Another way to add to the ABC-X Model is to incorporate chronic stress, or what one model calls "enduring vulnerabilities."[10] Enduring vulnerabilities are relatively stable family characteristics (e.g., personalities, disabilities) and backgrounds (e.g., trauma, chronic depression). Stress is the accumulation of daily hassles coupled with enduring vulnerabilities.

||||||||▶   **Application Activity 8.2:**
Framing Resources

1. Read Paul's testimony about his ministry in 2 Corinthians 11:16–12:10.

   • In terms of the stress models, list some of the stressors (A) Paul faced.

   • What do you think counted as resources (B) for Paul?

   • How did Paul frame (C) his experiences in stress-reducing ways?

2. Now read the following passages of Scripture: Philippians 4:6–8 and 2 Corinthians 4:16–18.

   • What kinds of resources did Paul suggest Christians draw upon to cope with stress?

   • How did Paul encourage Christians to perceive their circumstances?

The relationship between these stressors (A) and family well-being (X) is moderated by adaptive processes (B, C). This model helps clarify that the "A" (number and severity of stressors) may include long-standing patterns and dispositions. It also identifies positive communication as an adaptive process that impacts how family members appraise and cope with everyday stressors.

Circumplex Model of Family Functioning

This next model defines communication as essential for helping families successfully navigate stressful life events. Developed over 40 years ago,

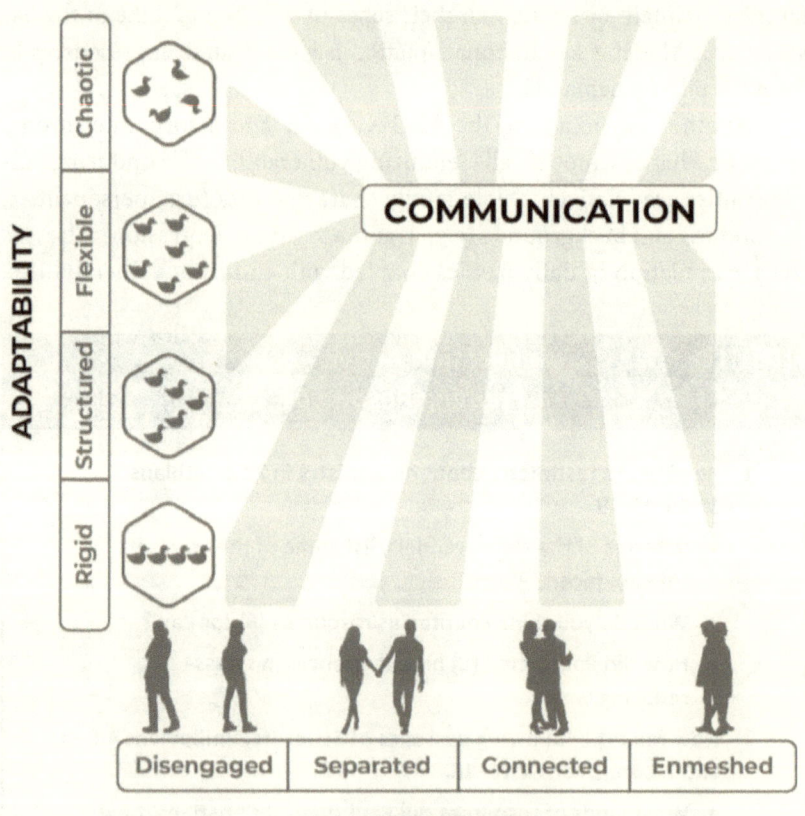

Figure 8.2: Olson's Circumplex Model of Family Functioning, based on David H. Olson, "Circumplex Model of Marital and Family Systems," *Journal of Family Therapy* 22, no. 2 (2000): 144–167.

Olson's Circumplex Model of Family Functioning is one of the most widely known theories of family functioning in the fields of communication and psychology. David Olson and his colleagues identify different types of families based on two dimensions—adaptability and cohesion.[11] Figure 8.2 portrays the Circumplex Model along with labels to clarify four different levels of both adaptability and cohesion.

Family adaptability refers to a family's ability "to change its power structure, role relationships, and relationship rules in response to situational and developmental stress."[12] The model identifies four different levels of family functioning based on adaptability. Ranging from high levels to low levels, these four family types are chaotic, flexible, structured, and rigid. Optimal family functioning occurs at the two mid-levels (flexible and structured), with both extremes (chaotic and rigid) considered to be ineffective. Too much adaptability results in limited leadership, lenient discipline, endless negotiations in decision-making, and dramatic role and rule shifts. Too little adaptability results in authoritarian leadership, overly strict discipline, little to no negotiation in decision-making, and rigid role and rule enforcement.[13]

Family cohesion refers to "the emotional bonding that family members have toward one another and the degree of individual autonomy they experience."[14] Families with high cohesion spend a great deal of time together and make major decisions collaboratively. Families with low cohesion spend little time with each other and make decisions without consulting other family members. The four different levels of family functioning based on cohesion, ranging from high to low, are enmeshed, connected, separated, and disengaged. Like flexibility, optimal family functioning occurs at the mid-levels of cohesion (connected and separated), with both extremes (enmeshed and disengaged) seen as problematic. Too much cohesion results in emotional co-dependence, blurred internal boundaries, strong parent-child coalitions, minimum private space, and almost exclusively shared decision-making. Too little cohesion results in minimal emotional bonding, open external boundaries, weak coalitions, maximum separate physical space, and autonomous decision-making.[15]

Although adaptability and cohesion are the two primary dimensions, Olson sees *communication* as critically important.[16] He argues that communication is a facilitating dimension that allows families to adjust their levels of adaptability and cohesion as they grow and change. Positive communication behaviors such as sending clear messages, listening, and self-disclosure are needed for optimal family functioning. In contrast, negative communication skills such as sending incongruent and disqualifying messages, poor problem-solving skills, and lack of empathy prevent families from adjusting successfully to stressful life events.

Researchers have applied this model to understand the role of family communication in creating resilience.[17] Families that communicate in ways that balance cohesion and adaptability have more resilient members, regardless of the type and severity of adversity they experience.[18] For example, in the face of a non-normative stressor like an unexpected hospitalization for a family member, resilient families move toward higher levels of cohesion and flexibility as they draw together during the crisis. Members may rearrange schedules to always have someone present at the hospital bedside (increased adaptability) and quickly arrange an information chain to share news about the patient. They may coordinate meals with each other (increased cohesion), with members taking on atypical roles in the family to accommodate the shifts in schedules. These changes in family dynamics build resilience through communication that balances cohesion and adaptability.

||||||||▶ **Application Activity 8.3:
Classify Family Adaptability and Cohesion**

- **Think about a movie that depicts family life. Pick a scene in the movie that involves normative, non-normative, or chronic stress.**
- **How did the family members account for the stress in terms of their adaptability and cohesion?**
- **Classify the family in terms of adaptability (from chaotic to rigid) and cohesion (from disengaged to enmeshed) providing examples to support your classifications.**

Family Resilience

Focusing on processes related to family stress and outcomes foreshadows how families become resilient. Family members' ability to cope and successfully adapt to adversity and stressful life events is referred to as family resilience.[19] From a communication perspective, resilience is developed, shaped, and maintained through our experiences and interactions with others. This means we can learn to communicate in ways that support the development of family resilience.

The Theory of Resilience and Relational Load (TRRL), developed by Tamara Afifi and her colleagues, is a communication-focused theory that explicitly links the ways in which we interact with each other as a key for handling stress and building family resilience.[20] It centers on how couples and families communicate during stressful events as well as their overall pattern of relational maintenance behaviors. According to the theory, it is the "prosocial, daily verbal and nonverbal behaviors, perceptions, and actions that allow relational partners and family members to become resilient and thrive."[21] Figure 8.3 depicts some of the elements of this theory. TRRL has ten propositions which we summarize in five key ideas here.[22]

1. When people invest in their relationships by maintaining them over-time, it builds reserves (emotional, psychological, relational, cognitive) that can be drawn from during relationally stressful moments.

2. Couples and families who have a strong communal orientation (i.e., those who view themselves on the same team with their partner or family), and who have similar levels of communal orientation, are more likely to invest in their relationships. Discrepancies in couples or families lead people to question the level of commitment to the relationship, which can increase relational load.

3. During stressful events, when we engage in secure appraisals (i.e., pro-relationship assessments of stress) and positive communication patterns, we can prevent the depletion of relational reserves because people feel validated and confident in their relationship, whereas threatening appraisals and negative communication patterns (i.e., self-preservation-focused assessments of stress and selfish communication) deplete reserves because people spend time defending themselves and regulating their emotions.

4. Relational load can influence perceptions of a communal orientation with their relational partner, making individuals feel as though they are no longer unified.

5. Depleted reserves (or few initial investments) can create relational load that can impact one's personal and relational health, whereas ample reserves facilitate resilience, thriving, and health (mental and physical health, relational health, efficacy, healthy behaviors).

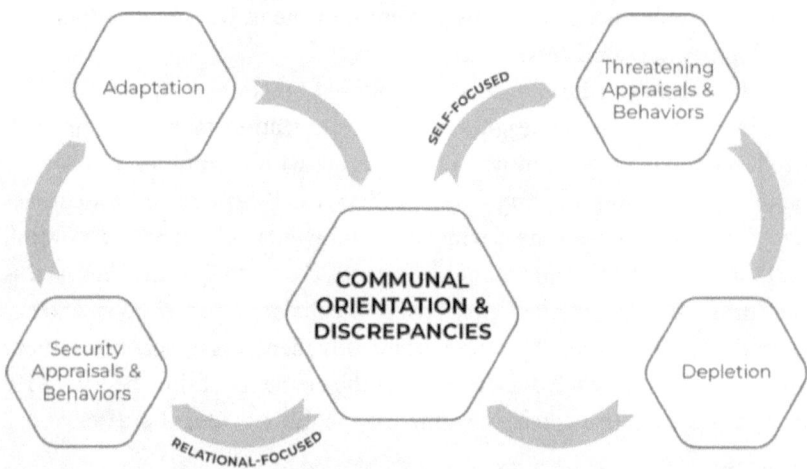

Figure 8.3: Theory of Resilience and Relational Load, based on Tamara D. Afifi, Anne F. Merrill, and Sharde Davis, "The Theory of Resilience and Relational Load," *Personal Relationships* 23, no. 4 (2016): 663–683.

Let's highlight a few aspects of this theory. In Chapter 5 we covered relational maintenance behaviors. These include verbal and nonverbal behaviors that help keep relationships strong, including positivity (e.g., complimenting one another), openness (e.g., sharing personal information), assurances (e.g., affirming commitment to each other), social networks (e.g., spending time together with common friends), and shared tasks (e.g., doing chores together).[23] These types of behaviors are investments in the relationship and should be deposited on an ongoing basis to build a healthy emotional reserve. Families then have "emotional currency," so to speak, and can make withdrawals from these reserves when confronted with stressful life events. Thus, the "emotional wealth" of the family accumulated over time serves as a buffer against the physical and psychological consequences of stress.

"We got this!" and "We are in this together!" reflect the mindset of those who have a communal orientation. TRRL holds that people will invest in their relationships and build emotional reserves when they are high in communal orientation and when all family members have similar levels of commitment to a communal orientation. When facing adversity, families with strong reserves make pro-relationship assessments (i.e., secure appraisals) of the stress of the situation. This leads to better family adaptation and health, reinforcing coupleness or family-orientedness, which in turn promotes higher investments in emotional reserves. In contrast, those families who lack reserves engage in more self-focused appraisals (i.e., relationship-threatening assessments of the situation) and conflict behaviors. These threatening appraisals deplete emotional resources, exacerbating the stress and increasing relational load. This can lead to negative health and relational outcomes and can challenge the "we are a team" orientation. This cycle is broken by building emotional reserves through regular use of communicative maintenance strategies. Thus, establishing patterns of positive daily communication before adversity comes is key for family resilience.

Practical Suggestions for Building Family Resilience

Creating resilience requires both proactive and reactive strategies. A *proactive strategy*, for example, is deliberately seeking out and participating in a faith community, realizing that this community is a resource to draw upon during times of adversity. A *reactive strategy* is reaching out to that community when already dealing with adversity. These strategies have both a buffering and a recovery effect, by providing protection from the full destructive force of hardship and by extending assistance in dealing with family hardships. Let's look at some of these strategies. We start by identifying communication-based strategies and end by offering faith-based perspectives for building resilience.

Communication-Centered Strategies

Communication scholar Patrice Buzzanell identifies five practical communication processes for developing and sustaining resilience in the face of abnormal stress and crisis.[24] *Crafting normalcy* is keeping the daily routine going the best you can. "Keep on keeping on" reflects this strategy. If saying evening prayers together is part of your normal routine, then continue this practice during times of crises. *Affirming identity anchors* is "a relatively enduring cluster of identity discourses upon which individuals and their familial, collegial, and/or community members rely when explaining who they are for themselves and in relations to each other."[25] Families may, for example, trust in biblical promise, anchoring their identities in Christ, and reminding family members during times of adversity of their position in Christ. *Maintaining and using communication networks* is building communities (e.g., family, church, work, civic groups) that we can rely on during rough times. Asking for practical help (e.g., a meal train), emotional support (e.g., a listening ear to vent frustrations), and informational support (e.g., pastoral counseling, advice from those who have gone through similar events) are ways to draw on support networks. *Putting alternative logics to work* acknowledges that during crises we may need to develop different practices or routines. If families are experiencing a financial stress, for example, they may opt for a much less expensive "staycation" as an alternative to a high-cost elaborate vacation. *Legitimizing negative feelings while foregrounding productive actions* is to acknowledge and legitimize our feelings and emotions during adversity while realizing that focusing on them is counterproductive and that time is best spent developing plans to navigate the crisis.

Another communication-based strategy is to encourage family members to construct shared narratives as a way to make sense of an adverse situation.[26] From interviews with fathers, mothers, and children who had dealt with financial hardship during the 1980 recession, Kristen Lucas and Patrice Buzzanell identified message-based strategies for dealing with the immediate hardship—for example, talk centered around tightening the belt and preparing for the hard times.[27] Messages were also shared that shaped the value systems and attitudes of the younger generation, reinforcing the importance of hard work, living within their means, and devising back-up plans. These conversations serve as teachable moments for building long-term resilience.

**|||||||| ▶   Application Activity 8.4:
Applying Strategies to a Family Crisis**

Describe a real or hypothetical family crisis, and then address the following:

- Discuss how you could build family resilience by implementing the strategies discussed (crafting normalcy, affirming identity anchors, maintaining and using communication networks, putting alternative logics to work, legitimizing negative feelings while foregoing productive actions, and constructing shared narratives).

- Which strategy do you see as most productive? Least productive? Explain.

Christian-Centered Strategies

Priest Christopher Krall suggests faith-based strategies that create resilience.[28] In his view, we should live in hope of a better world, engage in contemplation, hold onto community, and pray. We develop each of these ideas with additional thoughts for Christian families.

First, resilience comes from hope. Krall focuses attention on hoping for environments where all can feel safe and thrive—a world conducive to human flourishing. Hoping for a better life and circumstances undoubtedly breeds resilience. Christians also hope for a life to come—a resurrection and victory over death itself. As the Apostle Paul persuasively argued to the Corinthians, "if only for this life we have hope in Christ, we are of all people most to be pitied" (1 Cor. 15:19). Similarly, the author of Hebrews extols faithful men and women for welcoming hope-filled promises from afar and "longing for a better country—a heavenly one" (Heb. 11:16). Adopting a hope for heaven should not make people less hopeful about earth, but it should create resilience even in the face of death. As Krall concludes, "Stress and life's traumatic onslaught do not have to be overwhelming or paralyzing due to fear. Rather, with strength forged through faith, stress and even death are overcome."[29]

A second strategy for resilience-building is contemplation. Families might spend time considering their immediate and ultimate life purposes. They might have family discussions around ways their lives could benefit from Divine intervention. In addition to family meditations and discussions, individual meditation can build resilience by shaping our perceptions and appraisals of family situations and relationships. It can also imbue life with meaning and purpose. Krall argues, "People holding a faith-based perspective adapt to and endure stress greater than those who are overwhelmed by stress, who think they have no choice but to keep swimming through life's challenges with their own strength or who have no concept of the meaning or purpose of their lives."[30] Christians, however, can confess with Paul, "I delight in weaknesses, in insults, in hardships, in persecutions, in difficulties. For when I am weak, then I am strong" (2 Cor. 12: 9–10).

Third, resilient people do not isolate themselves but draw strength and hope from others. As Ecclesiastes 4:9–12 reminds us,

> Two are better than one, because they have a good return for their labor: If either of them falls down, one can help the other up. But pity anyone who falls and has no one to help them up. Also, if two

lie down together, they will keep warm. But how can one keep warm alone? Though one may be overpowered, two can defend themselves. A cord of three strands is not quickly broken.

Like Ruth in the opening example of the chapter, we can cling to important relationships. Jesus also modeled this. In one of his most stressful experiences in the Garden of Gethsemane, he invited Peter, James, and John to keep watch with him (Mark 14:32–42). There is wisdom in surrounding ourselves with loving relationships and communities.

Finally, resilience is enhanced by prayer. Prayer not only shifts our own perspectives, aligning them with God's (see Eph. 1:18–19), but also mobilizes things in the spiritual and natural realms. This two-fold nature of prayer is why missionaries like Oswald Chambers claim: "Prayer does not fit us for the greater works; prayer is the greater work."[31] When we spend time communicating with God (speaking and listening) our assessments of situations and people tend to change. We adopt the compassion of Jesus (see Matt. 9:36; Matt. 14:14). The Fruit of the Holy Spirit (Gal. 5:22) surfaces in our lives. Or like Job (38–40), our perspective changes when we recognize the awesomeness of God.

In addition, our prayers somehow result in tangible changes. Daniel (Chapter 9) fasted and prayed and received an angelic visit that affected nations. James (5:17) reasons: "Elijah was a man with a nature like ours, and he prayed earnestly that it would not rain; and it did not rain on the land for three years and six months." Joshua (10:12–15) in petition to God commanded the sun to stand still, and it did. Prayer is not merely meditative. Nor is it only about God listening to our thoughts. Prayer is an active engagement with God which holds the promise that "whatever you ask for in prayer, believe that you have received it, and it will be yours" (Mark 11:24; see also Matt. 21:22; John 15:7).

Hope, meditation, community, and prayer are four faith-based strategies for building resilience. More generally, many research studies support that relying on faith to cope with adversity is an effective strategy.[32] In one study, for example, 16 lower-income older adults who were living in extended-stay hotels and also experiencing health problems were interviewed about stressful housing conditions and strategies for coping and making sense of hardships.[33] Three faith-based themes emerged: God has plans ("God knows what he's doing"), God provides support ("He's never left my side"), and God enables deliverance ("I overcame that with God's hand on me"). This narrative analysis reveals how faith is a means for coping with stress ("God is my strength") and making sense of the adversity ("God's got this—he is in control").

Relying on faith in God during adversity is also a major theme in Scripture. Take, for example, Job, a man Scripture describes as "blameless and upright," who "feared God and shunned evil" (Job 1:1). God allowed Satan to take everything from Job except his life itself—Job's children, his wealth, and his health (Job 1:12–18; 2:7). In the midst of suffering, his faith in God sustained him. Despite Satan's relentless attacks, Job remained resilient.

Conclusion

Although stress is an inescapable part of life, we can learn strategies for managing stress well and building family resilience. You now understand some of the ways stress and vulnerabilities interact with your own resources, perspectives, and coping strategies to impact adaptation and coping. Key to building resilience is how family members communicate with each other before and during adversity. Positive interactions (e.g., complimenting and encouraging one another, openly sharing thoughts and feelings, spending time together) are investments in the family, and depositing this currency over time builds reserves to draw upon when faced with stress. Communication also helps us coordinate levels of adaptability and cohesion in families, strategically moving the family forward from dysfunctional family forms to more healthy forms.

We can also interact in ways to create a communal family orientation, by being intentional in the ways of expressing our family roles and responsibilities. Messages that convey the "we got this" orientation is one such strategy. Another strategy is to encourage family members to co-construct family narratives that reinforce "who we are" as a family. Reminding each other of Scripture that affirms the family's faith identity, praying for and encouraging each other, enacting rituals and routines, and simply "being present together" express the message that "we are in this together," helping build family resilience.

The Bible is filled with stories of individuals who showed great resilience in the face of adversity, from Paul who went back to Lystra in Asia Minor after the people in that city stoned and left him for dead (Acts 14:19–20) to Job who refused to curse God after losing everything (Job 1:22) to Ruth who persevered amid tragic circumstances. We can learn from them.

In this world, we, too, will "face trials of many kinds" (James 1:2), but as Scripture aptly reminds us, "We are hard pressed on every side, but not crushed; perplexed, but not in despair; persecuted, but not abandoned; struck down, but not destroyed" (2 Cor. 4:8–9).

Chapter 9

Communication Routines:
Doing Life Together

Chapter Summary: This chapter explores the role of communication for families as they make decisions and enact them. Just as businesses hold strategic planning meetings and establish budgets, so too should families. A biblically informed framework for families "doing life together" that centers on expectations, motivations, and coordination is presented. This framework privileges love as motivation and grace as an expression of that love. The chapter covers how families negotiate household chores, create budgets, and establish rules for technology and media, providing practical strategies for navigating the everyday, often mundane, tasks in ways that lead to family flourishing.

Introduction

ONE MAJOR ASPECT OF FAMILY COMMUNICATION has to do with setting up routines to manage a household. Someone must compost food waste and take out the garbage. Bills need to be paid. Laundry and dishes must be cleaned. Who changes the next dirty diaper? Does a family hire a cleaning service? How families decide who does what, when, and how are *family communication processes*. We term this aspect of family communication "doing life together." Thinking about, discussing, and practicing the "business" side of family creates a routine structure that facilitates peaceful, sustainable relationships.

Here is a story to focus our attention on the communication processes used to negotiate family life. Chapter 23 of Genesis relays negotiations that happened between the Jewish Patriarch Abraham and the Hittite people. His wife Sarah has died, and Abraham wants to purchase a burial plot. Listen to the exchange:

> He [Abraham] said, "I am a foreigner and stranger among you. Sell me some property for a burial site here so I can bury my dead."

> The Hittites replied to Abraham, "Sir, listen to us. You are a mighty prince among us. Bury your dead in the choicest of our tombs. None of us will refuse you his tomb for burying your dead."

> Then Abraham rose and bowed down before the people of the land, the Hittites. He said to them, "If you are willing to let me bury my dead, then listen to me and intercede with Ephron son of Zohar on my behalf so he will sell me the cave of Machpelah, which belongs to him and is at the end of his field. Ask him to sell it to me for the full price as a burial site among you."

> Ephron the Hittite was sitting among his people and he replied to Abraham in the hearing of all the Hittites who had come to the gate of his city. "No, my lord," he said. "Listen to me; I give you the field, and I give you the cave that is in it. I give it to you in the presence of my people. Bury your dead."

> Again, Abraham bowed down before the people of the land and he said to Ephron in their hearing, "Listen to me, if you will. I will pay the price of the field. Accept it from me so I can bury my dead there."

> Ephron answered Abraham, "Listen to me, my lord; the land is worth four hundred shekels of silver, but what is that between you and me? Bury your dead."

> Abraham agreed to Ephron's terms and weighed out for him the price he had named in the hearing of the Hittites: four hundred shekels of silver, according to the weight current among the merchants.

Modern negotiations in the U.S. often sound like the exact opposite of this conversation as each party wrangles to get the best deal. The seller asks a higher price than she thinks she will get. The buyer bids a lower price than he thinks he will get, and they meet in the middle. Abraham and Ephron's negotiations were dramatically different. In essence, Ephron says, "What is money between us? Let me be your servant. Let me meet your need with my resources!" Likewise, Abraham says, "I want to honor you and pay the full price. Don't undersell me because this is a family emergency." In a refreshing way, this scene illustrates how Christian families should treat one another. It pictures the servanthood Christ commanded (Mark 10:45) and how to prefer one another in honor (Rom. 12:10). It prizes people and relationships above things.

How families go about "doing life together" should also demonstrate this type of love for one another. Families, as we reviewed in Chapter 2, are a picture of redeemed relationships that God planned for us. Families mirror the kind of love that members of Christ's body should have for one another. Marriage is a picture of Christ and his people. The standard Jesus set for these relationships is nothing less than the same kind of love he had for us (John 13:34). Jesus taught about this in his Sermon on the Mount (Matt. 5–7): we should turn the other cheek, go the extra mile, pray for our enemies, forgive repeatedly, and love without reservation. Christian families are to live by God's standards for relationships, which go well beyond a set of "dos" and "don'ts." When it comes to how we handle the business side of our relationships, the Kingdom of God is one that prefers one another in love (Rom. 12:10) and leaves no debt outstanding but to love one another (Rom. 13:8).

In this chapter we consider a few areas of life where families must make decisions and negotiate actions for "doing life together." We highlight household chores, family budgeting, and rules for technology and media. These areas are by no means exhaustive. There are a host of other, often mundane, essential tasks in family life. Our goal is to emphasize that approaching family communication from a Christian perspective privileges love as our motive for "doing life together" and grace as our expression of that love.

Household Management

Life takes work. Most families not only have to earn a living through paid employment but also must manage tasks required to run their own households. The options available to families are to either hire a person or company to do the work or assign family members responsibility for the jobs. Look at this list of typical household chores.

- Shopping
- Paying bills
- Organizing family schedules
- Washing dishes
- Mowing the lawn
- Maintaining the car
- Washing clothes
- Transporting family members
- Planning family vacations
- Cleaning the house or apartment
- Determining investment strategies
- Completing routine home maintenance
- Cooking
- Home upgrades or remodeling

When babies are brought into homes, the amount of household labor increases substantially, adding to this list tasks such as changing diapers, dressing, and feeding young children, administering or arranging medical care, and so on.[1] Determining how these chores get done is one central aspect of "doing life together." We provide a framework for families that centers on expectations, motivations, and coordination.

Expectations

Did you have a cleaning chore chart as a kid? Did your elementary teacher rotate who was in charge of erasing the board or feeding the class hamster? These kinds of organizational structures assign work responsibilities for household and classroom management. They make expectations about chores explicit and accountable.

Families often hold and create work expectations—either explicitly or implicitly—that inform their routines. Gary Chapman shares a humorous story about this in one of his lectures about the five love languages. He grew up thinking that it was unmanly to vacuum. He had an expectation that only women should use a vacuum cleaner. He did not mind sweeping or mopping, he just had an expectation that he would never vacuum. When he got married, however, his wife had no such expectation. This did not go well. There were several arguments before the couple was able to identify the root of the issue. After uncovering and articulating the expectation, Gary decided he would rather show love to his wife by serving her, even if it meant vacuuming the floors, then continue with his belief that "real men don't vacuum."[2]

One of the first steps in having healthy family routines is to acknowledge and share expectations. As one friend shared, "Unspoken expectations become landmines in relationships!" Acknowledging expectations creates a space where discussion, negotiation, and collaboration can lead to family routines that honor one another. Sometimes this means you get your way. Sometimes it means you compromise. Sometimes it means you give up your way and change your expectations to serve your family. Identifying and articulating expectations can prevent malignant or false attributions and can avoid relational explosions.

IIIIIIII ▶ **Application Activity 9.1:**
Relationship Landmines

- What unspoken rules for housework have you adopted? Examples of these kinds of rules include, "Men should always take care of trash," or "Dishes should be clean every night before going to bed." Make a list of as many of these kinds of implicit expectations as you can.

- Now pair up with a partner and compare lists. Did your expectations jive? Did they contradict?

- Discuss how having these expectations might impact your relationships with roommates? With siblings? With a marriage partner?

Motivations

In addition to articulating expectations, families need to drill into their motivations. Do you want to have a clean home to impress others? Do you assign tasks to align with cultural expectations for what men or women should do? Is your reason for earning money to become wealthy, please a parent, give generously? We can have many different motivations for engaging in the tasks of life. 1 Corinthians 13 reminds us that if our motives are not based in love, then we fall short of honoring God.

Imagine a family in which members tried to outdo one another in service. If one person cooked a meal, someone else would do all the dishes and sweep and mop the floor to make sure the cook was served well. Someone else might take care of the family finances, but like a poker game, another family member would up the ante. "I'll see your administration of family resources and raise you by taking care of the trash and cleaning the toilets!" This kind of love for one another would create a competitiveness in the family to see who could love more and best. This imagination illustrates what the Bible might mean when it instructs us to "outdo one another in showing honor" (Rom. 12:10, ESV).

||||||||▶   Application Activity 9.2:
Rewriting the "Love Chapter" for Family Labor

- **Read 1 Corinthians 13.**
- **Go back and change the examples given throughout the chapter to apply to family labor. For example, the passage might start, "If I were to clean all the dishes in the house, but wasn't motivated by love, it would be like a dripping faucet."**
- **Be poetic, dramatic, creative, and have fun!**

Jonathan's family often repeats the cliché "many hands make light the work," and we have added the phrase "and a happy heart makes it go faster." This helps focus not only on the practical aspects of serving one another but also on our motivations for helping. Another phrase that focuses on motives mirrors how we want to obey God.[3] It reminds that true obedience is "right away, all the way, and with a happy heart." These expressions go beyond behavioral metrics and probe into our attitudes. They uncover the "heart" behind our actions and refocus on our motivations.

Coordination

Our expectations and motivations necessarily influence how we coordinate labor for and in the family. Practically, how we divide labor may need to rely on family meetings. Businesses rely on meetings to share information, solicit feedback, brainstorm and evaluate options, delegate tasks, and make collaborative decisions. These types of conversations are important to success in any business, and they are also important for coordinating family activities. Who will drop the kids at school, and who is in charge of dinner? When is the next doctor's visit scheduled? What was learned from the phone call with the bank about financing a home purchase? Family meetings can coordinate the mundane and monumental. Let's look at a few examples to see how expectations, motivations, and coordination play out in families.

Household Chores

When it comes to household chores, one of the most common areas of contemporary research tries to explain the persistent difference in men and women's time spent working around the house. According to 2019 national data, the average man spends about 1 hour and 39 minutes a day doing household chores, whereas the average woman spends 2 hours and 16 minutes a day.[4] Of course, these statistics do not account for the household responsibilities assigned to kids. But many academics have focused on this issue and proposed various explanations for these differences.

Social norms about housework and what is fair chore allocation is one explanation for gender-based differences in housework. From this view, gender differences are expected, with gender-norm conformity rather than gender-equity being the goal.[5] Others account for gender differences in housework allocation in terms of the type of household chores assigned.[6] Women primarily take responsibility for "female-typed" household chores (e.g., cooking, cleaning, grocery shopping), which require more daily input, whereas "male-typed" chores (e.g., lawn mowing, home and auto maintenance) are periodic.[7] Of course, some men cook and clean in their households more than women, but across the board, there are persistent gender differences in these tasks.[8] Other researchers account for macro-level forces and argue that because women bear children and primarily are the ones to care for infants, they are expected to work part-time and thus take on more household responsibilities.[9] Based on our model, these explanations point to differing expectations for men and women when it comes to the division of household labor.

Others explain the differences in workload divisions through a psychological approach. For example, one theory suggests that people have different thresholds for action.[10] Individuals have different levels of tolerance for clutter or dirt, so the one with the lowest threshold will be more motivated to clean before his or her partner because that person actually sees the dirt first. To explain the difference in male/female division of labor, this theory would suggest that the average woman's tolerance for an unclean home is lower than the average man's. Internalized pressure to be a "good wife" or "good mother" may also explain why women engage in more domestic labor.[11] Based on our model, probing these psychological processes helps to uncover the motivations for behavior.

Still another approach tries to integrate couples' philosophies toward marriage with their division of labor. For example, Niels Blom and colleagues present a theoretical depiction of how families might divide household and paid employment responsibilities.[12] They consider examples of egalitarian versus non-egalitarian partners and specialized versus non-specialized roles. In a *companionate marriage*, both spouses participate in paid employment equally and both participate in housework equally. In a *complementarity marriage*, a specialized couple would have an unequal division of labor. This could be pictured by a man who works 40 hours outside the home but does no household chores and a wife who does 20 hours of home-based labor per week but does not earn money in the labor force. There could also be mixtures in between these two archetypal marriages.

As we make decisions about how best to divide labor in a household, gender is only one variable that might be taken into account. Age, ability, interests, and experiences also play a role in who does what. Families should communicate with one another to set expectations and encourage love-motivated actions. Household chores can be coordinated through planning

---

|||||||| ▶ **Application Activity 9.3:**
Reflecting on Specialization

- Review the types of division of household labor (companionate, complementarity, a mixture). Which type of family did you come from? If you had two parents, how did they divide household and paid employment? How did it look if you had one parent?

- How were you involved in the family earning and household work? For example, did you get a job and pay rent? Buy your own car? Were you expected to do household chores? Cook for your siblings?

- Estimate how many hours per week you did household chores when you were under the age of 10? Between 10–13 years old? 14–17 years old?

meetings, checklists, and schedules that rotate responsibilities. Families can set routines for communication to avoid assumptive or unfair distributions of household labor. Engaging in clear communication allows for families to consider expectations, motivations, and coordination of household chores as they do life together.

Budgeting

Have you ever sat through a business or church budget meeting? There are often reports to review, discussions about upcoming expenses, and decisions to be made about the best strategies to reach goals. How about accounting—do you enjoy reconciling income and spending? For many, these kinds of meetings and tasks are tedious or boring, but they are essential. Effective management of family budgets has strong implications for family well-being. It makes sense, right? If parent spending is out of control, for example, then resources might not be available to provide for the basic needs of children. Every business needs to track expenses and receipts as does each family. Learning how to deal with family finances is one area where routines of communication can help. To do this well, remember that families should articulate expectations, reflect on motivations, and then coordinate the practical aspects of budgeting.

Our expectations and motivations about family budgets can be informed by our past experiences, family backgrounds, media influences, or even how our peers deal with money. The Bible offers many explicit guidelines and implies principles about spending and saving money, generosity, and what priority finances should take in our lives (see Box 9.4). It may take several conversations, time studying and reflecting, and family discussions to align understandings of money with Scripture and to articulate expectations about spending, saving, investing, and giving habits.

Practical coordination for spending takes place through setting and keeping a budget. In terms of communication, this means having regular budget meetings and holding each other accountable to disciplined spending habits. Budget meetings help set priorities and goals for spending and saving, define monthly spending categories, and determine spending caps in different areas.

Many interesting interaction dynamics occur in budget discussions. Because people come from different family backgrounds and have different experiences with money, holding a budget meeting forces couples and

Points to Ponder 9.4:
Scriptures on Work and Money

After reflecting on the Scriptures below, how do these teachings on work and money correspond with your upbringing? With your own practices? With media portrayals of money? With how you see friends treat work and finances?

- He who trusts in his riches will fall, but the righteous shall flourish as the green leaf. (Prov. 11:28)

- Do not wear yourself out to get rich; do not trust your own cleverness. Cast but a glance at riches, and they are gone, for they will surely sprout wings and fly off to the sky like an eagle. (Prov. 23:4–5)

- No one can serve two masters, for either he will hate the one and love the other, or he will be devoted to the one and despise the other. You cannot serve God and money. (Matt. 6:24)

- The rich rules over the poor, and the borrower is the slave of the lender. (Prov. 22:7)

- Lazy hands make for poverty, but diligent hands bring wealth. (Prov. 10:4)

- Dishonest money dwindles away, but whoever gathers money little by little makes it grow. (Prov. 13:11)

- Each man should give what he has decided in his heart to give, not reluctantly or under compulsion, for God loves a cheerful giver. (2 Cor. 9:7)

- Instruct those who are rich in this present world not to be conceited or to fix their hope on the uncertainty of riches, but on God, who richly supplies us with all things to enjoy. Instruct them to do good, to be rich in good works, to be generous and ready to share, storing up for themselves the treasure of a good foundation for the future, so that they may take hold of that which is life indeed. (1 Tim. 6:17–19)

- Not that I speak from want, for I have learned to be content in whatever circumstances I am. I know how to get along with humble means, and I also know how to live in prosperity; in any and every circumstance I have learned the secret of being filled and going hungry, both of having abundance and suffering need. I can do all things through him who strengthens me. (Phil. 4:11–13)

> ## Points to Ponder 9.4 *continued*:
> ## Scriptures on Work and Money
>
> - The generous will themselves be blessed, for they share their food with the poor. (Prov. 22:9)
> - A little sleep, a little slumber, a little folding of the hands to rest—and poverty will come on you like a thief and scarcity like an armed man. (Prov. 24:33–34)
> - A tithe of everything from the land, whether grain from the soil or fruit from the trees, belongs to the Lord: it is holy to the Lord. (Lev. 27:30)

families to get on the same page, literally. Their expectations, priorities, habits, goals, and dreams are put into a family budget form. Because money reflects priorities, desires, and dreams, it is important to listen closely during budget talks. Listen for expectations and motivations, not just spending limits in a certain category.

Coordinating expectations not only happens within families but also between families. Parents may expect to cut off all financial support once their child marries. Others may want to pay for mobile phone plans, to cover any fuel needed to visit them, or to share in-kind support like borrowing a car, including their married children on family vacations, or inviting their kids and grandkids over for a weekly meal together. The work of uncovering expectations within and between families and articulating these expectations is a challenge but worthwhile.

An interesting dynamic, called a *forced dichotomy*, occurs between couples and can show up in budgeting discussions. Whether two people are very similar to each other or very different, because there are only two, one person is forced to be the "most" while the other is the "least." For money, this forced dichotomy usually manifests in a spender/saver dynamic. One partner is a "wasteful spender" and the other a "miserly saver." When setting spending caps or holding each other accountable to them, the saver prioritizes building up a rainy-day fund or investing, whereas the spender is more inclined to splurge. Knowing about the forced dichotomy can help couples work together to understand their proclivities and hesitations, their strengths and weaknesses. Good communication is key to doing this effectively.

It should come as no surprise that family interaction around budgeting often looks different across different economic strata. In a fascinating book titled *Alone Together*, family interaction is depicted across different economic strata in the U.S.[13] Sociologists found that couples who do not have enough resources to make "ends meet" engage in high amounts of communication, but it is usually negative. They experience high stress trying to figure out what bills to pay or where to move or how they can stretch their finances. Couples with enough money to handle the daily demands of life (e.g., food, shelter, transportation) interact about as much as those in the lower strata, but their communication is more positive. These middle-class couples tend to enjoy each other and talk about important decisions as well as everyday life. Wealthy couples share the same household but live almost separate lives; they are alone together. On average, these couples spend limited time interacting together and more time engaged in work, hobbies, and independent pursuits. Interpreting these findings, it is important to understand that they apply to the average family in each stratum, not any particular family. For the average American family, it seems there may be a "sweet spot" for happy marriages. It seems that couples need neither too little nor too much wealth to flourish relationally, like the Proverb writer requests of God: "[G]ive me neither poverty nor riches, but give me only my daily bread. Otherwise, I may have too much and disown you and say, 'Who is the Lord?' Or I may become poor and steal, and so dishonor the name of my God" (Prov. 30: 8–9).

Creating a Family Budget

Many emerging adults have never set a budget or had to track their spending. Some do not know where to start. Here, we provide a basic guide to budgeting and then in the next section offer five tips on how to develop family budgeting routines. We assume that individuals and families should spend less money than they make each month. After all, the Bible warns that "the borrower is the slave of the lender" (Prov. 22:7, ESV). We also emphasize again that budgets reflect priorities. Family values are expressed through finances. We also strongly encourage you to create a budget for yourself now. Even if you are not in a relationship, you can ask parents or trusted mentors to help you apply the tips presented in this chapter.

Family budgeting is generally set on a monthly basis because rent/mortgage, utility bills, and other expenses generally happen every month, regardless of how income is earned. However, depending on your income schedule (e.g., salary paid monthly, hourly paid weekly, contracts paid per invoice), you may need to determine a cash-flow plan (i.e., how the timing of income corresponds with the timing of expenses). We encourage you to develop a monthly budget with many of the primary spending categories families experience. Conventional family budgeting advice recommends taking care of the four most important things first: food, shelter, utilities, and transportation. Other spending categories include things like clothing, medical needs, recreation/entertainment, and personal expenses. Developing a habit of generosity through tithing (giving away 10% of your earnings) is another biblical concept, so we also encourage this practice. Another standard to budgeting is to "pay yourself first," which means saving money each month for the future. Some recommend this should be about 10% of your income as well.

Practical Interaction Tips

Here are five practical tips for setting budgeting routines as a family. First, approach the management of the family budget as a team. There may be a tendency to look at individual habits, but for married couples and families who share a household budget, it is better to approach it as "doing life *together*." Take a class or training together on how to do budgets and how to invest. Meet a financial planner and do it together. Collaborate to set priorities and spending limits. Approach budgeting as a team.

Second, hold regular, monthly budget meetings. Set aside time each month to review the previous month's spending (e.g., How did you as a team stay within your limits?) and set new spending goals and categories in anticipation of the next month (e.g., Is there a holiday or birthday to account for in the upcoming month? Is there extra income like a sales bonus to allocate?). The frequencies of the meetings may become less important as couples have more experience together and more aligned priorities. Having a planned time to connect about family spending and consider the upcoming life events can prevent brief or hurried conversations, which can prevent meaningful conversations about expectations and priorities.

Third, hold one another accountable while being flexible. Implementing a budget requires self-discipline, monitoring, and accountability. You have to know how much you are spending and which category you are spending from. Sometimes you have to say "no" to yourself and to each other in order to achieve the goals you set. And even when you anticipate the upcoming month as best as you can, there are still unexpected events and emergencies. As a couple or family, you need to be able to adjust spending priorities based on emerging needs. If there is a sudden death and you need to get to a funeral, or if your car tire blows out, you need to be able to respond immediately. Having a "rainy day fund" (usually about $1,000 in cash or savings set aside for the unexpected) is a good way to stay flexible while sticking to your budget.

Fourth, in addition to budgeting meetings, hold sessions to dream. Talk about desires, life goals, and fun things. Then, prioritize saving for them. These wish list items could include almost anything: a vacation, kid's college fund, a jet ski, international travel, retirement, a quilting kit. The point is to have conversations periodically (maybe once every six to nine months or annually) where you check in with each other and learn about persistent and new spending dreams. Then you set goals and a plan for achieving them together.

Fifth and finally, get practical. Delegate the duties of budgeting. Someone needs to track expenditures within categories and report how, as a team, you did the previous month. Someone must pay the bills (or set up all the automated withdrawals). Someone has to make sure taxes are filed on time or designate beneficiaries or update the family will. It is fine to delegate to the person who is most interested, skilled, or willing to do these things, but both partners (and the kids, as they age) should be aware of the spending practices and financial processes in place for your family.

Technology in Families

There are plenty of other aspects of family life that benefit from thoughtful routines of communication. Family members approach technology and media use, for example, with varied expectations and motivations which must be coordinated into family routines. Is this a topic worthy of a family meeting? You bet it is! Recent surveys report that children between 8 and 12 years old average about five hours of screen media a day, and teenagers average over seven hours. What is amazing is that these figures do not even include screen time used for schoolwork.[14] The same survey found that nearly 70% of children have a smartphone by the age of twelve.

Paul Patton and Robert H. Woods Jr. advocate for thoughtful practices related to modern digital exposure in their book *Everyday Sabbath: How to Lead Your Dance with Media and Technology in Mindful and Sacred Ways*.[15] Following their lead, we encourage families to have conversations about technology that center on three practices. First, families should approach technology with *sacred intentionality*—reflecting on media use with the goal of determining patterns of strategic technology use and times when it is mindless or habitual. Second, *sacred interiority* emphasizes that families should consider the value and the effects of technology on family life. Finally, and perhaps most importantly, families need to have conversations about *sacred identity*—discerning how technology shapes their thinking about who they are as divinely created persons made in the image of God or influences them to believe otherwise.

Families need to make decisions regarding technology and media. For example, should parents restrict children's technology use? If so, in what areas—doing homework, playing games, connecting with peers? What are the expectations? What are the motives for restricting? What does restricting technology look like in everyday family life? We could also ask: is it good parenting to provide oversight in children's media use? If so, to what extent and with what technologies? These are decisions that families make, and they do so with varying degrees of intentionality. As one example, a study identified how parents mediated children's smartphone use and found that discussion-based active mediation was more desirable than restrictive mediation practice.[16] Discussion-based mediations offer children a stronger voice in the process than does a one-way system of parental rulemaking imposed on the children. Of course, we are not saying that no rules should be imposed, nor are we saying that parents should abdicate their final decision-making authority. Our point is that family members who have a stake in the outcome should be included as much as possible in the conversation to set expectations and to isolate motivations.

One additional consideration that families face when discussing technology, and other areas of life, is privacy. In a technological society, privacy has taken on new importance and meaning. Here are some privacy questions that families face with technology: Is it acceptable to share photos of your family vacation on social media platforms? How about "embarrassing" baby pictures? Should you post about your parents' divorce? Should parents have passwords to your social media accounts or vice versa? Communication Privacy Management Theory (CPM) was developed by Sandra Petronio and assumes that privacy is important for effective family functioning.[18] CPM asserts that what is considered private information is likely not to be the same for all family members. Private information is that which makes us feel vulnerable and is often information we want to determine when

---

IIIIIIII ▶   **Application Activity 9.5:**
                 Role of Technology

Think for a minute about interpersonal communication technology (ICT) from the past 30 years (e.g., email, text messages, mobile phones, social media, virtual reality headsets).

Discuss with a partner:

- When have you seen ICTs get out of whack/out of their proper place in your life?
- What role do these ICTs play in your family relationships?

Christian writer Andy Crouch suggests that technology is in its proper place when it helps us: (1) start great conversations, (2) bond with real people we have been given to love, (3) take care of the fragile bodies we inhabit, (4) acquire skills and mastery of domains that are the glory of human culture (e.g., sports, music), and (5) cultivate an awe for the created world we are part of and responsible for stewarding.[17] Consider each of these five expectations for the role of technology, and discuss with a partner:

- How has your family's use of ICTs matched these expectations? How has it diverged from these?
- What family routines do you think could keep ICTs in their proper place in your home?

---

and how it is revealed.[19] A parent, for example, may view family finances as private, whereas you may not. On the other hand, your mom may see your health issues as public, whereas you do not. Petronio suggests that we feel we "own" private information, and as owners, we set boundaries around our private information and expect others to respect them.[20]

These boundaries may be porous or fixed, which CPM describes as permeability. Families can have *high permeability* orientations, meaning that information is readily shared within and outside the family unit, whereas other families have *low permeability*, meaning the sharing of information both within and outside the family is highly restricted. Of course, *moderate permeability* is also an orientation; "these families are more judicious with choices about who knows information about family members, both among the individuals within the family and to those outside."[21] The theory also asserts that rules govern who we let inside our privacy boundaries and how. Finally, CPM recognizes the possibility of *boundary turbulence*, meaning there are mistakes and expectation violations when it comes to revealing and concealing private information.

To address the often disparate rules and expectations related to privacy, meta-communication (communication about communication) is needed. Conversations between family members can share their expectations or offer stories to illustrate times in which boundaries were crossed. Meta-communication can also include discussions about what communication rules a family wants to establish. Setting shared expectations can help prevent turbulence, but turbulence can also be resolved through negotiation and reformulation of boundary rules. In order to determine if it is appropriate, for example, to post about your parent's divorce, an understanding of your parent's privacy boundary expectations is needed. And, if in doubt, it is probably best to assume the information is private.

Conclusion

Household chores, budgeting, technology use, and managing private information, along with a myriad of other family activities, are all part of "doing life together." Every household has to find a way to manage. Across each domain, people bring expectations and motivations that should be coordinated together and clearly communicated with each other. Our interactions should reflect our desire to serve one another in honor and love (see 1 Peter 1:22; Gal. 6:2; Phil. 2:3; Mark 10:45). As the negotiations between Abraham and Ephron for Sarah's burial plot beautifully illustrate, families should prize people and relationships above things as they navigate life together.

PART III
Communication through Different Family Stages

This section of the book is divided into three subsections. The first focuses on marriage (Chapters 10, 11, and 12) and the second on parenting (Chapters 13 and 14). The final subsection considers family legacies (Chapter 15). We spend time discussing a Christian perspective on marriage, which we see as intrinsically linked to sexual practice, and reviewing theories and research that help explain communication in marriage, cohabitation, and other marriage-like expressions of family. We then turn to the life experiences of children in various contexts before reviewing how parents parent. These chapters cover topics like discipline, which impacts not only a child's behavior but also his or her spiritual formation. We then consider how families leave legacies. Children receive inheritances that go beyond wealth and include cultural practices as well as spiritual blessings and curses. Across all these topics, we integrate biblical perspectives with social scientific evidence to present a view of communication through different family stages.

Let's start our journey with courtship—how we find a life partner.

III.A: Marital Interaction

Chapter 10

Pathways to Marriage

Chapter Summary: The road to marriage is varied but most men and women will eventually marry. This chapter looks at how marriage relationships form by reviewing psychological, biological, and sociological perspectives on mate selection, or how individuals find a life partner. Next, the chapter looks at venues where couples meet and the central role communication plays in the courtship process. Biblically informed advice for making a decision on whom to marry concludes the chapter.

Introduction

ABRAHAM, ADVANCED IN YEARS, entrusted his faithful household steward to find a wife for his son Isaac. The servant was instructed to find Isaac a wife from Abraham's relatives, requiring him to travel to Nahor, Abraham's homeland. Before departing, the servant asked Abraham, "What if the woman is unwilling to come back with me to this land?" (Gen. 24:5). Abraham responded in faith: God "will send his angel before you, so you can get a wife for my son from there" (Gen. 24:7). When the servant came to the well on the outskirts of the city, he prayed:

> O Lord, God of my master Abraham, give me success today, and show kindness to my Master Abraham. See, I am standing beside this spring, and the daughters of the townspeople are coming out to draw water. May it be that when I say to a girl "Please let down your jar that I may have a drink," and she says "Drink, and I'll water your camels, too"—let her be the one you have chosen for your servant Isaac. By this I will know that you have shown kindness to my master. (Gen. 24:12–14)

Even before he finished praying, Rebekah appeared before the servant and did all the servant had prayed. The servant then worshipped: "Praise be to the Lord, the God of my master Abraham, who has not abandoned his kindness and faithfulness to my master" (Gen. 24:27).

The story unfolds with Rebekah telling her family about all that transpired at the well. Her brother hurried to the well to invite the servant to stay with them. As soon as Rebekah's father and brother knew that the servant's message was from the Lord, they said, "Here is Rebekah; take her and go, and let her become the wife of your master's son, as the Lord has directed." But wait, the story does not end there. Rebekah's family gives this young girl a choice as to whether she is willing to leave her homeland and become Isaac's wife: "So they called Rebekah and asked her, 'Will you go with this man?' She responded, 'I will go'" (Gen. 24:58).

This story is striking and instructive.[1] Take a moment and identify some courtship principles that can be gleaned from it. These principles might include actively searching (Abraham sent a servant to find a wife), praying (the servant prayed), involving the family and trusted counselors (Abraham and Rebekah's families), and identifying criteria for a life partner (Isaac's wife was Jewish, she was a "young woman," likely to match Isaac's age). Another criterion Abraham set was that the woman must be willing to relocate, to come live with Isaac (see Gen. 24:5–9). As a courtship principle, there needed to be a high level of alignment toward life goals. In this case, Isaac's life calling was to lay hold of God's promise to Abraham and his descendants, so his wife had to be in agreement with that dream and willing to relocate to support it. Notice also that the servant tested Rebekah's character. No doubt, watering the servant's camel was a lot of work for Rebekah (a camel drinks as much as 25 gallons of water).[2] This gesture shows that Rebekah's heart was kind and generous. The story also illustrates personal choice and family involvement. While not exhaustive, these courtship principles can offer some guidance for Christians as they endeavor toward marriage.

In this chapter, we look at how marriage relationships form by reviewing psychological, biological, and sociological perspectives on mate selection, or how we find a life partner. We then look at ways people meet and the central role communication plays in the courtship process. We include courtship in a book on family communication because marriages and families are not formed in a vacuum. A marriage is a merging of pre-existing family systems and experiences. If a woman grew up in the foster care system and meets a man who was raised by a single father, those childhood experiences impact the expectations, dispositions, and communication skills that the couple brings into their partnership. It is important to recognize the continuity between generations. While many models of attraction and interpersonal communication tend to theorize from assumption of autonomous and individualistic frameworks, we recognize and emphasize that a person's family and social context has profound impacts on the courtship experiences. We conclude the chapter by offering biblically informed advice for deciding whom to marry.

Finding a Life Partner

Courtship, which is often referred to in academic literature as mate selection, is more than finding a mate and is a much more complete relationship than mere sexual procreation. So we opt to use different terms. We begin by reviewing broad perspectives on why marriage occurs and how people enter into it. As we presented in Chapter 2, the Bible demonstrates that marriage was God's idea. Adam and Eve were the first married couple. (It must have been nice to have God as the matchmaker!) Ever since that time, however, there have been many factors involved in the courtship process.[3] We review psychological, biological, and sociological perspectives. All of these perspectives add value in understanding how people are thrust into relationships and how they move toward marriage.

IIIIIII ▶	Application Activity 10.1: Stages of Courtship

Take a few minutes to outline what the stages of relationships are that people experience on the path toward marriage. Identify the stages and describe verbal and nonverbal communication behaviors that people exhibit in each stage.

- For example, if you were attracted to someone, how would you get that person's attention?

- How would you let that person know your interest? What messages—verbal or nonverbal—would you send?

Psychological Forces

A psychological perspective on courtship privileges processes and forces within individuals that account for how they partner. There are many such theories, but we review needs and attachment theories.

Needs Theories. Needs theories explain why and how people couple. Based on this way of thinking we are motivated to form relationships to meet basic social and psychological needs. Will Schutz proposed that the three primary social needs that drive behavior are: (1) *inclusion*, to belong and to experience human connection and fellowship; (2) *control*, to have some influence over others and outcomes; and (3) *affection*, to give and to receive love and support.[4] Families are places where these needs can be met for many, but as children age, romantic relationships become a primary locus for fulfilling social needs. Perhaps this is one way to understand why God stated, "It is not good for the man to be alone. I will make a helper suitable for him" (Gen. 2:18). Men and women were made to reflect God as social and to fulfill each other's social needs.

In general, needs theories presume that we are motivated to behave in ways that fulfill our own needs. This, however, is only part of the story. Families often sacrifice for each other, and many parents put their children's needs above their own. How can this happen if we are primarily motivated to gratify our own desires? A biblical anthropology, or view of human beings, recognizes that one of God's most precious gifts to humanity is choice. We have the power to choose whether we fulfill our desires or deny them for a higher purpose. As Christ pleaded with his disciples,

> Whoever wants to be my disciple must deny themselves and take up their cross and follow me. For whoever wants to save their life will lose it, but whoever loses their life for me will find it. What good will it be for someone to gain the whole world, yet forfeit their soul? Or what can anyone give in exchange for their soul? For the Son of Man is going to come in his Father's glory with his angels, and then he will reward each person according to what they have done. (Matt. 16:24–26)

We are accountable to God for how we live, and he called us to subjugate our own needs, through our personal volition, to find his life in us.

Attachment Theory. Another popular psychological theory to explain how people form relationships is Attachment Theory. The theory describes

Points to Ponder 10.2:
Did God Create Us with a Hierarchy of Needs?

Perhaps one of the most famous needs theories is Abraham Maslow's "hierarchy of needs."[5] To briefly summarize Maslow, humans are motivated by striving to fulfill five basic needs—physiological, safety, belonging, esteem, and self-actualization—and that we first strive to meet lower-level needs (physiological needs, safety) followed by social needs (companionship, belonging, acceptance), and ultimately by needs for self-actualization. Coupling happens to fulfill these needs.

But wait! Did you notice that Maslow defines sex as a basic physiological need on par with food? And that sex, for Maslow, comes before the social need of companionship? More broadly, this theory seems to argue that we are motivated to find a life partner to fulfill our own needs. Is that a rather selfish perspective on relationships? These considerations beg the question: How well do you think Maslow's hierarchy aligns with a Christian perspective?

Does the view that we are motivated to fulfill our own needs tell the whole story? From a Christian perspective, we are commanded to look out not only for our own needs but also for the needs of others (Phil. 2:4). How are these needs met? Maslow proposes that our needs can be met through our efforts. However, the Bible teaches that only God can truly meet our needs because the most fundamental need we have is not self-actualization but salvation from our sin.[6] This relates to another concern with Maslow's theory: namely, Maslow started from a belief that human beings are intrinsically good. In his words, humanity's "inner nature, as much as we know of it so far, seems *not* to be intrinsically, primarily, or necessarily evil" (emphasis added).[7] This philosophy clearly diverges from a biblical perspective, which teaches that humans both bear the image of God (*imago Dei*; see Gen. 1:26–28) and are marred by sin through the Fall (see Chapter 4 for more details about the grand arc of Scripture).

A third critique of Maslow's theory is its ordering of needs. For example, sex is a basic need to Maslow, who viewed humans as essentially similar to animals. This view fits neatly with the sexual revolution of the 1960s and grants permission to exploit others to fulfill our own sexual desires. Yet, it contrasts sharply with the

> **Points to Ponder 10.2** *continued*:
> **Did God Create Us with a Hierarchy of Needs?**
>
> biblical view that sex is prohibited outside of marriage (e.g., Lev. 18, 20; Rom. 1:18–32; Col. 3:5). This ordering, even if only heuristic, suggests that we cannot seek companionship when hungry nor act courageously in ways that privilege others over our own safety. It is true that many act selfishly, but this is not the only way of being. Centuries of human experience, particularly in the context of altruistic behaviors in families, tell another story. Finally, is self-actualization really the pinnacle of human experience? From a Christian perspective, we could argue that self-actualization should be placed at the bottom of the chart for those who choose to put other "needs" above instinctual and social needs.[8] Regardless of our needs or their categories, God endowed us with an incredible gift of self-direction.
>
> In the end, what can we learn from Maslow's theory? What should we discard?

three primary ways in which people relate to others, classified as secure, avoidant, or ambivalent attachment. Originally proposed to explain child development, others have expanded the theory to describe adult romantic relationships. We review parent-child attachment in Chapter 13 but here consider it in terms of romantic partnering.

Research on adult attachment illustrates that a person's attachment style predicts how he experiences love. For example, in one set of studies researchers found that individuals with *secure attachment* report more positive experiences with love than those with avoidant or ambivalent styles. Securely attached individuals characterized their relationships as happy, friendly, and trusting. In contrast, with *ambivalent attachment*, individuals saw love as an obsession, as emotional highs and lows, or as extreme sexual attraction and jealousy. Those with *avoidant attachment* characterized love in terms of fear of intimacy, emotional highs and lows, and jealousy. Individuals with ambivalent and avoidant attachment styles also experienced shorter relationships than those with the secure attachment style.[9]

Research on attachment suggests that people develop sets of expectations and modes of relating with others, which begin in early childhood and persist into early adult romantic relationships. As a lifespan perspective teaches, however, childhood experiences are not deterministic. In fact, Beth Le Poire and her colleagues found that partner attachment style may better predict attitudes and behaviors than early parent-child attachment styles.[10] In other words, attachment styles may be less enduring than early theories purported.

Take a moment and reflect on how your early childhood attachments and interactions may have shaped your views of romantic relationships (e.g., fear of intimacy, intensity of jealousy, emotionally available/unavailable, feelings of being wanted/unwanted, and/or knowing you were loved/hated). If you experienced avoidant or ambivalent attachment in your early formative years, how do you think it might impact your romantic relationships? How might you move forward from here? If you were in a relationship with someone who had an avoidant or ambivalent attachment style, what kinds of messages do you think would be important to share with that person?

Certainly, our needs and experiences of attachment to others impact our courtship experiences. But we are more than our minds. Attraction is impacted by physical and sociological forces, as well.

Biological Forces

There are a number of studies and theories that offer biological explanations for attraction. Mating is, after all, a case of biological connection as much as it is psychological and social. And biologically, opposites attract. Males and females are the quintessential opposites as they possess complementary reproductive systems which God designed to be joined together.

Many theorists and researchers who study biological processes of attraction often defer to evolutionary thinking as part of their explanations. In this perspective, the ultimate goal of species survival features prominently. Affection Exchange Theory, for example, is a bio-evolutionary view of mate selection.[11] The theory is grounded in a set of beliefs that see humans as subject to the principles of natural and sexual selection. We are attracted, whether consciously or unconsciously, to those who offer the highest probability for procreation and survival. Physiological influences, such as hormones, affect this process. The theory contends that affectionate communication, both receiving and conveying affection, contributes to reproductive and survival success. For example, saying "I love you" and giving a hug signal to others that you are a "viable partner and a fit potential parent."[12]

Nonverbal pairing is another area of study that assumes human behavior is more akin to animals than not. Anthropologist David Givens groups nonverbal behaviors used in mate selection into five phases or functions: (1) attracting attention, (2) recognizing the other, (3) holding conversations, (4) touching, and (5) making love. The specific nonverbal tactics often differ for males and females but tend to align with one of these five functions.[13] As Helen Fisher in her book *Anatomy of Love* summarizes, "Like the smile, the sequential flirt, the coy look, the head toss, the chest thrust, and the gaze are probably all part of a standard human repertoire of gestures that, used in certain contexts, evolved to attract a mate."[14] While these behaviors may be attractive and do serve to gain attention, the ultimate evolutionary end of reproduction is not necessarily the only reason they exist. Psychological needs like attention, belonging, and feelings of self-worth also can explain why people flirt. Alternatively, an explanation could include that God is playful and fun. Many do not think of God as "fun" per se, but one Fruit of the Holy Spirit is joy (Gal. 5:22). A glimpse at the variety of odd and playful behaviors across the globe demonstrates this attribute of God. So an alternative explanation of the flirting facts is that because males and females reflect God's nature, they find ways to enjoy and be enjoyed by one another.

A fascinating biological experiment that examined attraction between men and women involved scented t-shirts. The experiment designed by Claus Wedekind took clean t-shirts and had men sleep in them.[15] Men were instructed to be hygienic and avoid scent-producing products (e.g., deodorant, pungent foods). Women who did not know who each t-shirt belonged to then smelled and ranked the t-shirts for their attractiveness. The genetic profile of immunities for the men and women was also measured. Results? Women were attracted to men with opposite immune profiles and not as attracted to men who were most similar to themselves. Essentially, these findings suggest that any potential offspring between the women and the men whom they found most attractive would be healthier because they would benefit from a wide set of immunities (i.e., different immune profiles of their parents). Findings are consistent with studies of other animals and have been replicated with varying success on new human populations, but the strength of this effect is relatively weak.[16]

So opposites attract, biologically, but there was a surprising reversal that the studies also found. Women taking oral contraceptives ("the pill") had a flipped attraction: they were most attracted to men whose immune profiles were similar to theirs.[17] This flipped attraction would mean that any future offspring from couples attracted to each other while women were on the pill would be least protected against potential sicknesses in the environment (see Motuk's *Scent of a Man* for an accessible review).[18] Further research verified the downstream effects, finding that children of couples who formed when a woman was on the pill were sick more frequently and considered less healthy than children of couples who met when not on the pill.[19] Attraction, of course, is more than meets the nose. Biological factors can only explain part of our choices.[20]

Sociological Forces

Others have looked at mate selection from sociological and economic perspectives. Often referring to the "marriage market," researchers predict who will marry whom. For example, you have probably heard the adage "birds of a feather flock together" or the saying that "opposites attract." These contradictory quips illustrate *homogamy* (literally "same marriage") and *heterogamy* ("different marriage"). Biologically, opposites attract, but sociologically people seem attracted to those with whom they share life experiences. In a study of couples who moved from "serious" relationships to engagement or marriage, homogamy of social variables (e.g., socioeconomic status, religious affiliation, race, education attainment, geographical location) was important, especially in early stages of the relationship. In later stages of the relationship, value and attitude compatibility were important. There was some evidence that heterogamy occurred toward later stages of relationships, but overall homogamy was the most important for finding a partner.[21]

Another way of looking at marriage markets is to zoom out and consider who is available—who are the eligible partners? Indeed, "the make-up of the population affects mate choice because it limits the field of marriageable partners."[22] Consider contemporary universities in the U.S. Because more women attend universities than men and there are about two female majors for every male in certain fields like communication and psychology, the chances of finding a marriage partner during college is good for heterosexual men but not as good for women. These structural variables (population size, sex ratios, education attainment) can all impact whom we date or marry.

Economists help explain marriage in terms of free market forces like supply, demand, and competition. Think of it like a big open market where men and women would shop for a spouse. What price would you have to

---

Points to Ponder 10.3:
What Does the Birth Control Pill Really Cost?

The vast majority of women (89%) report using oral contraception ("the pill") at some point in their lifetime, and an estimated 30 to 35% report current use.[23] Within churches there are debates about the morality of birth control (e.g., Should people prevent conception? Which methods are potential abortifacients?), but these debates go beyond our consideration here. Instead, we focus on how social forces related to the pill impact families. A lecture by an economist on this topic introduced some paradoxes.[24]

First, women on the pill compete with other women who are not on the pill for men to do less. Think of it in terms of the marriage market forces. There are two women, one on the pill and one not. The woman who is not taking birth control says to a man, "I'll give you sex if you will partner with me, but sex will require a promise that you contribute financially and relationally to any potential offspring that we produce." The woman on the pill says, "I'll give you sex to partner with me, and sex will not require any obligation for future investment." For the woman on the pill, there is less obligation and commitment required from potential sexual partners, which lowers the potential cost that men would have to pay to be partnered. That is, when women and men are using various birth control methods, it changes the cost-benefit calculations.

---

pay to get the best marriage partner? For example, in a market that is predominantly female, men have a market advantage (high supply of women), whereas women have a low supply of male partners with a high demand. Thus, the price women pay for men is higher than in a different market. Economists use social science research to set parameters for their models. Variables like physical attractiveness, athleticism, social standing, economic prosperity, and others become attributes of the product that make it worth the cost or not.

This economic exchange metaphor is consistent with a broad category of theories that help describe human behavior called social exchange theories.[25] This group of theories posits that people evaluate the costs and rewards of relating. According to the theory, people basically want to maximize rewards and minimize costs, but only insofar as it feels equitable. If

> ## Points to Ponder 10.3 *continued*:
> ## What Does the Birth Control Pill Really Cost?
>
> Another paradox is that since the introduction of oral contraceptives in the U.S., overall fertility dropped. This seems a natural and positive application. However, the drop in fertility was with married women primarily, and non-marital fertility has increased substantially since that time (i.e., women not married have more babies than before, with now over 40% of children born to unmarried parents).[26] Relatedly, this created a situation where those often best prepared in terms of education and financial resources to raise kids (married parents) are not having babies, and those least prepared (unmarried parents) are. More broadly, these changes illustrate ways various technologies, like contraceptives, can have sweeping effects on families and society.
>
> Given these paradoxes, what do you see as the pros and cons of using the pill? Other contraceptives? What advice would you give to a friend regarding the pill? How could these paradoxes inform a discussion with a partner about family planning?

costs are consistently higher than the rewards, they will either do something to increase their input or end the relationship. Another way that costs and rewards play out is through comparing their ratio against one's expectations for the relationship and available alternatives. If you expect that dating is only romantic but does not involve companionship and closeness, then you may seek fulfillment from other close friends and not a dating partner. Likewise, if there are many available alternatives, it may be easy to end a relationship. If there are few, then ending a relationship is weighed against the prospect of being single.

An extension of this way of thinking is found in Caryl Rusbult's Commitment Model.[27] This model is depicted in Figure 10.1 and includes three predictors of commitment, which are (1) how satisfied someone is with the relationship, (2) how much the person has invested in the relationship to date, and (3) the quality of available alternatives. Commitment, in turn, predicts how much the person continues to invest in maintaining the relationship (e.g., forgiveness, willingness to sacrifice). This theory makes commitment a hinge: a person's commitment is central to determining future investments in the relationship.

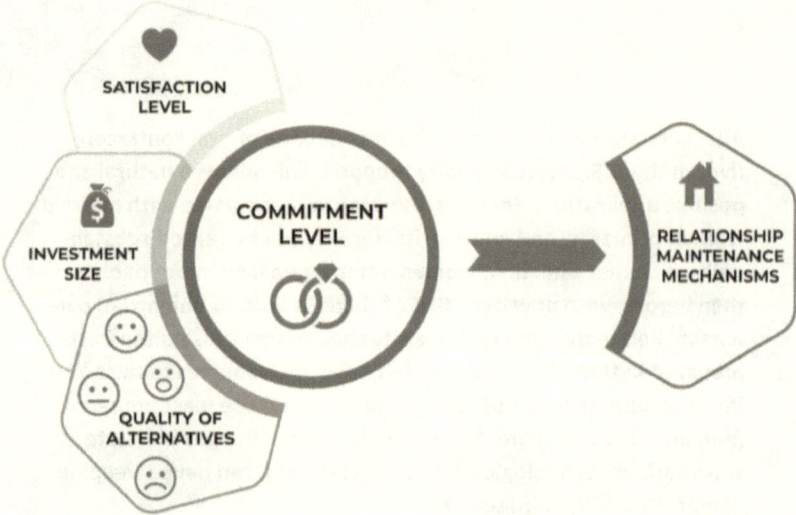

Figure 10.1: Commitment Model, based on Caryl E. Rusbult, Christopher R. Agnew, and Ximena B. Arriaga, "The Investment Model of Commitment Processes," in the *Handbook of Theories of Social Psychology*, eds. Paul A. M. Van Lange, Arie W. Kruglanski, and E. Tory Higgins (Thousand Oaks, CA: Sage, 2012), 218–231.

Commitment, from a Christian perspective, is not just a cost-benefit ratio nor is it solely about equity. Christianity does not teach that relationships should be 50/50. Rather, marital commitment should be total, complete: a 100/100 investment from both parties. During courtship, couples are charged to honestly determine if they can joyfully and completely commit their lives to one partner.

With this background on the psychological, biological, and sociological forces that influence how we choose a life partner, let's look at some of the ways people meet and the role communication plays in their courtship.

Routes toward Marriage

Pathways to marriage, at one time, followed the elementary-school rhyme: "First comes love, then comes marriage, then comes a baby in a baby carriage." New relationships were surrounded or embedded within social systems. Parents would know any potential suitors and their families. Uncles and aunts would be able to share opinions and evaluations of the relationship as it progressed, sometimes even chaperoning dates or coaching how to improve the relationship. Observing how potential suitors treated one's own parents and siblings provided opportunities for experiential information seeking. Courtship would move toward engagement and marriage, then the birthing of the next generation. There was a strong, communal vetting system and continued support for relationships.

Consider arranged marriages. They once were designed to bring political alliances or to pool family lands and resources.[28] Modern arranged marriages have moved away from resource aggregation, but still recognize that idealistic, romanticized views of love need to be supplemented with social support and an ardent commitment. According to one Indian couple who had an arranged marriage, "I would just honestly say, do not expect love to conquer all. Marriage is a lot about commitment and determination and saying 'I have to get through this and I have to make this work.'"[29] Additionally, from the very conception of an arranged marriage, parents are involved. Families often investigate potential spouses and broker initial meetings. This is not to say that the participants in an arranged marriage have no say in their pairing; indeed, most modern arrangements only progress with mutual consent and desire from both suitors. In this way, modern arranged marriages are different from the political and financial alliances of the past. Instead, they support a vetting process and connection between two family systems, not just individuals.

These somewhat nostalgic and historic experiences are no longer the most common path toward marriage and family formation.[30] American practices and rituals involving love, sex, and marriage have changed dramatically in a relatively short amount of time. Family sociologists Bradford Wilcox and Jeffrey Dew review three social revolutions from the past half-century that have greatly influenced marriages in the West.[31] The *psychological revolution*, sparked by the rise of expressive individualism, placed the emotional dimension of marriage above two other traditional characteristics of marriage in that it elevated personal fulfillment above the normative structure of a lifelong commitment and deprecated a view of marriage as a necessary prerequisite for childbearing. The *gender revolution*, sparked by more women joining the labor force, resulted in men taking on more domestic responsibilities associated with maintaining a family. It also redefined the role of fatherhood, especially encouraging fathers to be more emotionally involved in childcare.[32] Finally the *secular revolution*, marked by a move away from traditional religious practices, placed greater significance on marital unions to fulfill the emotional and spiritual aspects of life. For example, having the same level of education replaced being part of the same religion as the most important social force that predicted partnering.[33]

Together these changes have given rise to the "soulmate" model of marriage, an arrangement where people see marriage "as an expressive 'super-relationship' designed to secure them personal growth, emotional intimacy, and individual fulfillment."[34] Soulmate marriage is much more individualistic than days gone by, not requiring communal support, much less communal approval. This model is also not limited to marriage. Indeed, there are many individuals who are choosing not to marry at all. During courtship, it is important to reflect on your model of what marriage is, recognizing that these social revolutions have likely impacted everyone's views.

Research has compared couples who ascribe to different views of marriage.[35] In a study of 1,414 married men and women, researchers examined several beliefs couples had about marriage to determine how different types of marriages faired in terms of divorce and marital quality. For their study, they identified four types of marriages. First, those with a traditional view of marriage largely believed that marriage was permanent, gender specialized, and embedded in social networks and religious institutions (a view the researchers labeled as *religious companionate model*). Then, there were those with a soulmate model who viewed marriage as expressive, emotionally intimate, and aimed at personal fulfillment and growth. Soulmate model couples were less likely to see marriage as permanent, forming the second and third types of marriage: those who received marital support from their social network (*supported soulmate*) and those who didn't (*unsupported soulmate*). A fourth type of marriage, labeled the *secular institutional model*, believed marriage was permanent and gender specialized, but they were non-religious and did not receive support from their social networks. Results showed that those in religious companionate marriages were satisfied and stable as long as they also were emotionally connected. Those who ascribed to the soulmate model had equally high marital quality as the religious companionate couples but did not have as stable marriages. Both the supported and non-supported soulmate models reported higher conflict and higher divorce rates than religious companionate marriages. The secular institutional marriage couples without supportive social or religious connections reported the least satisfying and most unstable marriages.

From our view, those who are on the lookout for a life-partner should search for genuine friendship and deep connection with another person (like the soulmate model suggests), but only alongside and within supportive religious and social communities (like the religious companionate model). Scripture admonishes that "[p]lans fail for lack of counsel, but with many advisers they succeed" (Prov. 15:22), and that "victory is won through many advisers" (Prov. 11:14). Humbly receiving advice from those who know you well and love you, like parents, mentors, pastors, and friends, can help identify potential challenges for relationships and either encourage or deter the relationship based on their view of partner compatibility. As we demonstrate in Part II of this text, marital

||||||||▶   Application Activity 10.4: Digital Dating

So how do people today find dating partners? Many turn to the internet. Almost half of unmarried adults are users of dating apps and websites. Technology is now the most common way couples meet.[36] Additionally, about 39% of current married couples met online.[37] Surprisingly, some Christian groups seem to avoid digital dating, although the reason for this is unclear. According to Christian pollster George Barna, 75% of evangelicals state that they will never use digital dating, with only 10% having tried it.[38] Regardless, shifts in how couples meet, facilitated by technology, create new pathways and processes for couples to vet relationships and there are pros and cons to each of them.[39]

Think about some of the pros and cons of digital dating. On the pros, imagine a global, unbounded marriage market. The idea is that through the internet, users have the best chance of finding a lifelong partner. Limitations of few potential partners, geography, and nationality are removed. For cons, however, the process is individualized and potentially removed from familial, social, and accountability networks.

Discuss in a group:

- What experiences have you had with digital dating?
- What are some additional pros and cons you see in digital dating?
- Based on your experiences and observations, when do you think it is appropriate to transition from online to in-person dating?

communication includes deep connection with a friend, but also involves handling conflict well, forgiving to repair relationships, building resilience, and "doing life together." Taking a more comprehensive view of family communication builds the type of marriage that can be rewarding over decades, especially when reinforced and supported by social and religious networks. Adding the voices of trusted counselors can lead toward satisfying partnerships.

Communicating in Different Relationship Stages

From a communication perspective, there are boundaries about topics and levels of disclosure that occur at different stages of relationship. Irwin Altman and Dalmus Taylor's classic Social Penetration Model of layers of an onion is apropos.[40] We often share surface-level information with strangers and acquaintances. We introduce ourselves, share our name, occupation or field of study, and something about how long we have lived in a place or attended university. This basic information is publicly available to almost anyone, but as friendship develops, we share more of who we are. On the road toward exclusivity in relationships and marriage, individuals transform into couples. Given limited resources, such as time and energy, partners may withdraw from social networks as involvement with each other increases. Of course, complete withdrawal or domineering control by a partner can potentially signal abuse (see Chapter 12), but it is normative to privilege time with a romantic partner, cognitively retreating and solidifying coupleness.[41] Communicatively, this occurs as couples share more and more of who they are with each other and restrict what they share with others. You probably have lots of experience and ideas on how couples partner and what denotes their "status."

Another aspect of communication in coupling is what topics are allowable for discussion. For example, platonic friends do not often talk about what will happen when they have kids, nor do dating couples usually lead with that topic. It presumes a commitment level that is not yet achieved. Moving from casual dating to an exclusive relationship opens new topics for discussion. Similarly, moving from dating to engagement creates conversations not necessarily discussed beforehand. These might include questions like: Where will we live? Is it more important to have a house or live in an apartment? What priority level does saving have over spending? How will we handle transportation needs? Premarital counseling often intentionally introduces such topics for couples to discuss. There are excellent resources available to help navigate these conversations, including Focus on the Family's "Ready to Wed" pre-marital counseling curriculum.[42]

Dating also can be fraught with mixed-messages and uncertainty, especially in Christian circles. Some well-meaning Christians advise not dating at all. Others say that dating is acceptable only if it is clearly progressing toward marriage. Still others say that dating is a fun, low-stakes way to get to know someone without the pressure to marry. You may have heard all of these messages at some point. As we have presented, relationships progress, and we believe there are boundaries around topics that should be explored, but we also recommend that every couple engage in honest self-reflection and open conversation about several categories of conversation. Alliteration helps remember them:

- Faith
- Family
- Feelings
- Finances
- Friends
- Fun
- Future

Each category may include multiple sub-topics, and the conversations may integrate several of these categories. For example, a discussion of faith might include sharing things like, "What are some of the most significant spiritual experiences you have had?" "Who is Jesus to you?" "In what ways do your parents or family members practice their faith?" "How do you see faith impacting your daily or weekly schedule?" "What role do you see faith playing in decisions about having or raising children?" These sample questions demonstrate that conversations about faith might include someone's personal testimony as well as information about family background and projections into how faith would influence future family life.

Taking an approach where boundaries delineate different stages of relationships allows for freedom within boundaries. We believe these topics of conversations can happen, at different levels of specificity, for friends, dating partners, engaged, and even married couples. Within each conversational topic, questions can be fitted to a couple's current relationship.

Whereas dating couples may ask about each other's faith experiences, engaged couples can engage in more personal questions about faith. "What ways will *we* express faith?" "How will *we* structure *our* days to accommodate faith practices?" "What spiritual experiences do *we* dream about achieving?" The oft-quoted Scripture of Proverbs 4:23 instructs, "Above all else, guard your heart, for everything you do flows from it." One way to guard your heart is by setting communication boundaries, by avoiding topics or lines of questions for which you do not have a commiserate level of relationship. For example, without a commitment, casual dating partners should not presume a future or advisory role in someone's life. The instruction about guarding your heart goes on to say, "Keep your mouth free of perversity; keep corrupt talk far from your lips" (Prov. 4:24). Practically, setting verbal as well as nonverbal (kissing, sexual touch) boundaries will guard your heart and lips.

Planning a Wedding and a Marriage

When a couple decides to wed, there is often an engagement and wedding ceremony. These communication rituals can be brimming over with significance, either cultural or personal. For many, engagement includes giving a ring as a pledge of fidelity and a symbol of engagement. It may also include a nod to some relationally significant event (e.g., a favorite destination, recreating a couple's first date). These symbols communicate relational history and serve to signify commitment. Try identifying some of the ways in which couples marked their change in relationship as you listen to couples' engagement stories in Application Activity 10.5.

IIIIIIII ▶ **Application Activity 10.5:**
Engagement Stories

- Interview a couple who became engaged or married within the past year.
- Ask them to share the story of their engagement.
- Listen specifically for the types of interaction the couple reports as they recount their courtship (e.g., verbal phrases, nonverbal communication, gift exchanges). What types of symbols and messages did they report using in their engagement story?

Weddings are also symbol-laden events. In *Weddings as Text*, Wendy Leeds-Hurwitz observed an array of "intercultural" weddings in America and explains the symbols and rituals included and their significance.[43] For example, marrying under a canopy was a Jewish tradition that symbolized a new home being formed by the couple's wedding. While there are nonverbal symbols like these, wedding ceremonies usually include vows that are read or repeated before attendants or witnesses. These verbal commitments are often significant to the couple or to a community.

Conclusion

Rebekah had a choice whether or not to marry Isaac. With perhaps the exception of arranged marriages, most of us are able to choose whom we wish to marry. How do we make the decision? How do we find someone with whom we are compatible? First, it is important to note that compatibility is not just about both partners believing in God. Having homogamy of denominational doctrines, theology, or even political platforms is not the only foundation for good marriages. There should also be social (e.g., Do you like hanging out? Do you enjoy talking together? Do you both share and seek to know one another?), vocational (e.g., Where is this person going in life? Am I willing to go there?), and physical (e.g., Are you attracted to him/her physically?) connections.[44]

Gary Thomas, in his book *The Sacred Search*, offers four biblically informed considerations to winnow the potential pool of marriageable partners.[45] Think of these filters as comprehensive, not just theological. The first filter is whether they *confess Jesus Christ* as their Lord; this is a Scriptural mandate and not negotiable (2 Cor. 6:14; cf. Deut. 7:3–4; Amos 3:3). Is their devotion to God cultural or personal? Does a potential partner pursue Christ? The second filter is *wisdom*. Do they make sound financial decisions? Are they hard-working, peaceful, kind? Do you observe the Fruit of God's Spirit—love, joy, peace patience, kindness, goodness, faithfulness, gentleness, and self-control (Gal. 5:22–23)—in their interactions with you and others? The third filter involves *seeking advice* from trusted individuals. What do others, such as your parents or pastor, think about this person? You could ask trusted individuals questions like "Does this relationship seem like a fit to you?" "Are there any areas you are concerned about?" The final filter is *prayer*. Have you asked God to help you make a wise decision about selecting a life partner? Have you been listening to God, hearing and obeying him? These filters should help test compatibility.

As a final piece of advice, allow courtship to be a process. We will examine marital dynamics in the next two chapters, but it is important to differentiate the two. Courtship is not marriage, and it does not have to be fast. It is fascinating, too, that attraction and infatuation can alter brain chemistry in a way that limits thoughtful, reasoned decision making. This process can last for over a year.[46] One piece of advice, then, is that courtship should go through all seasons, so that time tests character and also enables clear-headed commitment. This is not always the case, and we are not advocating a strict ruleset. But as we discuss in more detail in the next chapter, marriage is a covenant. Without the sealing of that covenant, courtship, and even engagement, are distinct relationship stages. Ben Stuart observes, "In marriage the two become one. A dramatic reorienting takes place. But until that covenant happens, you are still two. You are separate. That means there is a measure of separation in your decisions. You are accountable before God for your own life."[47] Selecting a life-partner is one of the most significant decisions that a person makes. Allowing the selection to be a process, embedded in a supportive and loving community, will encourage success.

Chapter 11

Marriage as a Covenant and Sexual Communication

Chapter Summary: The Bible presents marriage as a covenant inaugurated through sexual intercourse. The chapter reviews this perspective and redefines other relationships, particularly cohabitation, according to this view. The chapter considers sexual relationships and both biblical and scientific perspectives on problematic sexual communication pathologies in relationships. It then addresses what love is and argues that Divine love provides a basis for Christian marital love. In the conclusion, the idea that marriage is a picture of Christ and the church is reviewed.

Introduction

MARRIAGE FROM A BIBLICAL PERSPECTIVE is a covenant, so understanding covenant provides a basis for understanding marriage from a Christian standpoint. There are a number of covenants discussed in Scripture. Cutting covenant was an ancient practice that communicated a promise and established the basis of a relationship. Covenantal partners made pacts with each other and almost always sealed these arrangements with the shedding of blood. A covenant created allies. It forged relationships, and it defined the rights and responsibilities of the parties involved.

Consider the covenants God made with Abraham. Sometimes called a feudal-vassal covenant (an agreement between a greater and lesser party), God required perfection from Abraham and, in exchange, promised offspring and perpetual inheritance (Gen. 15, 17). Abraham knew that his life could never be 100% perfect and had no power to produce offspring, yet these were the stipulations God made. Following the cultural custom, Abraham cut animals in half and let their blood drain onto the earth between the halves. Traditional practice stipulated that God and Abraham would each walk through the blood, signifying that if they did not keep their end of the agreement, then the other party had a right to kill them and trample their blood underfoot. In a dramatic and surprising turn, Scripture records that a firepot and a flaming torch passed through the blood which drained from the five sacrificed animals (Gen. 15:17–21). In symbolic terms, God agreed that if Abraham or his descendants did not keep their end of the deal, God would spill his own blood to maintain the agreement.[1] Through the symbolic language of the ancient tribal people, Christ's death on behalf of humanity was sealed through covenant.

Marriage, from a biblical perspective, is also a lifelong covenant between a man and a woman. It is an agreement that is inaugurated at the consummation of the marriage and lasts until one or both parties die. Like other covenants, marriage is sealed by blood. The marriage covenant is ratified by the breaking of a virgin's hymen (the thin layer of tissue that partially covers a woman's vagina) through first sexual intercourse. This blood is a marker of mutual commitment, chastity, and faithfulness between lovers.

Today, couples often do not think of marriage in terms of covenant. Instead, many see it as a contract or a commitment. Bill Strom has offered foundational assumptions that come with covenant, contract, and commitment types of thinking.[2] *Contractualism*, he argues, presumes that humans relate to accomplish purposes such as survival and personal happiness with a goal toward equitable outcomes for all parties. Contractual marriage is exemplified in prenuptial agreements (i.e., legal documents that specify asset allocation should the marriage fail). As long as one's spouse delivers more reward than costs, the relationship endures. *Committalism*, on the other hand, focuses on developing and maintaining mutual satisfaction through competent communication that expresses support and affection. Unsatisfactory relationships are due to poor skills but can be fixed through counseling and education. Finally, *covenantalism* views relationships as sacred trusts, authored by God, where moral agents (husband and wife) strive for "peace with self, others, and God."[3] Covenantal relating recognizes dependence on faith communities to keep us accountable for relational thriving and to sustain us during hardships.[4] In sum, although mutual satisfaction and equity are important, the Bible presents marriage as more than a type of contractual or committed relationship; it is also covenantal.

In our view, the marriage relationship is comprehensive, based on love, and aimed toward representing God to those inside and outside the family.

In this chapter, we discuss research related to cohabitation, which some view as an alternative to singleness and others view as a substitute or precursor to marriage.[5] We then turn to build the case from Scripture related to sexual experiences. Given the nature of marriage as a covenant and the fact that the process of inaugurating this covenant is sexual debut, it is important to discuss sexual communication as intrinsically linked with marriage and as an important personal, relational, and social phenomenon. We present the concept of soul ties followed by a discussion of problematic experiences of sex and sexual communication in relationships. Our chapter then turns to examine what love is and how Divine love provides a basis for Christian marital love. In our conclusion, we present the Biblical case for how marriage reflects the relationship between Christ and the church.

Cohabitation in Society

Living together without being married, termed cohabitation, is now the most common path toward marriage.[6] In the 1950s, cohabitation was rare, but it has increased as a practice over the decades.[7] Early research on cohabitation showed it to be problematic: divorce rates for those who

IIIIIIII ▶ **Application Activity 11.1:**
Motivations for Cohabitation

In groups, discuss the following:

- What are some motivations for cohabitation? In what ways, if any, do men and women differ in their motivations for cohabiting? What are some risks associated with cohabitation? Benefits?

- Why do emerging adults tend to prefer cohabitation over marriage?

- Read the section "Motivation to Cohabit." Compare the responses from your group discussion to these research findings. Do you agree, for example, that women see cohabitation as a step toward marriage, but men view it as a "test drive"? Why or why not?

cohabited were higher than non-cohabitors, and sexual and physical abuse as well as child abuse occurred at higher rates.[8] As more and more people have cohabited, many of these risks have been diffused. Union formation (i.e., when people begin living with a partner) and marriage were once synonymous but in the U.S. have increasingly diverged, with cohabitation taking the place of marriage for first union formation experience and nearly 75% of 30-year-olds reporting that they have cohabited before marriage.[9] In the U.S., the age of marriage has consistently increased, but the age of union formation has remained fairly steady at around 22 years old.[10] Most cohabiting unions dissolve rather than end in marriage, and the average cohabitation lasts about two years.[11] As the most common family experience for emerging adults, more than parenthood and marriage,[12] cohabitation merits more attention.[13]

Motivations to Cohabit

Men and women tend to view cohabitation very differently. They both agree that cohabitation is a good, pragmatic solution for testing compatibility, sharing costs, and spending more time together.[14] Men, however, endorse the idea that cohabitation is a good option for "testing" the relationship more than women. Other studies show that those who enter cohabitation as a test tend to have high levels of depressive symptoms, attachment insecurity, and negative communication.[15] Three times more than men, women expressed that "love" was the reason they decided to cohabit, and men nominated "sex" as their motivation four times more frequently than women.[16] Penelope Huang and colleagues include a quote from a young adult female participant in their study:

> Most girls want to have the connection with the guy and know that it's a relationship. 'Cause women, their number one thing in life is to have good relationships with people. That is the one thing that they strive for, the main thing that they strive for. Guys, the thing that they strive for is sex, so it's kind of a tradeoff.[17]

The same study found both men and women see cohabitation as temporary, but women see it as a transitional step toward marriage, whereas men view it as a relationship "test drive," a low-stakes trial for whether or not the relationship has long-term potential. These different motivations suggest different levels of commitment.

Sliding Versus Deciding

In fact, commitment and intentionality may be some of the differentiating factors between cohabitation that leads or does not lead to marriage. Scott Stanley and his colleagues propose that many couples are "sliding" into marriage rather than "deciding" to marry.[18] Based on studies of cohabitation, they suggest that cohabiting couples are subject to relational inertia, which carries them into cohabiting relationships and eventually into marriage. The processes leading to cohabitation are often convenience and pragmatics, where it is easier to continue a relationship than to end it.[19] Here are the primary arguments for how couples "slide" into marriage:

1. There are two types of commitment.

    a. *Dedication commitment* is an intentional "we-ness" in the relationship and demonstrated by a willingness to sacrifice for one's partner. An example of dedication might be an engagement proposal, which usually has a pledge (like an engagement ring) and is announced publicly to family and friends.

    b. *Constraint commitment* is based on forces that increase the cost of leaving. In other words, leaving the relationship takes more effort and coordination than remaining in the relationship. Finding a new place to live, for example, increases the costs of breaking off a cohabiting relationship and constrains the couple to make things work out.

2. Cohabitation is an ambiguous relationship state. It is ill-defined. It can mean different things from couple to couple and the status of the relationship is often not shared by men and women within a cohabiting union.

3. Cohabitation increases constraint commitment (e.g., shared lease agreement, joint mobile data plan, co-owned pet) but does not inherently increase levels of dedication.

4. Based on relationship inertia, some couples, who otherwise would not have married, end up married partly because they cohabit. This applies most to men, who are usually "swept into marriage by the growing inertia instead of entering marriage by way of a clear decision and fully formed level of dedication."[20]

The ideas of Stanley and colleagues on constraint commitment versus dedication provide a plausible explanation for the finding that some cohabiting couples exhibit higher risks (e.g., abuse, violence, later divorce) but those who are engaged prior to cohabiting seem to be immune to these risks.[21]

Cohabiting and marital relationships usually include both consensual sexual liaisons and a practically universal expectation for sexual exclusivity.[22] So what are the differences?

We see cohabitation as relationally similar to marriage with all of its rights and responsibilities, but lacking the formal approval and dedication of marriage as covenant. One definition of *cohabitation* is "living together in a marriage-like sexually intimate coresidential relationship."[23] But what cohabitation lacks is the same level of social legitimacy and communal, familial, and social support that is offered to married couples, though this is changing as society is increasingly accepting of cohabitation as a family form.[24] These differences between marriage and cohabitation also may play out in terms of expectations cohabitors and their partners have for themselves and each other, the demands partners are willing to put on each other, and also the communication patterns formed during the early days of the union. What do you see as the differences? How does your faith impact decisions to cohabit or not?

Meaning of Sexual Communication

Because sex is integral to marital and cohabiting relations, we believe it is important to provide a robust framework for understanding the meaning of sex. Following a natural law argument, we unpack our perspective on sex and sex differences to help frame an understanding of related verbal and nonverbal messages in marital unions. It can be easy to see sexual prohibitions in Scripture without recognizing the beauty, pleasure, and complex interdependence of God's design. Sex was God's idea, so let's unpack some fundamental truths about it.

To begin, it was God's idea to create two sexes who precisely complement each other. God made humans as male and female (Gen. 1:27). This means that men and women both bear the image of God. Said another way, without both males and females, we would have an incomplete picture of God's nature—God is both feminine and masculine. This means that both sexes are equally valuable and that each uniquely portrays aspects of God that the other cannot. J. Budziszewski, author of *On the Meaning of Sex*, draws out four truths related to sexual differences, which help develop our understanding.[25]

First, Budziszewski suggests there is a *duality of nature* in sexes. "Manhood and womanhood reflect the same human nature, and with equal fidelity and dignity, but they reflect different facets of it."[26] Society has historically fallen into one of two errors in thinking related to this duality. People sometimes believe that because the two sexes are different, one must be more valuable than the other. Another error of thinking is that because both sexes have equal worth, they must be exactly the same. Neither of these errors follows from the duality of nature.

A second duality seen in the sexes is a *duality of paths*. Budziszewski argues that the developmental trajectories of men and women are different, both in what they start with and what they end with. Physiologically this is obvious. Males enter puberty later than females. Neurological development also occurs later. This difference could help explain why women, on average, marry about two years earlier than men. Another difference is that men, on average, are taller and stronger than women. Their bone structure and muscle mass are different. Of course, this does not mean any particular male is always taller or stronger than any particular female, but it does display sexual differences.

The third duality is *body and soul unity*. People are more than physical; they also are spiritual. We have bodies, souls, and spirits. The body and soul are equally important in defining who we are. We err if we focus on purely physical without recognizing that what happens to our bodies impacts our souls and vice versa. If we do not recognize this unity, for example, we either dismiss physical differences between the sexes or make these differences all-important. When two people give themselves to each other wholly this means body and soul.

Finally, Budziszewski points out that sex differences create *polaric complementarity*. That is, men and women are different in corresponding ways. "Each sex completes what the other lacks, and helps bring the other into balance."[27] As evidenced by the process of procreating, there must be unity of complementary opposites. Without such unity, or coming together, procreation does not occur. This contrasts sharply with all other biological systems in the human body. By God's design, reproductive organs are the only "half" organs we possess. In some cases, we even have redundant organs, like kidneys. Digestion occurs completely without any additional, complementary organs needed, and it happens in essentially the same way in men and women. We have complete and whole respiratory systems to achieve the function of breathing. However, to achieve the purpose of procreating, men and women require the input of their polar complement.

Purpose by Design

A natural law perspective aligns with a Christian perspective and focuses attention on both design and meaning of sex. These purposes, according to Budziszewski, are *procreation* (bringing about and nurturing new life) and *union* ("the mutual and total self-giving and accepting of two polar, complementary selves in their entirety, soul and body").[28] Budziszewski states that "because of its potentiality for procreation—it [sex] also carries within it the potentiality for a powerful and distinct form of human love. This is why sex shakes us to the core, this is why it says, 'Now you will never be the same.'"[29] Procreation, by design, brings together opposites, and to rear infants and children who thrive by design, these opposites continue to be needed within a family.

The purpose of physical union that sex brings is obvious. Two whole persons join together into one. The process is even biologically reinforced. The hormone oxytocin is released physiologically, which enhances not only pleasure but feelings of connection. This same hormone is released in breast feeding, so that mothers feel more and more attached to the infants they nurse. But sex creates a union that is beyond the physical because our bodies work with our souls and include emotional, spiritual, and intellectual connection.[30] Unity of complementary opposites brings about synergy. Truly, a husband and wife form a family, where the family is greater than the sum of its individual parts.

To summarize, "Mutual and total self-giving, strong feelings of attachment, intense pleasure, and the procreation of new life are linked by human nature in a single complex of meanings and purpose."[31] Sex should not be reduced into mechanistic, biological terms nor should it be abstracted from the context of the marital relationship in which God intended for it to find expression. Budziszewski points out that when we try to pick and choose among the elements of our design without adopting a holistic, comprehensive perspective on the meaning of sex that is fundamentally attached to its design, then we encounter problems. For example, some would suggest that sex's purpose is pleasure, which Budziszewski counters. He presents a case that though sex is pleasurable, its purpose is not pleasure. When we pursue sex for the purpose of pleasure alone, we introduce pathologies to the design. By analogy, even if eating can be enjoyable, the purpose of eating and the body's digestive system which supports eating is nutrition. Pleasure is a natural by-product of the purpose. However, if we only ate ice cream and chocolate for pleasure, antithetic to its purpose, the consequence would bring about sickness. So, too, the natural design of sex is procreation and union, and if we pursued sex for pleasure alone, we would run into various social and personal pathologies.

Sex as Transcendence

As a final note, Budziszewski introduces the idea that even in the closest human act of relating, there is a separation that is inherent. That is, even in sex, there is an incomplete connection, which indicates a need for transcendence. From a Christian perspective, as fulfilling and enjoyable as sex can be in the context of marriage and supported by the potentiality for procreation and union, it belies a need for a greater, more intimate connection—a connection with God himself. As Saint Augustine—a man who had experienced quite a bit of sexual exploration before converting to Christianity— insightfully stated, "You have made us for yourself, O Lord, and our hearts are restless until they rest in You."[32] Even though sex brings together two polar, complementary individuals, there is a greater, more complete union with God that brings complete fulfillment.

Sexual Experience in Relationships

With a robust philosophical understanding of the meaning and purpose of sex, let's examine some of the evidence around sexual experiences in relationships. Globally, married couples report more frequent sex than unmarried singles.[33] In the U.S., 17 is the average age of sexual debut for women, and about half of women (54%) have experienced first sexual intercourse by the time they are 18 years old.[34] Findings also show that sex frequency for the average individual has decreased over the past 25 years, particularly within married and partnered (cohabiting) relationships.[35] This change is partly, but not fully, explained by the rise in age for first marriage. Despite the nearly universal expectation that married and cohabiting partners are sexually exclusive, evidence shows that cohabiting people more frequently engage in sexual relationships with multiple, concurrent partners.[36]

Many studies examine sexual satisfaction alongside communication, emotional intimacy, and other relationship variables. These findings support the idea that better communication is related to better sexual experience.[37] A measure of sexual communication could include items like, "If I want something different during sex, I say or show it" and "Generally speaking, I can express my sexual needs and desires well."[38] Regardless of relationship type (married, single, cohabiting), a German study found that when individuals had higher levels of sexual communication, they experienced higher levels of sexual satisfaction.[39] Others have shown that communication impacts both relationship and sexual satisfaction.[40] Sexual satisfaction predicted greater emotional closeness between couples,[41] and both communication and sexual satisfaction are independent contributors toward broader marital satisfaction.[42] Moreover, "women are more likely to report that they are sexually satisfied when they report that they share housework with their husbands,"[43] which indicates the importance of ongoing relationship connection. "What happens outside of the bedroom seems to matter a great deal in predicting how happy husbands and wives are with what happens in the bedroom."[44] In general, when couples have mastered the art of communication, it is evidenced in all aspects of their relationship, including how much they enjoy each other sexually.

Some have even found benefits to religiosity and sexual satisfaction. One study that looked at sexual frequency and satisfaction over an 18-month period found that when couples viewed sex as spiritually significant, they experienced lower declines in sexual frequency and satisfaction than those who did not view sex as sacred.[45] A sociological study found that religion and spirituality were associated with higher levels of sexual satisfaction, even after controlling for age and gender. The study showed that when people were more spiritually active, they were more sexually satisfied in marriage.[46]

Sexual Pathologies

To review, sex is a relational experience, a total self-giving designed for procreation and union. In many ways, marital sex goes back to the Garden of Eden and removes the fig leaves that have been over Adam and Eve ever since sin entered the world (Gen. 3:7). It redeems fallen humanity, in a sense, and couples can again be naked and unashamed (Gen. 2:25). It is also fundamental to human continuation. Without sex, there could be no natural propagation of humanity into the next generation. Perhaps because it is universal to human experience (not to all humans, though), sex is rife for wounding, hurt, and perversion. So, what is a Christian perspective on these issues?

The Bible teaches that sexual perversion of any kind, like fornication (sex before marriage), adultery (sexual liaisons with anyone other than a spouse), or lust (the desire for sex with anyone other than a spouse), can be construed as a pathology that attacks God's design for marriage. Breaking covenant through divorce and remarriage, serial cohabitation, or sexual liaisons with multiple partners is sinful. Scripture admonishes, "Flee from sexual immorality. All other sins a person commits are outside the body, but whoever sins sexually, sins against their own body" (1 Cor. 6:18). In the Sermon on the Mount, Jesus states,

> You have heard that it was said, "You shall not commit adultery." But I tell you that anyone who looks at a woman lustfully has already committed adultery with her in his heart. If your right eye causes you to stumble, gouge it out and throw it away. It is better for you to lose one part of your body than for your whole body to be thrown into hell. (Matt. 5:27–29)

Jesus interpreted the Law of Moses not simply according to the "dos" and "don'ts" of behavior but also according to cognitive and motivational factors. In this case, Jesus took adultery and redefined it as any type of perverse desire or lust.

Some Christian groups explain that sexual intercourse creates "soul ties" between partners, building on Genesis 2:24, which teaches that the man and woman "are no longer two, but one flesh" (Matt. 19:6; see also Mark 10:8). An example of soul ties shows up in Genesis, when Shechem sleeps with Dinah. The Scripture says Shechem "loved the young woman and spoke tenderly to her"; in the King James Version of this verse, it says that his soul cleaved to her (Gen. 34:3). The story assumes an understanding that the relationship was ungodly (it was sex outside of marriage) and illustrates in a dramatic way how the sons of Jacob "cut off" the soul ties. Having multiple partners, regardless of marital status, creates an attachment to multiple people—it inaugurates a covenant with consequences. Thus, sexual transgressions, whether committed prior to, during, or after marriage, need to be addressed. Let's look at two common issues modern marriages face: "duty sex" and pornography.

Duty Sex

Based on the results of an in-depth survey of over 20,000 married women, called the Bare Marriage Project, Sheila Wray Gregoire and colleagues share that many women experience sex as an obligation and as a trade-off.[47] Requiring sex as a duty or obligation of marriage, however, removes the mutual self-giving of it. This is a perversion of the unitive purpose of sex. Nevertheless, it happens. The study found that obligation-sex messages, especially among Christian circles, meant wives heard that if they did not give their husbands unconditional sex, then their husbands would commit sin (e.g., give in to lust, watch pornography, have an affair).[48] This type of manipulation wrongly applied Paul's teaching that

> [t]he husband should fulfill his marital duty to his wife, and likewise the wife to her husband. The wife's body does not belong to her alone but also to her husband. In the same way, the husband's body does not belong to him alone but also to his wife. Do not deprive each other [of sex] except by mutual consent and for a time, so that you may devote yourselves to prayer. (1 Cor. 7: 3–5a)

Duty sex can be manipulative and coercive, even leading to marital rape.

One female participant in the study shared that she used sex in order to get other things she wanted. This type of communication would say, "I don't really want you; I only want what you can give me." Sex becomes a means to an end—a means to get something from a partner, not give oneself to a partner. That type of manipulation says, "I will hold myself back from you until you give me what I want." It changes the nature of sex, and it ruins intimacy.[49] There is an old adage that goes: "Women trade sex for love, and men trade love for sex." In our view, prostituting sex for a price, whether it be relational or monetary, degrades both men and women. It casts aspersions on each person's motives and portrays men in overly stereotypical ways. Yet, as the quotation demonstrates, this type of communication can and does happen in marriages.

Both aspects of duty sex are manipulative and a misappropriation of power in relationships. Neither allow sex to be an expression of love. Neither enable the mutual self-giving and intimacy that is potential in sexual connection.

Pornography

Another pathology related to sex and sexual communication is pornography. The word literally means "writings about whores" and likely derived from erotic descriptions of sexual acts.[50] Today it subsumes a $13–14 billion industry[51] of movies, images, and internet sites designed to arouse sexual pleasure (which is more money spent on porn than on major league football, baseball, and basketball combined!).[52] While pornography can be a catch-all definition, individuals and couples in relationships have varied understandings of what is and is not considered porn.[53] From a biblical standpoint, we believe that anything a person seeks to encourage lustful thinking or action could be considered pornography (see Matt. 5:27–29).

Exposure to pornography has increased over the past half-century and generally is initiated during adolescence.[54] One study found that almost two-thirds of youth (93% of boys, 62% of girls) reported seeing online pornography before they reached the age of 18.[55] In a study of married and cohabiting couples (median age of 32 for males and 29 for females), descriptive analysis showed that males reported significantly more frequent porn use than females, with less than 2% of women using porn more than once a week compared to 26% of males.[56] Similarly, 64% of women reported no pornography use compared to only 27% of males.[57] An internet-based study that sought to expand the age-representativeness of pornography consumption rates demonstrated that for both men and women, consumption decreases with age but that men consumed an average of two to three times more minutes per week than women.[58] For Christians, there are large differences in porn consumption based on their level of participation in religion. For men under 50 years old, about 10% of Protestants and 20% of those in other religions who attended weekly services reported watching an X-rated film in the previous year, compared to about 45% and just over 50% of those who attended religious services about once per year.[59]

Pornography today is marked by accessibility, affordability, and anonymity.[60] There are many "free" porn internet sites and YouTube videos that seek to seduce users to visit their sites. This happens often in private locations and solitude, making the behavior anonymous. Sites are available 24 hours a day and 7 days a week. These characteristics may be some of the reasons pornography use has increased over the past several decades along with more accepting attitudes toward pornography use.[61]

Effects of Pornography

The effects of pornography use have implications for society, relationships, women, and men. In this section, we share consequences that fit with the normative use of pornography, where men are the predominant users and women are the predominant ones depicted. There are increasing numbers of women who use pornography relative to men, so the effects we list for men may also affect women and the effects on women can also relate to the experiences of men. We acknowledge this, but to illustrate the typical case, we separate our discussion into gendered experiences and examine each in turn.

Effects on Society. The social conditions in which pornography is produced are alarming. Anyone concerned about violence against women cannot in good conscience consume or endorse pornography use because a large proportion of pornography is produced by women who are enslaved as sex workers. These women did not choose their profession but were sold into slavery. They are systematically broken by pimps who force them to perform various sex acts.[62] According to a conversation kit about pornography produced by Axis, a ministry dedicated to contextualizing the Gospel into the lives and culture of contemporary adolescents, arguing against sex trafficking while using, purchasing, or supporting pornography would be like going to a protest against a political candidate while simultaneously donating to her campaign. Pornography is so interconnected with human trafficking that opposing one logically requires opposing the other, too.

Other social issues and consequences related to pornography are sexting and so-called revenge porn. *Sexting* is sending sexually explicit images or messages via social media or text messaging services, often between dating partners. Teenage boys and girls who engage in sexting are often attempting to portray themselves as attractive and to signal interest in sexual relations.[63] When couples share sexual images of one another, these images can be used in blackmail or in revenge. When a couple breaks-up, *revenge porn* is what happens when one partner shares sexting images through social media or with friends to shame a former partner. These relational and social consequences result from youth and young adults who are not just using pornography but are participating in producing these images and videos.

Effects on Relationships. Pornography use is consistently related to weakened relational commitment,[64] increased chances for divorce,[65] lower sexual quality for men and women, and more problematic communication patterns. To illustrate the first two effects, one study found: "Individuals who are 20 years old and do not begin consuming porn have about a 6% probability of getting divorced, while those who do add porn at this age have a 51% probability of getting divorced."[66] To illustrate its effects on communication, according to one of the largest detailed studies in the U.S., which included a sample of 1,755 heterosexual couples, findings showed less positive communication, more relational aggression, and lower relationship satisfaction (for men and women) among those who used pornography in their relationships.[67] A summary of 30 nationally representative studies demonstrated overwhelmingly that pornography use is associated with worse relationship outcomes for both men and women.[68]

Another relational impact comes from how pornography is typically used. Most users view pornography alone, with a minority viewing it alongside a current sexual partner; men are significantly more likely than women to view pornography by themselves and women are significantly more likely than men to view pornography with a sexual partner.[69] The context of pornography use and related sexual arousal can be considered in light of classical psychological conditioning. A behavior is reinforced because of the reward that comes from that behavior. In the case of viewing porn alone, sexual arousal and expression become an individual, not relational, experience.

One explanation for these deleterious effects on relationships could stem from the fact that pornography requires nothing from its users. Using pornography for sexual arousal or expression diverges from sex's unitive purpose. There is no listening, no caring, no sharing, no responding, no giving required. Instead, it provides instant sexual gratification that is isolating, not relational.

Effects on Women. For women, there are personal ramifications. Research has consistently found that a partner's porn use is related to lower self-esteem.[70] These results persist whether women have accepting or depreciating attitudes toward pornography.[71] Even previous partners' pornography use can impact women. In a study of 171 college women, porn use of a previous partner directly predicted women's reports of interpersonal sexual objectification and eating disorder symptoms.[72] Previous partner's use also influenced the extent to which women internalized cultural beauty standards, which indirectly predicted their body surveillance and body shaming. These personal consequences caused women to second-guess their attractiveness once partners started porn use and led to increased relationship anxiety and depressive experiences.

Effects on Men. Finally, pornography has deleterious implications for men. These can be summarized as changes in men's perceptions and addiction. A meta-analysis of studies on the effects of viewing pornography showed that it was related to increased aggression, violence, objectification (seeing women as only body parts), and instrumentalization (seeing women for one's own pleasure, as servile) toward women.[73] Even proponents of porn use admit: "Cognitively, pornography may prime, maintain, and reinforce offense supportive cognitions, for example, that women are constantly receptive to men's needs, deceptive, or treacherous."[74] These associations are not necessarily caused by porn use, but more likely, these behaviors and pornography influence each other: more porn leads to more sexual and relational experimentation, which leads to more porn use.

Another outcome for men is porn-induced erectile dysfunction. Some studies find no predictive or causal associations between men's pornography use and erectile dysfunction, but show that there are concurrent associations between these variables.[75] However, others offer evidence to show unprecedented historic increases in erectile dysfunction for men under 30 years old.[76] These dramatic increases (from 7% to 30% of men in just over a decade) do not necessarily show that pornography is the culprit. However, the dysfunction only occurs when men are with women and not when they are viewing pornography. In other words, men report being more sexually aroused from images and videos than from real women.

Perhaps even more disturbing than changes in beliefs and behaviors is that pornography is addictive; it can change how the brain is wired at a fundamental level. Neuroscience shows that sexual addiction to pornography is similar to drug addiction, gambling, or compulsive shopping.[77] Modern internet pornography invokes two features, supernovelty and superstimuli, which lead to increased addiction. First, *supernovelty* refers to the idea that there are endless images to see. This is the same feature used by social media to encourage continued viewing of their sites. A "news feed" will scroll endlessly on most social media sites, providing a continuous stream of novel pictures, videos, and posts. So, too, websites and mobile apps with pornographic images utilize supernovelty to encourage addiction.

The second feature is the use of *superstimuli*. Here is a summary that helps define superstimuli:

> Nobel prize winning scientist Nikolaas Tinbergen posited the idea of "supernormal stimuli," a phenomenon wherein artificial stimuli can be created that will override an evolutionarily developed

genetic response. To illustrate this phenomenon, Tinbergen created artificial bird eggs that were larger and more colorful than
actual bird eggs. Surprisingly, the mother birds chose to sit on
the more vibrant artificial eggs and abandon their own naturally
laid eggs. Similarly, Tinbergen created artificial butterflies with
larger and more colorful wings, and male butterflies repeatedly
tried to mate with these artificial butterflies in lieu of actual female butterflies.[78]

With computer image manipulation capabilities, many aspects of pornography are enhanced as superstimuli. Those who consider pornography
an art form assume that its viewers understand "pornographic material as
fictive and exaggerated representations of sex and sexuality."[79] However, giv-
en the natural inclination toward supernovelty and superstimuli, pornography has the ability to warp natural attractions. Men and women are attracted
to fake butterflies, chasing exaggerated images rather than real relationships.

Understanding Pornography from a Biblical Perspective

These consequences for society, relationships, women, and men show
that pornography is a counterfeit to God's design. It is important in relationships to understand that God designed sex and saw that it was good.
However, pornography exchanges God's good design for something fake.
In Romans 1:24–25, Paul describes sexual perversion as exchanging "the
truth about God for a lie." Static images and online videos are shallow,
two-dimensional representations of people. Even prostitution, hook-ups,
and friends-with-benefits encounters enable sexual expression and experimentation but avoid holistic relating, which purposes toward unity and the
potentiality for procreation. As Pope John Paul II insightfully noted, "The
problem with pornography is not that it shows too much of the person,
but that it shows far too little."[80] Men and women are more than their body
parts and designed to be fully sexually known in the context of a loving,
comprehensive, committed marriage.

What Does Love Have to Do with It?

To this point, we have not yet discussed the topic of love. Hopefully it is
clear that sex should be an expression of love, but love is more than sex.
The Bible has much to say about how we are to love one another, including

this verse in Proverbs 3:3–4: "Let love and faithfulness never leave you; bind them around your neck, write them on the tablet of your heart. Then you will win favor and a good name in the sight of God and man." Both men and women need love and are commanded to love one another. Paul instructs, "Submit to one another out of reverence for Christ" (Eph. 5:21), and "each one of you also must love his wife as he loves himself, and the wife must respect her husband" (Eph. 5: 33). Jesus taught, "My command is this: Love each other as I have loved you. Greater love has no one than this: to lay down one's life for one's friends" (John 15:12–13). Mutual, total self-giving is the hallmark of love.

There are some theories that try to understand love in adult romantic relationships. One is Sternberg's triangular theory. In this theory, love is seen in three components: passion, intimacy, and commitment.[81] *Passion* "refers to the drives that lead to romance, physical attraction, sexual

---

IIIIIIII ▶	Application Activity 11.2:
	Love in Poetry

Love has long been the subject of poetry, the theme of fiction, and also vital to human and Divine experience. Take a look at Shakespeare's Sonnet 116 about love. It was first published around 1609 AD. What are some of the aspects of love that the poet highlights?

Now look at Paul's letter to the Corinthians (1 Cor. 13:1–8) written around 53 AD. How are these two depictions of love similar? Where are they different?

From these two writings, what is the meaning of love for human relationships? For communication? How well do these descriptions apply to family as a whole, not just to couples/marriages?

Sonnet 116
   Let me not to the marriage of true minds
   Admit impediments. Love is not love
   Which alters when it alteration finds,
   Or bends with the remover to remove:
   O no! it is an ever-fixed mark
   That looks on tempests and is never shaken;

It is the star to every wandering bark,

Whose worth's unknown, although his height be taken.

Love's not Time's fool, though rosy lips and cheeks

Within his bending sickle's compass come:

Love alters not with his brief hours and weeks,

But bears it out even to the edge of doom.

If this be error and upon me proved,

I never writ, nor no man ever loved.[82]

1 Corinthians 13: 1–8

If I speak in the tongues of men or of angels, but do not have love, I am only a resounding gong or a clanging cymbal. If I have the gift of prophecy and can fathom all mysteries and all knowledge, and if I have a faith that can move mountains, but do not have love, I am nothing. If I give all I possess to the poor and give over my body to hardship that I may boast, but do not have love, I gain nothing.

Love is patient, love is kind. It does not envy, it does not boast, it is not proud. It does not dishonor others, it is not self-seeking, it is not easily angered, it keeps no record of wrongs. Love does not delight in evil but rejoices with the truth. It always protects, always trusts, always hopes, always perseveres. Love never fails.

consummation, and related phenomena in loving relationships."[83] This includes the "feelings" of being in love, butterflies in the stomach, and sexual and physical arousal that "lead to the experiences of passion in a loving relationship."[84] *Intimacy* is the friendship-aspect of a relationship. It is the "feelings of closeness, connectedness, and bondedness" that people experience.[85] Intimacy is not sexual in Sternberg's theory; it is more like an emotional connection. Finally, *commitment* is a person's active decision to love someone, which over the long-term maintains love in the relationship. It is volitional, a choice to love and persist in love.[86]

Because love is a universal human phenomenon (i.e., not the purview of only one nation or people group), the theory should apply to people in multiple countries. Recent research has tested this claim and found support for the cross-cultural applicability of the triangular theory of love.[87] Because the three anchors of the theory can operate independently, it allows for multiple combinations that result in different types of love. Figure 11.1 shows how passion, intimacy, and commitment combine to demonstrate different types of love. What kind of relationship has high passion and commitment but no intimacy? Sternberg calls this a fatuous (silly, pointless) love. It is like a fanatic of a pop singer or sports icon. The fan would have no real friendship (intimacy) with the object of the affection (passion), but he might show up at every concert or sporting event rain or shine (commitment).

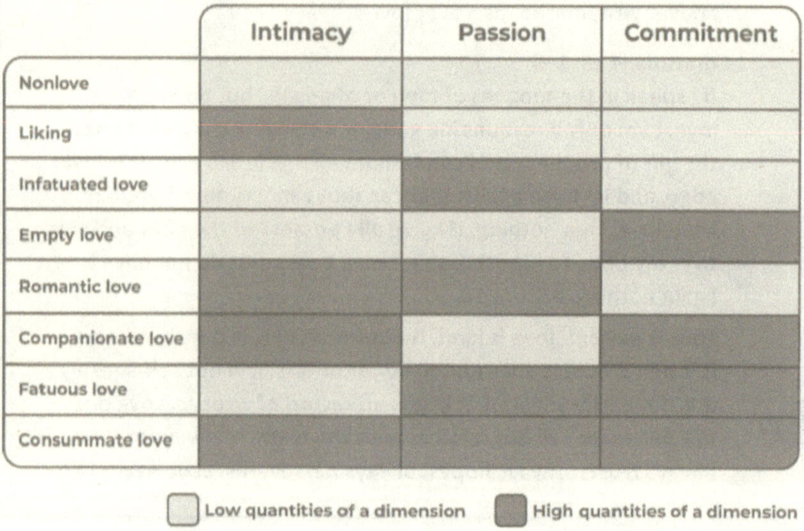

	Intimacy	Passion	Commitment
Nonlove	Low	Low	Low
Liking	High	Low	Low
Infatuated love	Low	High	Low
Empty love	Low	Low	High
Romantic love	High	High	Low
Companionate love	High	Low	High
Fatuous love	Low	High	High
Consummate love	High	High	High

Low quantities of a dimension   High quantities of a dimension

Figure 11.1: Sternberg's Triangular Theory of Love, based on Robert J. Sternberg, "A Triangular Theory of Love," *Psychological Review* 93, no. 2 (1986): 119–135.

Think about a long-term relationship. How do you think a couple moves through different types of love over time? For many, relationships begin through *liking* (high intimacy, low passion, and low commitment) or *infatuation* (high passion, low intimacy, and low commitment). As a relationship progresses, there are more types of love that become involved. For example, *romantic love* may best describe courtship when friendship blossoms and the emotional experience and erotic excitement of love are high, awaiting formal commitment in engagement and consummation in marriage. Ideally in marriage, all three aspects of love operate simultane-ously, which is labeled *consummate love*. Lovers in marriage enjoy exclusive and rewarding sex, appreciate an ever-developing friendship, and pledge fidelity to one another as long as they both shall live. But love is dynamic, not static. Good marriages are always developing, which means that love will also change over time.

There are likely times in every marriage when *companionate love* (low levels of passion) marks the relationship, for example, when physi-cal injuries or surgeries may preclude sex for a time. Alternatively, at mid-life when marriage takes center stage, couples often realize they have neglected to nurture their friendship (intimacy) during years of activities that focused on their children.[88] These couples likely continued sexual liaisons and maintained commitment toward one another but neglected their friendship. The dynamic nature of these factors also means that some relationships fail, and some marriages will end in divorce. When couples lose passion and intimacy in their marriage, their commitment may also wane. As Gary Thomas points out in *Sacred Marriage*, "Romantic love has no elasticity to it. It can never be stretched; it simply shatters. Mature love, the kind demanded of a good marriage, must stretch, as the sinful human

---

**IIIIIII ▶   Application Activity 11.3:
                    Model of Love**

Passion, intimacy, and commitment are the three dimensions of love articulated by Sternberg, but there are other theories of love, as well. Tobore Onojighofia Tobore, for example, proposed a qua-druple theory of love which includes attraction, connection, trust, and respect.[90]

In groups, develop a model of love and be ready to share your model. As you develop your model, you might consider some of the following questions:

- What are key dimensions that are part of your model of love?

- Do the dimensions operate independently, or do they work interdependently? For example, Tobore argues that if trust is compromised, it can lead to deteriorating connection and undermine respect.

- How might you visually represent your model?

---

condition is such that all of us bear conflicting emotions."[89] In terms of the triangular theory, Thomas is indicating that resolute commitment allows love to be sustained when passion and intimacy are low. Our point, here, is to consider ways that love changes as relationships in marriage also change.

Sternberg's theory focuses on adult relationships, but love is more fundamental to humanity. It can describe parent-child relationships, friendships, and even how we consider our enemies (see Matt. 5:43–44). Love should mark every relationship. C. S. Lewis took a slightly different approach in his essay *The Four Loves*.[91] He offers thoughts about the translation and application of four Greek words for love: *storge, philia, eros,* and *agape. Storge* is affection. Lewis likens this type of love to the care of a mother to her infant. *Philia* is friendship, the "crown of life."[92] This kinship occurs when two people share camaraderie over something in common. According to Lewis, it is the most time-consuming and least appreciated form of love. *Eros* is romantic, passionate love. It is a flame, and when the passion ends, eros is smothered. *Agape* is unconditional charity. According to Lewis, it is the ultimate aim of life for which all the other forms of love provide a training ground. Lewis describes it in Christian terms as God's unconditional love given to us through Jesus Christ.[93]

Lewis insinuates that love requires an interaction between vertical (Divine) and horizontal (human) love. The Apostle John claims that we are able to love because God loved us first (1 John 4:19). He reasons, "Whoever claims to love God yet hates a brother or sister is a liar. For whoever does not love their brother and sister, whom they have seen, cannot love God, whom they have not seen" (1 John 4:20). This sentiment is echoed by Gary Thomas, who writes, "Once we enter the marriage relationship, we cannot love God without loving our spouses well."[94] Love is central to the marital experience. More broadly, Divine love provides a basis for Christian love in all relationships.

Conclusion

One of the clearest teachings about marriage in the Bible is that it is a picture. Marriage illustrates on earth the relationship Christ has with his Bride. Thus, "Marriage should be honored by all and the marriage bed kept pure" (Heb. 13:4), and "[h]usbands should love their wives just as Christ loved the church and gave himself up for her" (Eph. 5:25), which is one reason that Christian marriage should be viewed as a covenant. This means that there is opportunity throughout the Bible for both literal and allegorical interpretations when it comes to understanding marital and sexual relations. Take Proverbs 31, for example. This passage portrays an industrious and empowered woman. She engages in managerial and executive tasks with compassion and competence. This description can also be read as a portrayal of the Bride of Christ. In an allegorical interpretation of a different passage, Hudson Taylor and others have read the Song of Songs as a depiction of the intimacy between Christ and the church.[95] In this poetic book, King Solomon represents Christ, and the Shulamite represents the Church, his Bride.

Because of the "profound mystery" (Eph. 5:32) demonstrated in marriage as a picture of Christ and the church, anything that detracts from the sexual, relational, loving, committed relationship of marriage maligns how God desires to demonstrate his love for us. Throughout the Old Testament, prophets indict the Israelites for adultery and prostitution when they would engage in idolatry (see Judges 2:16–23). When we substitute pornography for sexual intimacy, when we connect with multiple partners, when we float into and out of relationships, when we slide into cohabitation rather than decide to marry, we portray God's love in ways that diverge from his good design. God is totally faithful toward us, and he desires our faithful, exclusive devotion to him (see Exod. 20:3; Deut. 6:4) within a continuous and comprehensive, lifelong, loving covenantal relationship, just as marriage should portray.

Chapter 12

Struggling, Stymied, and Successful Marital Communication

Chapter Summary: This chapter shares both the good and bad of marital communication dynamics. It reviews Relational Turbulence Theory, arguing that healthy communication patterns during stressful transitional periods are especially critical for maintaining strong marital bonds. The chapter then turns to signs of struggling and stymied marriages, addressing topics including violence and divorce. It then covers three models—disillusionment, emergent stress, and enduring dynamics—that help explain why some couples have happy, stable marriages, some are stable but unhappy, and some marriages end. The chapter closes by discussing signs of a healthy relationship, offering practical suggestions for strengthening successful marriages even during times of stress and dissatisfaction.

Introduction

SIN'S LEGACY ACROSS GENERATIONS has been present since Adam and Eve. The impact of sin on family relations is profoundly illustrated in Genesis 4 when Cain kills his brother. Six generations later, Cain's offspring Lamech is the first recorded to practice polygamy (Gen. 4:19). Because one of his two wives was named Adah, which in Hebrew means "ornament," it is possible that Lamech took her as a trophy wife.[1] In the very limited record we have of this character, he boasts, "I have killed a man for wounding me, a young man for injuring me. If Cain is avenged seven times, then Lamech seventy-seven times" (Gen. 4:23–24). In this way, Lamech serves to illustrate the amplified effects of sin on human relations, including the

193

family: only a handful of generations after Cain, Lamech marries two women, likely commodifying one of them. God never intended murder nor polygamy. Yet, these practices have been evident since near the beginning of human history.

In this chapter, we consider the realities of sin's impact in marital relationships and also present some principles and practices that can lead to strong marriages. We begin by presenting Relational Turbulence Theory, arguing that healthy communication patterns during stressful transitional periods are especially critical for maintaining strong marital bonds. We then turn to signs of struggling marriages and address topics including partner violence and divorce. We then consider three marriage models—disillusionment, emergent stress, and enduring dynamics—that help explain why some marriages thrive, some struggle, and still others end. We close the chapter by discussing signs of a healthy relationship, offering practical suggestions for strengthening marriages, even during times of stress and dissatisfaction.

Relationships in Transition

The Relational Turbulence Theory tries to make sense of how couples think, feel, and communicate during times of transition, and to identify how healthy communication patterns help couples navigate transitions successfully.[2] Transitions can vary in valence (positive or negative), significance (major or minor), and abruptness (gradual or sudden). Examples of transitions that couples face include significant health issues, death of a loved one, birth of a child, or job loss.[3] Such transitions heighten uncertainty about what to expect from a partner and create opportunities to define the relationship. They result in new interaction patterns to accommodate the change and increase experiences of partner interference toward a person's goals and activities. Combined, these feelings of self, partner, and relationship uncertainty result in relational turbulence—"a quality of relationships characterized by feelings of chaos and a state of increased cognitive, emotional, and behavioral reactivity to relationship-relevant information."[4] To navigate these transitions, couples may benefit from engaging in four forms of transitional processing communication: (1) increasing interaction with each other by spending more time together, (2) promoting a sense of connection by engaging in relationship talk, (3) creating a sense of feeling situated by framing changes in their lives in a positive way, and (4) increasing confidence in the partnership by expressing relational commitment through verbal and nonverbal behaviors.[5]

The Relational Turbulence Theory highlights the importance of communication between partners during times of transition. Communication researchers Kellie Brisini and colleagues surveyed 311 married adults with at least one child.[6] These couples were asked to detail a major transition that occurred in the life of their child and describe the type of communication used to navigate the transition. Across all the responses, couples identified three major transition types for their child: puberty, transition to adulthood, and health crisis. The study also showed that a spouse's perception of how the partner communicated during transitions impacted outcomes. Specifically, relationship-focused communication was negatively related to partner uncertainty and interference from a partner but was positively related to facilitation with partner.

In other words, a husband could share a relationship-focused message with his wife like, "We're in this for the long haul," or "I know this is a hard time, but I'm not going anywhere." A wife might express, "This is really stressful, but I'm not giving up on us." These kinds of messages were related to lower levels of uncertainty and interference and higher levels of facilitation. Such messages verbally express what might be assumed by one person but unknown to her or his partner (remember, we cannot read minds!). The study also found that "married partners may benefit from attempts, not only to engage in transition processing communication, but to recognize their partner's communicative efforts."[7] As couples share relationship-building messages and appreciate one another's efforts to collectively transition their relationship, the turbulence they experience can become a time of growth to reify, not reject or redefine, their relationship. However, when couples do not navigate transitions well, it can lead to dissatisfaction.

Interactive Warning Signals

For marriages to thrive, we need to identify the signs that signal relationship trouble—what to look for, what to do and not to do, and how to spot when a relationship is in transition, which makes it susceptible to increased discord. Like a lighthouse that signals ships are approaching a rocky shoreline, recognizing communication patterns can warn couples that they are moving toward dangerous relational waters. A theme throughout the book is that communication plays a key role in whether relationships succeed or are stymied.

Famous for developing the "love lab"—a Seattle apartment with cameras in the rooms—John Gottman is one of the foremost experts on marriage and marital interaction. After coding hundreds of videos of couples interacting through daily events (e.g., cooking, watching television, eating together, reading magazines), specific interaction patterns were uncovered that can distinguish satisfied and dissatisfied couples.[8] Dissatisfied couples engage in more negativity in their communication and less positivity during conflict. They also engage in greater *reciprocity* of negativity. Instead of making "repair" attempts (reviewed in Chapter 7) that move the conversation or conflict toward collaboration, they reflect and even amplify the negativity they hear. The following are behaviors that often cascade into cycles of negativity, taken from Gottman's book *What Predicts Divorce?*[9]

Negativity Behaviors

- More disagreements compared to agreements
- Little humor, laughter, and reciprocated laughter
- Few assents, agreements, approval, and compliance
- Disagreements, criticisms, and put downs (verbal contempt)

Reciprocity of Negativity

- Lack of validation of expressed feelings
- Cross-complaining
- Deficiency in contracting sequences and negotiation
- Listener withdrawal from interaction
- Defensiveness, such as denying responsibility, yes-butting, and mindreading
- Defending oneself against complaints and confrontations
- Little editing, referring to chains of negativity that are interrupted by neutral statements that work to defuse the conflict
- Lack of feeling probes and meta-communication sequences that strive to repair communication
- Conflict across interactional tasks

The presence or absence of these signs does not automatically mean a marriage is good or bad, thriving or doomed. Instead, these are symptoms that signal trouble. Couples have the power to change their relationships and their communication.

Violence

For some, negative communication patterns escalate to the point of intimate partner violence. Interpersonal violence is defined by a range of couple communication behaviors, which include sexual violence, stalking, physical violence, and psychological aggression. The Centers for Disease Control and Prevention in the U.S. provided estimates for these experiences from 2015 data.[10] It reports that in their lifetime, 18% of women have experienced sexual violence and 10% have been stalked. Almost one-third (31%) have experienced physical violence in their lifetime. Identical levels of physical violence victimization were experienced by men (31%), with substantially lower levels of sexual violence (8%) and stalking (2%). Both sexes also reported approximately equal levels of psychological aggression (36% of women; 34% of men). This data support previous research that identified two subtypes of intimate partner violence in couples, neither of which was God's intent for families.

Michael Johnson and Kathleen Ferraro differentiate between common couple violence and intimate terrorism, which we characterize here.[11] *Common couple violence* is perpetrated by both men and women, is not likely to escalate over time, generally is isolated to a single event, and, although it can include verbal abuse as well as physical violence, it rarely involves psychological abuse. The so-called common couple violence is the only type of partner violence found in a general population (i.e., non-clinical, non-distressed samples). A typical common couple violence event happens when a couple loses their temper during an argument and resorts to physical violence.

Intimate terrorism, however, looks very different. It is almost exclusively perpetrated by men who use physical violence as one tactic in a pattern of control. Terrorism within relationships also can escalate over time and will include psychological abuse. The pattern might involve a man demanding that his partner stop communicating with friends, not leave their apartment, or never drive anywhere without him. This essentially cuts off any supportive relationships or social connections that could contradict his control over his girlfriend, fiancé, or wife. Physical violence is used to enforce these demands. These abusers typically are diagnosed with some emotional or psychological problem.

It is important to recognize the communication that characterizes violence, particularly violence in an abusive relationship.[12] Relational abuse usually occurs in a cycle that has three main stages: there is (1) a violent incident, (2) a repentant apology with a honeymoon phase, then (3) escalating tension/aggression, which erupts into another violent incident.[13] It can be difficult to recognize if you are in a cycle of abuse. Victims of abuse usually deny that their partner is an abuser or write-off the incident as a one-time event. Often domestic abuse victims want to see the best in their abuser and believe their partners will change. However, without intervention, the cycle can continue and even escalate over years.

The different phases of the cycle are marked by different communication habits, which can be "warning signs" that a person is in an abusive relationship. Violent incidents can include things like hair pulling, slapping, physical punishments, restricting movements, or intentionally causing pain or discomfort (like taking away clothes or blankets to make someone cold). In addition to physical abuse, there can be signs of emotional or verbal abuse, too. The National Domestic Violence Hotline lists several of these, including:

- Preventing or discouraging you from spending time with friends, family members, or peers
- Telling you that you never do anything right
- Insulting, demeaning, or shaming you, especially in front of other people
- Pressuring you to have sex or perform sexual acts you are not comfortable with
- Controlling finances in the household without discussion, including taking your money or refusing to provide money for necessary expenses
- Destroying your belongings or your home[14]

After a violent incident, the next phase is an apology and honeymoon period, which is violence free. The abuser apologizes and often seems quite sincere while promising never to abuse again. This phase usually involves renewed attention, care, politeness, and gifts that dote on the abused. In this phase a victim of abuse might drop legal charges or agree to give the relationship another chance. However, the next phase of the cycle includes reverting to old patterns where the abuser puts limits on what their partner can do, demands more control of the relationship, and is less and less tolerant of disagreement. Victims often re-engage in soothing or appeasing behaviors during this phase. Established patterns of communication reemerge and lead to a new violent incident, where the cycle begins again.

Verbal, emotional or psychological, and physical abuse can all be damaging but sometimes hard to recognize. If you read these signs and can see how they are part of your own relationship or someone you know, please get help! Abusers sometimes track online activity or check on cell phone use, so in those cases it can be helpful to use a public computer (like in a library or school) or to borrow a friend's phone to call for help. There are several free services for domestic or intimate partner violence, including the National Hotline: 1.800.799.SAFE (1-800-799-7233). There are often local shelters—some exclusively for women and children—that give abused people a safe place to go (see www.domesticshelters.org to search by location).

Sometimes it takes an outside force to help someone see they are within the cycle of abuse. If you know someone who seems to be withdrawing from friendship because of a relationship they are in, who is harder to reach than before, or who covers signs of physical abuse, it is worth having a confidential, honest conversation where you express your concerns. Violence was not part of God's design, but it has been part of human experience ever since Cain killed his brother. Family violence, in particular, can be traumatic because it introduces abuse into the very relationships that are supposed to be safest. There are avenues for help and we encourage you to be courageous and reach out.

Divorce

You have probably heard the statistics: about half of first marriages end in divorce with even more for second or third marriages. You may have also heard that the divorce rate stabilized and is dropping. A broad look at divorce shows that it increased substantially across the 1900s, peaked in the 1980s, then stabilized and declined since the 2000s.[15] Divorce rates are considerably higher for younger than for older individuals and for less educated compared to college-educated adults.[16] According to a recent analysis of marriage and divorce rates (measured as the number of newly reported incidents of divorce per 1,000 from the appropriate population), the 1960s saw a divorce rate of 9.6, which increased to around 15 in the 1970s and up to a peak of 22 in the 1980s.[17] Since the 1980s, the divorce rate has steadily decreased and has reached the lowest point since the 1970s at around 15 per 1000 women.[18] However, over the same time period the marriage rate has been in a steady decline from 68.8 in the 1980s down to 35 in 2010 and to 33.2 per 1000 in 2019.[19] So, while divorce has decreased about 35% since the 1980s, marriage has decreased almost 50% in the past 40 years.

Moreover, there has been a widening gap between those who have a stable marriage and those who divorce.[20] Over half of divorces occur in the first seven years of marriage, while midlife is a second crisis point for marriage, a time in which marital satisfaction is often at its lowest point.[21]

Points to Ponder 12.1: No-fault Divorce

There once was a time in America, still practiced in some religious communities and countries, where a spouse had to present legal grounds for divorce. Many saw these laws as a restrictive holdover from the nation's founding Judeo-Christian ethic. Indeed, recognizing that all communication is interdependent (that is, it both causes and happens in response to others' communication) means that it would be very difficult to pin responsibility on one party without the other party being culpable too. In the U.S., "no-fault" divorce laws have been in place in 46 states since the 1970s and in all states since 1985.[22] Passing these laws removed the burden of proof for causes like adultery, cruelty, or abandonment. Instead, more ambiguous causes like "insupportability" were introduced, making legal divorce accessible to anyone.[23] Around the time these laws were ratified across the nation, there was a substantial increase in the divorce rate. Because of these increases, coupled with the legal changes, some presented evidence showing that passing the no-fault divorce laws caused more divorces,[24] while others demonstrated with evidence that a social movement termed the "divorce revolution" was already underway[25] and that the legal changes simply caught up with the social practice.[26] While both arguments have some credence, more generally these trends show that it can be important to consider policy in light of social practice and social practice in light of policy.

Divorce rates are also rising among adults aged 50 and older—a trend known as the "gray divorce revolution."[27] Given how common divorce is, you probably know quite a few people who have directly experienced divorce. Research has investigated both the antecedents and consequences of divorce. We look at these in turn but stress that even though a relationship may have risk factors, that does not mean that a divorce is inevitable. There are often choices that couples can make, including how they communicate and react to one another, that can impact the direction their marriage goes.

Predicting Divorce

Research over many decades has uncovered sociological and demographic predictors of divorce.[28] Dropping out of high school or earning only a high school diploma, getting married as a teenager, having a baby before being married, poverty, and unemployment are some of these factors.[29] Having parents who have divorced, being divorced yourself, marrying interracially, and cohabiting premaritally are also risk factors associated with divorce.[30]

Extra-marital affairs also predict divorce, with estimates between 20 to 40% of marriages ending due to infidelity.[31] Interviewing 53 divorced individuals, Shelby Scott and her colleagues found that the most commonly reported reasons for divorce were lack of commitment, infidelity, and conflicts/arguments, with the "final straw" most commonly reported as infidelity, domestic violence, and substance abuse.[32] Despite these reasons, there is evidence that couples who stay married despite infidelity report an increase in marital satisfaction over time, and that these couples do not differ from non-infidelity couples in marital stability or satisfaction.[33]

Of course, there are interaction patterns that lead to divorce. Some of the same patterns associated with relational conflict presented in Chapter 6—like Gottman's four horsemen of criticism, defensiveness, contempt, and stonewalling—can lead couples down a pathway toward divorce. Other patterns that researchers have identified include attitudes toward commitment. One study that compared first and second marriages found that individuals who hold a negative view of divorce (e.g., seeing divorce as morally wrong, believing that marital problems can and should be solved) are less likely to take steps to end their marriage and are more optimistic that marital quality will improve.[34] The study found that these couples have reason to be optimistic because "commitment to staying married even through

rough times is generally associated with improvements in relationship quality over time."[35]

Another communication pattern that predicts divorce is the demand-withdraw sequence. This pattern, not surprisingly, occurs when one partner pushes for a response, but the other partner pulls away. This typically plays out as a wife presents challenges and demands and her husband emotionally or physically withdraws.[36] John Gottman and Nan Silver suggest that wives, in particular, should be careful not to begin conflict discussions with "harsh start-ups" and that husbands should remain open to their wife's influence.[37] More generally, the presence of the demand-withdraw sequence signals that couples should pay attention to how they say something as much as to what they say. A preponderance of negativity can signal trouble for a marriage.

Houston and colleagues set out to test three explanatory models that predict not only divorce but also what leads to being happily married.[38] The *Disillusionment Model* argues that couples have unrealistic idealizations of their partner and marriage, so during courtship they do not engage in conflict. These illusions become difficult to maintain after the wedding (or after cohabitation) because couples are together more continuously, so conflict increases, diverging from their fairy tale script of "happily ever after." Decreases in love lead to negative sentiment, which leads to distress and divorce. The *Emerging Stress Model* suggests that newlyweds are deeply in love, so they express high levels of love and low levels of negativity. However, they experience declines in romantic attraction early in marriage (partly because marriage is more holistic, including "doing life together," not just emotional sharing) and thus couples experience increased negativity early in the relationship, which predicts distress and divorce. Finally, the *Enduring Dynamics Model* proposes that interpersonal communication patterns established during courtship will persist throughout marriage. If dynamics involve healthy communication patterns, then they will continue. If dynamics are primarily negative, then negativity will continue in marriage, eventually leading to divorce.

Houston and colleagues analyzed 156 couples across four different time points.[39] The first three time points happened during their first three years of marriage and the fourth was a 13-year follow-up. This longitudinal data allowed an intense investigation of early marital dynamics that could predict outcomes over a decade later. They distinguished *married-happy* (68 couples) from *married-unhappy* (32 couples) and those who *divorced-quickly* (around or before the second anniversary, 10 couples), *divorced-early* (between 2–7 years, 21 couples), or divorced-later (after more than 7 years, 25 couples). The study found that "disillusionment may distinguish those who divorce from those who stay married,"[40] but "the timing of divorce depended on how spouses felt about each other and got along with each other as newlyweds."[41] Married-happy couples exhibited stronger romantic bonds as newlyweds (i.e., more deeply in love, more responsive personality, less ambivalence, and less frequent negativity) than married-unhappy couples and divorce-early couples. However, married-happy and divorce-later couples were similar to each other. Together, these findings show that the first two to three years of a marital relationship are really important for predicting both divorce and happiness 13 years out. In other words, it is necessary to have realistic expectations of what marriage entails (to prevent disillusionment and divorce), and it is equally important to develop positive communication routines (to promote enduring dynamics and happiness).

Another study of the causes of divorce found that one predominant reason couples divorce is because they gradually grow apart.[42] Couples feel a diminished sense of closeness, feel unappreciated by their spouse, or feel unloved. This finding corroborates evidence that there are two primary timeframes when divorce happens.[43] The first occurs around seven years into a marriage (early divorce). The second happens when a couple's first child reaches 14 years of age (later divorce). Based on analysis of video recordings of couples engaged in a marital conflict discussion, couples' negative affect (e.g., complaining, criticizing) predicts early divorce, but it is the *absence* of positive affect (e.g., assent, humor, laughter) which predicts later divorce. Intense fighting can make marriages end quickly, but boredom and disinterested interactions lead to a passionless, detached marriage and later divorce.

Effects of Divorce

Research outlines several effects of divorce for adults and children. For adults, divorce is associated with short- and long-term declines in economic well-being (which is greater for women than men), decrease in physical health and perceived well-being, lower levels of mental health, and increase in mortality rates after divorce.[44] Divorced adults, compared to their married counterparts, experience poorer self-concept, more social isolation, less satisfying sex lives, and more stressful life events.[45] Both men and women also report an appreciable decline in overall life satisfaction after divorce unless the dissolved marriage was highly distressed.[46] A recent summary admits that there is "particularly strong evidence that divorce has negative effects on mental health of adults—but also that these effects are temporary."[47] For some adults, consequences of divorce persist until another marital relationship replaces the disrupted one while for others the consequence of divorce mostly subside after two to three years.[48] Of course, many factors play a role in adults' adjustment to divorce, including the role of spirituality (i.e., the extent to which one views divorce as a spiritual failure or sacred loss).[49]

For children, one of the most detrimental consequences of divorce is family instability. Children fare best when some semblance of order, routine, and stability is maintained in their lives. As a 2020 review concluded, "the more family structure transitions children face, the lower their level of well-being on average."[50] This pattern applies across multiple domains of well-being, including problem behavior, emotional health, socioeconomic attainment, and relationship stability in adulthood.[51] Children experience less support, fewer interactions, fewer rules, harsher discipline from divorced parents than married parents.[52] Relocating to a new neighborhood, which is common after divorce, also disrupts a child's peer relationships at a time when social support from peers may be most crucial. In the long term, children of divorce achieve lower levels of education and financial success.[53]

To help understand the specific stresses that college students of divorced parents face, Mick Cunningham and JaneLee Waldock interviewed 20 university students.[54] Common across interviews, students reported difficulty coordinating logistics with their moms and dads and difficulty integrating their lives with their parents. A recurring stressor involved scheduling.

Students felt trapped trying to coordinate equal time with both parents and figuring out how to spend holidays. Young adult children reported feeling guilty for choosing to spend more time with one parent than another because they recognized that parents may view time allocation as a measure of how much their child loves each of them. The phrase "I feel like I am always trying to please people" characterized the frustration with the "politics of time obligation."[55] Figuring out how to spend time took effort, which college students knew full well. Another stressor related to feelings of loss and sadness about how divorce has changed the family. This loss is characterized by the phrase, "my ideal home is no longer there."[56] For many, "going home" is not an easy place to identify.

Why does divorce hurt children? Chris Segrin and Jeanne Flora offer three possible explanations.[57] The first is a *parental absence* perspective. The argument here is that parenting is hard work and that children fare better when two rather than one parent is caring for them. We would add that children of divorce lose not just an extra set of parenting hands, but that there are particular ramifications for the absence of either a father or mother. A second explanation is the *economic disadvantage* perspective. Divorce often lowers the social economic status for the children and their parents, and this lower status is associated with poorer well-being. This is especially pronounced for women post-divorce.[58] The third explanation for how divorce hurts children is a *family conflict* perspective. The increased interparental conflict and acrimonious relationships between spouses could explain why some children suffer. It may be easy to see these explanations as distinct on paper, yet in real life they can happen simultaneously and together attribute to the experiences of children of divorce.

**||||||||▶ Application Activity 12.2:
A Good Divorce**

With a partner, discuss the following:

- Is there such a thing as a "good divorce"? Why or why not?
- What would make a "good divorce"?
- Read the excerpt below, do you agree that communication is key to a "good divorce"? What other factors should be considered?

Some sociologists, family therapists, and court systems support the notion of a "good divorce." The argument is that divorce can result in minimum distress—emotionally, physically, and economically—for both parents and their children if the parents engage in cooperative co-parenting behaviors. The best outcomes occur when both parents are active in the parenting process by talking with and providing emotional support for their children as well as assisting in daily activities such as helping with homework and monitoring their children's attitudes and behaviors. Children of divorce fare better when the parents communicate regularly, maintain consistency in rules

---

IIIIIIII ▶	Application Activity 12.2 *continued*: A Good Divorce

across households, and support each other in parenting decisions and roles.

A major factor in distinguishing between a "good" and "bad" divorce is how parents communicate with each other following the divorce. Constance Ahrons identified five groups of post-divorce parenting styles.[59] Two groups were associated with a "good divorce": cooperative colleagues (marked by moderate levels of interaction and high-quality communication) and perfect pals (marked by high levels of interaction and high quality of communication). The other three groups were not: angry associates (marked by infrequent exchanges and moderate quality of communication), fiery foes (marked by low levels and poor-quality interaction), and dissolved duos (marked by little or no communication). Some research on children who experienced a "good divorce" and those who did not show some benefits.[60] Youth whose parents maintained a "good divorce" exhibited fewer behavioral problems and rated their paternal relationships more positively than youth from other post-divorce forms; however, these children were no better off with respect to other indicators such as self-esteem, grades, substance abuse, and life satisfaction. Thus, "a good divorce is not a panacea for improving children's well-being in post-divorce families."[61] So, having a positive post-divorce co-parenting relationship is better for kids than not having one, but only along some dimensions.

Return to the discussion with a partner.

- Think about a divorced couple you know well. How would you classify their communication style—cooperative colleagues, perfect pals, angry associates, fiery foes, or dissolved duos?

- How, if at all, did the style impact the well-being of the child/children?

- Should Christians embrace the idea of a "good divorce"? Why or why not?

206

Christian Perspective on Divorce and Remarriage

Given the prevalence of divorce, you almost undoubtedly have encountered it in one way or another and probably have formed your own opinions on divorce and marriage. Perhaps you have witnessed your parents' divorce or know a close friend who is divorced. We have, too. While some are conflict-ridden and lead to heartache, some are mutual and result in thriving new marriages. So, what is a Christian or biblical approach to understanding divorce?

The book *Divorce and Remarriage: Four Christian Views* lays out approaches that range from acceptance to prohibition, giving biblical evidence for each.[62] Indeed, there are a wide variety of perspectives, even within Christianity. And the debates are not new. The Church of England originated as a response to Catholic restrictions over divorce and remarriage. Even centuries before the Anglican Church formed, people held contrasting views about divorce.

A passage in the Gospels records a time when a group of religious scholars asked Jesus, "Is it lawful for a man to divorce his wife for any and every reason?" (Matt. 19:3). Jesus's response offered a clear position statement: God created marriage between one man and one woman who, when joined through sexual union, should never again be separated. Traditional wedding ceremonies often conclude with this quotation, "What therefore God hath joined together, let not man put asunder" (Mark 10:9, KJV). The religious scholars, however, pointed out that the ancient and religiously sanctioned practice did not match this position. "'Why then,' they asked, 'did Moses command that a man give his wife a certificate of divorce and send her away?'" (Matt. 19:7). Jesus did not deny the reality of the practice, nor did he compromise his position. He stated that "Moses permitted you to divorce your wives because your hearts were hard. But it was not this way from the beginning. I tell you that anyone who divorces his wife, except for sexual immorality, and marries another woman commits adultery" (Matt. 19: 8–9). This response must have seemed extreme to Jesus's followers. Matthew records that the disciples commented, "If this is the situation between a husband and wife, it is better not to marry." Again, Jesus's response about eunuchs is uncompromising (see Matt. 19:10–12).

Perhaps, like the disciples, many today would feel that if there is no way out of a marriage—if divorce is not an option—then it would be better not to marry. Indeed, this may partly explain why cohabitation has increased so dramatically. However, one interpretation of Jesus's statements is that he is articulating an ideal that is intrinsically linked to a practice of sexual exclusivity and fidelity. He teaches that "two become one flesh" and that remarriage is equivalent to adultery (sexual infidelity). Paul echoes this teaching to the new believers in Corinth: "A wife must not separate from her husband. But if she does, she must remain unmarried or else be reconciled to her husband. And a husband must not divorce his wife" (1 Cor. 7:10). The author of Hebrews also picks up on the explicit link between chastity and marriage: "Marriage should be honored by all, and the marriage bed kept pure, for God will judge the adulterer and all the sexually immoral" (Heb. 13:4). From this perspective, serial cohabitation is as problematic as divorce and remarriage. These passages, from our view, teach that marriage commitment is designed to be for life. It is a covenant. Ideally, there should be no divorce. Furthermore, there should be complete sexual abstinence outside the context of marriage.

One reason we believe Jesus maintained that divorce was a compromise that moved away from God's design is because the Bible displays the marital relationship as a picture of how Christ relates to his Bride, as we review in the conclusion of Chapter 11. Think of Hosea. He was commanded by God to love a prostitute and marry her (Hos. 1:2), and then when she cheated on him and became enslaved again to a pimp, to buy her back (Hos. 3:1–3). We might be too quick to write off Hosea's story as fiction or as an allegory, but that sells the tale short. Every marriage is a picture of Christ and his Bride (Eph. 5:32), and Christ's love is relentless even in the face of our infidelity toward him. His commitment is unwavering, evidenced by his death on the cross. Marriage is also a total commitment through the point of death.

With such a view, it can be tempting to align with a position that there are no grounds for divorce—period. However, theologians often contend that there are at least two biblically based reasons for divorce: infidelity and desertion (see Matt. 19; 1 Cor. 7:10–16). Additionally, some consider any act that would be similarly disruptive to the marriage (like infidelity or desertion) to fall within the biblical grounds for divorce.[63] Practically, abuse or even the threat of imminent harm warrants leaving immediately to find safety. It may also require marital separation, in which the couple or family lives apart. A survey of 1,000 Protestant pastors found that 55% believed that divorce may be the best response to domestic violence and less than 5% believed that divorce in these cases was never an option.[64] Our goal is not to debate "acceptable" reasons for divorce. Instead, we point out that Jesus's teaching acknowledges the reality of the social practice, but simultaneously holds that God's original design was different.

In sum, the widespread practice of divorce gives evidence of a long-standing divergence between God's design and social practice. This divergence creates a complexity within human relations that God never intended, but that is not beyond his grace. As Scripture teaches, "[W]here sin increased and abounded, grace (God's unmerited favor) has surpassed it and increased the more and superabounded" (Rom. 5:20, AMPC). Christianity does not condemn those who have been divorced, been sexually promiscuous, engaged in homosexual acts, or had multiple partners. With all types of sin, there are consequences (see Rom. 6:23), but God's grace "superabounds"! Recall that the religious leaders of Jesus's day brought a woman caught in the act of adultery, and after dismissing her accusers, Jesus asked, "Has no one condemned you?" She replied, "No one, sir," and Jesus comforted, "*Then neither do I condemn you.* Go now and leave your life of sin" (John 8:9–11, emphasis added). There is room to consider both parts of what Jesus said. There is a deliberate decision we must make to "sin no more" (John 8:11, KJV). But the truth of the first part of Jesus's statement is also echoed throughout the New Testament: "[T]here is now no condemnation for those who are in Christ Jesus. For in Christ Jesus the law of the Spirit of life set you free from the law of sin and death" (Rom. 8:1–2). Part of leaving a life of sexual sin is to break soul ties to live in complete spiritual freedom. Scripture teaches that Christ became sin for us so that we can become the righteousness of God in him (2 Cor. 5:21). In other words, Christ has taken the punishment for broken covenants; we must appropriate his forgiveness. So, whatever you have experienced personally or within your social circles, we encourage you to seek to be like Jesus and to maintain the standard of God's good design, but also to exhibit love, grace, forbearance, forgiveness, and humility.

Building Healthy Marital Relationships

It is important, sometimes critical, to understand signs of abuse and a struggling marriage and to consider divorce. But one of our goals throughout the book is to teach communication practices and principles that can promote positive and enduring relationships. Even during times of stress or when interaction patterns signal relationship trouble, there are ways to alter marital communication that can help move it in a positive direction. Not every time, but sometimes after a separation, counseling, and genuine change, families can be reunited and reconciled. Marriage, across the board, has been shown to benefit those involved,[65] but unhappy marriages do not accrue the same benefits.[66] In this final section, we review practices that can decrease the propensity for divorce and build thriving marital relationships.

Taking a perspective of marriage as covenant means that our communication should reflect this perspective. Bill Strom and Divine Agodzo have identified six covenantal principles.[67] Expressions and attitudes about marriage that reflect these six are:

- We are part of a community, and relational flourishing is not possible apart from community.

- We are motivated by love to do what is best for each other.

- We take responsibility for our words and actions, knowing that they can breathe life or death into our relationship.

- We will make vows to each other, agreeing to live out those promises.

- We desire to change together toward a shared vision, holding each other accountable to that vision.

- We are committed to our relationship until death do we part.

A covenantal relationship adheres to all six principles and can lead to a thriving marriage. In particular, it removes doubt and uncertainty about the relationship. A devoted, stalwart commitment provides relationship stability that allows for imperfections, confession of mistakes, forgiveness, healing, and growth. As Scripture states, "love covers over a multitude of sins" (1 Peter 4:8). Covenantal communication opens relational possibilities and vulnerabilities that are often masked or marginalized in other types of relationships. The distinction between a committed and a covenantal relationship, argues psychologist Greg Smalley, helps us answer the question, "Isn't living together in a committed relationship just as good as marriage?" Smalley answers, "no"; the marital covenant creates a "level of safety and security" and allows couples to "experience a profound vulnerability and openness that can't happen in other relationships."[68]

Observing thousands of couples and learning from relationship "masters" and the "disasters," John Gottman and Nan Silver distill *Seven Principles for Making Marriage Work*.[69] Principles include knowing and appreciating your spouse, choosing to give attention and to engage with her, accepting her influence, appropriately dealing with conflict, committing to work through disagreements, and letting the relationship become a special, meaningful place in your lives. While we recommend the book as a helpful resource for any marriage, we look at each of these seven principles in more detail.

The first principle is that couples should enhance their "love maps." A love map includes details about each other's world. Beyond favorite color or cuisine, do you understand each other's goals, fears, and hopes? In their book, Gottman and Silver offer several listening and learning activities to improve your love maps.

The second principle is to nurture fondness and admiration. Rehearsing what made you fall in love in the first place is a great practice to stoke your affection for your partner. Fondness can also grow by reminiscing on happy or funny events from the past. Noticing the things at which your partner excels, and commenting on them, is another place to maintain admiration. Gottman and Silver say that this will fan the flames in your relationship and argue that fondness and admiration are antidotes for contempt.

Turning toward each other, as opposed to turning away or turning against each other, is the third principle that makes marriage work. After coding hundreds of videos of couples interacting through daily events (e.g., cooking, watching television, eating together, reading magazines), Gottman and his research team noticed a pattern. They watched what happened when one partner made a bid for their partner's attention, affection, humor, or support. In general, unhappy couples might ignore or actually pull away from their partner's bid (turn away). Really unhealthy couples might turn the bid into an argument or accusation (turn against). The happiest and most relationally healthy couples choose to engage emotionally with one another. They turned toward each other and responded to one another's desires for relationship.

The fourth key for making marriage work is to accept influence. This involves not just conceding arguments or showing respect. It also means considering each other's ideas and feelings as well as sharing in decision making. One of the aspects of love is that it never seeks its own way (1 Cor. 13). Are all the decisions made by only one partner? Accepting influence means being willing to yield your own prerogative in order to learn and appreciate your spouse.

Gottman and Silver share that both husbands and wives should accept influence from the other, but in their research with thousands of couples, it is usually husbands who are most resistant to accepting influence. In the Christian church there are numerous teachings about headship and the roles of men and women. Some would contradict Gottman's principle of accepting influence from wives because these would argue that wives should submit to the authority of their husbands. While we acknowledge a diversity of perspectives in this area, we believe that accepting influence, as Gottman describes it, does not usurp any God-given authority structures in the family. This teaching, instead, aligns with what Paul writes in Ephesians. The verse, before offering specific instructions for wives and husbands, first says, "Submit to one another out of reverence for Christ" (Eph. 5:21). Learning to accept influence from a partner is the fourth key that helps relationships thrive.

The fifth and sixth principles for making marriage work have to do with inevitable conflicts that come in marriage relationships. In Chapters 6 and 7 we talked about what motivates conflict and how to handle it with grace and forgiveness. As Scripture says, we should owe nothing to others but the continual debt of love (Rom. 13:8).

To review briefly, Gottman and Silver present that there are two types of conflicts that emerge—solvable and unsolvable problems. The fifth principle is to solve solvable conflicts. Gottman and Silver encourage couples to soften the ways they bring up conflicts, learn and make and accept *repair attempts*, which are any ways that partners' communication seeks to keep the conversation moving in a positive direction. It is also important to keep calm during conflict discussions. Finally, recognizing that we all have faults and that we all make mistakes encourages us to be gracious toward one another and come up with positive solutions to our solvable problems.

The sixth principle is to overcome gridlock. For unsolvable conflicts, it is important to continue a dialogue about them. Gottman and Silver suggest that couples seek to understand the cause(s) of the problem by becoming "dream detectives."[70] They believe that couples can try to uncover hidden (or unspoken) dreams, pressing to understand the roots of the conflict, not just what appears on the surface. Doing this requires you to be an ACE listener and to draw out others' deep thoughts (see Chapter 5).

The final principle that Gottman and Silver identify for making marriage work is to create shared meaning. Relationships, and families in general, can create an inner life together—"a culture rich with symbols and rituals."[71] Developing and rehearsing inside jokes is one example of how families do this. More profoundly, sharing a sense of shared vision or shared mission for your marriage and family can be deeply meaningful. Recounting family stories, such as your engagement, sweet wedding day memories, significant moments in your life with Christ, answered prayers, humorous anecdotes about children, all help set family values and develop shared meaning.

Other ways to build a healthy marriage are to establish or re-emphasize connection rituals (see Chapter 5). Try reviewing the five love languages. Are you consistently communicating love through gifts, quality time, words of encouragement, acts of service, and physical touch? If you share love through all channels, you will be sure to speak your spouse's primary

---

**||||||||▶ Application Activity 12.3:
Creating Intimacy**

Douglas Kelley's Intimacy in Personal Relationships study uncovered six contexts for developing intimacy.[72] He asked people to share their experiences with intimacy and love. Findings show that talk, sex, play, grief, conflict, and forgiveness all bring couples closer. Participants described a time where these different contexts created intimacy. In small groups, do the same. Specifically,

- Describe a time where _____ (talk, play, sex, grief, conflict, forgiveness) has demonstrated or created intimacy in one of your relationships.

- Which of these contexts created the deepest intimacy? Why?

- What themes about intimacy are uncovered in the shared stories?

Kelley frames the results of his work in terms of The Model of Intimate Relating: The Process of Discovery and Connection. As the title of the model suggests, Kelley argues that intimacy requires *discovery* (gaining informational, social, physical, and psychological/ emotional access to one another) and *connection* (feeling "close," understood, and accepted).

- Reflecting once again on a time where _____ (talk, play, sex, grief, conflict, forgiveness) has demonstrated or created intimacy in one of your relationships, frame these experiences in terms of Kelley's Model of Intimate Relating. In what ways did these experiences build (or perhaps, failed to build) intimacy through discovery and connection?

---

love language at some point, and odds are that you will fill their love tank. Which rituals are present in your relationship that embody passion, intimacy, and commitment?

Another practical way to enhance marriage is through the *Love Dare*, a forty-day devotional with daily challenges for showing love to your spouse.[73] This *New York Times* best-seller is based on the 2009 Christian film *Fireproof*, which traces the story of a struggling marriage that reforms through a re-dedication toward the character's marriage and consistent, devoted love.[74]

At the core of these kinds of activities is a push toward holistic connection with one another. Busyness can rob relationships of emotional connection and push lovers toward selfishness instead of intentionally delving into the inner lives of one another through active listening and supportive communication. Spending ten minutes a day in quality conversation—for example, no talking about kids, schedules, or household budget—can take a marriage from good to great.[75] There are plenty of resources and advice about how to improve your marriage, but the bottom line is that to have a thriving marriage you must not only decide to invest in it, you must also follow through in communication.

Conclusion

We started this chapter looking at Lamech as an example of sin's legacy in marriage. We reviewed problematic communication patterns including violence and divorce and then transitioned to consider how to develop enduring dynamics that will build stable and happy marriages. We conclude the chapter by looking at a couple in the New Testament who exhibited a healthy marriage.

During Paul's second missionary trip he met a Jewish couple, Aquila and Priscilla, in Corinth. This tentmaking couple invited Paul to work alongside and stay with them "because he [Paul] was a tentmaker as they were" (Acts 18:3). Although there are not many great examples of powerhouse couples in the Bible, Aquila and Priscilla stand out. From the handful of times they are mentioned in Scripture, we can draw some lessons about Christian marriage. First, this couple worked together. Aquila and Priscilla are mentioned seven times in the New Testament, but they are never mentioned alone. They are also listed as both Priscilla and Aquila and as Aquila and Priscilla, implying perhaps that both the wife and husband were equals in life and ministry. They faced hard times together (Acts 18:2), served as missionaries (Acts 18:18), and risked their lives for the Gospel (Rom. 16:3–4). Based on Scripture, it also seems they stayed on the lookout for ways to help others. When a young, articulate disciple named Apollos began to publicly debate the Jews about Jesus, "Priscilla and Aquila . . . invited him to their home and explained to him the way of God more adequately" (Acts 18:26). They also opened their home to host the local gathering of believers, as we learn from a greeting Paul sends to the congregation "that meets at their house" (1 Cor. 16:19). Navigating toward these outcomes must have required Priscilla and Aquila to nurture their love for one another, create intimacy, avoid violence, and heed any relational warning signs that surfaced. All relationships struggle at times, and what distinguishes those that succeed from those that are stymied is a stalwart commitment coupled with caring communication.

III.B: Parent-child Interaction

Chapter 13

Children in Multiple Family Contexts

Chapter Summary: The introduction of children into family systems is a profound but normative life stressor. Baby talk starts to echo through households. Chores change as do arguments about who does what. The contexts in which children grow are varied, as well. This chapter provides a demographic view of children's living arrangements and covers various theories that describe parent-child and family relationships, including Attachment Theory, family communication patterns, and parenting styles. Topics like linguistic development, sibling communication, sibling rivalry, and birth order effects are introduced. The chapter presents a biblical case for parenting in ways that reflect and honor God.

Introduction

JESUS WAS BORN INTO AN EARTHLY FAMILY. In many ways, he was an ordinary boy. We can imagine him growing from an infant, "wrapped in swaddling clothes, lying in a manger" (Luke 2:12, KJV), to a toddler playing tag under the watchful eyes of his parents. We can celebrate with Jesus's parents as they dedicate him to the Lord (Luke 2:21–40). We can visualize Jesus's mother and father walking alongside their son as they journey to the temple in Jerusalem to celebrate the Feast of the Passover when Jesus was about 12 years old (Luke 2:41). As they travel, we can picture Jesus's father and uncles instructing him about Jewish laws and customs, including the purpose of the Passover and the significance of the temple (see Exod. 12:24–28; Deut. 6). We can even feel the anxiety Jesus's parents experience when, on their way back home from the feast, they realize that Jesus is not among their traveling companions (Luke 2:43–44), and the relief they must feel when after three days of searching they find him in the temple courts (Luke 2:46). We can imagine Jesus listening to his mother, learning his father's trade, playing with his siblings, and going to the local synagogue with his family. "It was within the nurturing care of his earthly family that 'Jesus grew in wisdom and stature, and in favor with God and men'"[1] (Luke 2:25), and that Jesus was prepared for his earthly ministry.

In this chapter, we present a biblical case for raising children in ways that reflect and honor God's plan. A biblical perspective fundamentally embraces children as a gift from God. Psalm 127:3–5 reads, "Children are a heritage from the Lord, offspring a reward from him. Like arrows in the hands of a warrior are children born in one's youth. Blessed is the man whose quiver is full of them." Our chapter begins by overviewing aspects of child development, including family demographic contexts, sibling relationships, and language acquisition. We then turn to various theories that describe parent-child and family relationships: Attachment Theory, family communication patterns, and parenting styles. We end by presenting researched and biblically informed traits and practices linked to effective parenting, including how parents and children can talk about taboo topics like sex and drug use.

Context of Children

The contexts in which children grow are diverse. Each family is different, not only genetically but also circumstantially. Living arrangements, household composition, neighborhoods, cultural and social situations, and even historic moments often start out and develop differently in families. A model to help characterize such development is the Bioecological Model.[2] This model proposes overlapping, interdependent, and dynamic systems. These include biological, microsystems (e.g., family, school, church), mesosystems (e.g., the mutual influence of church and school, the interactions between family and church), and exosystems (e.g., government structures, extended family systems). These interfacing systems are couched within broader macrosystems (e.g., cultural/ideological influences) and chronosystems (e.g., historic setting). None of the systems are static—that is, all of them are developing simultaneously and interact with each other to influence how individuals and families grow.

In the U.S., the living situations for children are diverse and dynamic. As a breakdown by percentages, about 60% of children live with their

> ## Points to Ponder 13.1:
> ## International Babies
>
> In a fascinating depiction of infancy in various nations, documen-
> tarist Thomas Balmès followed the first year of life of four babies
> in four very different cultural settings.[3] Pre-birth rituals, feeding,
> cleaning, crawling, and first steps are all portrayed, and they are
> radically different in each country. The available resources, lan-
> guages, cultural practices, parental roles and expectations as well
> as living arrangements all diverge substantially in the different con-
> texts. The documentary serves to portray ways that macrosystems
> and microsystems surrounding children influence how they devel-
> op. It also widens the lens through which we see babies, expanding
> cultural, economic, and ethnic approaches to birth and babyhood.
> Watch the movie and see what you learn!

married, biological parents and an additional 3% with their cohabiting,
biological parents; 24% live in single-parent households (with 97% of these
living with a mother and 3% living with a father); 9% live in stepfamilies;
and the remaining 4% in other living arrangements (e.g., with a grandparent, in foster care).[4] This cross-sectional look at living arrangements gives
some idea of family experiences, but masks the dynamic nature of family
and household transitions.

Demographers have used longitudinal data sets to explore household
stability and instability. Overall, they estimate that children experience an
average of 3.4 moves (transitions to new addresses) between birth and adulthood and an additional 4.8 family composition changes.[5] These family changes include things like the birth of new siblings, family members moving out,
parental divorce or remarriage, stepsiblings joining a household, introduction of new cohabiting partners, or uncles or aunts moving in.[6] Most changes
children experience are normative (e.g., birth of a sibling), but some are non-
normative. In addition, there are differences by education and ethnicity where
children of college-educated parents and Asian Americans experience fewer
transitions across the board.[7] One study found that almost half of children
(45%) experience a living arrangement where they are "doubling up," which is
defined as a time when "a nuclear family coresides with other adults, such as
grandparents, other extended family, or friends,"[8] and over a third of children
born to single mothers will live in a stepfamily before reaching adulthood.[9]

Everyone experiences some form of family and household transition. Jesus, for example, likely witnessed the early death of his earthly father, Joseph. This is perhaps why nothing of the life of Joseph is mentioned in Scripture after Jesus's twelfth birthday and why Jesus, as the eldest son, took on the responsibility of caring for Mary and then passed that responsibility to his disciple John while hanging on the cross (John 19:26–27). Transitions are normal but can bring a mixed set of consequences for children. Moving from a single-mother family to a stepfamily, for example, generally adds resources and economic advantage. It also may bring more supportive relationships; however, it often breeds more complex interpersonal dynamics as children navigate multiple or changing household rules and relationships.[10]

Children with Parents

Looking at how families differ from the perspective of parents, William Bradford Wilcox and Elizabeth Marquardt describe adults with and without children "to determine how parenthood is linked to the[ir] emotional welfare."[11] They reason that children thrive when parents are happy and stable; therefore, it is useful to look not just at the demographic conditions of childhood but also at the social and cultural dynamics within families where children live. Findings show that married parenting is different from parenting outside of the marital context. For example, married fathers and mothers indicate that their "life has an important purpose" more than their married counterparts who are childless. Married parents, compared to unmarried parents, are less likely to be depressed and more likely to be happy. Parenting, however, is associated with lower levels of marital happiness compared with childless couples, at least for the first several years after babies enter the home. These differences indicate a trade-off between purpose and satisfaction for parents versus non-parents. Focusing on married parents, the researchers report social, cultural, and relationship factors that impact satisfaction and likelihood of divorce. The best outcomes for married parents (which by extension help children) occur when couples report high levels of education, adequate social support, low levels of financial strain, equitable division of household labor, shared religious involvement and a belief that "God is the center of their marriage,"[12] enjoyable sex lives, and above average daily generosity (defined as "the virtue of giving good things to [one's spouse] freely and abundantly").[13] These findings are nicely summarized in the report subtitle: *How Parenthood Makes Life Meaningful and How Marriage Makes Parenthood Bearable.*[14] Let's now turn to understand better another important aspect of the family context: siblings.

Children with Siblings

Pope John Paul II is attributed with saying that the best gift you can give a child is siblings.[15] Sibling relationships are pervasive, with about 82% of kids living with siblings.[16] These relationships are arguably the most important and enduring relationships people experience. They typically are the longest relationship a person has in a lifetime, with some estimating that we spend about one-third of our lives residing with siblings.[17] By middle childhood, the time spent with siblings commonly outstrips that spent with parents,[18] and a typical 11-year-old spends about 33% of her out-of-school hours with siblings.[19] Sibling relationships are generally viewed as involuntary until at least emerging adulthood. These relationships often have shared histories of formative experiences and shared parents, which makes them distinct from other friendships or relationships.[20] Sibling relationships also offer potential resources, support, and protection.[21] Other unique characteristics are that sibling relationships often resemble, in terms of power and closeness, peer friendships and, somewhat paradoxically, siblings often experience both a high level of conflict and a high level of closeness.[22]

Of course, not all sibling relationships look alike. One typology of sibling relationships identifies five types.[23] *Intimate* sibling relationships are marked by a high level of closeness and emotional interdependence; siblings share a history of positive experiences and consider each other friends. *Congenial* siblings are also emotionally involved and provide support upon request; they consider themselves "good" friends. They are also more likely to disagree and argue than intimate siblings. *Loyal* siblings share a heightened recognition of the importance of the sibling bond and sense of obligation to offer support. *Apathetic* siblings are indifferent toward each other, making little effort to offer instrumental or emotional support; contact with each other is minimal. Finally, *hostile* sibling relationships are characterized by siblings overtly rejecting requests for help and avoiding contact with each other. These siblings experience high levels of envy, resentment, and aggression toward each other. Not surprisingly, intimate and congenial sibling relationships are overall most positive, as marked by commitment and trust, communication and relational satisfaction, and liking and loving. Individuals who classified their sibling relationship as intimate/ congenial report that their siblings used relational maintenance behaviors at a higher rate than those individuals who classified their sibling relationships as loyal, apathetic, or hostile.[24]

The nature of the parent-child relationship might also impact the strength of the sibling bond. In the absence of parental support and as a way to compensate for the lack of resources, siblings may forge a strong bond.[25] Siblings can provide instrumental and emotional support for each other and can help each other develop skills such as problem-solving, negotiation, sharing, cooperation, and empathy.[26] Siblings can also teach each other negative behaviors. Studies have shown that positive sibling relationships are linked to prosocial behaviors and negative sibling relationships associated with behavioral problems.[27] Given that an older sibling often wields more power in the relationship than a younger one,[28] researchers suggest that parents pay particular attention to older siblings' behaviors, as these "may be likely to cascade downstream to both younger sibling behavior and the quality of sibling interaction."[29]

Sibling relationships are not static and often change over the lifespan. It is not unusual for younger siblings to engage in more negative antisocial interaction than older sibling pairs.[30] Young siblings may compete for resources from their parents, such as time, attention, and money. This competition may create sibling rivalry. Studies have looked at sex differences in sibling rivalry, but findings are mixed. One study, for example, found that pairs of boys reported more feelings of rivalry than did pairs of girls and cross-sex siblings,[31] while another study reported more competition and conflict between sisters than brothers.[32] Although some studies suggest that sibling rivalry continues late into adulthood,[33] overall sibling rivalry seems to peak during adolescence and decrease over the lifespan.[34] By the time siblings reach emerging adulthood, their interactions often resemble their interactions with peers, and siblings at this life stage may even serve as each other's confidants.[35] One of God's greatest blessings in a parent's life is seeing his or her children's relationships with each other strengthen as they move into adulthood (Ps. 133:1).

With the introduction of siblings comes an introduction of birth order. Some estimate that there are over 2,000 psychological studies that explore birth order![37] This has given rise to several publications and popular books on the subject. For example, Kevin Leman argues in *The Birth Order Book: Why You Are the Way You Are* that "why you are the way you are" is because of your birth order.[38] Are you a first-born child? Middle? Last born? An only child? Leman argues that your birth order can dramatically shape your personality.

IIIIIIII ▶ **Application Activity 13.2:**
Sibling Relationships

Do you have one or more siblings? If so, answer the following questions as you reflect on your relationships with your siblings. If not, reflect on the following questions thinking of a sibling pair that you know well.

1. Describe the nature of the communication between the siblings. How would you classify the sibling relationship—intimate, congenial, loyal, apathetic, or hostile?[36] Would you classify the relationship differently at different life stages? Explain.

2. This typology was developed to classify adult sibling relationships. Do you think this typology is helpful in thinking about younger sibling pairs? Why or why not?

3. In what ways do you think the mother-child or father-child relationships influence how siblings communicate with each other?

Born to Rebel, a book by Frank Sulloway, compares first- and later-born children on five key personality dimensions: conscientiousness, agreeableness, openness to experience, extraversion, and neuroticism.[39] This book reports that firstborn children are dutiful, hardworking, self-disciplined, organized; that is, they are more conscientious than later-born children. However, firstborn children also tend to be anxious and prone to depression and feelings of vulnerability, traits associated with neuroticism. In contrast, later-born children are agreeable (acquiescent, easygoing, tender-minded), open to experience (prone to fantasy, attentive to inner feelings, attracted to novelty), and are extraverts (affectionate, excitement seeking, fun-loving).

How strong do you think the link between birth order and personality is? Here is a list from *The Birth Order Book*:

- **Firstborn traits**: Perfectionist, reliable, conscientious, list maker, well organized, hard driving, natural leader, critical, serious, scholarly, logical, does not like surprises, loves computers

- **Middle child traits**: Mediator, compromising, diplomatic, avoid conflict, independent, loyal to peers, many friends, a maverick, secretive, unspoiled

- **Last born (baby) traits**: Manipulative, charming, blames others, attention seeker, tenacious, people person, natural salesperson, precocious, engaging, affectionate, loves surprises

- **Only child traits**: Little adult by the age of seven; very thorough; deliberate; high achiever; self-motivated; fearful; cautious; voracious reader; black and white thinker; uses "very," "extremely," and "exactly" a lot; cannot bear to fail; has very high expectations for self; more comfortable with people who are older or younger[40]

Do the traits that align with your birth order seem accurate to you? Do the traits resonate with your own or others' experiences based on birth order?

After reading the birth order characteristics, what do you think are the dynamics in families that might explain these persistent characterizations of birth order effects? We believe that birth order effects are largely the function of different family environments and communication dynamics. Firstborn siblings may shoulder more responsibility in raising younger siblings than do later-born siblings. This might account for why younger siblings see their older sibling as bossy. This might also account for the belief that firstborn children are more organized and natural born leaders than later-born children. Firstborn children often learn to play independently (because there are no near peers in the house), while later-born children have playmates. In their earliest years of development, firstborn children also have the undivided attention of their parents, while the introduction of additional children divides parents' attention. Parents' interactions with firstborn children may also be quite different than their interactions with later-born. We are all familiar with the "babies of the family" getting away with things that older siblings did not. Could this help account for why last born children tend to be characterized as manipulative, attention-seeking, or charming? Alternatively, parents' experience level for parenting infants is non-existent for firstborn children but increases with each additional child. Parents are learning to parent, so it is reasonable that they will treat subsequent children differently based on their accumulated experiences. Parents' gender-based expectations of children may also play a role. The oldest born daughter, for example, may have more responsibility for helping with the younger siblings than does the oldest born son. Cultures also differ in expectations of children of different birth orders.[41]

Despite its popularity, "empirical research on birth order and personality has consistently revealed only sporadic links between personality and birth order."[42] The bottom line: while birth order may shape your personality and behavior, playing a role in explaining "why you are the way you are," other factors such as family dynamics, gender-role expectations, and culture also are key influences on differences between siblings.[43]

Communication Development Processes

Despite the varied contexts in which children are born and reared, there is something that is common across all settings. Children learn to communicate. It is actually remarkable that one of the very first acts of a zygote is to communicate. The new confluence of egg and sperm send signals to the mother's body to prepare the uterus for implantation. It is safe to say that human communication is universal and fundamental. The persistence and cross-cultural fact of human communication and language acquisition has led to two theoretical camps:[44] The Chomsky camp argues that language ability is innate, a biologically hardwired ability. The Skinner camp believes that

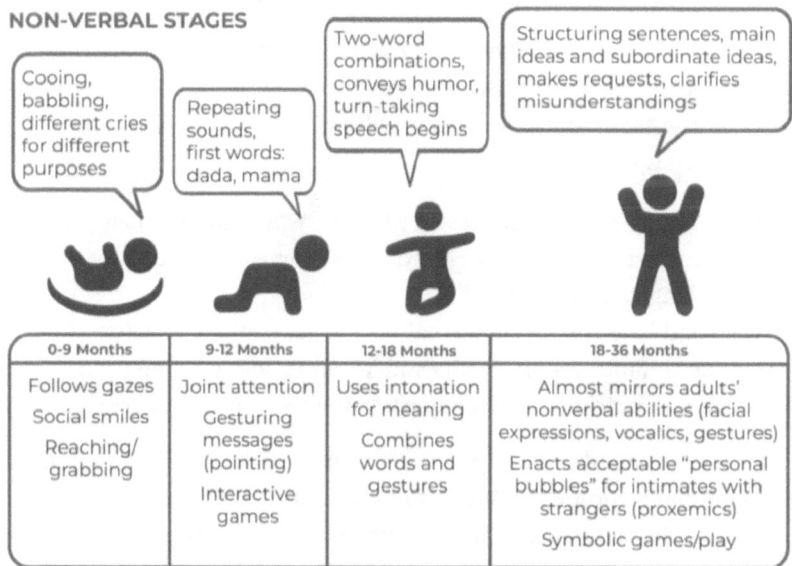

NON-VERBAL STAGES

0-9 Months	9-12 Months	12-18 Months	18-36 Months
Follows gazes Social smiles Reaching/grabbing	Joint attention Gesturing messages (pointing) Interactive games	Uses intonation for meaning Combines words and gestures	Almost mirrors adults' nonverbal abilities (facial expressions, vocalics, gestures) Enacts acceptable "personal bubbles" for intimates with strangers (proxemics) Symbolic games/play

Figure 13.1: Language Development Processes for Infants and Children, based on Carol A. Miller and Laura S. DeThorne, "Communication Development, Distributed across People, Resources, and Time," in *The Handbook of Lifespan Communication*, ed. Jon F. Nussbaum (New York: Peter Lang, 2014); Thomas J. Socha and Julie Yingling, *Families Communicating with Children* (Malden, MA: Polity Press, 2010).

language is culturally imprinted, a learned behavior. These nature versus nurture debates have amassed evidence on both sides. Which do you think it is?

Regardless of how we develop language, there are milestones that children typically surpass. A newborn has very different communication abilities than an 18-month-old than a 3-year-old. Carol Miller and Laura DeThrone give an excellent multi-functional timeline for how speech/language, nonverbal behavior, and socio-emotional expression develop.[45] Thomas Socha and Julie Yingling also offer a developmental timeline for understanding how infants and children acquire and use language in relational contexts.[46] We include a simplistic depiction of some of these developmental milestones in Figure 13.1.

For language development, there is no more intriguing Bible story than the Tower of Babel. In the biblical narrative it is a significant historic event that forever impacted language. The story starts by noting, "Now the whole world had one language and a common speech" (Gen. 11:1). The people decided to build a tower and make a name for themselves.

> But the Lord came down to see the city and the tower the people were building. The Lord said, "If as one people speaking the same language they have begun to do this, then nothing they plan to do will be impossible for them. Come, let us go down and confuse their language so they will not understand each other." (Gen. 11:5–7)

There are numerous perspectives on why God would confuse language, and it can be interesting to discuss. How do you imagine that the tower of Babel impacted language acquisition?

Beyond language or nonverbal behaviors, families socialize children to become communicators. Socha and Yingling offer guiding principles of positive communication with children.[47] Their six principles are:

1. Families should teach positive communication by "scaffolding" communication experiences to benefit children.[48] Parents should make the most of teachable moments in everyday activities and interactions.

2. Families should remember that they are both parenting and modeling parenting as they communicate with their children. Socha and Yingling ask, "Will hearing that message in the future make me feel proud of my parenting?"[49]

3. Family communication should take a disposition of continuous improvement, allowing potential in children to be realized, not squashed. Opening possibilities and imagination for children means sometimes encouraging creativity by ignoring the feasibility of children's ideas and suggestions. Accommodating the absurd along with a child can help facilitate potential. For an entertaining, but poignant satire about parenting in ways that encourage creativity, check out *Ten Ways to Destroy the Imagination of Your Child* by Anthony Esolen.[50]

4. Families should work to be positive in their interactions in order to maximize learning and promote forgiveness. Making mistakes is inevitable. Parents and children should work to create a supportive rather than defensive climate.

5. Positive communication in families should result in the best outcomes for children. Families should invest in providing the needed knowledge, skills, and experiences to set their kids up for life. This is a long-term investment strategy that reduces problems and promotes resilience.

6. "Families should use positive communication with children as a means to increase happiness."[51] Socha and Yingling suggest this happens when families (1) create a positive communication climate in everyday life, (2) encourage children to develop virtuous character, and (3) coach children as they encounter difficult situations in life. The home should be a safe space for children to explore ideas, get advice, and find loving support.

These guidelines provide some practical handrails for enhancing positive communication with children. Some of the theoretical underpinning for these types of recommendations comes from a suite of ideas on parent-child interactions. Family is a primary locus for training infants, toddlers, young children, and even adolescents, so what happens in a family impacts children long after they leave the home.[52] These parent-child interaction theories emphasize different aspects of how family communication matters. We review Attachment Theory, family communication patterns, and parenting styles.

Attachment Theory

John Bowlby argued that a secure parent-child attachment is essential for healthy emotional development. As a psychologist of the 1960s, Bowlby was heavily influenced by Freud's psychoanalytic perspective and also by behaviorist paradigms. In many ways, Bowlby designed Attachment Theory to "accommodate all those phenomena to which Freud called attention."[53] His theory was based on observing mother-infant interactions and theorizing how these behaviors and experiences translated into mental representations about the self and others. Later conceptualizations summarized attachment as interactive responses that are habituated over time.[54] Attachment styles, from a communication perspective, are "chronic interpersonal styles that reflect people's general beliefs about themselves and others—beliefs about whether the self is worthy of care and affection, and beliefs about whether other people are generally dependable and responsive."[55] These beliefs manifest into four attachment styles: secure, avoidant, anxious-ambivalent, and disorganized.

Bowlby suggested that a *secure attachment* provides a child with the comfort and security needed to construct healthy mental models of self and social life. When infant caregivers are available, responsive, and affectionate, kids feel safe to explore the world around them with the assurance that someone will respond helpfully if needed. *Avoidant attachment* showed up when infants displayed unusual independence and autonomy. This attachment style develops from unavailable, cold, and non-responsive caregivers. A third style, *anxious attachment*, develops when early caregiver interaction is inconsistent or the caregiver responds in unpredictable ways. An additional attachment style was proposed to explain seemingly "conflicted, disoriented, or fearful behavior shown by infants toward their caregiver" and was labeled *disorganized attachment*.[56] Bowlby believed that once established—usually around one to two years of age—attachment styles are relatively stable throughout the rest of a person's life.

In the general population (i.e., those not seeking psychological counseling or not distressed), the majority of children are securely attached to their mothers and fathers. When there are dozens or hundreds of studies on a particular topic, like attachment, a meta-analysis looks across a large number of studies to estimate how the variables or constructs work in general. A study using this methodology estimated the proportion of attachment styles in the general population. For children under two years old, the study found 62% of kids were securely attached, 15% were avoidant, 9% anxious, and 15% were classified as disorganized attachment.[57] For children in clinical or distressed samples, the proportions were nearly reversed. Only 9% of maltreated children were classified as secure attachment, 28% avoidant, 15% anxious, and nearly half (48%) exhibited disorganized attachment.[58]

Given these differences in parent-child communication, it is not surprising that secure attachment has been linked with a host of positive outcomes. A meta-analysis of attachment and regulation of emotion found that securely attached children were happier, less sad, and showed more ability to control or regulate their emotions. Secure children also used more positive coping strategies, including seeking social support.[59] Other meta-analytic studies showed that insecurely attached youth experience higher levels of depression[60] and more eating disorders.[61] These findings replicate a number of other review studies that detail benefits that come from secure attachment for children and youth.

Attachment can be thought of as a relational foundation that parents provide their children. Because infant interaction primarily occurs within family settings, parent-child interaction becomes a template or set of expectations for how to communicate. With babies, it is easy to view attachment as a one-way process: parents set the stage onto which their children debut. However, children are active communication agents, and regardless of their attachment style, they influence the interactions that occur. A common sequence of interaction could be when a parent instructs a child, the child ignores or disobeys, the parent yells, the child continues to ignore or disobey, so the parent yells more with a changed tone of voice, so the child responds.[62] This type of escalation results as an *inter*action, which is dependent on both parent and child communication decisions.

||||||||▶ **Application Activity 13.3:**
Attachment and God

Psychologists have found that individuals' beliefs about God boil down into two broad categories:[63] (1) "a kindly or benevolent God (e.g., 'forgiving,' 'loving,' 'merciful') and (2) a wrathful or authoritarian God (e.g., 'critical,' 'punishing,' 'stern')."[64]

- Which view of God do you tend to hold?
- How do you think your childhood attachment experiences inform this view?

||||||| ▶ Application Activity 13.3 *continued*:
Attachment and God

One of the amazing teachings of Scripture is the paradox of a loving *and* just God. Both views of God are accurate, in a sense. Many
other world religions, and even some Christian teaching, focus on
the wrathful, authoritarian nature of God. However, the Bible clearly teaches that Christ bore the wrath of God on behalf of humanity
(see Isa. 53:4–6; John 3:36; 2 Cor. 5:21). God is loving and merciful, eager to be reconciled to humankind, including you personally
(Rom. 5:10; 2 Cor. 5:20). The story of Jesus's death, burial, and resurrection is one where God himself removed sin and every other
barrier that stood in the way of connecting with him. God is love
(1 John 4:16). In the midst of our own mistakes and transgressions,
God loved us. As Ephesians 2:4–5 (NASB) clearly teaches, "But God,
being rich in mercy, because of his great love with which he loved
us, even when we were dead in our wrongdoings, made us alive together with Christ (by grace you have been saved)." The Bible does
not gloss over the wrath of God, but displays how, in benevolence,
Christ absorbed it.

Many have a tendency to understand God based on their own experiences—good and bad—with parents. We anthropomorphize God.
This can leave a stumbling block for many who were not securely
attached to their mothers and fathers (some 38% of children), or
for those who grew up without a father or family at all. It is God
who removes the barriers to our knowing and loving him fully. In
Colossians 2:8–15, Paul warns that we should not let existing philosophies or prevailing beliefs in this world take us captive. God has
made us alive with Christ, has forgiven all our sins, has canceled our
debt, taking it away and nailing it to the cross, and has disarmed
our accusers. God's grace, fully displayed through Christ, allows us
to have confident, secure, and direct attachment to God.

- Reflect on these ideas. In what ways could a "secure
  attachment" to God change the way you feel? Act?

Family Communication Patterns Theory

Family Communication Patterns (FCP) Theory developed as a confluence
of two separate theories. One line of thinking was aimed at classifying

different marital types. This research identified traditional, independent, and separate marriages based on couples' ideology and level of interdependence.[65] From this theory, FCP focuses on different types of families. Another area of research was geared toward understanding how families processed one-way, mass media messages that they encountered through television.[66] This theory proposed that to interpret new media messages, people either focused on inherent characteristics of the message they saw or they deferred to how their social network (family) responded to the message. From this theory, FCP offers two dimensions or orientations toward family interaction.

Merging these lines of research, FCP describes two different family communication orientations which makes four family types. First, *conversation orientation* refers to "the degree to which families create a communication environment in which all family members are encouraged to participate in unrestrained interaction about a wide range of topics," stressing the importance of openly sharing ideas, expressing concerns, and participating in decision-making.[67] This does not describe the amount of communication that happens in a family, but characterizes the general disposition of a family toward expressiveness. Second, *conformity orientation* refers to "the degree to which family communication stresses a climate of homogeneity of attitudes, values, and beliefs," emphasizing uniformity and obedience to parents, with parents often making decisions without consulting the children.[68] These two orientations are considered orthogonal, that is, they operate independently from each other.

Crossing these two orientations, like the x and y axes of a graph, creates four family quadrants, which depict four family types: (1) protective (high conformity, low conversation), (2) pluralistic (low conformity, high conversation), (3) consensual (high conformity, high conversation), and (4) laissez-faire families (low conformity, low conversation). Unlike attachment styles, FCP does not theorize that any one type of family is better than another.[69] For example, a conformity orientation might be done in love, so it could be an overall positive orientation for a family. However, conformity could be demanded without relational warmth, which could lead to an overall negative experience.[70] Neither is a high conversation orientation theorized to be better than a low conversation orientation.

Empirical research on FCP, however, demonstrates that families with high conversation orientation, regardless of their conformity orientation, tend to result in better psychological, social, and behavioral outcomes for children and youth. In one observational study, conversation orientation—operationalized by coding parent-child communication, listening, and warmth—was inversely related to youth behavior problems; that is, when there were high levels of warmth, there were low levels of youth behavior problems.[71] A cross cultural study found that across the U.S., China, and Saudi Arabia conversation orientation was a positive predictor of both collaboration and compromise conflict styles, whereas conformity orientation predicted accommodation and avoidance conflict styles.[72] Similarly, research reported a positive association between conversation orientation and young adults' perceptions of co-parental communication quality, but it was negatively associated with conformity orientation.[73] Mental health, lower stress levels, and more communication ability were all related to higher levels of conversation orientation.[74] Based on a meta-analysis of FCP, conversation orientation consistently benefitted youth and young adults, but associations with conformity orientation were mixed.[75] Therefore, while theoretically all family types are equal, empirical findings suggest that consensual and pluralistic families benefit children the most.

Parenting Styles

A final broad theory of family interactions emerged from qualitative observations of parenting. Diane Baumrind introduced three parenting styles: authoritative, authoritarian, and permissive.[76] *Authoritative* parents are "warm, firm, and accepting of their [child's] needs for psychological autonomy."[77] Like secure attachment, authoritative parents balance authority and connection, structure and relationship. An authoritative parent provides "an emotional climate of warmth and involvement intended to encourage a child's independence and autonomous self-expression."[78] This parent type also engages in confrontative control (e.g., demanding, firm, instructive) rather than coercive control (e.g., intrusive, manipulative, punitive, restrictive).[79] Research consistently has shown that authoritative parents provide the best chance for their children and youth to thrive. Around the year 2000, Laurence Steinberg, the then-president of the Society for Adolescents, presented: "We can stop asking what type of parenting most positively affects adolescent development. We know the answer to this question."[80]

The other two parenting styles—authoritarian and permissive—fall out of balance on one side or the other of authoritative parenting. On the one hand, *authoritarian* parents are firm but lack connection and warmth.

They prize structure over relationship and authority over connection. A *permissive* parent, on the other hand, prizes warmth over firmness. They lack structure and authority. Steinberg concluded, "The challenges ahead involve finding ways to educate adults with regard to how to be authoritative, and help those who are not authoritative to change."[81]

Developing Strong Families

Just as evidence clearly points to the fact that authoritative parenting with appropriate autonomy granting is best for kids, the evidence also links secure attachment and high conversation orientation (i.e., consensual and pluralistic families) to better outcomes for children and youth. Although the Bible does not clearly command "thou shalt be authoritative parents," we can safely assume that God intended for children to thrive. Thus, the attributes of parents and parenting that lead to secure, communicatively oriented, and authoritative parenting honor God. In the Shema of Deuteronomy 6:7, for example, parents are instructed to respond to children's questions and maintain an ongoing relationship "when you sit at home and when you walk along the road, when you lie down and when you get up." This teaching suggests that parents have authority over their children, but they are also to maintain an open relationship with them.

Consistently, research on families and family interaction points to the positive, overlapping qualities of parents. For example, Nick Stinnett and John DeFrain identified six characteristics of strong families, including a commitment to one another, mutual appreciation, open communication, shared time together, attentiveness to spirituality, and adaptability.[82] Similarly, the pro-family Christian organization Focus on the Family describes seven traits of effective parenting, which are "well researched, based on the foundations provided through Scripture, enriched by years of application in family counseling settings, as well as the great research surrounding the authoritative style of parenting."[83] Its model includes adaptability, respect, intentionality, love, boundaries, grace and forgiveness, and gratitude. These typologies overlap and could be essentialized in this way: healthy families prioritize positive relationships based on mutual respect through quality communication.

Important Parent-Child Conversations

Strong families persist and grow across time. Of course, there will be some times when different traits are absent or stunted, but in general, families should continually exhibit and pursue traits of strong families. This includes a need to encourage open, honest, and direct conversations across all subjects, even taboo topics.

Two specific topics that have garnered research attention are parent-child conversations about sex and drugs. These are among the most avoided parent conversation topics for adolescents and young adults, especially with fathers and stepparents.[84] Yet, parents should weigh in on even these taboo topics. As summarized in a research study about drug talks, "Youth hear direct messages about substances from media, peers, and prevention programs, and thus parents, too, should join the conversation with their youth about substances."[85] The same could be said about sex. Television and movies, peers, teachers, and classroom curricula and discussions all vie for youth's attention and invite (sometimes demand) conformity to their views on sex. Parents need to address these issues. Evidence shows that parents are an important influence throughout childhood and early adolescence. Even as peer influence increases during adolescence, parental influence remains strong.[86]

As you might expect from the review of different parenting theories, findings show that when parents and children share expressive and warm relationships when talking about topics like drugs, children do best. For example, when family environments are characterized by high conversation orientations and parents directly discuss drug-use expectations, the children report the lowest levels of substance use, which contrasts with the least effective family environments that are not expressive and where parents avoid directly addressing the topic of substances or substance use.[87] Similarly, a European study that collected data from multiple countries showed that families with warm relationships (i.e., authoritative and permissive) reported significantly less substance use than families with low warmth (i.e., neglectful or authoritarian parents).[88]

Other communication studies confirm that having some conversation is better than no conversation, and having direct conversations about drug use and expectations, rather than merely hinting about it, is most effective for preventing early substance use.[89] In general, research supports the claim that parents can help their children navigate decisions around drug use.

So, what does a "drug talk" sound like, and when does it happen?

Family communication scholar Michelle Miller-Day set out to answer these questions.[90] She studied freshmen entering college and asked them to share about their experiences as youth. From this data, she developed a typology of "drug talks" that ranged from ongoing conversations that parents initiated and had with their children to one-time lectures. Some parents also avoided directly talking about the subject and only hinted their positions on drugs, whereas others were explicit. This created four groups: direct ongoing, direct situated, indirect ongoing, and indirect situated types of conversations. A final category was youth who had never had a "drug talk" with their parents.

Research with over 2,000 early adolescents showed that most 7th through 9th graders reported having situated direct (32%) and ongoing direct (25%) conversations. About 31% reported one of the indirect styles, and only about 8% were in the "never talked" category.[91] The study also included messages youth recalled hearing from their parents. Below is a summary of three trends in these messages within each style:

> First, indirect styles demonstrated more variation in the messages. While direct styles almost uniformly conveyed "don't do drugs," indirect styles included everything from "it's your choice" and "they know I won't" messages. Second, responses coded into the ongoing direct style shared that the impetus for the ongoing messages came from life circumstances, such as school programming, drug treatment programs, and parental occupations. Finally, a large proportion of messages coded into the "never talked" style also was coded as "they know I won't." So while youth reported that their parents never talked with them, they also shared reasons why they have not had drug talks. Most of these responses shared that youth were trusted to make good decisions.[92]

Ironically, the study showed that youth in the "never talked" style, although they reported that their parents could trust them not to use drugs, were the group that reported the highest levels of drug use. These trends in messages heard by youth also point to the interface between family and other spheres of society.

In terms of talking about sex, a line of research has examined "memorable messages" teenagers and young adults hear from their family members.[93] Qualitative analysis of these types of messages show that they are impactful,[94] can be absorbed from family interactions or come specifically from fathers, mothers, siblings, and society,[95] and often share different guidance and expectations for daughters and sons.[96] For example, women receive more negative messages about sex (e.g., consequences for having sex including pregnancy and sexually transmitted infections), whereas men receive more messages about the pleasure of sex.[97] As well, mothers' messages assume that men tend to initiate sex, so women must be sexual gatekeepers.[98] A consistent finding is that most messages are negatively framed, meaning that messages include warnings, express harmful or hurtful experiences with sex and reproductive health, or share that sex should be reserved for marriage or loving, committed relationships.[99] Similarly, studies suggest that with "transparent and supportive conversations, women noted transitioning to a deeper understanding and acceptance of their bodies, functions, and sexuality."[100] Many of these studies focus on sexual empowerment, especially for women. From our view, parents should share direct messages within the context of warm, supportive relationships. Moreover, offering a positive view of sex as God's design (see Chapter 11) before offering any warnings or prohibitions may help adolescents and young adults gain a holistic and mature view of their own bodies and sexuality.

Research supports the idea that parents should have open lines of communication and share direct socializing messages across a variety of topics, like drugs, sex, dating, religion, and major life-decisions. Equally important to sharing their perspective is listening, allowing children to question, explore, reason, and discuss their opinions and experiences. Connecting parents and children in open, honest conversation creates space for relationships to flourish.

Conclusion

While each individual child has just one family experience, children as a group have diverse experiences. It can be tempting to think that whatever we encountered as kids (be it good or bad) is normal, but there are an array of family environments and communication events that children face. In this chapter, we overviewed these situations, considered parents' experiences with children, siblings, language development, and parent-child communication theories. We also presented some of the best parenting practices for having drug-talks, sex-talks, and other important, taboo conversations. Families are the most important context for children. As Scripture records, it was within the context of the family that Jesus "grew and became strong; he was filled with wisdom, and the grace of God was upon him" (Luke 2:40).

Chapter 14

Parental Modeling across Spiritual and Practical Domains

Chapter Summary: The central Jewish prayer, the Shema, is couched within a family model for integrating God into family life: "These words, which I am commanding you today, shall be on your heart. You shall teach them diligently to your children. . ." (Deut. 6:4–9, NASB). There are parallels between God's command to Adam to be fruitful and multiply and Jesus's command to his followers to go and make disciples. This parallel implies that there is no better opportunity to disciple than in the family. This chapter includes models for child-training, such as behavior modification (reinforcement), social learning, and psychological control techniques, and their consequences. It also describes some fundamental parenting skills that consistently result in more well-adjusted children and adults and concludes with a passage about discipline from the Book of Hebrews.

Introduction

THIS CHAPTER IS ABOUT COMMUNICATION between parents and children, including how parents discipline their kids. Take a minute and write down the first three to five words that come to mind when you hear the word "discipline." Did you write things like "being grounded," "spanking," "time-out," or "no screen time"? Now think about an Olympic athlete. When we say the word "discipline" in the context of an elite competitor, what comes to mind? Write down the first three to five words you think of. Did you write words like "intense training," "regimented," "routine," "coaching," or "healthy diet"? The root word for discipline really is disciple.[1] It is associated with learning and discernment more than some form of punishment or behavioral control. Discipline is synonymous with training. In the context of family communication, parents disciple (not just discipline) their children. Let's look at discipleship more closely.

When asked, "What is the most important commandment?" Jesus responded by quoting the Shema: "Love the Lord your God with all your heart and with all your soul and with all your mind" (Matt. 22:36–40), which comes from Deuteronomy. Here it is in context.

> Hear, O Israel: The Lord our God, the Lord is one. Love the Lord your God with all your heart and with all your soul and with all your strength. These commandments that I give you today are to be on your hearts. *Impress them on your children.* Talk about them when you sit at home and when you walk along the road, when you lie down and when you get up. Tie them as symbols on your hands and bind them on your foreheads. Write them on the doorframes of your houses and on your gates. (Deut. 6:4–9, emphasis added)

The greatest commandment was to be taught and modeled in families. The passage emphasizes this context again in verses 20 to 25. God was commanding parents to disciple their children into faithful, comprehensive love for God.

The discipleship theme is also seen in the parallels between God's first commandment and Jesus's last commandment on Earth. After his death and resurrection, Jesus gives the command to "go and make disciples of all nations" (Matt. 28:19–20). He is charging his followers with the responsibility to reproduce themselves throughout the world in every nation. This "Great Commission" parallels God's first command to Adam and Eve. In the beginning, God blessed humankind and instructed them: "Be fruitful and increase in number; fill the earth and subdue it" (Gen. 1:28). There was an expectation and an empowerment for humans not only to reproduce but also to bring all of creation under God's dominion. The parallels are striking, and most people will never have a better opportunity to "go and make disciples" than in their own homes.

In this chapter we review research on parenting alongside biblical analysis. We begin with a differentiation between mothering and fathering. We then turn to understanding discipline in families. We include both classic and contemporary models of parenting, such as behavior modification, social learning, psychological control techniques, and emotion coaching. We also include tips for applying parenting practices in ways that result in positive outcomes for children and adults. At the end of the chapter, we return to consider discipline and discipleship from the Book of Hebrews.

Parenting Versus Mothering and Fathering?

Let's start with mothering and fathering. In the Hebrew lexicon of the Old Testament, there is no word for "parent," per se. The position and activity of parenting is described through the roles of father and mother. This is not to say that parents or parenting is not a viable concept, but it brings up an interesting consideration. Can parenting roles best be understood as mothering and fathering?

A passage in the New Testament, which in Greek does include a term for parent, illustrates ways that mothers and fathers may differ in their parenting approaches. Aligning with the idea that the Body of Christ is the family of God (as presented in Chapter 2), Paul addresses the congregation in Thessalonica as "brothers and sisters" (1 Thess. 2:1). He continues the familial analogy and describes aspects of relating in ways that reflect mothering and fathering. He says that like a mother, his teammates "cared for you" and were "delighted to share with you . . . [their] lives" (1 Thess. 2:7-8). And "exhorting and encouraging . . . as a father would his own children" (1 Thess. 2:11, NASB), Paul's team urged the congregation to live up to the family name (1 Thess. 2:11-12). Mothers and fathers both are depicted as loving, but their modes of communication appear different. Mothers cared and shared, while fathers encouraged and urged.

While there are many overlaps and similarities, some social science evidence supports the idea that fathers and mothers also play distinct roles in the parenting enterprise. This is a logical extension of evidence that males and females are different and polaric complements (see Chapter 11). For example, evidence from observations of male and female infants as they are born (and therefore before they can be socialized into certain behavior patterns) shows that differences in behavioral proclivities are natural. Female infants tend to be more wakeful, look around more, and make eye-contact after birth more than male infants.[2] Extending these findings into adulthood, Michael Lamb and colleagues, in their biosocial theory of fatherhood, present empirical evidence demonstrating that fathers and mothers engage with children differently.[3] In general, these findings show that mothers and fathers interact verbally with different styles. Mothers tend to be more soothing and rhythmic in their vocalizations toward their infants. Fathers, however, are more explosive, unpredictable in both physical and verbal interactions. In addition, fathers engage in more play activities with children than mothers. Other research into social perception demonstrates that tasks like bathing, lap-sitting, and kissing children are viewed as more socially appropriate for mothers than for fathers.[4] Theories that predict a father's investment in a child propose that father involvement is based on a man's belief about his role and sociodemographic factors.[5] For example, paternity certitude is one of the cognitive predictors for fathers investing in children. This concept only applies to fathers because pregnancy and birth experiences make motherhood a certainty. Indeed, research and theory over the past few decades has argued for a more comprehensive understanding of fatherhood as a distinct role and activity from motherhood.[6]

Drawing distinctions between men and women and between fathers and mothers can help to illuminate the contributions of each sex and the importance of complementary influences. Too often, social science has attempted to gloss over gender as an important construct or to write off differences as individual rather than patterns that reflect design. Unfortunately, examining only "caregiver" effects or "parenting" influences potentially obscures how men and women uniquely enact their roles in ways that can benefit children within the dynamics of a loving union of polar complements (i.e., biblical marriage covenant).

One important way that family communication and childhood outcomes are impacted is through the absence of a father. Fatherlessness or father-absence is not just correlated with negative child, adolescent, and young adult outcomes, but also actually causes some of these harms.[7] The National Fatherhood Initiative reports data from the United States Census Bureau showing that one in four children experience fatherlessness (i.e., they live without a co-residential father, stepfather, or adoptive father). According to the report, children who experience fatherlessness are:

- At four times a greater risk of poverty,
- Seven times more likely to experience teen pregnancy,
- More likely to experience behavioral problems,
- More likely to be victims of child abuse or neglect,
- Twice as likely to die as an infant,

- More likely to abuse drugs and alcohol,
- More likely to commit a crime and to be incarcerated,
- Twice as likely to drop out of high school,
- And twice as likely to be obese.[8]

The research clearly shows the impact father-absence can have on boys and girls. Research affirms that children do best when reared by their own, married biological parents in stable and loving homes.[9]

To be clear, these harms are not an indictment on single mothers, grandparents, or others who fill a parenting void. Nor are these general statistics a sentencing or prognosis for individual children who grow up without a father. Differences in outcomes are not because youth are "more problematic or psychologically disturbed than youth in two-parent biological families, but the relational ambiguity and inconsistency as well as the situational complexity of stepfamily living make life more difficult to manage. Relating becomes more strenuous and less stable."[10] People often cope with hard situations in remarkable ways, and generally, having at least one quality, supportive parent-child relationship will trump negative contexts, experiences, and events.[11]

The interplay between family communication and family form has yet to be fully described. Focused studies of communication in multiple family forms, particularly communication of fathers and mothers, will help to improve understanding of the unique contributions fathers and mothers make toward children and adolescents as well as ways that family form interacts with parents' abilities to communicate.[12] As honest social inquiry progresses, we hypothesize that children will continue to be resilient to the variety of family forms they might experience throughout their lifespan and that God's design for married parenting will shine through as the most beneficial family form society can achieve.

Discipline

One specific way that mothers and fathers influence their children is through discipline. As we presented, discipline means training, with parents making disciples of their kids.

Family is a power system that God created, where children by design are under parental authority.[13] This design orders three unique roles—fathers, mothers, and children—into a structure that mirrors the triune God.[14] Family roles, all equally valued, each have responsibilities. Children are to obey their parents: "Honor your father and mother, so that you may live long in the land the Lord your God is giving you" (Exod. 20:12); "Children obey your parents in the Lord, for this is right" (Eph. 6:1; see also Col. 3:20). "Obey" (*hupakouo*) in Ephesians and Colossians is a compound Greek word for "under" and "hear."[15] It implies listening in subordination, giving heed to one's parents. Obeying parents is where most children first learn to submit to authority. Mothers and fathers also have responsibilities. These duties include teaching (Deut. 4:10), training (Eph. 6:4), disciplining (Prov. 13:24), loving (Titus 2:4), and serving as godly role models (Deut. 4:9). Family structure, then, creates a power system of authority and submission.

Think about when a child is born. As helpless infants, unable to move or feed themselves, parents hold near absolute authority over children, a power to protect and nurture. There is still an interaction between parents and children, and babies still influence family dynamics profoundly, but babies have little inclination and even less choice about whether to comply. When children are young, this power structure is necessary as it helps to ensure a child's safety and learning. As children mature into adolescents and adults, however, they seek out autonomy, and this developmental process requires a renegotiation of the parent-child power structure.[16] One helpful concept to distinguish between a healthy and an unhealthy renegotiation process is the differentiation of self. [17]

Family therapist Murray Bowen proposed that to develop in a healthy way, children have to learn to differentiate from their parents.[18] Each person is unique. Even in families that share many commonalities, kids need to grow in their autonomy and unique identity. The differentiation process is both psychological and interpersonal.[19] Psychologically, children need to decrease their reliance on others' emotions to determine their own, and they need to maintain a well-defined sense of self and personal conviction. Interpersonally, differentiating children need to allow space for intimacy—not cutting off completely from others, but also not fusing with others' attitudes, beliefs, and behaviors.

Studies have found that differentiating from parents is beneficial across racial categories[20] and with both genders.[21] A review of multiple studies found that low levels of differentiation are associated with chronic anxiety, poor marital satisfaction, and psychological distress.[22] Conversely, young adults who reported differentiation were less controlling, less neurotic, less distant, less socially inhibited, more assertive, less overly-accommodating, less self-sacrificing, and less needy than people who did not have high levels of differentiation.[23] To summarize: "differentiation of self plays a central role in healthy adult development."[24] The inherent power structure of early childhood needs to realign and be reassigned as children age in order to develop mature, contributing family members.

Control and Influence

A helpful framework for understanding the process of differentiation from the perspective of parenting can be to imagine two independent dimensions of discipline: control and influence. When babies are born, parents have almost zero influence over cognitive processes, like decision making, and total control over physical processes, like bathing and feeding. As children age and become capable of more self-care and reasoning, control decreases and influence increases. A two-year-old may throw a fit about not getting an ice cream cone but has no power to purchase one himself. Parents have the "power of the purse string" as well as the threat of force, because they are bigger and stronger than their young child.[25] They also have some influence. Through some of the discipline techniques we describe later in this chapter, parents can coach their children, offer advice, or develop systems of reward and punishment.

These influence processes may continue to develop as children age into youth and adulthood. As new life events take place (e.g., buying a first car, applying for a mortgage, having a baby), adults often seek their parents' advice or ask for them to share their experiences. Control also can, and should, decrease as children and youth age. As we reviewed in the previous chapter, autonomy-granting is an important parenting function. It can be difficult for some parents to relinquish control over their children because it comes with the opportunity to fail and experience pain. However, without the opportunity to experience autonomy, children may never mature or effectively differentiate from their parents. The popular *Love and Logic* parenting book is based on this premise; that is, we love our children so much that we set appropriate boundaries (control), but we also allow our children to make their own decisions (influence), experiencing the natural and logical consequences of those decisions.[26]

Consider Figure 14.1. It includes dimensions of control and influence as percentages on the y-axis and across the bottom of the chart is a child's age. At birth, control is near 100% and influence is near 0%. As the child ages, these parenting dimensions begin to shift, but the graph is unfinished. Where do you think the lines of control and influence should cross? In other words, when should parents begin exerting more influence than control over their children?

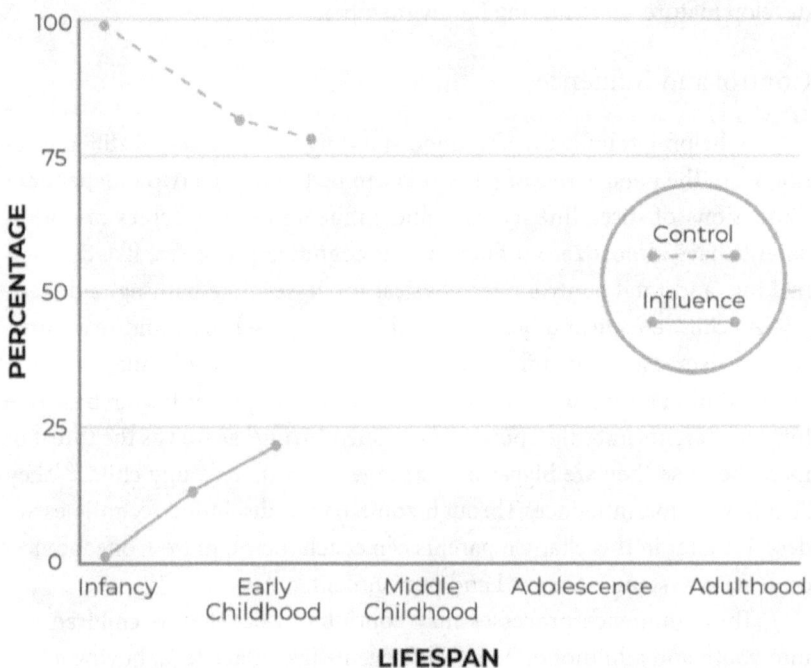

Figure 14.1: Influence and Control.

If parents are to wisely wield influence and control, they need strategies or parenting practices to utilize. Measures of parenting practices include a variety of specific tactics. For example, in a compendium of discipline techniques, Murray Straus and Angèle Fauchier list the following: corporal punishment (e.g., spanking), deprivation of privileges (e.g., taking away a toy), diversion (e.g., distracting from one behavior with another task or toy), explanation or teaching (e.g., lecturing, reminding about rules), ignoring misbehavior (e.g., walking into a different room), penalty tasks (e.g., assigning extra chores), psychological aggression (e.g., yelling, shaming child), reward (e.g., praising, giving money for good behavior), and monitoring (e.g., checking to see if behavior is complete, saying "I've got my eye on you").[27] These specific practices are helpful for training children. For the most part, they derive from a few basic theories of how people learn and how parents train. Let's turn to look at the theories that underlie such a diverse array of parenting practices.

Classical/Operant Conditioning

Have you ever heard of Pavlov's dogs? A Skinner box? One line of questioning that psychologists pursued was how people learn to behave in certain ways. The result is what we often call classical conditioning, or behavior modification. The premise of conditioning is that people tend to do things that are rewarding and tend to avoid things that are not. This is why it is usually easier to eat foods you like (maybe ice cream) and harder to eat foods you do not like (maybe raw cauliflower). Even if you know eating something does not match your goals, because it is enjoyable it is easy to develop a habit of it. Conditioning aims to associate behaviors that are desired with rewards that may have nothing to do with that specific behavior. Consider again the eating example. You may reward yourself for a strenuous workout with a protein-packed ice cream milkshake. The workout is not inherently pleasurable, but the reward of a delicious ice cream will encourage the behavior. Parenting through various forms of conditioning is quite common.

To explain the theory best, we first must clarify some terms. In the theory, *reinforcement* aims to strengthen or encourage a behavior, while *punishment* aims to weaken a behavior.[28] Both reinforcement and punishment can operate through positive and negative mechanisms. In the theory, *positive* means "adding" something new, like a plus sign, which introduces something to either reinforce or punish. *Negative* means "removing," like a minus sign, which takes something away in order to reinforce or punish. Behavior modification techniques, then, occur when a desired behavior is strengthened through adding something rewarding (*positive reinforcement*) or removing something unpleasant (*negative reinforcement*), or through weakening an undesired behavior through adding something unpleasant (*positive punishment*) or through removing rewards (*negative punishment*).

So, if a parent tells a teenager, "I'm taking away the keys to your car if you stay out past curfew," what type of behavior modification technique is it? First, ask yourself, "Is the aim to strengthen or weaken a behavior?" In this case, the goal is to weaken the behavior of missing curfew. Then ask, "Is something being added or taken away?" Here, the keys (driving privileges) are being taken away. Because the goal of the discipline is to weaken a behavior by taking something away, it is negative punishment. If we reframed the goal as strengthening the behavior of abiding by curfew, then the technique would be negative (taking away keys) reinforcement (strengthening curfew compliance). It can be difficult to distinguish between negative punishment and negative reinforcement because it depends on how the conditioning goal is framed. As another example, consider when a parent tells a child, "If you do well in school this term, I'll give you $5 for each 'A' and $2 for each 'B'!" Again, ask whether the goal is to strengthen or weaken a behavior and is something being added or taken away? In this case, the goal is to strengthen getting good grades by adding a monetary reward, so it is a positive reinforcement technique.

||||||||▶ Application Activity 14.1:
Marriage Behavior Modification

Behavior modification techniques do not just work in parent-child relationships. Check out the article "What Shamu Taught Me about a Happy Marriage" by Amy Sutherland for examples of how it can be applied to romantic relationships.[29]

- How have you used behavior modification techniques in your relationships with siblings, roommates, or dating partners?
- What are the pros and cons of using behavior modification in your relationships?

Research on operant conditioning is extensive. It generally shows that reinforcement is a more sustainable and long-lasting training technique than punishment. It helps transfer behaviors from being externally motivated toward intrinsically motivated. Psychologists have identified several potential problems with using punishment.[30] For example, punishment is often a quick fix. It tends to suppress behavior, not deter it completely. In other words, when the threat of punishment is no longer present, the behavior may surface again. Punishment also has a tendency to increase aggression because punishment is not pleasant. Additionally, punishment may inadvertently model unwanted behaviors. While reinforcement is aimed at strengthening behaviors that a parent would want to see their children replicate, punishment focuses on behaviors that are unwanted without necessarily demonstrating behaviors that are expected or desired. Kids are left guessing what they should do, even if it is clear what they should not do. For these reasons, many psychologists caution against punishment and advocate instead for exclusive use of positive reinforcement. While we believe there can be a time and place for punishment that results in immediate obedience (e.g., when imminent danger looms), a pattern of punishment over reinforcement and other tactics can be problematic.

Points to Ponder 14.2:
To Spank or Not to Spank?

Spanking is a subset of other forms of physical (corporal) punishment. It weakens a behavior because it introduces something undesirable (i.e., positive punishment). Many either prohibit or endorse spanking without considering research on it. And the research is divided. Some show that spanking harms children, and others show that spanking leads to long-term positive benefits. From our view, if parents put parameters around spanking or other power-based positive punishment tactics in age-appropriate, child-specific, and relationship-grounded ways, then it can enhance benefits without introducing harm. When used outside of these bounds, however, it certainly can damage children. Like yelling or other forms of punishment, spanking can result in expedient compliance, which sometimes is necessary to preserve the health and safety of young children (e.g., stop a child from poking a pen into an electric outlet). But it should be used within parameters. We list some points to clarify how and when spanking might be appropriate.

1. Physical abuse and severe corporal punishment (e.g., hitting, pushing, grabbing, shoving, slapping in the face, boxing the ears, shaking, beating with a stick, throwing things) harms children and is *never* appropriate discipline.

2. Spanking is not abuse and is defined by the following criteria:

   a) "spanking is physically non-injurious,

   b) intended to modify behavior,

   c) administered with an opened hand to the extremities or buttocks,"[31] and

   d) "inflicts a minor, temporary level of physical pain, if that."[32]

3. Spanking is most effective for children between the ages of 2–6 years old and introduces harm when used with children younger than 18-months or after puberty.[33]

4. Spanking is beneficial for gaining compliance (it can be helpful to enforce other forms of discipline, like time-out), and it may be especially useful for controlling a child's defiant non-compliance.[34]

5. Parents should be calm and in control of their own emotions when spanking, never angry.

6. Spanking should be used sparingly, within the bounds of an overwhelmingly positive and loving relationship, as part of a wide array of parenting discipleship practices.[35]

As research on mother's discipline of toddlers concludes, "behavior improves when mothers skillfully vary their disciplinary tactics to fit the type of noncompliance."[36] There are numerous options for training children. Spanking is only one. Knowing more about a variety of discipline tactics will enable appropriate measures that fit with each novel situation.

Social Learning (Cognitive) Theory

Behavior modification techniques learned from operant conditioning are only part of the story of how parents train (disciple) their children. Social Learning Theory (later called Social Cognitive Theory), proposed by Albert Bandura, expanded on behaviorist ideas and suggested that people also learn from observation, making decisions based on their assessment of the outcomes they witness. Bandura reasoned that "although behavior can be shaped into new patterns . . . by rewarding and punishing consequences, learning would be exceedingly laborious and hazardous if it proceeded solely on this basis."[37] In the family context, children watch others (e.g., siblings, parents, aunts, uncles). They imitate their actions when they seem rewarding and avoid behavior patterns that seem to result in punishment or undesired consequences. Sayings like "some things are caught, not taught" and "the apple doesn't fall far from the tree" reflect the fact that kids often imitate family members.

The basic concept of the theory is easy to grasp. Parents model all kinds of behaviors and in so doing set expectations that their children carry with them into society and into future relationships. How parents engage in conflict-resolution discussions (e.g., calmly arguing, yelling, demand-withdrawal) models how children will engage in these conversations. Routinely kids will mimic these behaviors when they disagree with siblings. But these behaviors also come up again when people enter their own romantic relationships. Families develop routines that model expectations about how people should display physical affection (or not), whether to gossip about others (or not), how to eat healthy foods, what kinds of sleep patterns are good, as well as a host of other arenas. Families define what is "normal" for their kids, especially when they are young. Social Learning Theory offers some insight into these processes and introduces some helpful concepts that describe how children might evaluate what they observe.[38]

Psychological Control Techniques

Moving even further away from behavioral control, some parents rely on psychological techniques to socialize children. You have probably heard of a parent using "reverse psychology" to trick a child into doing something. Or maybe someone you know is good at "guilt tripping." These are forms of psychological control, defined as a process by which parents exert dominance over their children by controlling their thoughts and feelings rather than just behavior.[39] Psychological control entails "the relative degree of emotional autonomy that the parent allows."[40] It encourages dependence on a parent through demeaning or invalidating feelings, limiting verbal and emotional expression, withdrawing love and approval, using guilt induction, instilling anxiety, or attacking a child verbally.[41] While psychological manipulation tends to be more efficient at gaining compliance than physical control, it also is more insidious.[42]

Communication scholars have explored the interpersonal power dynamics of psychological control and theorized "inconsistent nurturing as control" and "necessary convergence communication."[43] *Inconsistent Nurturing as Control Theory* argues that intermittent rewarding (inconsistent nurturing behavior) reinforces undesired behavior.[44] Applying this theory to discipline, parents using inconsistent nurturing behaviors are using rewards and punishments that ultimately reinforce an unwanted action from their child. When a parent nurtures, soothes, calms, or pays attention to a child exclusively when disciplining her, the child may see these warm behaviors as a reward (even if accompanied by a punishment) and thus the child is encouraged rather than discouraged from performing the unwanted behavior. In fact, parental attention itself might perpetuate undesirable child or adolescent behavior because the child may feel it is better to get some attention from a parent than to be ignored.

Another application of psychological control is necessary *convergence communication*.[45] Michelle Miller-Day relates that Necessary Convergence Communication Theory "emerged from an extensive ethnographic study of three generations of women in six families (grandmothers, mothers, and adult daughters) and the discovery that the submissive daughters in three of these families accounted for all of the self-reported behavioral problems (e.g., eating disorders, substance abuse, and suicidality)."[46] She witnessed a particular interaction script where a submissive partner uncritically accepted or converged with the social meanings of a dominant partner. For example, an adult woman might talk about how she really liked her new haircut, but when her mother expressed disapproval, she started seeing flaws in her hair and changed her perspective to match her mother's.[47] These women, even though grown with their own kids, had not ever fully differentiated from their mothers. The convergence communication pattern predicted self-harming behaviors in the women.

Both of these family communication theories pinpoint problematic parenting practices. As with other types of training, moderation and wisdom are needed to guide appropriate use. Absolute conformity through manipulation is detrimental, but increasing influence can be beneficial. Let's look at one more parenting theory that utilizes a coaching model.

Emotion Coaching

John Gottman not only studied marriages but also wrote about parenting.[48] His research aligns well with Socio-Emotional Learning Theory (SEL), a popular perspective that describes five basic skills children develop as they mature.[49] According to CASEL, the Collaborative for Academic, Social, and Emotional Learning,

> SEL is the process through which all young people and adults acquire and apply the knowledge, skills, and attitudes to develop

healthy identities, manage emotions and achieve personal and collective goals, feel and show empathy for others, establish and maintain supportive relationships, and make responsible and caring decisions.[50]

People need to be able to recognize emotional experiences in themselves and others, act appropriately and empathetically, and make healthy decisions. Bringing SEL concepts into practice can take work.

In the family, Gottman suggests a five-step process for training (discipling) children.[51] He calls it *emotion coaching*. Emotion coaching can be used for children or teenagers, but it may require slightly different approaches for different ages. There is not always time or an appropriate space for emotion coaching, but incorporating this model into parenting is a dynamic way to balance behavioral control, modeling, and psychological control.

Step 1 requires noticing low-intensity emotions. Attuning to others' emotions requires parents who have learned to be socially aware themselves. It also involves becoming a student of a child's nonverbal messaging. Emotions are often expressed nonverbally, especially in infants and younger children. Recognizing low intensity emotions can prevent them from escalating into high-intensity outbursts. More generally, this points to a need for parents to be involved in their children's lives. There should be rituals for connecting between mothers and fathers, between a parent and each child, and for the entire family. Sometimes termed monitoring, when parents know their child—likes and dislikes, typical day and routines, and friends—the child tends to do better.

In Step 2, emotion coaches see these low-intensity emotions as an opportunity for connection and training. Recognizing how a child feels is not about spying on his or her every move but aims to establish points of connection. Rather than dismiss or ignore the emotion, a parent can capitalize on the moment to coach the child through his or her feelings.

Step 3 validates a child's emotions and offers empathy. This may be through soothing, a hug, or verbally validating a child's emotion. Saying "it's tough to feel left out" can make an empathy bridge between the parent and child. If the child is mad at the parent—when enforcing a family rule, for example—it may be more appropriate to wait or separate as a way of expressing empathy.

In Step 4, the parent can help the child to verbalize or label the emotion. Questions that probe for specific emotions (e.g., frustrated, annoyed) and not just generic (e.g., mad) can help the child develop a wider emotional register with a corresponding vocabulary.[52] Labeling an emotion can help clarify how a child is feeling and why. It also lends itself toward connection as the child has the opportunity to narrate the experiences that led to the emotion.

The last step, Step 5, is to help the child problem-solve. Notice that this step is different from validating emotions. Parents socialize children into appropriate behaviors (e.g., "We can feel mad without tackling our brother") and setting appropriate limits (e.g., "I love that you are generous, but dogs do not need ice cream"). Helping children to brainstorm actions that stem from their emotions and then to think through the implications of their actions can model desirable ways for resolving future conflicts, as well.

These five steps to emotion coaching boil down to being attentive, seizing opportunities for connection and coaching, engaging in emotional labeling, and brainstorming appropriate responses. More generally, adopting the role of a coach encourages influence that can last a lifetime. It provides parents a chance to connect emotionally, share stories or similar experiences, offer advice, and deepen relational intimacy with their children.

||||||| ▶   Application Activity 14.3:
Classifying Parenting Practices

Now that you have seen some of the "behind the scenes" theories of discipline, see if you can classify different parenting practices.

- Think of several common parenting practices. Some of these may include time-out, getting grounded, or spanking. Make your own list.

- Now, see if you can classify each of these based on the theory that underlies them. For example, spanking is based on operant conditioning as positive punishment.

- Think about Jesus's relationship with his disciples, described in the Gospels. What are some of the techniques of disciple-making that we see Jesus employ? Make a list of other types of techniques Jesus used to train his followers. How could these techniques be incorporated into parenting practice?

Discipline to Disciple

Family interventions are one way to distill what kinds of parenting practices prove important for rearing children.[53] Almost all of the scientifically tested and effective parenting interventions that demonstrate improvements in child and youth outcomes teach a few basic parenting skills. These include:

1. Reducing coercive interactions (e.g., minimizing psychological control, ceasing harsh punishment)

2. Reinforcing prosocial behavior (e.g., rewarding desired actions and traits)

3. Listening, being responsive to a child, and improving communication (e.g., using emotion coaching, improving relational warmth)

4. Monitoring and setting appropriate limits (e.g., exerting appropriate control and influence)[54]

These basic skills centrally revolve around communication. A comprehensive discipleship involves communicating unconditional rather than manipulative or conditional love, praising success and rewarding good character, continually developing the unique parent-child relationship, and using parental authority to establish clear expectations and appropriate boundaries.

Practically, discipline is an ever-evolving, customized aspect of a relationship. Each new situation potentially calls for a novel disciplinary approach. Therefore, the greater the repertoire of parenting practices available, the better a trainer each parent will be. Drawing from across the literature and the biblical models, we believe all discipline should be age-appropriate, child-specific, and relationship-grounded. Let's break that down.

Age-appropriate

Obviously, a teenager is different from a 2-year-old. Both need love and both need training. However, the tactics and techniques for training an infant are different from what works well for a toddler, which differ for training a teenager. A lecture is not appropriate or effective for a 6-month-old any more than spanking is for a 16-year-old. Knowing how to train in ways that are developmentally appropriate is a key to effective discipline.

||||||||| ▶   **Application Activity 14.4:**
          When Does Someone Become an Adult?

Different cultures have different rites of passage that mark the entrance into adulthood. The Quinceañera, Bar Mitzvah, and Sweet Sixteen are all markers of one's entrance into adulthood. In his book, Chris Bruno claims that "Boys are Born. Men are Made"[55] and articulates a plan for creating rites of passage to turn a boy into a man. In a group, discuss the following:

- What rites or rituals mark entry into adulthood today?

  If "adulting" is a verb, what actions does it entail?

- Why is becoming an adult important? Why is it unimportant?

At the turn of the millennium, demographers and psychologists described a new life stage labeled "emerging adulthood," which spans about a decade from when high school ends until one enters into traditional family roles in society (e.g., marriage).[56] Here are some of its defining characteristics:[57]

- It is the age of identity exploration, of trying out various possibilities, especially in love and work.
- It is the age of instability.
- It is the most self-focused age of life.
- It is the age of feeling in-between, in transition, neither adolescent nor adult.
- It is the age of possibilities, when hopes flourish, when people have an unparalleled opportunity to transform their lives.

Discuss these characteristics of emerging adulthood in light of parenting in age-appropriate ways. How should parents engage with young adults? What levels of autonomy, control, and influence should parents of college students have? How do young adults honor their parents as they gain autonomy, explore viable career options, and pursue independence?

Child-specific

Each child is different. Some are self-motivated, and others are externally motivated. Some thrive with autonomy, while others wither. Some watch an instructional video and can replicate it easily, while others may want detailed, step-by-step written instructions with illustrations. Because each child is different, a one-size-fits-all approach to parenting does not work well. Certainly, there are practices that can work for many different people, but recognizing and honoring the individuality of each child provides a foundation for relationship and correction that results in maturity.

Relationship-grounded

Finally, all discipline should be grounded in relationship. As meta-analysis of spanking showed, ill effects of corporal punishment were mediated by a positive and warm parent-child relationship. Similarly, research explained seemingly contradictory findings that boys with high levels of testosterone either outshined other boys in academics and leadership or outshined other boys in how much they got into trouble at school.[58] The difference? The ones with good parent-child relationships exhibited positive traits, and the ones with negative relationships exhibited problematic behaviors. Punishment and reinforcement, modeling, and emotion coaching all are predicated on relationship. Indeed, "mother" and "father" are relational terms; they make no sense without a child. Consequently, all discipline should be grounded in relationship.

Points to Ponder 14.5: Tips for Disciplining Kids

- **PUNISH PUNISHABLE OFFENSES ONLY. Do not punish children for being children. Sometimes babies cry. Toddlers may not learn a rule the first time it is introduced. These things are normal. Making messes or imperfectly performing chores and tasks is part of learning. Sometimes adolescents struggle and fail math exams. Iterative improvement is a normal part of growing. Making mistakes is not always a punishable offense, even if they are frustrating. Determine what is punishable and what is not.**

- **SET AND COMMUNICATE EXPECTATIONS. The old saying "If you aim at nothing, you hit it every time" applies directly to training behaviors. When the Pettigrew kids were toddlers and fairly young children, we would go through a little routine of setting expectations when we went somewhere new. For example, when we parked the family car in front of a restaurant (because** memories do not last too long for a 3-year-old), we would take a minute to set some clear expectations. We would ask the kids, "Are we going to run inside?" The kids would chorus, "No!" "Are we going to sit or climb on the table?" "No!" "Are we going to eat with forks?" "No—oh, yes!" Then we would close with a final question to lighten the mood, something like, "Are we going to have fun?" "Yes!" and then pile out of the car. When there are clear expectations, it is a lot easier to hold kids accountable to them.

- ALLOW NATURAL CONSEQUENCES TO TEACH. The book *Parenting with Love and Logic* makes a good case for some ways to allow natural consequences to be a teacher.[59] In many ways, natural consequences, like falling without a safety net, are automatically age appropriate. This is not absolute, of course. The classic "visual cliff" experiment shows that young crawling babies will fall down the stairs without any care because they have limited depth perception and no comprehension of the cause-effect sequence of falling. Yet, for the most part, allowing kids to experience failure when young can prevent severe consequences later in life.

- STICK TO THE CONSEQUENCES. Setting consequences is so much easier than sticking to them. If your teenager knows that a curfew violation results in being "grounded" for two days, then stick to it. It is not a time to negotiate the consequences even if there is a long-anticipated school dance the next day. Set consequences when stakes and emotions are low, and then stick to them when the stakes and emotions are high. Consistency provides necessary stability and predictability, which ultimately demonstrates love.

- ACKNOWLEDGE GOOD BEHAVIOR. As we discussed in Chapter 5, there are many ways to encourage others. Using the CPA framework, for example, parents should encourage their children, with their character (C) being encouraged more than their performance (P) or appearance (A). Learning and speaking a child's "love language" is another way to enhance connection. In any case, following a "catch 'em being good" approach will help kids to feel valued and loved, not just corrected.

Points to Ponder 14.5 *continued*:
Tips for Disciplining Kids

- FRAME CORRECTION IN THE AFFIRMATIVE. A tip for training young kids is to communicate in affirmative ways. This does not just mean being encouraging; it is normal to correct a child. But it does mean that parents have to be mindful of how to share correction. You have probably heard of the "recency effect," where people tend to remember the last thing you say. For kids around 1 to 3 years old, there is a hyper-recency effect. So, if you say, "Please be nice and don't throw your toys," a kid might not process the entire sentence and might recognize just a couple words like "Throw your toys." Happy that you obviously think throwing toys is as much fun as he does, your child may repeat the action with glee. If you see the behavior as willful defiance and punish your son, then it can lead to confusion and hurt feelings. Framing correction in the affirmative, without using negation, is a way to be clearer, especially for young children. In this case, you would say, "Please keep your toys in your hands," or "Can you roll me the truck"? Speaking in concrete terms about the behaviors you want to see will make parent-child communication clearer.

- CLARIFY THE MEANING BEHIND THE MESSAGE. As children age, they start to interpret the subtext of the discipline they receive. Take, for example, if a family prizes their white living room furniture. They saved up to buy it, and only guests are ever hosted in the living room. If a parent habitually says things like "Get off the couch," "Don't touch that," "Can you please go to your room to play?," and "You can watch TV in your room," then that child will eventually start to hear or interpret the "relational content" of the message.[60] They may hear, "Things are more important than you," or "You're not wanted," or "I don't want to spend time with you." While the parents' intentions may be to preserve the couch, and it may be appropriate to teach responsibility or stewardship, it is important to recognize that messages define relationships and have subtext. Parents should clarify how messages are to be interpreted. This often takes place through *metacommunication*—communication about communication.[61] When we repeat certain messages, it may be helpful to clarify the meaning of the messages.

Conclusion

To conclude this chapter, we return to Scripture. Discipline requires a heart that desires the best for the one being trained. As Hebrews 12:5–6 reminds us (quoting Proverbs 3:11–12), "My son, do not make light of the Lord's *discipline*, and do not lose heart when he *rebukes* you, because the Lord *disciplines* the one he loves, and he *chastens* everyone he accepts as his son" (emphasis added).

There are three primary Greek words for training in this passage: discipline, rebuke, and chasten. Strong's[62] Greek dictionary defines each.[63]

- **Discipline** here is defined as a "tutorage (education or training)," a trainer, and to train up (educate). Discipline obviously is synonymous with teaching.

- **Rebuke** means "to confute, admonish: convict, convince, and tell a fault." Rebuking is a process that proves someone or a concept as irrefutably wrong. The idea is that in light of the rebuke, there is no way to be defensive or hold the previous opinion. It forces confession (which literally means saying the same thing).

- **Chasten** means to "flog, literally or figuratively." Flogging refers to ideas like Proverbs 23:13–14: "Do not withhold discipline from a child; if you punish them with the rod, they will not die. Punish them with the rod and save them from death." In a translation of the Aramaic equivalent of the New Testament, the Passion Translation adds the following footnote to the word chasten: "The Aramaic word for 'draws you to himself' is *nagad*, which can mean 'scourge' (severely punish) or 'to attract,' 'to draw,' or 'tug the heart.' The Greek is 'The Lord scourges [chastises] every son he receives.'"[64] In this way, chastening brings a child close to the father.

These three words work together in the context of a father-son relationship, specifically described as loving and encouraging. The context is just as important to note as the specific words used to describe discipline. Reflecting on all that we have covered about parental training, meditate on Hebrews 12:5–11 (The Passion Translation):

And have you forgotten his encouraging words spoken to you as his children? He said, "My child, don't underestimate the value of the discipline and training of the Lord God, or get depressed when he has to correct you. For the Lord's training of your life is the evidence of his faithful love. And when he draws you to himself, it proves you are his delightful child."

Fully embrace God's correction as part of your training, for he is doing what any loving father does for his children. For who has ever heard of a child who never had to be corrected? We all should welcome God's discipline as the validation of authentic sonship. For if we have never once endured his correction it only proves we are strangers and not sons.

And is not it true that earthly fathers are respected even though they correct and discipline? Then we should demonstrate an even greater respect for God, our spiritual Father, as we submit to his life-giving discipline. Our parents corrected us for the short time of our childhood as it seemed good to them. But God corrects us throughout our lives for our own good, giving us an invitation to share his holiness. Now all discipline seems to be painful at the time, yet later it will produce a transformation of character, bringing a harvest of righteousness and peace to those who yield to it.

May we all experience loving discipline that results in righteousness and peace!

III.C: Family Legacy

Chapter 15

Family Legacy: Material, Spiritual, and Relational Inheritance

Chapter Summary: Family relationships, both immediate and extended, usually persist until death and can leave a mark that lasts even beyond the grave. This chapter focuses on legacy. It covers topics related to financial inheritance, guidance for end-of-life conversations, and the ways in which immediate and extended families contribute toward cultural legacies. The chapter then defines and illustrates how a spiritual legacy is passed from generation to generation. It concludes with an encouragement to consider the kind of communication legacy that children might inherit from their parents as well as what they will leave behind.

Introduction

FAMILY IS, BY NATURE, A SELF-PROPAGATING, multigenerational institution. Indeed, the human family began with Adam and Eve and persists today. Way beyond genetic information, parents pass on resources, values, and skills as well as spiritual blessings and curses. An intriguing way to learn about these intergenerational transmissions can be to follow the genealogies of the Bible. Take Noah, for example. After the great flood, the Bible records a story where Shem and Japheth honor their father, whereas Ham dishonors him (Gen. 9). As a result, Noah cursed Ham's son and blessed Shem and Japheth. Looking forward through history, Ham's offspring become the Canaanites, and the tribes that emerge from Shem's line become the Israelites. Generations later, the nation of Israel defeats the nations of the Canaanites, fulfilling the words Noah spoke over his sons centuries earlier. Some might write this off as a coincidence of history, but the Bible includes several examples of how blessings and curses flow through family lines.

In this chapter, we look at how families not only share genetic information with the next generation but also how they leave a legacy in other ways. *Family legacy* can be defined as "shared practices, beliefs, and other psychological materials within a family that are passed on from one generation to another and that develop through communication and interaction among family members."[1] Family legacies serve to shape individual identities, link younger and older generations, and provide continuity of family values—those things which are significant and important to a family—across generations.[2] The famous developmental psychologist Erik Erikson theorized that the two final life stages that individuals face are tensions between generativity versus stagnation and integrity versus despair.[3] These final stages typically begin in mid to late adulthood (ages 40–65+) and continue through the end of life. Both are outward-facing, pushing people to ask themselves questions like, "What does my life mean?," "How am I pouring into the next generation?," and "What am I leaving behind?" Coming to terms with death—not just in the abstract, but in the reality of personal mortality—and "getting your affairs in order" is family business. Families pass on tangible resources, cultural beliefs and practices, and spiritual legacies. Parents can also leave a relational and communication inheritance to their children. We look at each in turn.

Financial Inheritance

Let's start with leaving a financial legacy, because that is what is most often associated with the concept of inheritance. Assets like a family home, vehicle, business, savings, and retirement accounts are often passed from one generation to the next. As Proverbs 19:14 states, "Houses and wealth are inherited from parents." Transmitting material goods is "a normative experience which all families face, regardless of their social and cultural background and the economic value of their assets."[4] Many older adults report giving an average of 10% of their income to their adult children.[5] Leaving an inheritance to children is a meaningful event for many older adults, regardless of the amounts they give. Research shows that older adults often begin with a disposition toward equal bequests for all their biological offspring.[6] In terms of inheritance, blood relations (biological children) tend to receive more and take priority over other family relations, like stepchildren.[7] But fairness for most older adults also means taking into account the value of certain assets, the needs of their specific children, and the ways their children have cared for them in later life in order to ensure equitable (not necessarily equal) distributions.[8]

Despite the fact that most parents leave an inheritance for their children, most children do not know their parents' intentions nor do they have realistic expectations about the amounts or process of receiving an inheritance.[9] Some families avoid conversations about inheritance because it admits parents' mortality. Others avoid such conversations because it seems insensitive, like all they care about from their parents is money. Yet, communicating about inheritance can prevent conflict, which "may in turn contribute to preserving the integrity of the family as a social institution and build social capital."[10] Interviews with older adults revealed that communicating about inheritance can help avoid conflict and preserve biological ties. Interviews also showed that children resist having these discussions but that older adults have a keen desire that their children carry out their inheritance wishes.[11]

Charles Collier advises that engaging in a conversation with parents about inheritance can create an opportunity for connection, education, openness, and even logistical planning because leaving an inheritance is both a legal and a family matter.[12] For example, a legal death certificate is required to transfer funds to beneficiaries, and some banks will freeze accounts for a certain number of days before assets can be transferred. In some cases, based on state law, a probate court will rule on the legality of a last will and testament or assign a legal executor who is the only person authorized to conduct business on behalf of a deceased person. Engaging in conversations about financial inheritance before death happens can provide clarity, coordinate necessary logistics, and give a space for candid conversations between aged parents and their adult children.

A fixed reality in the human experience is that life on earth ends. As Scripture teaches, "[I]t is appointed for men to die once, but after this the judgment" (Heb. 9:27, NKJV). Only while living is there opportunity to prepare for death, spiritually and practically. Here are some of our tips for conversation topics or details to address.

- Discuss a last will and testament and final wishes with loved ones.

- Determine who will assume power of attorney for a parent should he become incapacitated. Whoever takes the responsibility should be well acquainted with the parent's wishes and able to make decisions the way the aged parent would make them.

- Plan a funeral with your parents (including specifics such as whether to cremate or not, where ashes or remains should be spread or buried, if there are special songs to sing or poems to read, if the person wants to have a funeral, graveside service, or host a memorial service, and if there is a significant person to officiate).

- Assign beneficiaries to bank and savings accounts (including 401k plans, Individual Retirement Accounts, mutual funds), or place accounts in multiple names with rights of survivorship.

- Place titles and deeds to all secured assets (e.g., vehicles, properties) in multiple names with rights of survivorship. Alternatively, assign all assets to beneficiaries in a legally executed last will and testament.

Just as family communication includes "doing life together," it also includes walking upon the threshold of death together.

Communicating at Death

While we are discussing end-of-life communication, it is important to note that atop the practical conversations, we should also have sentimental and spiritual conversations. Life is certainly more than money. Reminiscing about good times or expressing appreciation for how someone has impacted your life are helpful and can translate into significant memories after someone passes away. When people are dying, many also wish to have a final confession. This can take place with a pastor or priest, but sometimes it is done with a family member. It can be freeing for the confessor to hear that God offers forgiveness through Christ. Anyone can encourage a confessor with the Scripture in 1 John 1:9: "If we confess our sins, he is faithful and just and will forgive us our sins and purify us from all unrighteousness." As life ends, it is appropriate and helpful to communicate that you know that death is imminent. At this time, messages should express love, stay positive, confirm individual identity (e.g., "You are my son, and you always will be"), address spiritual beliefs, and encompass everyday talk.[13] Expressing your love and saying "goodbye" can also be important messages, both for the survivors and for the one who is dying.

Most of us only spend time with a few family members, like grandparents, parents, or other close relatives, when they are at the point of death. Some medical personnel, like hospice nurses and doctors, have more regular experience being with people as they pass into the afterlife. Writing for a "virtual" hospice organization, Reverend Glen Horst enumerates tips for talking to people who are dying.[14] He adds that it can be just as important to ask for forgiveness as to offer it. Leaving things unsaid can become a source of regret for many. He also suggests that caregivers should "freely" and "often" say "I love you." Finally, he reminds that "touch talks too" and encourages holding hands or touching arms to communicate presence and love, even when words are no longer possible.[15] When Diane's father-in-law was passing from this life to the next, a caring individual took a picture of her husband holding the hand of his father—a powerful and cherished reminder of the gift of touch.

||||||||▶   **Application Activity 15.1:**
Let's Eat and Talk about Death

The book *Let's Talk about Death (over Dinner)*,[16] along with the website "Death over Dinner,"[17] encourages individuals to host a dinner gathering to talk about end-of-life issues.

- If you were invited to one of these dinner parties, would you go? Why or why not?
- If you were to host one of these parties, what topics would you hope to address?
- Have you had end-of-life conversations with family members? If so, share your experiences and reflect on the value of these conversations.

Cultural Legacy

Another way of thinking about family legacy is to consider ways family members pass on their values as well as their ethnic, national, or cultural practices. These are often communicated through specific rituals, as we reviewed in Chapter 5. Determining how to imbue rituals with significance is a challenge all families face, and it largely depends on how the ritual is framed and practiced. Families can employ traditions from their broader cultural heritage (e.g., celebrating Hanukkah, wearing a bright red Chinese wedding dress, giving gifts at Christmas) or can impart rituals particular to their family (e.g., eating chili crab at Thanksgiving). Passing down a cultural legacy can happen simply by routine, but it is most powerful when the "why" behind a ritual is communicated clearly.

||||||||▶ **Application Activity 15.2:**
Family Values

In describing your family, what are some values that have been passed down to you? These could be things like an interest in politics, an appreciation for hiking and hunting, the importance of training for a sport, a focus on health, or an emphasis on education. Family values can also include the importance of your cultural or national heritage.

- List at least three values your family has passed down to you.
- How did you first encounter these values?
- How were they reinforced or emphasized in your family?
- Which family members helped shape your understanding of these values?

Kin Networks and Legacy

Leaving a cultural legacy is not only the purview of a person's immediate family. Larger kin networks also play a part in developing the lives of the next generation. Grandparent-grandchild interactions, for example, are the most common form of intergenerational relationship and can influence grandchildren in profound ways.[18] To a large extent, the interactions that grandchildren have with their grandparents becomes a basis for their understanding of older adults in society and a template for how to interact with them.[19] Obviously, factors like geographic proximity, age, ability, and health of a grandparent are salient predictors of the grandparent-grandchild relationship quality.[20] The sex of the grandparent and grandchild and also whether they are paternal or maternal grandparents (and the relationships a grandchild's father or mother have with their parents) can also influence the grandparent-grandchild relationship.[21] In general, healthy maternal grandmothers in their mid-60s have the closest relationships and most frequent interaction with their grandchildren.[22]

A study specifically designed to learn about the faith-related influence of grandparents found that grandchildren were more susceptible to influence in cognitive aspects of religion (i.e., values, motivations) than spiritual disciplines (i.e., religious practices like prayer and Bible reading).[23] This study summarized the findings as an admonition to grandparents: "To have the best opportunity in shaping your grandchildren's faith formation, practice your own faith passionately, consistently, and publicly so they can see how Christ has transformed you."[24] In this way, grandparents can support, or potentially subvert or circumnavigate a parent's influence on their grandchildren's spiritual development.[25] Through positive interactions and through passive and active ways, grandparents can transmit spiritual, cultural, and family values.

Other kin relationships are also important. "Aunting" and "uncleing" are often forgotten influences in children's lives. There is a wide variance in how aunts and uncles are expected to fulfill their roles as kin, but research on aunt and uncle communication shows that these kin can take on parenting roles, be actors or organizers in extended family rituals and gatherings, and can be a source of support and guidance.[26] Equal numbers are involved and non-involved, and aunts tend to take a different role than uncles in their relationships with the next generation.[27] Sometimes aunts and uncles provide tangible and relational resources. All these ways of cross-generational interaction can shape the culture and values that are adopted by the next generation.

A pastor in Seattle shared the story of how he converted to Christianity, which started with an all-expense paid trip by his agnostic uncle. With no children of his own, the uncle of this now-pastor nephew felt he was frittering away his talent and potential in college. As a successful scholar, editor, and teacher, his uncle believed that experiencing different cultures could open his nephew's eyes to the plight of the impoverished, the beauty in diversity of cultural expression, and ultimately to the importance of education. This uncle sponsored a global excursion with only a couple of rules. For travel, lodging, and most meals, his nephew was to travel like a backpacker (e.g., stay in cheap hostels, use public buses and trains, eat street food). But he was to spare no expense on cultural experiences, such as museums and fine art performances (e.g., theater, ballet, opera, symphony). Finally, the nephew was to journal about his experiences along the way. He went to dozens of countries over an entire year.

Cut off from everything that was familiar and with very limited communication back home (it was pre-cellphone days), his experiences were eye-opening, but the nephew ultimately was very lonely. While disembarking from a ship at port, an English-speaking stranger struck up a conversation. The stranger was passionate about Jesus, seemed to instantly perceive the nephew's loneliness, and with incredible, inexplicable insight into his personal life and situation persuaded the nephew to seek God. He ended the conversation by giving the nephew a Bible. Although the two never met again, the encounter had lasting impact. The entire trip changed dramatically as the nephew began voraciously devouring God's Word and as he nurtured a personal relationship with God through prayer. Simultaneously, his cultural survey took on a new, spiritual dimension as he began to love the people he met because he embraced the reality that God created each one. Although conversion to Christianity was not his uncle's intent, his generosity changed his nephew's life. This story dramatically illustrates how extended kin networks can shape the experiences of the next generation.

Religious Cultural Legacy

Because the focus of this text is Christianity and family communication, we want to draw attention particularly to how families transmit religious and spiritual practices from one generation to the next. As many children become youth, religion becomes merely a social club devoid of any spiritual substance. Estimates vary, but churches report that around 40 to 70% of youth cease attending services and programs after high school.[28] The Fuller Youth Institute, a seminary group that translates research findings into ministry resources, explains that many youth see religion like a jacket they can put on or take off depending on their circumstances.[29]

American youth have mostly adopted what has been described as the *de facto* religion of America: "moral therapeutic Deism."[30] This view portrays God as distant and uninvolved, advocates that people should be good to each other, and sees the ultimate purpose of life as being happy. This view of God and religion stands in contrast to a vibrant relationship with Jesus Christ, the Father, and the Holy Spirit. It also diverges from classic and contemporary teachings on Christianity. Yet, as recently as 2021, moral therapeutic Deism characterized about 40% of American adults under 50 years old.[31]

For families to transmit a culture of spiritual and religious involvement, youth must be part of an authentically spiritual and genuinely relational faith community. The Fuller Youth Institute claims that although parents are decidedly the most influential people in youth's spiritual development, they are necessary but not sufficient. Churches and parents transmit "sticky faith" when youth are surrounded by at least five adults who know them and support their spiritual development.[32] This implies that participating in religious activities, like attending church meetings or reading Christian books, for example, is not enough to see the next generation own their faith. Indeed, religious practices have value in positioning people to experience God, but as Jesus lamented over the religious of his day, "You study the Scriptures diligently because you think that in them you have eternal life. These are the very Scriptures that testify about me, yet you refuse to come to me to have life" (John 5:39–40). As with other aspects of faith, there should be an alignment between our motives and actions that bring us into closer relationship with God, and such authentic faith in the home and community propagates in the next generation.

What are some practical ways parents might consider instilling an authentic faith in their children? A family might spend time articulating a faith-based mission statement, go on a mission trip together, or attend a spiritual conference as the main activity in a family vacation. Parents engaging in conversations with strangers or co-workers about their beliefs can be an eye-opening experience for themselves and their children. Practicing evangelism is an excellent way to refine and reinforce your own beliefs, gaining an understanding of what you believe within a pluralistic ideological landscape. It also can enhance your love for all people. If a relationship with God is essential to your family experience, your time and priorities will reflect that reality. A family might spend time in prayer together or memorizing and meditating on the same Bible passage. These types of experiences can set families on a course to experience God together and to transmit their faith to the next generation.

Spiritual Disciplines

Another strategy for transmitting authentic faith within a community is to practice spiritual disciplines. These time-tested practices position families and communities to experience God. Richard Foster describes several spiritual disciplines that have persisted across centuries. His book *Celebration of Discipline: The Path to Spiritual Growth*[33] provides a theological rationale and biblical case for each discipline. He also offers tips on how to practically perform each discipline. For example, Foster not only makes a clear biblical case for fasting but also gives advice on how to prepare your spirit, mind, and body to fast, what the experience of multi-day fasting is like physically and mentally, and how to break a fast in ways that correspond with your physiological needs. The practices he outlines are as relevant today as they were for ancient Christian communities.

Foster's book is divided into three groups of practices that draw individuals, families, and congregations closer to God. Inward disciplines include meditation, prayer, fasting, and study. Outward disciplines include simplicity, solitude, submission, and service. Finally, corporate disciplines include confession, worship, guidance, and celebration. Spiritual disciplines can be practiced religiously without any real spiritual result, so they are not a formula that guarantees faith will be transmitted from one generation to the next. However, celebrating spiritual disciplines and engaging with these practices provides an opportunity for children, youth, and parents in families to genuinely experience God, giving them a shared spiritual experience. As these authentic experiences accumulate, odds are that youth in families will experience God as a communicating Agent and, out of that radical reality, develop a personal relationship with the Father, Son, and Holy Spirit.[34]

A challenging and encouraging book chapter on spiritual disciplines comes from Dallas Willard's dense treatise, *The Spirit of the Disciplines: Understanding How God Changes Lives*.[35] Willard was a philosophy professor at University of Southern California and a mentor to Richard Foster. Amid a rather heady treatment of spiritual disciplines, Willard exemplifies how practical, mundane, and experiential spiritual disciplines really are. He argues that the Apostle Paul held a realistic psychology that propelled him toward a disciplined life. Willard explains that Paul understood that "if a convert's habits remain the same they will realize little in the life of Christ."[36] He describes three stages of transformation. First, we are baptized into Christ. Second, we "consciously and purposefully regard ourselves as 'dead to sin and alive to God in union with Jesus Christ' (Rom. 6:11, NEB)."[37] Third, we train our bodies and habits automatically to produce righteousness. Like muscle memory for a piano or tennis player, we discipline our lives to respond joyfully and consistently out of the indwelt life of Christ.

Spiritual disciplines are not easy. They are a training regimen designed to "put to death the misdeeds of the body" (Rom. 8:13). This happens by the power of the Spirit of God at work in our own spirits, but it does not happen without our involvement, which is where spiritual disciplines come in. The aim of the disciplines is not discipline, but something that transcends discipline. As Willard points out, the purpose of practicing piano is not to become good at practice, but to become excellent at playing piano. So, too, the goal of spiritual disciplines is not to have a disciplined life but to live out of the power of God's Spirit daily.

Families can model, encourage, train, and participate in spiritual disciplines together. Integrating confession, worship, guidance, and celebration into family routines creates a powerful opportunity to experience God. Fasting can also be practiced as a family or as an individual. When the kids were all under 6 years old in Jonathan's family, one year for Good Friday the family did a fast in which they only ate black beans all day to remember the costly sacrifice of Christ on the cross. We picked black beans so the food would be plain, but also so the kids would be able to eat as much as they wanted throughout the day. In some ways, the fast backfired. Two of the kids enjoyed the black beans so much they asked to eat them all the next day, too! For them, black beans felt like a treat instead of a solemn remembrance.

Parents can also model routines that support individual disciplines of study and prayer or incorporate these practices into family time. The possibilities for training and practicing spiritual disciplines as a family are only limited by creativity. There is no wrong way to do it, as long as the goal remains to connect with the Father and become like Christ, by the power of the Holy Spirit, in all that is said and done.

Spiritual Legacy

Beyond routines like religious practice, it is important to distinguish that parents also leave a spiritual legacy for their children, their children's children, and the generations to come. Blessings and curses transcend generations. Our first parents' sin, for example, has passed to each person born through the lineage of Adam and Eve. So, too, Christ's righteousness has passed to all people who are born again (see John 3). As Romans 5:18–19 states,

just as one trespass resulted in condemnation for all people, so also one righteous act resulted in justification and life for all people. For just as through the disobedience of the one man the many were made sinners, so also through the obedience of the one man the many will be made righteous.

Leaving a spiritual, generational inheritance is part and parcel of family existence.

An illustration of this type of generational legacy was presented in a publication from the year 1900 comparing two American families. A pastor and educator named A. Winship published a review that compared the family lines of Max Jukes (a pseudonym) and Jonathan Edwards.[38] Both Edwards and Jukes lived in New England during the 1700s. Edwards was a famous American Christian clergyman, theologian, author, college president, and leader in the First Great Awakening. Jukes settled in the woods of New York and was characterized as a "jolly good fellow and not very bad. He was popular and he could tell a good story that made everybody laugh."[39] However, "he would not go to school, because he did not like it. He would not stay in evenings, for he did not like that. . . . He would not work for he did not like it."[40] The contrast between their family lines is stark.

Doubtless, some of Winship's analysis is limited and is lost to history, but much is documented in his publication *Jukes-Edwards: A Study in Education and Heredity*.[41] His findings have been summarized as follows:

Jonathan Edwards' legacy includes: 1 U.S. Vice-President, 1 dean of a law school, 1 dean of a medical school, 3 U.S. Senators, 3 governors, 3 mayors, 13 college presidents, 30 judges, 60 doctors, 65 professors, 75 Military officers, 80 public office holders, 100 lawyers, 100 clergymen, and 285 college graduates. Jukes' descendants included: 7 murderers, 60 thieves, 190 prostitutes, 150 other convicts, 310 paupers, and 440 who were physically wrecked by addiction to alcohol. Of the 1,200 descendants that were studied, 300 died prematurely.[42]

Winship offers some explanations that might explain the differences. He notes that Mrs. Sarah Edwards had direct and consequential influence over the household and the Edwards children. Winship also posits that differences could be explained by the fact that education remained prominent in the Edwards family line and absent in the Jukes line. Also, both families married partners of similar social and economic capital, thus perpetuating their socioeconomic position. Whatever the social mechanisms, we believe there are also spiritual forces at work. There are blessings that follow from loving and obeying God, and they can persist across generations.

Think of the promises God gave to Abraham. Genesis records that Abraham was to inherit the land of Canaan through offspring he and his wife Sarah would birth. This happens generations later when the twelve tribes of Abraham's grandson Jacob come out of 400 years of slavery! Even further down the family line, the Messiah, Jesus Christ, fulfills one of the promises given to Abraham. Galatians 3:16 instructs that "the promises were spoken to Abraham and to his seed. Scripture does not say 'and to seeds,' meaning many people, but 'and to your seed,' meaning one person, who is Christ." Promises given to a father were fulfilled through later generations.

Author and pastor Dutch Sheets calls the spiritual connection between generations the "synergy of the ages."[43] He teaches that children should pray that God brings to fruition promises he made to their parents and grandparents. "God's plan is always for the present generation to build on the strengths of the previous. This is the synergy of the ages—multiplied power through generational agreement and honor."[44] From this perspective, our prayers today may play out in our children's or grandchildren's lives. Indeed, "there is an aspect of our spiritual walk that stretches beyond the boundaries of our window on earth."[45] Families gain a spiritual inheritance from their ancestors and leave one for their progeny.

Points to Ponder 15.3:
Generational Curses

If generational blessings are passed down, then is it equally true that curses can flow across generational lines? The example of Noah and his sons at the beginning of the chapter suggests that they can. Passages like Deuteronomy 5:8–10 also express that curses are passed down:

> You shall not make for yourself an image in the form of anything in heaven above or on the earth beneath or in the waters below. You shall not bow down to them or worship them; *for I, the Lord your God, am a jealous God, punishing the children for the sin of the parents to the third and fourth generation of those who hate me*, but showing love to a thousand gen-

erations of those who love me and keep my commandments. (emphasis added)

This passage shows that anything that a family places above God is an idol, and idolatry carries generational curses.

Generational curses can come from intentional dedication to various gods (a common practice in many parts of Asia upon the birth of a child) as well as cult agreements, oaths, or pacts (such as those used in Freemasonry). Because of Jesus's death and resurrection, the power of generational curses, including the curse of Adam and Eve's original sin, is broken and this victory can be applied to each Christian's life. As Paul writes, "The sting of death is sin, and the power of sin is the law. But thanks be to God! He gives us the victory through our Lord Jesus Christ" (1 Cor. 15:56–57). "Christ has redeemed us from the curse of the law, having become a curse for us (for it is written, 'Cursed is everyone who hangs on a tree')" (Gal. 3:13). Regardless of a person's background, Christ begins a new life and can free each person from spiritual curses.

A simple process to break generational curses is to repent, renounce, and replace. We repent of the idolatry that resulted in the curse (Acts 3:19), renounce the hold the curse held on our lives (Titus 2:12; 2 Tim. 2:19), and replace the curse with a blessing by inviting the Holy Spirit to fill us anew (Matt. 12:43–45). Further teaching that delves into these topics and gives practical steps toward breaking the power of generational curses is included in the books *Bondage Breaker* and *Victory over the Darkness* by Neil T. Anderson,[46] *Deliverance from Evil Spirits* by Francis MacNutt,[47] and *Operating in the Courts of Heaven: Granting God the Legal Rights to Fulfill His Passion and Answer our Prayers* by Robert Henderson.[48]

Communicating a Blessing

One key to imparting a spiritual legacy, sometimes overlooked, is communicating a blessing. Genesis 49 records the blessings Jacob bestowed on his sons. As the patriarch of the family, it was Jacob's responsibility and privilege to speak his blessing over his sons. He followed his father's example. Isaac blessed Jacob with these words:

> May God give you heaven's dew and earth's richness—an abundance of grain and new wine. May nations serve you and peoples bow down to you. Be lord over your brothers, and may the sons of your mother bow down to you. May those who curse you be cursed and those who bless you be blessed. (Gen. 27:28–29)

This blessing that Isaac gave was certainly passed down from Abraham to whom God said, "I will bless those who bless you and curse those who curse you; and all the families of the earth will be blessed through you" (Gen. 12:3). The spiritual legacy that passed from God to Abraham to Isaac to Jacob to the 12 tribes of Israel illustrates the importance of communicating blessing across generations.

For some, communicating a blessing may seem mysterious or daunting. In Scripture, the blessing is communicated from fathers to sons. What about daughters? What about mothers? Was the patriarchal blessing just a cultural artifact? We are convinced that there are blessings that both mothers and fathers can impart to daughters and sons. There are a variety of resources that explain spiritual blessings in more detail. One we recommend is *Blessing Your Spirit: With the Blessings of Your Father and the Names of God* by Sylvia Gunter and Arthur A. Burk.[49] It includes scriptural meditations and blessings that can be read aloud for individuals or families. Included here are some blessings from Scripture that mothers and fathers can speak over their children. We have edited the language of some to make them easier to read aloud over a family.

Numbers 6: 24–26

The Lord bless you
   and keep you;
the Lord make his face shine on you
   and be gracious to you;
the Lord turn his face toward you
   and give you peace.

Deuteronomy 28:6–9

May God bless you when you come in and when you go out.
May the Lord grant that the enemies who rise up against you will

be defeated before you, even though they come at you from one direction let them flee from you seven ways!

May the Lord send a blessing on your barns and on everything you put your hand to.

May he bless you in the land he is giving you.

May the Lord establish you as his holy people, as he promised you on oath, as you keep the commands of the Lord your God and walk in obedience to him.

2 Corinthians 9:8–10

May God bless you abundantly, so that in all things at all times, you have all that you need, and may you abound in every good work. Now may he who supplies seed to the sower and bread for food also supply and increase your store of seed and enlarge the harvest of your righteousness.

Ephesians 1:17–19

May the God of our Lord Jesus Christ, the glorious Father, give you the Spirit of wisdom and revelation, so that you may know him better. I pray that the eyes of your heart may be enlightened in order that you may know the hope to which he has called you, the riches of his glorious inheritance in his holy people, and his incomparably great power for us who believe.

2 Peter 1:2–3

Grace and peace be yours in abundance through the knowledge of God and of Jesus our Lord. May his divine power grant you everything you need for life and godliness.

Communication Legacy

Finally, we believe that families leave a communication legacy. There is ample evidence that one generation does indeed shape the world of the next. This happens directly and indirectly. Parents train their kids, influence nieces and nephews, and impact grandkids through their direct interactions with them. They also indirectly influence the generations that follow, leaving behind tangible, cultural, and spiritual inheritances. Relationally, too, we leave behind an inheritance. If a child is trained to be assertive and loving, and experiences the blessings of these ways of relating, odds are that the child will train her children to be the same way. Thus, parents have indirect influence on their grandchildren and subsequent generations through the ways their children parent. The relational strengths that parents model with each other, friends, acquaintances, and strangers can be passed down and create a starting point for how the next generation will relate to one another. This kind of communication legacy is mediated by individual personalities and other influences. But we want to encourage you to consider ways that you have inherited a communication legacy from your family and be intentional about the kind of communication legacy you want to leave behind. Do you want your grandchildren to say you were the best listener? That you were an encourager? Compassionate? That you truly loved your enemies? That you never met a stranger and showed Christ's love to everyone you met? Start practicing communicating today in ways you want to be remembered.

Conclusion

Research confirms the importance of legacy. One study sought to uncover the "kinds of legacy-leaving that are appreciated and wished for by surviving children."[50] This study asked adults who lost a parent at a young age about their memories and knowledge of their parents and ways those memories were kept alive. Participants said that leaving possessions, photos, videos, and written communication helped them remember their parents, assured them that their parents loved them, and reminded them of their parents' pride in them. Without these reminders, participants experienced pain or regret. As one respondent shared, "I don't remember my dad ever saying, like, 'I love you,' or, 'I'm proud of you,' or, you know, 'I know you're going to [do] great things,' or something like that. So, uhm I think that would actually be helpful for the surviving parent, because they can always, like, you know, reference back to that encounter."[51] The interviewees also mentioned that surviving kin should continue to talk about the deceased parent. One participant shared, "I talk to my grandmother, and she'll have great stories that I love hearing. Or my aunt, about when she [my mother] first met my father. Or, my dad might throw something in (pause) and sometimes it's hard—but I love hearing it (pause) 'cause it gives me a better understanding of who she was."[52] For those who have experienced loss, it is not absence itself that makes the heart grow fonder, but in absence it is communication that nurtures memories and helps fill the void left by death. Communication helps create family legacy.

Perhaps you have not thought much about what kind of legacy you want to leave behind, but it is never too early to start. Will your relationships with siblings, friends, and family be characterized by incredible rituals of connection? Will your marriage be one where forgiveness flows freely to heal the inevitable conflicts, disagreements, and misunderstandings of life? How resilient will your family be? Will others notice that the way you coordinate life's demands is marked by a grace and peace that could only come from God? It has been said that everyone's tombstone will have a birthdate and a date of death, but what matters is the dash in between. We hope that you take what you have learned in *Family Communication and the Christian Faith* and both the good and the bad that you have inherited—materially, spiritually, and relationally—and pass on something even better to the generations that follow!

Notes

Foreword

[1] Perry L. Glanzer, "Marriage as a Required Liberal Arts," *Christian Scholar's Review*, May 27, 2022, https://christianscholars.com/marriage-as-a-required-liberal-art/

[2] John Wesley, *A Plain Account of Christian Perfection* (London: Epworth Press, 1952), 87.

[3] Deborah Tannen, *The Argument Culture: Moving from Debate to Dialogue* (New York: Random House, 1998).

Authors' Note: What Do We Mean by "Christian Faith"?

[1] C. S. Lewis, *Mere Christianity* (New York: Collins, 2012).

[2] Dennis Bratcher, "Christian Creeds, Confessions, and Catechisms," The Voice, 2018, http://www.crivoice.org/creeds.html

[3] J. Warner Wallace, *Cold-Case Christianity: A Homicide Detective Investigates the Claims of the Gospel* (Colorado Springs, CO: David C. Cook, 2013); Lee Strobel, *The Case for Christ* (Grand Rapids, MI: Zondervan, 1998).

[4] Howard G. Hendricks and William D. Hendricks, *Living by the Book: The Art and Science of Reading the Bible* (Chicago: Moody Publishers, 2007); Kay Arthur, David Arthur, and Paul De Lacy, *How to Study Your Bible: Discover the Life-Changing Approach to God's Word* (Eugene, OR: Harvest House).

[5] dc Talk and the Voice of the Martyrs, *Jesus Freaks: Stories of Those Who Stood for Jesus: The Ultimate Jesus Freaks* (Tulsa, OK: Albury Publishing, 1999).

[6] Marvin R. Wilson, *Our Father Abraham: Jewish Roots of the Christian Faith* (Grand Rapids, MI: Wm. B. Eerdmans, 1998).

[7] Jonathan Pettigrew, *Stepfather-Stepson Communication: Social Support in Stepfamily Worlds* (New York: Peter Lang, 2014).

[8] Jonathan Pettigrew and Robert H. Woods Jr., *Professing Christ: Christian Tradition and Faith Learning Integration in Public Universities* (Pasco, WA: Integratio Press, 2022).

[9] Mary Anne Fitzpatrick and Diane M. Badzinski, "All in the Family: Interpersonal

Communication in Kin Relationships," in *The Handbook of Interpersonal Communication*, eds. Mark L. Knapp and Gerald R. Miller (Beverly Hills, CA: Sage, 1985), 687–736.

[10] Quentin J. Schultze and Diane M. Badzinski, *An Essential Guide to Interpersonal Communication: Building Great Relationships in the Age of Social Media with Faith, Skill, and Virtue* (Grand Rapids, MI: Baker Academics, 2015).

Chapter 2: Understanding Family

[1] United Nations, "Universal Declaration of Human Rights," 1948, http://www.un.org/en/universal-declaration-human-rights

[2] Chris Segrin and Jeanne Flora, *Family Communication*, 3rd ed. (New York: Routledge, 2019).

[3] Frederick S. Wambodt and David Reiss, "Defining a Family Heritage and a New Relationship Identity: Two Central Tasks in the Making of a Marriage," *Family Process* 28, no. 3 (September 1989): 315–355.

[4] Douglas Kelley, *Marital Communication* (Cambridge: Polity Press, 2012), 3–9.

[5] Lynn H. Turner and Richard West, *Perspectives on Family Communication*, 3rd ed. (New York: McGraw Hill, 2013), 9.

[6] Jacob E. Cheadle, Paul R. Amato, and Valerie King, "Patterns of Nonresident Father Contact," *Demography* 47 (2010): 205–225.

[7] Adam Reed and Jonathan Pettigrew, "Standing Tall, Bending Low" (unpublished manuscript, January 31, 2019). Typescript.

[8] Jack O. Balswick and Judith K. Balswick, *The Family: A Christian Perspective on the Contemporary Home*, 3rd ed. (Grand Rapids, MI: Baker Academic, 2007), 361.

[9] Francis Chan, *Letters to the Church* (Colorado Springs, CO: David C. Cook, 2018), 69–72.

[10] United Nations, "Universal Declaration of Human Rights."

[11] Robert P. George, *In Defense of Natural Law* (New York: Oxford University Press, 2001).

[12] Allan Carlson and Paul Mero, *The Natural Family: A Manifesto* (Dallas, TX: Spence Publishing, 2004), https://www.worldcongress.pl/docs/en/pdf/the_natural_family.pdf

[13] Ibid., 1.

Chapter 3: Family, Faith, and Society

[1] United Nations, "Universal Declaration of Human Rights," 1948, http://www.un.org/en/universal-declaration-human-rights

[2] "The Truth Project," directed by Del Tackett (Focus on the Family, 2011).

[3] Tim Hansel, *You Gotta Keep Dancin': In the Midst of Life's Hurts, You Can Choose Joy!* (Elgin, IL: David C. Cook, 1985), 41.

[4] Michael Rutter, Celia Beckett, Jenny Castle, Emma Colvert, Jana Kreppner, Mitul Mehta, Suzanne Stevens, and Edmund Sonuga-Barke, "Effects of Profound Early Institutional Deprivation: An Overview of Findings from a UK Longitudinal Study of Romanian Adoptees," *European Journal of Developmental Psychology* 4, no. 3 (2007):

332–350. See also Kirsten Weir, "The Lasting Impact of Neglect," *Monitor on Psychology* 45, no. 6 (June 2014): http://www.apa.org/monitor/2014/06/neglect

[5] Melissa Fay Green, "30 Years Ago, Romania Deprived Thousands of Babies of Human Contact: Here's What's Become of Them," *The Atlantic*, July/August 2020, https://www.theatlantic.com/magazine/archive/2020/07/can-an-unloved-child-learn-to-love/612253/

[6] Neel Burton, "When Homosexuality Stopped Being a Mental Disorder," *Psychology Today*, September 18, 2015, https://www.psychologytoday.com/us/blog/hide-and-seek/201509/when-homosexuality-stopped-being-mental-disorder

[7] Pew Research Center, "Same-sex Marriage around the World," October 28, 2019, https://www.pewforum.org/fact-sheet/gay-marriage-around-the-world/

[8] CNN Fact Sheet, "Same Sex Marriage Fast Facts," August 11, 2020, https://www.cnn.com/2013/05/28/us/same-sex-marriage-fast-facts/index.html

[9] John G. Roberts, Chief Justice, "Dissenting, Obergefell v Hodges Supreme Court of the United States," 576 U.S., 4, https://www.bshrlaw.com/sites/481/uploaded/files/Roberts_CJ_dissenting_OBERGEFELL__v_HODGES_Slip_Copy2.pdf

[10] Robert P. George and Jean Bethke Elshtain, eds., *The Meaning of Marriage: Family, State, Market, and Morals* (Strongsville, OH: Scepter Publishers, 2006).

[11] Allan Carlson and Paul Mero, *The Natural Family: A Manifesto* (Dallas, TX: Spence Publishing, 2004), https://www.worldcongress.pl/docs/en/pdf/the_natural_family.pdf

[12] David Blankenhorn, *The Future of Marriage* (New York: Encounter Books, 2009).

[13] Anthony Esolen, *Defending Marriage: Twelve Arguments for Sanity* (Charlotte, NC: Saint Benedict Press, 2014).

[14] Blankenhorn, *The Future of Marriage*.

[15] Stephanie Coontz, "The World Historical Transformation of Marriage," *Journal of Marriage and Family* 66, no. 4 (2004): 974–979.

[16] Stephanie Coontz, *Marriage, A History: How Love Conquered Marriage* (New York: Penguin Books, 2004), 5.

[17] Ibid.

[18] Ibid., 4.

[19] Coontz, "The World Historical Transformation of Marriage."

[20] Pamela J. Smock and Christine R. Schwartz, "The Demography of Families: A Review of Patterns and Change," *Journal of Marriage and Family* 82, no. 1 (2020): 9–24.

[21] Ibid.

[22] Ibid.

[23] Pew Research Center, "Marriage and Cohabitation in the U.S.," November 6, 2019, https://www.pewresearch.org/social-trends/2019/11/06/marriage-and-cohabitation-in-the-u-s/

[24] Lydia R. Anderson, "High Schools Seniors' Expectations to Marry," *Family Profiles*, FP-16-14 (Bowling Green, OH: National Center for Family & Marriage Research, 2016), https://www.bgsu.edu/content/dam/BGSU/college-of-arts-and-sciences/NCFMR/documents/FP/anderson-hs-seniors-expectations-marry-fp-16-14.pdf

[25] Valerie Schweizer, "The Retreat from Remarriage, 1950–2017," *Family Profiles*, FP-19-17 (Bowling Green, OH: National Center for Family & Marriage Research, 2019), https://www.bgsu.edu/ncfmr/resources/data/family-profiles/schweizer-retreat-remarriage-fp-19-17.html

[26] Smock and Schwartz, "The Demography of Families."

[27] Ibid.

[28] Ibid.

[29] W. Bradford Wilcox and Elizabeth Marquardt, eds., *State of Our Unions 2010: When Marriage Disappears: The Middle America* (Charlottesville, VA: The National Marriage Project, 2010), http://stateofourunions.org/2010/SOOU2010.pdf

[30] Smock and Schwartz, "The Demography of Families."

[31] Pew Research Center, "Marriage and Cohabitation in the U.S."

[32] Ibid.

[33] Smock and Schwartz, "The Demography of Families."

[34] "'Demographic Winter' Leading to Decline in Fertility Worldwide," *Rhode Island Catholic*, November 29, 2018, https://thericatholic.com/stories/demographic-winter-leading-to-decline-in-fertility-worldwide,10328

[35] Emily Schodelmeyer, "Fewer Married Households and More Living Alone," United States Census Bureau, August 9, 2017, https://www.census.gov/library/stories/2017/08/more-adults-living-without-children.html

[36] Smock and Schwartz, "The Demography of Families."

[37] Dennis Thompson, "U.S. Grandparents Are Raising Millions of Kids, and It's Tough," *U.S. News and World Report*, August 4, 2020, https://www.usnews.com/news/health-news/articles/2020-08-04/us-grandparents-are-raising-millions-of-kids-and-its-tough

[38] Pew Research Center, "U.S. Has World's Highest Rate of Children Living in Single-Parent Households," December 12, 2019, https://www.pewresearch.org/fact-tank/2019/12/12/u-s-children-more-likely-than-children-in-other-countries-to-live-with-just-one-parent/

[39] Andrew J. Cherlin, *The Marriage-Go-Round: The State of Marriage and the Family in America Today* (New York: Random House, 2009).

[40] Ibid., 19.

[41] Dennis Hiebert, *Sweet Surrender: How Cultural Mandates Shape Christian Marriage* (Eugene, OR: Cascade Books, 2013).

[42] Ray S. Anderson and Dennis B. Guernsey, *On Being Family: A Social Theology of the Family* (Grand Rapids, MI: William B. Eerdmans Publishing, 1985), 11.

Chapter 4: Theory and Theology

[1] James Pedlar, "Christ as the Good Samaritan," James Pedlar: Theologian and Pastor, July 3, 2010, https://jamespedlar.ca/2010/07/03/christ-as-the-good-samaritan/

[2] Em Griffin, Andrew Ledbetter, and Glenn Sparks, *A First Look at Communication Theory*, 9th ed. (New York: McGraw Hill, 2014), 5.

[3] M. James Jordan, *The Ancient Road Rediscovered: What the Early Church Knew* (Taupo, New Zealand: Fatherheart Media, 2014).

[4] Joshua J. Knabb and Matthew Y. Emerson, "'I Will Be Your God and You Will Be My People': Attachment Theory and the Grand Narrative of Scripture," *Pastoral Psychology* 62 (2013), 830.

[5] Quentin J. Schultze, *Communication for Life: Christian Stewardship in Community and Media* (Grand Rapids, MI: Baker Academic, 2000).

[6] Emmanuel S. A. Ayee, "Human Communication Revisited—A Biblical

Perspective," *Bulletin for Christian Scholarship* 78, no. 1 (2013): 8.

[7] James Sire, *The Universe Next Door: A Basic Worldview Catalog*, 6th ed. (Downers Grove, IL: InterVarsity Press, 2020).

[8] Bill Strom and Divine Agodzo, *More Than Talk: A Covenantal Approach to Everyday Communication*, 5th ed. (Dubuque, IA: Kendall Hunt, 2018).

[9] Ibid., 318.

[10] Dawn O. Braithwaite, Paul Schrodt, and Kristen Carr, "Introduction: Meta-Theory and Theory in Interpersonal Communication," in *Engaging Theories in Interpersonal Communication: Multiple Perspectives*, 2nd ed., eds. Dawn O. Braithwaite and Paul Schrodt (Los Angeles, CA: Sage, 2015), 11.

[11] Ryan S. Bisel, "Reconciliation and Critique: Option Three at Areopagus," in *Professing Christ: Christian Tradition and Faith-Learning Integration in Public Universities*, eds. Jonathan Pettigrew and Robert H. Woods Jr. (Pasco, WA: Integratio Press, 2022), 22.

[12] Griffin et al., *A First Look at Communication Theory*, 5.

[13] Chris Segrin and Jeanne Flora, *Family Communication*, 3rd ed. (New York: Routledge, 2019), 26.

[14] Marianne Dainton and Elaine D. Zelley, *Applying Communication Theory for Professional Life: A Practical Introduction*, 3rd ed. (Thousand Oaks, CA: Sage, 2015), 3.

[15] Dawn O. Braithwaite, Elizabeth A. Suter, and Kory Floyd, *Engaging Theories in Family Communication: Multiple Perspectives*, 2nd ed. (New York: Routledge, 2018).

[16] Sandra Metts and Bryan Asbury, "Theoretical Approaches to Family Communication," in *The SAGE Handbook of Family Communication*, eds. Lynn H. Turner and Richard West (Los Angeles, CA: Sage, 2015), 43.

[17] Christina G. Yoshimura and Kathleen M. Galvin, "General Systems Theory: A Compelling View of Family Life," in *Engaging Theories in Family Communication: Multiple Perspectives*, 2nd ed., eds. Dawn O. Braithwaite, Elizabeth A. Suter, and Kory Floyd (New York: Routledge, 2018), 164–74.

[18] Ludwig von Bertalanffy, *General System Theory: Foundations, Development, and Applications* (New York: George Braziller, Inc., 1968).

[19] Dennis Bratcher, "Christian Creeds, Confessions, and Catechisms," The Voice, 2018, http://www.crivoice.org/creeds.html

[20] Michelle Goh, "The Care of Ageing Persons: A Trinitarian Perspective," *The Australasian Catholic Record* 94, no. 3 (2017): 262.

[21] Ibid.

[22] Walter R. Fisher, *Human Communication as Narration: Toward a Philosophy of Reason, Value, and Action* (Columbia, SC: University of Southern Carolina Press, 1987).

[23] William G. Kirkwood, "Narrative and the Rhetoric of Possibilities," *Communication Monographs* 59, no. 1 (1992): 30–47.

[24] Robin P. Clair, Stephanie Carlo, Chervin Lam, John Nussman, Canek Phillips, Virginia Sanchez, Elaine Schnabel, and Liliya Yakova, "Narrative Theory and Criticism: An Overview toward Clusters and Empathy," *The Review of Communication* 14, no. 1 (2014): 1–18.

[25] Jody Koenig Kellas and Haley Kranstruber Horstman, "Communicated Narrative Sense-Making: Understanding Family Narratives, Storytelling, and the Construction of Meaning through a Communicative Lens," in *The SAGE Handbook of Family Communication*, eds. Lynn H. Turner and Richard West (Los Angeles, CA: Sage, 2015), 76–90.

[26] Jody Koenig Kellas, "Narrating Family: Introduction to the Special Issue on Narrative and Storytelling in the Family," *Journal of Family Communication* 10, no. 1 (2010): 3.

[27] Jody Koenig Kellas and April R. Trees, "Family Stories and Storytelling: Windows into the Family Soul," in *The Routledge Handbook of Family Communication*, 2nd ed., ed. Anita L. Vangelisti (New York: Routledge, 2013), 391–406.

[28] Nancie Hudson, "When Family Narratives Conflict: Autoethnography of My Mother's Secrets," *Journal of Family Communication* 15, no. 2 (2015): 113–129.

[29] Segrin and Flora, *Family Communication*, 53.

[30] Leslie A. Baxter and Dawn O. Braithwaite, "Relational Dialectical Theory: Crafting Meaning from Competing Discourses," in *Engaging Theories in Interpersonal Communication: Multiple Perspectives*, eds. Leslie A. Baxter and Dawn O. Braithwaite (Thousand Oaks, CA: Sage, 2008), 359.

[31] Melissa W. Framer, "Torah-Observant Jewish Married Couples: The Influence of Mandated Abstinence of Physical Touch and Marital Maintenance" (PhD diss., Tempe, Arizona State University, 2020).

[32] Parker K. Palmer, *The Promise of Paradox: A Celebration of Contradictions in the Christian Life* (San Francisco, CA: Jossey-Bass, 2008), xxix.

[33] Paul B. Baltes, "Theoretical Propositions of Life-Span *Developmental Psychology*: On the Dynamics between Growth and Decline," *Developmental Psychology* 23, no. 5 (1987): 611–626.

[34] Loretta L. Pecchioni, Kevin B. Wright, and Jon F. Nussbaum, *Life-span Communication* (Mahwah, NJ: Lawrence Erlbaum, 2005), 5–9.

[35] Jon F. Nussbaum, ed., *The Handbook of Lifespan Communication* (New York: Peter Lang, 2014).

Chapter 5: Rituals for Connection: Creating Rhythms for Healthy Relationships

[1] Judy C. Pearson, Jeffrey T. Child, and Anna F. Carmon, "Rituals in Dating Relationships: The Development and Validation of a Measure," *Communication Quarterly* 59, no. 3 (2011): 360.

[2] Steven J. Wolin and Linda A. Bennett, "Family Rituals," *Family Process* 23, no. 3 (1984): 401.

[3] Linda A. Bennett, Steven J. Wolin, and Katharine J. McAvity, "Family Identity, Ritual and Myth: A Cultural Perspective on Life Cycle Transition," in *Family Transitions: Continuity and Change over the Life Cycle*, ed. Celia Jaes Falicov (New York: Guilford, 1988), 211–234.

[4] Grace M. Viere, "Examining Family Rituals," *The Family Journal: Counseling and Therapy for Couples and Families* 9, no. 3 (2001): 285.

[5] Ibid., 285–88.

[6] See Leslie A. Baxter, "Symbols of Relationship Identity in Relationship Cultures," *Journal of Social and Personal Relationships* 4, no. 3 (1987): 261–280; Carol J. S. Bruess and Judy C. Pearson, "Interpersonal Rituals in Marriage and Adult Friendship," *Communication Monographs* 64, no. 1 (1997): 25–46.

[7] Leslie A. Baxter, "Forms and Functions of Intimate Play in Personal

Relationships," *Human Communication Research* 8, no. 3 (1992): 336–363.

[8] Wolin and Bennett, "Family Rituals."

[9] Wendy Leeds-Hurwitz, *Wedding as Text: Communicating Cultural Identities through Rituals* (New York: Routledge, 2002).

[10] Viere, "Examining Family Rituals," 285.

[11] Bruess and Pearson, "Interpersonal Rituals."

[12] Steve Shadrach, *The Fuel and the Flame: Ten Keys to Ignite Your Campus for Jesus Christ* (Authentic Publishing: Tyrone, GA, 2003), 285.

[13] Kathryn Dindia and Daniel J. Canary, "Definitions and Theoretical Perspectives on Maintaining Relationships," *Journal of Social and Personal Relationships* 10, no. 2 (1993): 163–173.

[14] Dawn O. Braithwaite, Jaclyn S. Marsh, Carol L. Tschampl-Diesing, and Margaret S. Leach, "'Love Needs To Be Exchanged': A Diary Study of Interaction and Enactment of the Family Kinkeeper Role," *Western Journal of Communication* 81, no. 5 (2017): 601–618.

[15] Laura Stafford and Daniel J. Canary, "Maintenance Strategies and Romantic Relationship Type, Gender, and Relational Characteristics," *Journal of Social and Personal Relationships* 8, no. 2 (1991): 217–242.

[16] Andrew M. Ledbetter, Heather Stassen, Azhanni Muhammad, and Ephraim N. Kotey, "Relational Maintenance as Including the Other in the Self," *Qualitative Research Reports in Communication* 11, no. 1 (2010): 21–28.

[17] Arthur P. Aron, Debra J. Mashek, and Elaine N. Aron, "Closeness as Including Other in the Self," in *Handbook of Closeness and Intimacy*, eds. Debra. J. Mashek and Arthur P. Aron, (Mahwah, NJ: Lawrence Erlbaum, 2004), 27–41.

[18] See also Arthur P. Aron, Gary Lewandowski, J. Debra Mashek, and Elaine Aron, "The Self-Expansion Model of Motivation and Cognition in Close Relationships," in *The Oxford Handbook of Close Relationships*, eds. Jeffry A. Simpson and Lorne Campbell (Oxford: Oxford University Press, 2013), 90–115.

[19] Ledbetter et al., "Relational Maintenance," 22.

[20] Ibid., 27.

[21] Marianne Dainton and Scott A. Myers, *Communication and Relationship Maintenance* (San Diego, CA: Cognella, 2020).

[22] Elizabeth Dorrance Hall and Jenna McNallie, "The Mediating Role of Sibling Maintenance Behavior Expectations and Perceptions in the Relationship between Family Communication Patterns and Relationship Satisfaction," *Journal of Family Communication* 16, no. 4 (2016): 386–402.

[23] Alan K. Goodboy, Scott A. Myers, and Brian R. Patterson, "Investigating Elderly Sibling Types, Relational Maintenance, and Lifespan Affect, Cognition, and Behavior," *Atlantic Journal of Communication* 17, no. 3 (2009): 140–148.

[24] Scott A. Myers and Kelly G. Odenweller, "The Use of Relational Maintenance Behaviors and Relational Characteristics among Sibling Types," *Communication Studies* 66, no. 2 (2015): 238–255.

[25] Gary Chapman, *The Five Love Languages: The Secret to Love That Lasts* (Chicago: Northfield, 2015).

[26] Ibid., 56.

[27] Nichole Egbert and Denise Polk, "Speaking the Language of Relational Maintenance: A Validity Test of Chapman's Five Love Languages," *Communication Research Reports* 23, no. 1 (2006): 19–26.

[28] Laura Stafford, Marianne Dainton, and Stephen Haas, "Measuring Routine and Strategic Relational Maintenance: Scale Revision, Sex versus Gender Roles, and the Prediction of Relational Characteristics," *Communication Monographs* 67, no. 3 (2000): 306–323.

[29] Ibid.

[30] Selena Bunt and Zoe J. Hazelwood, "Walking the Walk, Talking the Talk: Love Languages, Self-Regulation, and Relationship Satisfaction," *Personal Relationships* 24, no. 2 (2017): 287.

[31] John Gottman and Julie Gottman, "The Natural Principles of Love," *Journal of Family Theory and Review* 9, no. 1 (2017): 7–26.

[32] Gottman and Silver, *The Seven Principles*.

[33] Baxter, "Forms and Functions."

Chapter 6: Rules for Conflict: Establishing Parameters for Hard Conversations

[1] Angie Williams and Jon Nussbaum, *Intergenerational Relationships across the Lifespan* (New York: Routledge, 2001).

[2] Howard J. Markman, Scott M. Stanley, and Susan L. Blumberg, *Fighting for Your Marriage: Positive Steps for Preventing Divorce and Preserving a Lasting Love* (San Francisco: Jossey-Bass Publishers, 1994).

[3] Ken Sande, "Getting to the Heart of Conflict," Relational Wisdom 360, https://rw360.org/getting-to-the-heart-of-conflict/

[4] Ibid.

[5] Tim Muehlhoff, *Defending Your Marriage: The Reality of Spiritual Battle* (Downers Grove, IL: InterVarsity Press, 2018).

[6] C. S. Lewis, *The Screwtape Letters*, C. S. Lewis Signature Classic Series (San Francisco: Harper, 2001), 13; see also https://www.thespiritlife.net/about/81-warfare/warfare-publications/1879-chapter-4-the-screwtape-letters-cs-lewis

[7] Quentin J. Schultze, "The 'God-Problem' in Communication Studies," *Journal of Communication and Religion* 28, no. 1 (2005): 1–22.

[8] Lewis, *The Screwtape Letters*, 16.

[9] Joyce L. Hocker and William Wilmot, *Interpersonal Conflict*, 10th ed. (Boston: McGraw Hill, 2018), 3.

[10] Lynn H. Turner and Richard West, *Perspectives on Family Communication*, 5th ed. (Boston: McGraw Hill, 2018), 247.

[11] Quentin J. Schultze and Diane M. Badzinski, *An Essential Guide to Interpersonal Communication: Building Great Relationships in the Age of Social Media with Faith, Skill, and Virtue* (Grand Rapids, MI: Baker Academics, 2015).

[12] Ibid.

[13] Markman, Stanley, and Blumberg, *Fighting for Your Marriage*.

[14] Mengyu (Miranda) Gao, Han Du, Patrick T. Davies, and E. Mark Cummings, "Marital Conflict Behaviors and Parenting: Dyadic Links Over Time," *Family Relations* 68, no. 2 (2018): 1–15.

[15] John M. Gottman and Nan Silver, *The Seven Principles for Making Marriage Work: A Practical Guide from the Country's Foremost Relationship Expert* (New York:

Harmony Books, 2015).

[16] Ibid.

[17] Ibid.

[18] Ibid.

[19] Ibid.

[20] Ibid., 34.

[21] Ibid.

[22] Ibid., 47.

[23] John M. Gottman and Nan Silver, *What Makes Love Last?: How To Build Trust and Avoid Betrayal* (New York: Simon & Schuster, 2012). See also "The Love Quiz: Are You Experiencing Negative Sentiment Override?", Gottman Institute, https://www.gottman.com/blog/quiz-negative-sentiment-override/

[24] Gottman and Silver, *The Seven Principles*, 51.

[25] Markman, Stanley, and Blumberg, *Fighting for Your Marriage*.

[26] Ralph H. Kilmann and Kenneth W. Thomas, "Interpersonal Conflict-handling Behavior as Reflections of Jungian Personality Dimensions," *Psychological Reports* 37, no. 3 (1975): 971–980. See also Jack O. Balswick and Judith K. Balswick, *The Family: A Christian Perspective on the Contemporary Home*, 3rd ed. (Grand Rapids, MI: Baker Academic, 2007), 262.

[27] Balswick and Balswick, *The Family*.

[28] Muehlhoff, *Defending Your Marriage*.

[29] Ibid., 55.

[30] Ken Sande, *The Peacemaker: A Biblical Guide to Resolving Personal Conflict*, 3rd ed. (Grand Rapids, MI: Baker Books, 2004).

[31] Ken Sande and Kevin Johnson, *Resolving Everyday Conflict* (Grand Rapids, MI: Baker Books, 2015).

[32] Ibid., 145.

[33] Ibid., 219.

[34] Markman, Stanley, and Blumberg, *Fighting for Your Marriage*.

[35] Tim Muehlhoff, *I Beg to Differ: Navigating Difficult Conversations with Truth and Love* (Downers Grove, IL: InterVarsity Press, 2014).

[36] Ibid., 151.

Chapter 7: Repairing Relationships: Offering and Receiving Forgiveness

[1] Anita L. Vangelisti and Linda P. Crumley, "Reactions to Messages That Hurt: The Influence of Relational Context," *Communication Monographs* 64, no. 3 (1998): 173–96; Anita L. Vangelisti, "Messages That Hurt," in *The Dark Side of Interpersonal Communication*, eds. William R. Cupach and Brian H. Spitzberg (Hillsdale, NJ: Erlbaum, 1994), 53–82.

[2] Vangelisti, "Messages that Hurt."

3 Ibid.

[4] Laura K. Guerrero, Peter A. Andersen, Peter F. Jorgensen, Brian H. Spitzberg, and Sylvie V. Eloy, "Coping with the Green-Eyed Monster: Conceptualizing and Measuring Communicative Responses to Romantic Jealousy," *Western Journal of Communication*

59, no. 4 (1995): 270–304; Vangelisti and Crumley, "Reactions to Messages that Hurt."

[5] Ibid.

[6] Guerrero et al., "Coping with the Green-Eyed Monster."

[7] Vangelisti and Crumley, "Reactions to Messages that Hurt."

[8] Guerrero et al., "Coping with the Green-Eyed Monster."

[9] Ibid.

[10] Ibid.

[11] M. James Jordan, *The Ancient Road Rediscovered: What the Early Church Knew* (Taupo, New Zealand: Fatherheart Media, 2015), 183.

[12] Adapted from Guerrero et al., "Coping with the Green-Eyed Monster."

[13] Janet R. Meyer and Kyra Rothenberg, "Repairing Regretted Messages: Effects of Emotional State, Relationship Type, and Seriousness of Offense," *Communication Research Reports* 21, no. 4 (2004): 348–56.

[14] Deboran Nin, "I Forgave My Cheating Husband," *Hamasa Magazine*, April 20, 2018, https://www.hamasamagazine.com/2018/04/16/forgave/

[15] Ken Sande, *The Peacemaker: A Biblical Guide to Resolving Personal Conflict*, 3rd ed. (Grand Rapids, MI: Baker Books, 2004).

[16] Douglas L. Kelley, "Communicating Forgiveness," in *Making Connections: Readings in Relational Communication*, 5th ed., ed. Kathleen M. Galvin (New York: Oxford Press, 2011), 203.

[17] Robert Enright and Jeanette Knutson, "Be Your Best Self: Giving and Receiving Forgiveness: A Guided Curriculum for Children Ages 11–14 (Grade 7 in the US, Year 9 in the UK) within a Christian Context," International Forgiveness Institute (2010).

[18] Julie H. Hall and Frank D. Fincham, "Self-Forgiveness: The Stepchild of Forgiveness Research," *Journal of Social and Clinical Psychology* 24, no. 5 (2005): 621–637.

[19] Frank D. Fincham, "Toward a Psychology of Divine Forgiveness," *Journal of Spirituality and Religion* (2020): 1–11.

[20] "Substitutionary Atonement," Moody Bible Institute, https://www.moodybible.org/beliefs/positional-statements/substitutionary-atonement/

[21] As cited in Douglas L. Kelley, *Just Relationships: Living Out Social Justice as Mentor, Family, Friend and Lover* (New York: Routledge, 2017), 117–118.

[22] Everett L. Worthington, *Forgiving and Reconciling: Bridges to Wholeness and Hope* (Downers Grove, IL: InterVarsity Press, 2003), 73–74.

[23] Sande, *The Peacemaker*.

[24] Lewis B. Smedes, *Forgive and Forget: Heal the Hurts We Don't Deserve* (New York: HarperCollins, 1996); Douglas L. Kelley, Vincent R. Waldron, and Dayna N. Kloeber, *A Communicative Approach to Conflict, Forgiveness, and Reconciliation* (New York: Routledge, 2019).

[25] Neil T. Anderson, *Victory over Darkness: Realize the Power of Your Identity in Christ* (Bloomington, MN: Bethany House, 2000); Neil T. Anderson, The Bondage Breaker: Overcoming *Negative Thoughts,*Irrational Fears,*Habitual Sin (Eugene, OR: Harvest House, 2019).

[26] Enright and Knutson, "Be Your Best Self."

[27] Kelley, *Just Relationships*.

[28] Ibid., 122.

[29] Everett L. Worthington, Constance B. Sharp, Andrea J. Lerner, and Jeffrey R. Sharp, "Interpersonal Forgiveness as an Example of Loving One's Enemies," *Journal of Psychology & Theology* 34, no. 1 (2006): 32–42.

[30] Ibid.

[31] Ibid., 33.

[32] Ibid.

[33] Ibid.

[34] Kelley, Waldron, and Kloeber, *A Communicative Approach to Conflict*, 104.

[35] Ibid., 104–105.

[36] Kelley, "Communicating Forgiveness."

[37] Ibid.

[38] Andy J. Merolla and Shuangyue Zhang, "In the Wake of Transgressions: Examining Forgiveness Communication in Personal Relationships," *Personal Relationships* 18, no. 1 (2011): 79–95.

[39] Pavica Sheldon, Eletra Gilchrist-Petty, and James A. Lessley, "You Did What? The Relationship between Forgiveness Tendency, Communication of Forgiveness, and Relationship Satisfaction in Married and Dating Couples," *Communication Reports* 27, no. 2 (2014): 78–90.

[40] Timothy Edwards, Elizabeth B. Pask, Robert Whitbred, and Kimberly A. Neuendorf, "The Influence of Personal, Relational, and Contextual Factors on Forgiveness Communication Following Transgressions," *Personal Relationships* 25, no. 1 (2018): 4–21.

[41] Larry D. Ellis, *Forgiveness: Unleashing a Transformational Process* (Denver: Adoration, 2010), 66.

[42] Enright and Knutson, "Be Your Best Self."

Chapter 8: Cultivating Resilience: Communication Strategies for Adapting to Stress

[1] Alicia Besa Panganiban, "Theology of Resilience amidst Vulnerability in the Book of Ruth," *Feminist Theology* 28, no. 2 (2020): 182–97.

[2] Heather M. Helms, Kaicee B. Postler, and David H. Demo, "Everyday Hassles and Family Relationships," in *Family & Change: Coping with Stressful Events and Transitions*, 6th ed., eds. Kevin R. Bush and Christine A. Price (Los Angeles: Sage, 2021), 27–54.

[3] Hamilton I. McCubbin and Joan M. Patterson, "Family Adaptation to Crisis," in *Family Stress, Coping, and Social Support*, eds. Hamilton I. McCubbin, A. Elizabeth Cauble, and Joan M. Patterson (Springfield, IL: Thomas Books, 1982), 26–47.

[4] David H. Olson, Yoav Lavee, and Hamilton I. McCubbin, "Types of Families and Family Response to Stress across the Family Life Cycle," in *Social Stress and Family Development*, eds. David M. Klein and Joan Aldous (New York: Guilford Press, 1988), 19.

[5] See Reuben Hill, *Families Under Stress* (New York: Harper & Brothers, 1949); Reuben Hill, "Generic Features of Families Under Stress," *Social Casework* 39, no. 2–3 (1958): 139–150.

[6] Hamilton I. McCubbin and Joan M. Patterson, "The Family Stress Process: The Double ABC-X Model of Adjustment and Adaptation," in *Social Stress and the Family: Advances and Developments in Family Stress Theory and Research*, eds. Hamilton I. McCubbin, Marvin B. Sussman, and Joan M. Patterson (New York: The Haworth Press, 1983), 7–37.

[7] Ibid.

[8] Michael Rosino, "ABC-X Model of Family Stress and Coping" in *The Wiley Blackwell Encyclopedia of Family Studies*, ed. Constance I. Shehan (New York: Wiley Blackwell, 2016), 1–6.

[9] Yoav Lavee, Hamilton I. McCubbin, and Joan M. Patterson, "The Double ABC-X Model of Family Stress and Adaptation: An Empirical Test by Analysis of Structural Equations with Latent Variables," *Journal of Marriage and Family* 47, no. 4 (1985): 811–825.

[10] Benjamin R. Karney and Thomas Nelson Bradbury, "The Longitudinal Course of Marital Quality and Stability: A Review of Theory, Method, and Research," *Psychological Bulletin* 118, no. 1 (1995): 3–34.

[11] See David H. Olson, "Circumplex Model of Marital and Family Systems: Assessing Family Functioning," in *Normal Family Processes*, 2nd ed., ed. Froma Walsh (New York: Guilford Press, 1993), 104–137; David H. Olson, Candyce Smith Russell, and Douglas H. Sprenkle, *Circumplex Model: Systematic Assessment and Treatment of Families* (New York: Haworth Press, 1989).

[12] David H. Olson and Hamilton I. McCubbin, "Circumplex Model of Marital and Family Systems V: Application to Family Stress and Crisis Intervention," in *Family Stress, Coping, and Social Support*, eds. Hamilton I. McCubbin, A. Elizabeth Cauble, and Joan M. Patterson (Springfield, IL: Thomas Books, 1982), 51.

[13] David H. Olson, Douglas H. Sprenkle, and Candyce Smith Russell, "Circumplex Model of Marital and Family System: 1. Cohesion and Adaptability Dimensions, Family Types, and Clinical Applications," *Family Process* 18, no. 1 (1979): 12.

[14] Ibid., 5.

[15] David H. Olson, "Circumplex Model of Marital and Family Systems," *Journal of Family Therapy* 22, no. 2 (2000): 144–167.

[16] Olson, Russell, and Sprenkle, *Circumplex Model*.

[17] Kristen Carr, "Communication and Family Resilience," in *The International Encyclopedia for Interpersonal Communication*, eds. Charles R. Berger and Michael E. Roloff (New York: Wiley Blackwell, 2016), 236–244; Kristen Carr and Jody Koenig Kellas, "The Role of Family and Marital Communication in Developing Resilience to Family-of-Origin Adversity," *Journal of Family Communication* 18, no. 1 (2018): 68–84.

[18] Carr and Koenig Kellas, "The Role of Family and Marital Communication."

[19] Carr, "Communication and Family Resilience," 239.

[20] Tamara D. Afifi, Anne F. Merrill, and Sharde Davis, "The Theory of Resilience and Relational Load," *Personal Relationships* 23, no. 4 (2016): 663–683.

[21] Ibid., 664.

[22] Tamara D. Afifi and Kathryn Harrison, "Theory of Resilience and Relational Load (TRRL): Understanding Families as Systems of Stress and Calibration," in *Engaging Theories in Family Communication: Multiple Perspectives*, 2nd ed., eds. Dawn O. Braithwaite, Elizabeth A. Suter, and Kory Floyd (New York: Routledge, 2018), 324–336.

[23] See Laura Stafford and Daniel J. Canary, "Equity and Interdependence as Predictors of Relational Maintenance Strategies," *Journal of Family Communication* 6, no. 4 (2006): 227–254; Marianne Dainton and Scott A. Myers, *Communication and Relationship Maintenance* (San Diego: Cognella, 2020).

[24] Patrice M. Buzzanell, "Resilience: Talking, Resisting, and Imagining New Normalcies into Being," *Journal of Communication* 60, no. 1 (2010): 1–14.

[25] Ibid., 4.

[26] Jennifer A. Theiss, "Family Communication and Resilience," *Journal of Applied Communication Research* 46, no. 1 (2018): 10–13.

[27] Kristen Lucas and Patrice Buzzanell, "Memorable Messages of Hard Times: Constructing Short- and Long-Term Resiliencies through Family Communication," *Journal of Family Communication* 12, no. 3 (2012): 189–208.

[28] Christopher Krall, "'Resilient Faithfulness': A Dynamic Dialectic between the Transcendent and Physical Dimensions of the Human Person," *Journal of Moral Theology* 9, no. 1 (2020): 168–189.

[29] Ibid., 189.

[30] Ibid., 187–188. 31 Oswald Chambers, "Utmost for His Highest," October 17, 2020, http://myreligion.com.ng/2020/10/october-17-2020-my-utmost-for-his-highest-devotional-topic-the-key-of-the-greater-work/

[32] See Caroline Campbell and Sandra Bauer, "Christian Faith and Resilience: Implications for Social Work Practice," *Social Work & Christianity* 48, no. 1 (2021): 28–51.

[33] Terri Lewinson, Katherine Hurt, and Anne K. Hughes, "'I Overcame That with God's Hand on Me': Religion and Spirituality among Older Adults to Cope with Stressful Life Situations," *Journal of Religion and Spirituality in Social Work: Social Thought* 34, no. 3 (2015): 285–303.

Chapter 9: Communication Routines: Doing Life Together

[1] Natasha Quadlin and Long Doan, "Sex-Typed Chores and the City: Gender, Urbanicity, and Housework," *Gender & Society* 32, no. 6 (2018): 789–813.

[2] Gary Chapman, "Essentials of Healthy Marriages," YouTube, April 24, 2015, https://www.youtube.com/watch?v=vM1LzhHQcf0

[3] Kely Braswell, *Independent Me: Learning to Relate to Spiritual Authority* (All Peoples Church, 2014).

[4] U.S. Bureau of Labor Statistics, "American Time Use Survey," 2019, https://www.bls.gov/charts/american-time-use/activity-by-hldh.htm

[5] Gigi Foster and Leslie S. Stratton, "What Women Want (Their Men to Do): Housework and Satisfaction in Australian Households," *Feminist Economics* 25, no. 3 (2019): 23–47.

[6] Chiung-Ya Tang and Melissa A. Curran, "Marital Commitment and Perceptions of Fairness in Household Chores," *Journal of Family Issues* 34, no. 12 (2013): 1598–1622.

[7] Javier Cerrato and Eva Cifre, "Gender Inequality in Household Chores and Work-Family Conflict," *Frontiers in Psychology*, August 3, 2018, https://www.frontiersin.org/articles/10.3389/fpsyg.2018.01330/full

[8] Arlie R. Hochschild and Anne Machung, *The Second Shift: Working Families and the Revolution at Home* (New York: Penguin Group, 2012).

[9] See Livia Sz. Oláh, Daniele Vignoli, and Irena E. Kotowska, "Gender Roles and Families," in *Handbook of Labor, Human Resources and Population Economics*, ed. Klaus F. Zimmermann (Switzerland: Springer, 2021), 1–28.

[10] Andréanne Charbonneau, Mylène Lachance-Grzela, and Geneviève Bouchard, "Threshold Levels for Disorder, Inequity in Household Labor, and Frustration with the Partner among Emerging Adult Couples: A Dyadic Examination," *Journal of Family*

Issues 42, no. 1 (2021): 176–200; Jess K. Alberts, Sarah J. Tracy, and Angela Trethewey, "An Integrative Theory of the Division of Domestic Labor: Threshold Level, Social Organizing and Sensemaking," *Journal of Family Communication* 11, no. 1 (2011): 21–38.

[11] Niels Blom, Gerbert Kraaykamp, and Ellen Verbakel, "Couples' Division of Employment and Household Chores and Relationship Satisfaction: A Test of the Specialization and Equity Hypotheses," *European Sociological Review* 33, no. 2 (2017): 195–208.

[12] Ibid.

[13] Paul R. Amato, Alan Booth, David R. Johnson, and Stacy J. Rogers, *Alone Together: How Marriage in America is Changing* (Cambridge, MA: Harvard University Press, 2007).

[14] Victoria Rideout and Michael B. Robb, *Common Sense Census: Media Use by Tweens and Teens* (San Francisco: Common Sense Media, 2019), https://www.commonsensemedia.org/press-releases/the-common-sense-census-media-use-by-tweens-and-teens-new-research-finds-youtube-videos-beat-out-tv-and

[15] Paul D. Patton and Robert H. Woods Jr., *Everyday Sabbath: How to Lead Your Dance with Media and Technology in Mindful and Sacred Ways* (Eugene, OR: Cascade Books, 2021).

[16] Wonsun Shin and Hye Kyung Kim, "What Motivates Parents to Mediate Children's Use of Smartphones?: An Application of the Theory of Planned Behavior," *Journal of Broadcasting and Electronic Media* 63, no. 1 (2019): 144–59.

[17] Andy Crouch, *The Tech-Wise Family: Everyday Steps for Putting Technology in Its Proper Place* (Grand Rapids, MI: Baker Books 2017), 20–21.

[18] Sandra Petronio, "Communication Privacy Management Theory: Understanding Families," in *Engaging Theories in Family Communication: Multiple Perspectives*, 2nd ed., eds. Dawn O. Braithwaite, Elizabeth A. Suter, and Kory Floyd (New York: Routledge, 2018), 87–97.

[19] Jeffrey T. Child and Sandra Petronio, "Privacy Management Matters in Digital Family Communication," in *Family Communication in the Age of Digital and Social Media*, ed. Carol J. Bruess (New York: Peter Lang, 2015), 35.

[20] Petronio, "Communication Privacy Management Theory."

[21] Ibid., 91.

Chapter 10: Pathways to Marriage

[1] For an application of Isaac and Rebekah's love story to courtship practices, see Gary Thomas, *The Sacred Search: What If It's Not about Who You Marry, But Why?* (Colorado Springs, CO: David C. Cook, 2013), 71–76.

[2] Ibid., 73.

[3] Adrienne R. Brown, "High School Seniors' Expectations to Marry, 2020," *Family Profiles, FP-22-04* (Bowling Green, OH: National Center for Family & Marriage Research, 2020), https://www.bgsu.edu/ncfmr/resources/data/family-profiles/brown-high-school-seniors-expectation-to-marry-2020-fp-22-04.html

[4] William C. Schutz, *FIRO: A Three-Dimensional Theory of Interpersonal Behavior* (New York: Holt, Rinehart and Winston, 1958).

[5] Abraham H. Maslow, *Toward a Psychology of Being*, 2nd ed. (New York: Van Nostrand Reinhold, 1968).

[6] Jim A. McCleskey and Larry Ruddell, "Taking A Step Back—Maslow's Theory of

Motivation: A Christian Critical Perspective," *Journal of Biblical Integration in Business* 23, no. 1 (2020): 6–16.

[7] Maslow, *Toward a Psychology of Being*, 3–4.

[8] For additional Christian critiques of Maslow's Hierarchy of Needs Theory, see Susan Mettes, "Ministry after Maslow: Maslow's Hierarchy of Needs Has Leavened the Teaching in American Churches. That's a Problem," *Christianity Today* 65, no. 5 (2018): 38–43; and Kent W. Seibert, "Taking a Step Forward: Maslow and Christian Management," *Journal of Biblical Integration in Business* 23, no. 1 (2020): 17–20.

[9] Cindy Hazan and Phillip Shaver, "Romantic Love Conceptualized as an Attachment Process," *Journal of Personality and Social Psychology* 52, no. 3 (1987): 511–24.

[10] Beth Le Poire, Julie Haynes, Jennifer Driscoll, Bennett N. Driver, Tracy F. Wheelis, Mary Kay Hyde, Matthew Prochaska, and Laurie Ramos, "Attachment as a Function of Parental and Partner Approach-Avoidance Tendencies," *Human Communication Research* 23, no. 3 (1997): 413–441.

[11] Kory Floyd, Colin Hesse, and Mark Alan Generous, "Affection Exchange Theory: A Bio-Evolutionary Look at Affectionate Communication," in *Engaging Theories in Family Communication: Multiple Perspectives*, 2nd ed., eds. Dawn O. Braithwaite, Elizabeth A. Suter, and Kory Floyd (Thousand Oaks, CA: Routledge, 2018), 17–26.

[12] Ibid., 18.

[13] David Givens, *Love Signals: A Practical Field Guide to the Body Language of Courtship* (New York: St. Martin's, 2005).

[14] Helen Fisher, *Anatomy of Love: A Natural History of Mating, Marriage, and Why We Stray* (New York: W.W. Norton & Company, 2016), 7.

[15] Claus Wedekind, Thomas Seebeck, Florence Bettens, and Alexander J. Paepke, "MHC-Dependent Mate Preferences," *Biological Sciences* 260, no. 1359 (1995): 245–249.

[16] Jamie Winternitz, J. L. Abbate, E. Huchard, J. Havlíček, and L. Z. Garamszegi, "Patterns of MHC-Dependent Mate Selection in Humans and Nonhuman Primates: A Meta-Analysis," *Molecular Ecology* 26, no. 2 (2017): 668–688.

[17] Claus Wedekind and Sandra Füri, "Body Odor Preference in Men and Women: Do They Aim for Specific MHC Combinations or Simply Heterozygosity?," *Proceedings of the Royal Society B: Biological Sciences* 264 (1997): 1471–1479.

[18] Alison Motluk, "Scent of a Man," *New Scientist*, February 10, 2001, http://motluk.com/stories/ns.scent.of.a.man.html

[19] Sheer Birnbaum, Gurit E. Birnbaum, and Tsachi Ein-Dor, "Can Contraceptive Pill Affect Future Offspring's Health? The Implications of Using Hormonal Birth Control for Human Evolution," *Evolutionary Psychological Science* 3 (2017): 89–96.

[20] For a critique of the evolutionary perspective, see John H. Harvey and Amy Wenzel, "Theoretical Perspectives in the Study of Close Relationships," in *The Cambridge Handbook of Personal Relationships*, eds. Anita L. Vangelisti and Daniel Perlman (New York: Cambridge University Press, 2006), 37–38.

[21] Alan C. Kerckhoff and Keith E. Davis, "Value Consensus and Need Complementarity in Mate Selection," *American Sociological Review* 27, no. 3 (1962): 295–303.

[22] Catherine A. Surra, "Research and Theory on Mate Selection and Premarital Relationships in the 1980s," *Journal of Marriage and Family* 52, no. 4 (1990): 849.

[23] Catherine Pakaluk, "To Have and To Have Not: Marriage and Childbearing in the Age of the Pill," *Baby Makes Three: Social Scientific Research on Successfully Combing Marriage the Parenthood*, Princeton University, June 16–19, 2010.

[24] Ibid.

[25] Marianne Dainton and Elaine D. Zelley, *Applying Communication Theory for Professional Life: A Practical Introduction* (Thousand Oaks, CA: Sage, 2005).

[26] Centers for Disease Control and Prevention, "Unmarried Childbearing," National Center of Health Statistics, 2019, https://www.cdc.gov/nchs/fastats/unmarried-childbearing.htm

[27] Caryl E. Rusbult, Christopher R. Agnew, and Ximena B. Arriaga, "The Investment Model of Commitment Processes," in *The Handbook of Theories of Social Psychology*, eds. Paul A. M. Van Lange, Arie W. Kruglanski, and E. Tory Higgins (Thousand Oaks, CA: Sage, 2012), 218–231.

[28] Stephanie Coontz, *Marriage, A History: How Love Conquered Marriage* (New York: Penguin Books, 2004).

[29] Jonathan Pettigrew, "Arranged Love? An Indian Case-Study" (unpublished manuscript, 2005).

[30] Michael J. Rosenfeld, Reuben J. Thomas, and Sonia Hausen, "Disintermediating Your Friends: How Online Dating in the United States Displaces Other Ways of Meeting," *Proceedings of the National Academy of Sciences of the United States of America* 116, no. 36 (2019): 17753–17758.

[31] W. Bradford Wilcox and Jeffrey Dew, "Is Love a Flimsy Foundation? Soulmate versus Institutional Models of Marriage," *Faculty Publications* 4517 (2010), https://scholarsarchive.byu.edu/facpub/4517

[32] David G. Blankenhorn, *Fatherless America: Confronting Our Most Urgent Social Problem* (New York: HarperCollins, 1996).

[33] Matthijs Kalmijn, "Shifting Boundaries: Trends in Religious and Educational Homogamy," *American Sociological Review* 56, no. 6 (1991): 786–800.

[34] Wilcox and Dew, "Is Love A Flimsy Foundation," 689.

[35] Ibid.

[36] Rosenfeld, Thomas, and Hausen, "Disintermediating Your Friends."

[37] Ibid.

[38] "Trends of Redefining Romance Today," Barna, February 9, 2017, https://www.barna.com/research/trends-redefining-romance-today/

[39] Jennifer L. Gibbs, Nicole B. Ellison, and Chi-Hui Lai, "First Comes Love, Then Comes Google: An Investigation of Uncertainty Reduction Strategies and Self-Disclosure in Online Dating," *Communication Research* 38, no. 1 (2011): 70–100.

[40] Irwin Altman and Dalmus A. Taylor, *Social Penetration: The Development of Interpersonal Relationships* (New York: Holt, Rinehart and Winston, 1970).

[41] Catherine A. Surra, "Courtship Types: Variations in Interdependence between Partners and Social Networks," *Journal of Personality and Social Psychology* 45, no. 2 (1985): 357–75.

[42] Ready to Wed," Focus on the Family, https://www.focusonthefamily.com/marriage/ready-to-wed/; see also Greg Smalley and Erin Smalley, *Ready to Wed: 12 Ways to Start a Marriage You'll Love* (Carol Stream, IL: Tyndale House Publishers, 2015).

[43] Wendy Leeds-Hurwitz, *Weddings as Text: Communicating Cultural Identities through Rituals* (Mahwah, NJ: Lawrence Erlbaum, 2002).

[44] Ben Stuart, *Single, Dating, Engaged, Married: Navigating Life and Love in the Modern Age* (Nashville, TN: Thomas Nelson, 2017).

[45] Thomas, *The Sacred Search*, 65–66.

[46] Arthur Aron, Helen Fisher, Debra J. Mashek, Greg Strong, Haifang Li, and

Lucy L. Brown, "Reward, Motivation, and Emotion Systems Associated with Early-Stage Intense Romantic Love," *Journal of Neurophysiology* 94, no. 1 (2005): 327–337; for an accessible review, see W. Jess Gill, "Hold on Tight! The Neurochemistry of Infatuation and Lifelong Love," The American Association of Christian Counselors, https://www.aacc.net/2020/02/06/hold-on-tight-the-neurochemistry-of-infatuation-and-lifelong-love/

[47] Stuart, *Single, Dating, Engaged, Married*, 101.

Chapter 11: Marriage as a Covenant and Sexual Communication

[1] For a thoughtful, culturally-grounded presentation of these ideas, see Ray Vander Laan, "That the World May Know. The True Easter Story," Focus on the Family, 2002, video.

[2] William Strom, "Contractualism, Committalism, and Covenantalism: A Worldview Dimensional Analysis of Human Relating," *Communication Studies* 64, no. 4 (2013): 353–373.

[3] Ibid., 360.

[4] See Bill Strom, "Relational Resilience amidst the Pandemic: Contract and Covenant Orientations Predict Struggle and Thriving During Social Lockdown," *Journal of Communication and Religion* 44, no. 4 (2021): 45–62.

[5] Lauren E. Harris, "Committing Before Cohabiting: Pathways to Marriage among Middle-Class Couples," *Journal of Family Issues* 42, no. 8 (2021): 1762–1786.

[6] Paul Hemez, "Young Adulthood: Cohabitation, Birth, and Marriage Experiences," *Family Profiles, FP-18-22* (Bowling Green, OH: National Center for Family & Marriage Research, 2018), https://www.bgsu.edu/ncfmr/resources/data/family-profiles/hemez-young-adults-cohab-birth-mar-fp-18-22.html

[7] Catherine A. Surra, "Research and Theory on Mate Selection and Premarital Relationships in the 1980s," *Journal of Marriage and Family* 52, no. 4 (1990): 849.

[8] David Popenoe and Barbara Dafore Whitehead, "'Should We Live Together?': What Young Adults Need to Know about Cohabitation before Marriage," (Piscataway, NJ: The National Marriage Project, 2002), http://nationalmarriageproject.org/wp-content/uploads/2013/01/ShouldWeLiveTogether.pdf

[9] Sharon Sassler and Daniel T. Lichter, "Cohabitation and Marriage: Complexity and Diversity in Union-Formation Patterns," *Journal of Marriage and Family* 82, no. 1 (2020): 35–61.

[10] Wendy D. Manning, "Young Adulthood Relationships in an Era of Uncertainty: A Case for Cohabitation," *Demography* 57, no. 3 (2020): 799–819.

[11] Kasey J. Eickmeyer and Wendy D. Manning, "Serial Cohabitation in Young Adulthood: Baby Boomers to Millennials," *Journal of Marriage and Family* 80, no. 4 (2018): 826–840.

[12] Hemez, "Young Adulthood."

[13] Manning, "Young Adulthood Relationships."

[14] Penelope M. Huang, Pamela J. Smock, Wendy D. Manning, and Cara A. Bergstrom-Lynch, "He Says, She Says: Gender and Cohabitation," *Journal of Family Issues* 32, no. 7 (2011): 876–905.

[15] Galena K. Rhoades, Scott M. Stanley, and Howard J. Markman, "Couples'

Reasons for Cohabitation: Associations with Individual Well-Being and Relationship Quality," *Journal of Family Issues* 30, no. 2 (2009): 238–258.

[16] Huang et al., "He Says, She Says."

[17] Ibid., 887.

[18] Scott M. Stanley, Galena Kline Rhoades, and Howard J. Markman, "Sliding Versus Deciding: Inertia and the Premarital Cohabitation Effect," *Family Relations* 55, no. 4 (2006): 499–509.

[19] Rhoades, Stanley, and Markman, "Couples' Reasons for Cohabitation"; Huang et al., "He Says, She Says."

[20] Stanley, Rhoades, and Markman, "Sliding Versus Deciding," 505.

[21] Ibid.

[22] Brandon G. Wagner, "Marriage, Cohabitation, and Sexual Exclusivity: Unpacking the Effect of Marriage," *Social Forces* 97, no. 3 (2019): 1231–1256.

[23] Sassler and Lichter, "Cohabitation and Marriage," 36.

[24] Huang et al., "He Says, She Says."

[25] J. Budziszewski, *On the Meaning of Sex* (Wilmington, DE: Intercollegiate Studies Institute Books, 2014).

[26] Ibid., 40.

[27] Ibid., 41.

[28] Ibid., 24.

[29] Ibid., 27.

[30] Ibid.

[31] Ibid., 29.

[32] Saint Augustine of Hippo, 354–430, *The Confessions of Saint Augustine*, translated by Rex Warner (New York: Mentor, 1963), 1.1.1; See also Justin Taylor, "An Analysis of One of the Greatest Sentences Ever Written," 2017, https://www.thegospelcoalition.org/blogs/justin-taylor/an-analysis-of-one-of-the-greatest-sentences-ever-written/

[33] Philipp Ueffing, Aisha N. Z Dasgupta, and Vladimira Kantorova, "Sexual Activity by Marital Status and Age: A Comparative Perspective," *Journal of Biosocial Science* 50, no. 6 (2020): 860–884.

[34] Brianna M. Magnusson, Jennifer A. Nield, and Kate L. Lapane, "Age at First Intercourse and Subsequent Sexual Partnering among Adult Women in the University States, A Cross-sectional Study," *BMC Public Health* no. 15 (2015), 96.

[35] Jean M. Twenge, Ryne A. Sherman, and Brooke E. Wells, "Declines in Sexual Frequency among American Adults, 1989–2014," *Archives of Sexual Behavior* 46, no. 8 (2017): 2389–2401.

[36] Wagner, "Marriage, Cohabitation, and Sexual Exclusivity."

[37] Elyakim Kislev, "Does Marriage Really Improve Sexual Satisfaction? Evidence from Pairfam Dataset," *The Journal of Sex Research* 57, no. 4 (2020): 470–481; Samantha Litzinger and Kristian Coop Gordon, "Exploring Relationships among Communication, Sexual Satisfaction, and Marital Satisfaction," *Journal of Sex Marital Therapy* 31, no. 5 (2005): 409–424.

[38] Kislev, "Does Marriage Really Improve Sexual Satisfaction?"

[39] Ibid.

[40] E. Sandra Byers and Stephanie Demmons, "Sexual Satisfaction and Sexual Self-Disclosure within Dating Relationships," *Journal of Sex Research* 36, no. 2 (1999): 180–189.

[41] Hana Yoo, Suzanne Bartle-Haring, Randal D. Day, and Rashmi Gangamma,

"Couple Communication, Emotional and Sexual Intimacy, and Relationship Satisfaction," *Journal of Sex Marital Therapy* 40, no. 4 (2014): 275–293.

[42] Litzinger and Gordon, "Exploring Relationships."

[43] William Bradford Wilcox, *The State of Our Unions 2011: When Baby Makes Three: How Parenthood Makes Life Meaningful and How Marriage Makes Parenthood Bearable* (Charlottesville, VA: National Marriage Project, University of Virginia, 2011), 36. http://stateofourunions.org/2011/SOOU2011.pdf

[44] Ibid.

[45] Krystal M. Hernandez-Kane and Annette Mahoney, "Sex through a Sacred Lens: Longitudinal Effects of Sanctification of Marital Sexuality," *Journal of Family Psychology* 32, no. 4 (2018): 425–434.

[46] Stephen Cranney, "The Influence of Religiosity/Spirituality on Sex Life Satisfaction and Sexual Frequency: Insights from the Baylor Religion Survey," *Review of Religious Research* 62, no. 2 (2020): 289 314.

[47] Sheila Wray Gregoire, Rebecca Gregoire Lindenbach, and Joanna Sawatsky, *The Great Sex Rescue: The Lies You've Been Taught and How to Recover What God Intended* (Grand Rapids, MI: Baker Books, 2021).

[48] Ibid.

[49] Ibid., 159.

[50] Gert M. Hald and Neil M. Malamuth, "Pornography," in *International Encyclopedia of the Social & Behavioral Sciences*, 2nd ed., ed. James D. Wright (Oxford: Elsevier, 2015), 613–618.

[51] Gert M. Hald, Christopher Seaman, and Daniel Linz, "Sexuality and Pornography," in *The APA Handbook of Sexuality and Psychology*, Vol 2: Contextual Approaches, eds. Deborah L. Tolman and Lisa M. Diamond (Washington, DC: American Psychological Association, 2014), 3–35.

[52] Joseph Price, Rich Patterson, Mark Regnerus, and Jacob Walley, "How Much More XXX is Generation X Consuming? Evidence of Changing Attitudes and Behaviors Related to Pornography Since 1973," *Sex Roles* 53, no. 1 (2016): 12–20; Frank Rich, "Naked Capitalist," *New York Times*, May 20, 2001, https://www.nytimes.com/2001/05/20/magazine/naked-capitalists.html

[53] Hald, Seaman, and Linz, "Sexuality and Pornography."

[54] Price et al., "How Much More XXX is Generation X Consuming?"

[55] Chiara Sabina, Janis Wolak, and David Finkelhor, "The Nature and Dynamics of Internet Pornography Exposure for Youth," *CyberPsychology & Behavior* 11, no. 6 (2008): 1–3.

[56] Franklin O. Poulsen, Dean M. Busby, and Adam M. Galovan, "Pornography Use: Who Uses It and How It Is Associated with Couple Outcomes," *Journal of Sex Research* 50, no. 1 (2012): 72–83.

[57] Ibid.

[58] Ingrid Solano, Nicholas R. Eaton, and K. Daniel O'Leary, "Pornography Consumption, Modality and Function in a Large Internet Sample," *Journal of Sex Research* 57, no. 1 (2020): 92–103.

[59] Lyman Stone, "The Truth about Conservative Protestant Men and Porn," Institute of Family Studies, June 19, 2019, https://ifstudies.org/blog/the-truth-about-conservative-protestant-men-and-porn

[60] "Connecting Parents, Teens, & Jesus in a Disconnected World," Axis.org. See also Al Cooper, ed., *Sex and the Internet: A Guidebook for Clinicians* (New York:

Routledge, 2002).

61 Andrew Dugan, "More Americans Say Pornography Is Morally Acceptable," Gallup, June 5, 2018, https://news.gallup.com/poll/235280/americans-say-pornography-morally-acceptable.aspx

62 "Nefarious: Merchant of Souls; Human Trafficking Documentary – Full Movie," June 16, 2020, https://www.youtube.com/watch?v=MFaDHgXPbUg

63 Joris Van Ouytsel, Yu Lu, Youngu Shin, Brianna L. Avalos, and Jonathan Pettigrew, "Sexting, Pressured Sexting and Associations with Dating Violence among Early Adolescents," *Computers in Human Behavior* 125 (in press).

64 Nathaniel M. Lambert, Sesan Negash, Tyler F. Stillman, and Frank D. Fincham, "A Love That Doesn't Last: Pornography Consumption and Weakened Commitment to One's Romantic Partner," *Journal of Social and Clinical Psychology* 31, no. 4 (2012): 410–438.

65 Samuel L. Perry and Cyrus Schleifer, "Till Porn Do Us Part? A Longitudinal Examination of Pornography Use and Divorce," *Journal of Sex Research* 55, no. 3 (2018): 284–296.

66 Ibid., 291.

67 Brian J. Willoughby, Jason S. Carroll, Dean M. Busby, and Cameron C. Brown, "Differences in Pornography Use among Couples: Associations with Satisfaction, Stability, and Relationship Processes," *Archives of Sexual Behavior* 45, no. 1 (2016): 145–158.

68 Samuel L. Perry, "Pornography and Relationship Quality: Establishing the Dominant Pattern by Examining Pornography Use and 31 Measures of Relationship Quality in 30 National Surveys," *Archives of Sexual Behavior* 49, no. 4 (2020): 1199–1213.

69 Hald, Seaman, and Linz, "Sexuality and Pornography."

70 Destin N. Stewart and Dawn M. Szymanski, "Young Adult Women's Reports of Their Male Romantic Partner's Pornography Use as a Correlate of Their Self-Esteem, Relationship Quality, and Sexual Satisfaction," *Sex Roles* 67, no. 5–6 (2012): 257–271; Dawn M. Szymanski, Chandra E. Feltman, and Trevor L. Dunn, "Male Partners' Perceived Pornography Use and Women's Relational and Psychological Health: The Roles of Trust, Attitudes, and Investment," *Sex Roles*, no. 5–6 (2015):187–199; Tracy L. Tylka and Ashley M. Vroon Van Diest, "You Looking at Her 'Hot' Body May Not be 'Cool' for Me: Integrating Male Partners' Pornography Use into Objectification Theory for Women," *Psychology of Women Quarterly* 39, no. 1 (2015): 67–84.

71 Szymanski, Feltman, and Dunn, "Male Partners' Perceived Pornography Use."

72 Tylka and Van Diest, "You Looking at Her 'Hot' Body."

73 Elizabeth Oddone-Paolucci, Mark Genius, and Claudio Violato, "A Meta-Analysis of the Published Research on the Effects of Pornography," in *The Changing Family and Child Development*, eds. Claudio Violato, Elizabeth Oddone-Paolucci, and Mark Genuis (Farnham, UK: Ashgate Publishing Ltd., 2000), 48–59.

74 Hald and Malamuth, "Pornography," 616.

75 Joshua B. Grubbs and Mateusz Gola, "Is Pornography Use Related to Erectile Functioning? Results from Cross-Sectional and Latent Growth Curve Analyses," *Journal of Sexual Medicine* 16, no. 1 (2019): 111–125.

76 John D. Foubert, "The Public Health Harms of Pornography: The Brain, Erectile Dysfunction, and Sexual Violence," *Dignity: A Journal of Analysis of Exploitation and Violence* 2, no. 3, article 6, https://digitalcommons.uri.edu/dignity/vol2/iss3/6

77 Christopher M. Olsen, "Natural Rewards, Neuroplasticity, and Non-drug Addictions," *Neuropharmacology* 61, no. 7 (2011): 1109–1122.

[78] Todd Love, Christian Laier, Matthias Brand, Linda Hatch, and Raju Hajela, "Neuroscience of Internet Pornography Addiction: A Review and Update," *Behavior Sciences* 5, no. 3 (2015): 388–433.

[79] Hald, Seaman, and Linz, "Sexuality and Pornography," 6.

[80] John Paul II, "The Redemption of the Body and Sacramentality of Marriage (Theology of the Body)," Libreria Editrice Vaticana, 2005, https://d2y1pz2y630308.cloudfront.net/2232/documents/2016/9/theology_of_the_body.pdf. This work is a compilation of the weekly audiences of His Holiness Pope John Paul II between September 5, 1979 and November 28, 1984. See also Karl MacMillan, "Pornography's Technological Handmaiden," *Humanum: Issues in Family, Culture & Science* 1 (2018), https://humanumreview.com/articles/old-friends-pornography-and-technology

[81] Robert J. Sternberg, "A Triangular Theory of Love," *Psychological Review* 93, no. 2 (1986): 119–135.

[82] Shakespeare, sonnet 116, http://www.shakespeare-online.com/sonnets/116.html

[83] Sternberg, "A Triangular Theory of Love," 119.

[84] Ibid.

[85] Ibid.

[86] Ibid.

[87] Piotr Sorokowski, Agnieszka Sorokowska, Maciej Karwowski, Agata Groyecka, Toivo Aavik, Grace Akello, Charlotte Alm, et al., "Universality of the Triangular Theory of Love: Adaptation and Psychometric Properties of the Triangular Love Scale in 25 Countries," *Journal of Sex Research* 58, no. 1 (2021): 106–115.

[88] Vincent Waldron and Douglas Kelley, *Marriage at Midlife: Counseling Strategies and Analytical Tools* (New York: Springer, 2009).

[89] Gary Thomas, *Sacred Marriage: What If God Designed Marriage to Make Us Holy More Than to Make Us Happy?* (Grand Rapids, MI: Zondervan, 2000), 15–16.

[90] Tobore Onojighofia Tobore, "Toward a Comprehensive Theory of Love: The Quadruple Theory," *Frontiers in Psychology* 19 (2020), https://www.frontiersin.org/articles/10.3389/fpsyg.2020.00862/full

[91] C. S. Lewis, *The Four Loves* (New York, Harcourt Brace, 1960).

[92] Ibid., 57.

[93] Ibid.

[94] Thomas, *Sacred Marriage*, 42.

[95] J. Hudson Taylor, *Union and Communication: Thoughts on Song of Solomon* (Minneapolis, MN: Bethany House, 2000); Sharon Jaynes, *Lovestruck: Discovering God's Design for Romance, Marriage, and Sexual Intimacy from the Song of Solomon* (Nashville, TN: Nelson Books, 2019).

Chapter 12: Struggling, Stymied, and Successful Marital Communication

[1] James Strong, *Strong's Exhaustive Concordance of the Bible: Updated and Expanded Edition* (Peabody MA: Hendrickson Publishers, 2007), H5710.

[2] Leanne K. Knobloch, Denise Haunani Solomon, Jennifer A. Theiss, and Rachel M. McLaren, "Relational Turbulence Theory: Understanding Family Communication during Times of Change," in *Engaging Theories in Family Communication: Multiple*

Perspectives, 2nd ed., eds. Dawn O. Braithwaite, Elizabeth A. Suter, and Kory Floyd (New York: Routledge, 2018), 255–265; Denise Haunani Solomon and Kellie St. Cyr Brisini, "Relational Uncertainty and Interdependence Processes in Marriage: A Test of Relational Turbulence Theory," *Journal of Social and Personal Relationship* 36, no. 8 (2019): 2416–2436.

[3] Kellie St. Cyr Brisini, Denise Haunani Solomon, and Jon Nussbaum, "Transitions in Marriage: Types, Turbulence, and Transition Processing Activities," *Journal of Social and Personal Relationships* 35, no. 6 (2018): 831–853.

[4] Ibid., 833.

[5] Ibid., 849.

[6] Kellie St. Cyr Brisini and Denise Haunani Solomon, "Children's Transitions and Relational Turbulence in Marriage: Can Transition Processing Communication Help?" *Journal of Family Communication* 20, no. 1 (2020): 82–96.

[7] Ibid., 93.

[8] John Mordechai Gottman, *What Predicts Divorce? The Relationship between Marital Processes and Marital Outcomes* (Hillsdale, NJ: Erlbaum, 1994).

[9] Ibid., 64–65.

[10] Sharon G. Smith, Xinjian Zhang, Kathleen C. Basile, Melissa T. Merrick, Jing Wang, Marcie-jo Kresnow, and Jieru Chen, "National Intimate Partner and Sexual Violence Survey: 2015 Data Brief—Updated Release," Center for Disease Control, November 2018, https://www.cdc.gov/violenceprevention/pdf/2015data-brief508.pdf

[11] Michael P. Johnson and Kathleen J. Ferraro, "Research on Domestic Violence in the 1990s: Making Distinctions," *Journal of Marriage and Family* 62, no. 4 (2000): 948–963.

[12] For a review, see Dudley D. Cahn, ed., *Family Violence: Communication Processes* (New York: SUNY Press, 2010).

[13] "Step by Step Guide to Understanding the Cycle of Violence," Domestic Violence: It's Everybody's Business, https://domesticviolence.org/cycle-of-violence

[14] "Warning Signs of Abuse: Knowing What to Look For," National Domestic Violence Hotline, https://www.thehotline.org/identify-abuse/domestic-abuse-warning-signs/

[15] "100 Years of Marriage and Divorce Statistics United States, 1867–1967," *Vital and Health Statistics* 21, no. 4 (December 1973), https://www.cdc.gov/nchs/data/series/sr_21/sr21_024.pdf; Wendy Wang, "The U.S. Divorce Rate Has Hit a 50-Year Low" (Charlottesville, VA: Institute of Family Studies, 2021), https://ifstudies.org/blog/the-us-divorce-rate-has-hit-a-50-year-low

[16] R. Kelley Raley and Megan M. Sweeney, "Divorce, Repartnering, and Stepfamilies: A Decade in Review," *Journal of Marriage and Family* 82, no. 1 (2020): 81–99.

[17] Wang, "The U.S. Divorce Rate."

[18] Leslie Reynolds, "Divorce Rate in the U.S.: Geographic Variation, 2019," *Family Profiles, FP-20-25* (Bowling Green, OH: National Center for Family & Marriage Research, 2020).

[19] Wang, "The U.S. Divorce Rate."

[20] W. Bradford Wilcox and Elizabeth Marquardt, *State of Our Unions 2010: When Marriage Disappears: The New Middle America* (West Chester, PA: Broadway Publications, 2011).

[21] John Mordechai Gottman and Robert Wayne Levenson, "The Timing of Divorce: Predicting When a Couple Will Divorce over a 14-Year Period," *Journal of*

Marriage and Family 62, no. 3 (2000): 737–745.

[22] Joanna L. Grossman, Ellen K. Solender, and Elicia Grilley Green, "No-Fault Divorce: The Case Against Repeal," SMU Dedman School of Law, 2018, https://www.smu.edu/-/media/Site/Law/clinics/elmo-b-hunter/No-Fault-Divorce-Historical-041218-final.pdf; Paul A. Nakonezny, Robert D. Shull, and Joseph Lee Rodgers, "The Effect of No-Fault Divorce Law on the Divorce Rate across the 50 States and Its Relation to Income, Education, and Religiosity," *Journal of Marriage and Family* 57, no. 2 (1995): 477–488.

[23] Grossman, Solender and Green, "No-Fault Divorce."

[24] Nakonezny, Shull, and Rodgers, "The Effect of No-Fault Divorce Law on Divorce Rate."

[25] Norval D. Glenn, "A Reconsideration of the Effect of No-Fault Divorce on Divorce Rates," *Journal of Marriage and Family* 59, no. 4 (1997): 1023–1025.

[26] Grossman, Solender, and Green, "No-Fault Divorce."

[27] Susan L. Brown, I-Fen Lin, "The Gray Divorce Revolution: Rising Divorce among Middle-Aged and Older Adults, 1990–2010," *The Journals of Gerontology: Series B* 67 no. 6 (November 2012): 731–741.

[28] See review, Raley and Sweeney, "Divorce, Repartnering, and Stepfamilies."

[29] Paul R. Amato, "Research on Divorce: Continuing Trends and New Developments," *Journal of Marriage and Family* 72, no. 3 (2010): 650–666.

[30] Ibid.

[31] David C. Atkins, Donald H. Baucom, and Neil S. Jacobson, "Understanding Infidelity: Correlates in a National Random Sample," *Journal of Family Psychology* 15, no. 4 (2002): 735–749; Rebeca A. Marin, Andrew Christensen, and David C. Atkins, "Infidelity and Behavioral Couple Therapy: Relationship Outcome over 5 Years Following Therapy," *Couple and Family Psychology: Research and Practice* 3, no. 1 (2014): 1–12.

[32] Shelby B. Scott, Galena K. Rhoades, Scott M. Stanley, Elizabeth S. Allen, and Howard J. Markman, "Reasons for Divorce and Recollections of Premarital Intervention: Implications for Improving Relationship Education," *Couple and Family Psychology: Research and Practice* 2, no. 2 (2013): 131–145.

[33] Marin, Christensen, and Atkins, "Infidelity and Behavioral Couple Therapy."

[34] Sarah W. Whitton, Scott M. Stanley, Howard Markman, and Christine A. Johnson, "Attitudes toward Divorce, Commitment, and Divorce Proneness in First Marriages and Remarriages," *Journal of Marriage and Family* 75, no. 2 (2013): 276–287.

[35] Ibid., 286.

[36] Andrew Christensen and Christopher L. Heavey, "Gender and Social Structure in the Demand/Withdrawal Pattern of Marital Conflict," *Journal of Personality and Social Psychology* 59, no. 1 (1990): 73–81.

[37] John M. Gottman and Nan Silver, *The Seven Principles for Making Marriage Work: A Practical Guide from the Country's Foremost Relationship Expert* (New York: Harmony Books, 2015).

[38] Ted L. Houston, John P. Caughlin, Renate M. Houts, Shanna E. Smith, and Laura J. George, "The Connubial Crucible: Newlywed Years as Predictors of Marital Delight, Distress, and Divorce," *Journal of Personality and Social Psychology* 80, no. 2 (2001): 237–252.

[39] Ibid.

[40] Ibid., 246.

[41] Ibid., 247.

[42] Lynn Gigy and Joan Kelly, "Reasons for Divorce: Perspectives of Divorcing Men and Women," *Journal of Divorce and Remarriage* 18, no. 1 (1992): 169–187.

[43] Gottman and Levenson, "The Timing of Divorce."

[44] Raley and Sweeney, "Divorce, Repartnering, and Stepfamilies."

[45] Paul R. Amato, "The Consequence of Divorce for Adults and Children," *Journal of Marriage and Family* 62, no. 4 (2000): 1269–1287.

[46] Paul R. Amato and Bryndl Hohmann-Marriott, "A Comparison of High- and Low-Distress Marriages That End in Divorce," *Journal of Marriage and Family* 69, no. 3 (2007): 621–638.

[47] Raley and Sweeney, "Divorce, Repartnering, and Stepfamilies," 92.

[48] Amato, "The Consequence of Divorce for Adults and Children."

[49] See, for example, Elizabeth J. Krumrei, Annette Mahoney, and Kenneth I. Pargament, "Divorce and the Divine: The Role of Spirituality in Adjustment to Divorce," *Journal of Marriage and Family* 71, no. 2 (2009): 373–383.

[50] Raley and Sweeney, "Divorce, Repartnering, and Stepfamilies," 88.

[51] Ibid.

[52] Amato, "The Consequence of Divorce for Adults and Children."

[53] Paul R. Amato and Alan Booth, *A Generation at Risk: Growing Up in an Era of Family Upheaval* (Cambridge MA: Harvard University Press, 1997).

[54] Mick Cunningham and JaneLee Waldock, "Consequences of Parental Divorce during the Transition to Adulthood: The Practical Origins of Ongoing Distress," in *Divorce, Separation, and Remarriage: The Transformation of Family*, eds. Giovanna Gianesini and Sampson Lee Blair (United Kingdom: Emerald Group Publishing, 2016), 199–228.

[55] Ibid., 212.

[56] Ibid., 217.

[57] Chris Segrin and Jeanne Flora, *Family Communication*, 3rd ed. (New York: Routledge, 2019).

[58] Amato, "The Consequence of Divorce for Adults and Children."

[59] Constance Ahrons, *The Good Divorce: Keeping your Family Together When Your Marriage Comes Apart* (New York: HarperCollins, 1994).

[60] Paul R. Amato, Jennifer B. Kane, and Spencer James, "Reconsidering the 'Good Divorce,'" *Family Relations* 60, no. 5 (2011): 511–524.

[61] Ibid., 522.

[62] H. Wayne House, *Divorce and Remarriage: Four Christian Views* (Downers Grove, IL: InterVarsity Press, 1990).

[63] Rebecca Randall, "Wayne Grudem Changes Mind About Divorce in Cases of Abuse," *Christianity Today*, November 26, 2019, https://www.christianitytoday.com/news/2019/november/complementarian-wayne-grudem-ets-divorce-after-abuse.html

[64] Bob Smietana, "How Pastors Perceive Domestic Violence Differently," *Christianity Today*, February 20, 2017, https://www.christianitytoday.com/news/2017/february/how-pastors-perceive-domestic-violence-lifeway-autumn-miles.html

[65] Linda Waite and Maggie Gallagher, *The Case for Marriage: Why Married People are Happier, Healthier and Better Off Financially* (United Kingdom: Crown Publishing Group, 2001).

[66] Elizabeth M. Lawrence, Richard G. Rogers, Anna Zajacova, and Timothy Wadsworth, "Marital Happiness, Marital Status, Health, and Longevity," *Journal Happiness Studies* 20 (2019): 1539–1561.

[67] Bill Strom and Divine Agodzo, *More than Talk: A Covenantal Approach to Everyday Communication*, 5th ed. (Dubuque, IA: Kendall/Hunt Publishing, 2018).

[68] Greg Smalley, "9 Reasons to Get Married," Focus on the Family, April 29, 2021, sec. "Marriage Creates a Safe Relationship Where You Can Reach the Deepest Level of Intimacy and Connection," https://www.focusonthefamily.com/marriage/9-reasons-to-get-married/

[69] Gottman and Silver, *The Seven Principles for Making Marriage Work*.

[70] Ibid., 225.

[71] Ibid., 243–244.

[72] Douglas L. Kelley, *Intimate Spaces: A Conversation about Discovery and Connection* (San Diego: Cognella, 2021).

[73] Alex Kendrick and Stephen Kendrick, *The Love Dare: New Revised Edition* (Nashville, TN: B & H Publishing Group, 2013).

[74] *Fireproof*, directed by Alex Kendrick (Sony Pictures Home Entertainment, January 27, 2009).

[75] Terri L. Orbuch, *5 Simple Steps to Take Your Marriage From Good to Great* (Austin, TX: River Grove Books, 2015).

Chapter 13: Children in Multiple Family Contexts

[1] "The Purpose of the Family," Focus on the Family, June 29, 2017, para. 5, https://www.focusonthefamily.com/parenting/the-purpose-of-the-family/

[2] Urie Bronfenbrenner, "Developmental Research, Public Policy, and the Ecology of Childhood," *Child Development* 45, no. 1 (1974): 1–5; Urie Bronfenbrenner and Pamela A. Morris, "The Bioecological Model of Human Development," in *The Handbook of Child Psychology*, 6th ed., eds. William Damon and Richard M. Lerner (Hoboken, NJ: Wiley, 2006), 793–828.

[3] *Babies*, directed by Thomas Balmès (Studio Canal, 2010).

[4] Pamela J. Smock and Christine R. Schwartz, "The Demography of Families: A Review of Patterns and Change," *Journal of Marriage and Family* 82, no. 1 (2020): 9–35.

[5] R. Kelly Raley, Inbar Weiss, Robert Reynolds, and Shannon E. Cavanagh, "Estimating Children's Household Instability between Birth and Age 18 Using Longitudinal Household Roster Data," *Demography* 56, no. 5 (2019): 1957–1973.

[6] Hope Harvey, "Cumulative Effects of Doubling Up in Childhood on Young Adult Outcomes," *Demography* 57, no. 2 (2020): 501–528; Kristin L. Perkins, "Changes in Household Composition and Children's Educational Attainment," *Demography* 56, no. 2 (2019): 525–548.

[7] Raley et al., "Estimating Children's Household Instability."

[8] Harvey, "Cumulative Effects," 502.

[9] William S. Aquilino, "The Life Course of Children Born to Unmarried Mothers: Childhood Living Arrangements and Young Adult Outcomes," *Journal of Marriage and Family* 58, no. 2 (1996): 293–310.

[10] Jonathan Pettigrew, *Stepfather-Stepson Communication: Social Support in Stepfamily Worlds* (New York: Peter Lang, 2014).

[11] William Bradford Wilcox and Elizabeth Marquardt, *The State of Our Unions 2011: When Baby Makes Three: How Parenthood Makes Life Meaningful and How Marriage Makes Parenthood Bearable* (Charlottesville, VA: National Marriage Project,

University of Virginia), 5.

[12] Ibid., 32.

[13] Ibid., 38.

[14] Ibid.

[15] Tom Hoopes, "I Like Having a Lot of Siblings Because . . .", *Ex Corde*, November 23, 2020, https://excorde.org/2020/i-like-having-a-lot-of-siblings-because#:~:text=St.,are%20always%20necessary%20or%20best

[16] Susan M. McHale, Kimberly A. Updegraff, and Shawn D. Whiteman, "Sibling Relationships in Childhood and Adolescence," *Journal of Marriage and Family* 74, no. 5 (2012): 913–930.

[17] Mary Anne Fitzpatrick and Diane M. Badzinski, "All in the Family: Interpersonal Communication in Kin Relationships," in *The Handbook of Interpersonal Communication*, eds. Mark L. Knapp and Gerald R. Miller (Beverly Hills, CA: Sage, 1985), 687–736.

[18] Susan M. McHale, Shawn D. Whiteman, Ji-Yeon Kim, and Ann C. Crouter, "Characteristics and Correlates of Sibling Relationships in Two-Parent African American Families," *Journal of Family Psychology* 21, no. 2 (2007): 227–235.

[19] Susan M. McHale and Ann C. Crouter, "The Family Contexts of Children's Sibling Relationships," in *Sibling Relationships: Their Causes and Consequences*, ed. Gene H. Brody (Norwood, NJ: Ablex Publishing, 1996), 173–196.

[20] Alan C. Mikkelson, "Adult Sibling Relationships," in *Widening the Family Circle: New Research on Family Communication*, 2nd ed., eds. Kory Floyd and Mark T. Morman (Los Angeles: Sage, 2014), 19–34.

[21] Patrick T. Davies, Lucia Q. Parry, Sonnette M. Bascoe, Meredith J. Martin, and E. Mark Cummings, "Children's Vulnerability to Interparental Conflict: The Protective Role of Sibling Relationship Quality," *Child Development* 90, no. 6 (2019): 2118–2134.

[22] Mikkelson, "Adult Sibling Relationships."

[23] Deborah T. Gold, "Sibling Relationships in Old Age: A Typology," *International Journal of Aging and Human Development* 28, no. 1 (1989): 37–51; see also Deborah T. Gold, "Siblings in Old Age: Something Special," *Canadian Journal of Aging* 6, no. 3 (1987): 199–215.

[24] Scott A. Myers and Kelly G. Odenweller, "The Use of Relational Maintenance Behaviors and Relational Characteristics among Sibling Types," *Communication Studies* 66, no. 2 (2015): 238–255.

[25] Avidan Milevsky, *Sibling Relationships in Childhood and Adolescence: Predictors and Outcomes* (New York: Columbia University Press, 2011).

[26] Alison Pike, Joanne Coldwell, and Judith F. Dunn, "Sibling Relationships in Early/Middle Childhood: Links with Individual Adjustment," *Journal of Family Psychology* 19, no. 4 (2005): 523–532.

[27] Alison Pike and Bonamy R. Oliver, "Child Behavior and Sibling Relationship Quality: A Cross-Lagged Analysis," *Journal of Family Psychology* 31, no. 2 (2017): 250–255.

[28] Wyndol Furman and Richard P. Lanthier, "Personality and Sibling Relationships," in *Sibling Relationships: Their Causes and Consequences*, ed. Gene H. Brody (Norwood, NJ: Ablex Publishing, 1996), 127–146.

[29] Pike and Oliver, "Child Behavior and Sibling Relationship Quality," 254.

[30] Scott A. Myers and Alan K. Goodboy, "Perceived Sibling Use of Verbally Aggressive Messages across the Lifespan," *Communication Reports* 23, no. 1 (2006): 1–11.

[31] Victor G. Cicirelli, *Sibling Relationships across the Lifespan* (New York Plenum Press, 1995).

[32] Victoria H. Bedford, "Ambivalence in Adult Sibling Relationships," *Journal of Family Issues* 10, no. 2 (1989): 211–224.

[33] Ibid.

[34] Michele Van Volkom, Carly Machiz, and Ashely E. Reich, "Sibling Relationships in the College Years: Do Gender, Birth Order, and Age Spacing Matter?" *North American Journal of Psychology* 13, no. 1 (2011): 35–50; see also Mikkelson, "Adult Sibling Relationships."

[35] Pike, Coldwell, and Dunn, "Sibling Relationships in Early/Middle Childhood."

[36] Gold, "Sibling Relationships in Old Age."

[37] Frank J. Sulloway, "Birth Order," in *Encyclopedia of Creativity*, vol. 1, eds. Mark A. Runco and Steven R. Pritzker (San Diego, Academic Press, 1999), 189–202.

[38] Kevin Leman, *The Birth Order Book: Why You Are the Way You Are* (Grand Rapids, MI: Fleming H. Revell, 1998).

[39] Frank J. Sulloway, *Born to Rebel: Birth Order, Family Dynamics, and Creative Lives* (New York: Vintage Books, 1997).

[40] Leman, *The Birth Order Book*, 15.

[41] Suzanne Degges-White, *Sisters and Brothers for Life: Making Sense of Sibling Relationships in Adulthood* (Lanham, MD: Rowman & Littlefield, 2017).

[42] April Bleske-Rechek and Jenna A. Kelley, "Birth Order and Personality: A Within-Family Test Using Independent Self-Reports from Both Firstborn and Later-born Siblings," *Personality and Individual Differences* 56 (2014), 15.

[43] Leman, *The Birth Order Book*.

[44] Thomas J. Socha and Julie Yingling, *Families Communicating with Children* (Malden, MA: Polity Press, 2010).

[45] Carol A. Miller and Laura S. DeThorne, "Communication Development, Distributed across People, Resources, and Time," in *The Handbook of Lifespan Communication*, ed. Jon F. Nussbaum (New York: Peter Lang, 2014).

[46] Socha and Yingling, *Families Communicating with Children*, 46–47.

[47] Ibid., 138–142.

[48] Ibid., 138.

[49] Ibid., 139.

[50] Anthony Esolen, *Ten Ways to Destroy the Imagination of Your Child* (Wilmington, DE: ISI Books, 2010).

[51] Socha and Yingling, *Families Communicating with Children*, 141.

[52] Hannos Petras and Zilo Sloboda, "An Integrated Prevention Science Model: A Conceptual Foundation for Prevention Research," in *Defining Prevention Science*, eds. Zilo Sloboda and Hannos Petras (New York: Springer, 2014), 251–273; see also Eugene R. Oetting and Joseph F. Donnermeyer, "Primary Socialization Theory: The Etiology of Drug Use and Deviance," *Substance Use and Misuse* 33, no. 4 (1998): 995–1026.

[53] Kim Bartholomew, "Avoidance of Intimacy: An Attachment Perspective," *Journal of Social and Personal Relationships* 7, no. 2 (1990), 148.

[54] Clyde Hendrick and Susan S. Hendrick, "Attachment Theory and Close Adult Relationships," *Psychological Inquiry* 5, no. 1 (1994): 38–41.

[55] Brooke C. Feeney and Nancy L. Collins, "Predictors of Caregiving in Adult Intimate Relationships: An Attachment Theoretical Perspective," *Journal of Personality and Social Psychology* 80, no. 6 (2001), 973.

[56] Pehr Granqvist, L. Alan Stroufe, Mary Dozier, et al., "Disorganized Attachment in Infancy: A Review of the Phenomenon and Its Implications for Clinicians and Policy-Makers," *Attachment & Human Development* 19, no. 6 (2017), 537.

[57] Marinus H. Van Ijzendoorn, Carlo Schuengel, and Marian J. Bakermans-Kranenburg, "Disorganized Attachment in Early Childhood: Meta-analysis of Precursors, Concomitants, and Sequelae," *Development and Psychopathology* 11, no. 2 (1999): 225–250.

[58] Ibid.

[59] Jessica E. Cooke, Logan B. Kochendorfer, Kaela L. Stuart-Parrigon, Amanda J. Koehn, and Kathryn A. Kerns, "Parent–Child Attachment and Children's Experience and Regulation of Emotion: A Meta-Analytic Review," *Emotion* 19, no. 6 (2019): 1103–1126.

[60] Anouk Spruit, Linda Goos, Nikki Weenink, Roos Rodenburg, Helen Niemeyer, Geert Jan Stams, and Cristina Colonnesi, "The Relation between Attachment and Depression in Children and Adolescents: A Multilevel Meta-Analysis," *Clinical Child and Family Psychology* Review 23, no. 1 (2020): 54–69.

[61] Aida Faber, Laurette Dubé, and Bärbel Knäuper, "Attachment and Eating: A Meta-Analytic Review of the Relevance of Attachment for Unhealthy and Healthy Eating Behaviors in the General Population," *Appetite* 123, no. 1 (2018): 410–438.

[62] See, for example, Albert Bandura, "Self-Efficacy: Toward a Unifying Theory of Behavioral Change," *Psychological Review* 84, no. 2 (1977): 191–215; Robert E. Larzelere, Sada J. Knowles, Carolyn S. Henry, and Kathy L. Ritchie, "Immediate and Long-Term Effectiveness of Disciplinary Tactics by Type of Toddler Noncompliance," *Parenting* 18, no. 3 (2018): 141–171.

[63] Frank D. Fincham, "Towards a Psychology of Divine Forgiveness," *Psychology of Religion and Spirituality*, https://doi.org/10.1037/rel0000323

[64] Ibid., 6.

[65] Mary Anne Fitzpatrick, *Between Husbands and Wives: Communication in Marriage* (Newbury Park, CA: Sage, 1988).

[66] Jack M. McLeod and Steven H. Chaffee, "Interpersonal Approaches to Communication Research," *American Behavioral Scientist* 16, no. 4 (1973): 469–499.

[67] Ascan F. Koerner and Paul Schrodt, "An Introduction to the Special Issue on Family Communication Patterns Theory," *Journal of Family Communication* 14, no. 1 (2014): 5.

[68] Ascan F. Koerner and Mary Anne Fitzpatrick, "Toward a Theory of Family Communication," *Communication Theory* 12, no. 1 (2002): 85.

[69] Ibid.

[70] Colin Hesse, Emily Rauscher, Rebecca Goodman, and Monica Couvrette, "Reconceptualizing the Role of Conformity Behaviors in Family Communication Patterns Theory," *Journal of Family Communication* 17, no. 4 (2017): 1–19.

[71] Martha A. Rueter and Ascan F. Koerner, "The Effect of Family Communication Patterns on Adopted Adolescent Adjustment," *Journal of Marriage and Family* 70, no. 3 (2008): 714–727.

[72] Xiaowen Guan and Xiaohui Li, "A Cross-Cultural Examination of Family Communication Patterns, Parent-Child Closeness, and Conflict Styles in the United States, China, and Saudi Arabia," *Journal of Family Communication* 17, no. 3 (2017): 223–237.

[73] Paul Schrodt and Jenna Shimkowski, "Family Communication Patterns and

Perceptions of Coparental Communication," *Communication Reports* 30, no. 12 (2015): 1–12.

[74] Paul Schrodt and Andrew M. Ledbetter, "Communication Processes That Mediate Family Communication Patterns and Mental Well-Being: A Mean and Covariance Structures Analysis of Young adults from Divorced and Nondivorced Families," *Human Communication Research* 33, no. 3 (2007): 330–356; Paul Schrodt, Andrew M. Ledbetter, Kodiane A. Jernberg, Lara Larson, Nicole Brown, and Katie Glonek, "Family Communication Patterns as Mediators of Communication Competence in the Parent-Child Relationship," *Journal of Social and Personal Relationships* 26, no. 6–7 (2009): 853–874; Paul Schrodt, Andrew M. Ledbetter, and Jennifer F. Ohrt, "Parental Confirmation and Affection as Mediators of Family Communication Patterns and Children's Mental Well-Being," *Journal of Family Communication* 7, no. 1 (2007): 23–46.

[75] Paul Schrodt, Paul L. Witt, and Amber S. Messersmith, "A Meta-Analytical Review of Family Communication Patterns and Their Associations with Information Processing, Behavioral, and Psychosocial Outcomes," *Communication Monographs* 75, no. 3 (2008): 248–269.

[76] Diana Baumrind, "Current Patterns of Parental Authority," *Developmental Psychology* 41, no. 1 (1971): 1–103.

[77] Laurence Steinberg, "We Know Some Things: Parent-Adolescent Relationships in Retrospect and Prospect," *Journal of Research on Adolescence* 11, no. 1 (2001), 13.

[78] Diana Baumrind, "Authoritative Parenting Revisited: History and Current Status," in *Authoritative Parenting: Synthesizing Nurturance and Discipline for Optimal Child Development*, eds. Robert E. Larzelere, Amanda Sheffield Morris, and Amada W. Harrist (American Psychological Association, 2013), 14.

[79] Ibid.

[80] Steinberg, "We Know Some Things," 13.

[81] Ibid.

[82] Nick Stinnett and John DeFrain, *Secrets of Strong Families* (Boston: Little, Brown and Company, 1985).

[83] "7 Traits of Effective Parenting," Focus on the Family, para. 1 https://www.focusonthefamily.com/parenting/the-7-traits-of-effective-parenting/

[84] Tamara D. Golish and John P. Caughlin, "'I'd Rather Not Talk about It': Adolescents' and Young Adults' Use of Topic Avoidance in Stepfamilies," *Journal of Applied Communication Research* 30, no. 1 (2002): 78–106.

[85] Jonathan Pettigrew, Michelle Miller-Day, YoungJu Shin, Janice L. Krieger, and Michael L. Hecht, "Parental Messages about Substance Abuse in Early Adolescence: Extending a Model of Drug-Talk Styles," *Heath Communication* 33, no. 3 (2018), 357.

[86] Karol L. Kumpfer, Rose Alvarado, and Henry O. Whiteside, "Family-Based Interventions for Substance Use and Misuse Prevention," *Substance Use and Misuse* 38, no. 11–13 (2003): 1759–1787; Maury Nation, Cindy Crusto, Abraham Wandersman, Karol L. Kumpfer, Diana Seybolt, Erin Morrissey-Kane, and Katrina Davino, "What Works in Prevention: Principles of Effective Prevention Programs," *American Psychologist* 58, no. 6–7 (2003): 449–456.

[87] Hye Jeong Choi, Michelle Miller-Day, YoungJu Shin, Michael L. Hecht, Jonathan Pettigrew, Janice L. Krieger, Jeong Kyu Lee, and John W. Graham, "Parent Prevention Communication Profiles and Adolescent Substance Use: A Latent Profile Analysis and Growth Curve Model," *Journal of Family Communication* 17, no. 1 (2017), 27–28.

[88] Amador Calafat, Fernando García, Montse Juan, Elisardo Becoña, and Jose

Ramon Fernández-Hermida, "Which Parenting Style Is More Protective Against Adolescent Substance Use? Evidence within the European Context," *Drug and Alcohol Dependence* 138 (2014): 185–192.

[89] Pettigrew et al., "Parental Messages about Substance Abuse in Early Adolescence."

[90] Michelle Miller-Day, "Talking to Youth about Drugs: What Do Late Adolescents Say about Parental Strategies?" *Family Relations* 57, no. 1 (2008): 1–12.

[91] Pettigrew et al., "Parental Messages about Substance Abuse in Early Adolescence."

[92] Ibid., 353–354.

[93] Jennifer M. Heisler, "They Need to Sow Their Wild Oats: Mothers' Recalled Memorable Messages to Their Emerging Adult Children Regarding Sexuality and Dating," *Emerging Adulthood* 2, no. 4 (2014): 280–293; Lydia Kauffman, Mark P. Orbe, Amber L. Johnson, and Angela Cooke-Jackson, "Memorable Familial Messages about Sex: A Qualitative Content Analysis of College Student Narratives," *Electronic Journal of Human Sexuality* 16 (2013): 1–10.

[94] Angela Cooke-Jackson, Mark P. Orbe, Amber L. Johnson, and Lydia Kauffman, "Abstinence Memorable Message Narratives: A New Exploratory Research Study into Young Adult Sexual Narratives," *Health Communication* 30, no. 12 (2015): 1201–1212; Jacqueline N. Gunning, Angela Cooke-Jackson, and Valerie Rubinsky, "Negotiating Shame, Silence, Abstinence, and Period Sex: Women's Shift from Harmful Memorable Messages about Reproductive and Sexual Health," *American Journal of Sexuality Education* 15, no. 1 (2019): 1–27.

[95] Kauffman et al., "Memorable Familial Messages about Sex."

[96] Heisler, "They Need to Sow Their Wild Oats."

[97] Gunning, Cooke-Jackson, and Rubinsky, "Negotiating Shame, Silence, Abstinence, and Period Sex"; Kauffman et al., "Memorable Familial Messages about Sex."

[98] Heisler, "They Need to Sow Their Wild Oats."

[99] Gunning, Cooke-Jackson, and Rubinsky, "Negotiating Shame, Silence, Abstinence, and Period Sex"; Cooke-Jackson et al., "Abstinence Memorable Message Narratives"; Kauffman et al., "Memorable Familial Messages about Sex."

[100] Gunning, Cooke-Jackson, and Rubinsky, "Negotiating Shame, Silence, Abstinence, and Period Sex," 22.

Chapter 14: Parental Modeling across Spiritual and Practical Domains

[1] Cameron Lee, "Parenting as Discipleship: A Contextual Motif for Christian Parent Education," *Journal of Psychology and Theology* 19, no. 3 (1991): 268–277.

[2] Allan C. Carlson, *Family Questions: Reflections on the American Social Crisis* (New Brunswick, NJ: Transaction, 1988).

[3] Michael E. Lamb, Joseph H. Pleck, Eric L. Charnov, and James A. Levine, "A Biosocial Model Perspective on Paternal Behavior and Involvement," in *Parenting Across the Lifespan: Biosocial Dimensions*, eds. Jane B. Lancaster, Jeanne Altmann, Alice S. Rossi, and Lonnie R. Sherrod (New York: Routledge, 1987), 111–142.

[4] Jennifer A. Kam, "Nonverbal Behaviors That Contribute to Healthy or

Destructive Family Functioning," in *Nonverbal Communication Reader: Classic and Contemporary Readings*, 3rd ed., eds. Laura K. Guerrero and Michael L. Hecht (Long Grove, IL: Waveland, 2008), 360–369.

[5] Green Litton Fox and Carol Bruce, "Conditional Fatherhood: Identity Theory and Parental Investment Theory as Alternative Sources of Explanation of Fathering," *Journal of Marriage and Family* 63, no. 2 (2001): 394–403.

[6] Allan C. Carlson, "The Androgyny Hoax," in Family Questions: Reflections on the American Social Crisis (New Brunswick, NJ: Transaction Books, 1990), 29–47; William J. Doherty, Edward F. Kouneski, and Martha F. Erickson, "Responsible Fathering: An Overview and Conceptual Framework," *Journal of Marriage and Family* 60, no. 2 (1998): 277–292; Michelle Miller and L. Edward Day, "Family Communication, Maternal and Paternal Expectations, and College Students' Suicidality," *Journal of Family Communication* 2, no. 4 (2002): 167–184; Jonathan Pettigrew, *Stepfather-Stepson Communication: Social Support in Stepfamily Worlds* (New York: Peter Lang, 2014).

[7] David G. Blankenhorn, *Fatherless America: Confronting Our Most Urgent Social Problem* (New York: HarperCollins, 1996); Sara McLanahan, Laura Tach, and Daniel Schneider, "The Causal Effects of Father Absence," *Annual Review of Sociology* 39 (2013): 399–427.

[8] Christopher A. Brown, "The Proof Is In: Father Absence Harms Child Well-Being," *Huffington Post*, May 13, 2014, https://www.huffpost.com/entry/the-proof-is-infather-abs_b_4941353

[9] For review, see Allan Carlson and Paul Mero, *The Natural Family: A Manifesto* (Dallas, TX: Spence Publishing, 2004), https://www.worldcongress.pl/docs/en/pdf/the_natural_family.pdf; Maggie Gallagher, "(How) Does Marriage Protect Child Well-Being?" in *The Meaning of Marriage: Family, State, Market, and Morals*, eds. Robert P. George and Jean Bethke Elshtain (Dallas, TX: Spence Publishing, 2006): 197–212; The Witherspoon Institute, *Marriage and the Public Good: Ten Principles* (Princeton, NJ: The Witherspoon Institute, 2006), https://www.bigskyworldview.org/content/docs/links/MarriageandThePublicGoodTenPrinciples.pdf

[10] Pettigrew, *Stepfather-Stepson Communication*, 159.

[11] For review, see Alison Clarke-Stewart and Judy Dunn, *Families Count: Effects on Child and Adolescent Development* (Cambridge University Press, 2006).

[12] For example, Vincent Waldron and Thomas Socha, eds., *Communicating Fatherhood* (in press); Allison M. Alford and Michelle Miller-Day, eds., *Constructing Motherhood and Daughterhood across the Life Span* (New York: Peter Lang, 2019); Michelle Miller-Day, *Communication among Grandmothers, Mothers, and Adult Daughters: A Qualitative Study of Women across Three Generations* (Mahwah, NJ: Lawrence Erlbaum, 2004).

[13] William J. Goode, "Force and Violence in the Family," *Journal of Marriage and Family* 33, no. 4 (1971): 624–636.

[14] "The Truth Project," directed by Del Tackett (Focus on the Family, 2011).

[15] James Strong, *Strong's Exhaustive Concordance of the Bible: Updated and Expanded Edition* (Peabody MA: Hendrickson Publishers, 2007), H5710.

[16] Joseph P. Allen and Deborah Land, "Attachment in Adolescence," in *The Handbook of Attachment: Theory Research, and Clinical Applications*, eds. Jude Cassidy and Phillip R. Shaver (New York: Guilford Press, 1999), 319–335; Laurence Steinberg, "We Know Some Things: Parent-Adolescent Relationships in Retrospect and Prospect," *Journal of Research on Adolescence* 11, no. 1 (2001), 1–19.

[17] Murray Bowen, *Family Therapy in Clinical Practice* (New York: Jason Aronson, 1978).

[18] Ibid.

[19] Elizabeth A. Skowron and Myrna L. Friedlander, "The Differentiation of Self Inventory: Development and Initial Validation," *Journal of Counseling Psychology* 45, no. 3 (1998): 235–246; Elizabeth A. Skowron and Thomas A. Schmitt, "Assessing Interpersonal Fusion: Reliability and Validity of a New DSI Fusion with Others Subscale," *Journal of Marital and Family Therapy* 29, no. 2 (2003): 209–222.

[20] Elizabeth A. Skowron, "Differentiation of Self, Personal Adjustment, Problem Solving, and Ethnic Group Belonging among Persons of Color," *Journal of Counseling and Development* 82, no. 4 (2004): 447–456.

[21] Skowron and Friedlander, "The Differentiation of Self Inventory."

[22] Richard B. Miller, Shayne Anderson, and Davelyne Kaulana Keala, "Is Bowen Theory Valid?: A Review of Basic Research," *Journal of Marital and Family Therapy* 30, no. 4 (2004): 452–466.

[23] Elizabeth A. Skowron, Krystal L. Stanley, and Michael D. Shapiro, "A Longitudinal Perspective on Differentiation of Self, Interpersonal and Psychological Well-Being in Young Adulthood," *Contemporary Family Therapy: An International Journal* 31, no. 1 (2009): 3–18.

[24] Elizabeth A. Skowron, Stephen R. Wester, and Razia Azen, "Differentiation of Self Mediates College Stress and Adjustment," *Journal of Counseling and Development* 82, no. 1 (2004): 14.

[25] Goode, "Force and Violence in the Family."

[26] Foster Cline and Jim Fay, *Parenting with Love and Logic: Teaching Children Responsibility*, 3rd ed. (Colorado Springs, CO: NavPress, 2020).

[27] Murray A. Straus and Angèle Fauchier, "Preliminary Manual for the Dimensions of Discipline Inventory (DDI) 1," Family Research Laboratory, (Durham, NH: University of New Hampshire).

[28] Saul McLeod, "What Is Operant Conditioning and How Does It Work?: How Reinforcement and Punishment Modify Behavior," *Simply Psychology*, 2018, https://www.simplypsychology.org/operant-conditioning.html

[29] Amy Sutherland, "What Shamu Taught Me about a Happy Marriage," *New York Times*, October 11, 2019, https://www.nytimes.com/2019/10/11/style/modern-love-what-shamu-taught-me-happy-marriage.html

[30] McLeod, "What Is Operant Conditioning and How Does It Work."

[31] Stanford B. Friedman and Kenneth S. Schonberg, "Consensus Statements," *Pediatrics* 98, no. 4 (1996), 853.

[32] Diana Baumrind, Robert E. Larzelere, and Philip A. Cowan, "Ordinary Physical Punishment—Is It Harmful? Comment on Gershoff (2002)," *Psychological Bulletin* 128, no. 4 (2002), 581.

[33] Ibid.

[34] Ibid., 580–589.

[35] Robert E. Larzelere, Sada J. Knowles, Carolyn S. Henry, and Kathy L. Ritchie, "Immediate and Long-Term Effectiveness of Disciplinary Tactics by Type of Toddler Noncompliance," *Parenting, Science, and Practice* 18, no. 3 (2018): 151–171.

[36] Ibid., 167.

[37] Albert Bandura, *Social Learning Theory* (Englewood Cliffs, NJ: Prentice-Hall, 1977), 145.

[38] For review, see Alesia Woszidlo and Adrianne Kunkel, "Social Learning Theory: An Emphasis on Modeling in Parent-Child Relationships," in *Engaging Theories in Family Communication: Multiple Perspectives*, 2nd ed., eds. Dawn O. Braithwaite, Elizabeth A. Suter, and Kory Floyd (New York: Routledge, 2018), 290–299.

[39] Brian K. Barber "Parental Psychological Control: Revisiting a Neglected Construct," *Child Development* 67, no. 6 (1996): 3296–3319.

[40] Marjory Roberts Gray and Laurence Steinberg, "Unpacking Authoritative Parenting: Reassessing a Multidimensional Construct," *Journal of Marriage and Family* 61, no. 3 (1999): 575.

[41] Barber, "Parental Psychological Control"; Brian K. Barber and Elizabeth Lovelady Harmon, "Violating the Self: Parental Psychological Control of Children and Adolescents," in *Intrusive Parenting: How Psychological Control Affects Children and Adolescents*, ed. Brian K. Barber (American Psychological Association, 2002), 15–52; Earl S. Schaefer, "Children's Reports of Parental Behavior: An Inventory," *Child Development* 36, no. 2 (1965): 413–424; Laurence Steinburg, Julie D. Elmen, and Nina S. Mounts, "Authoritative Parenting, Psychosocial Maturity, and Academic Success among Adolescents," *Child Development* 60, no. 6 (1989): 1424–1436.

[42] Brian K. Barber, ed., *Intrusive Parenting: How Psychological Control Affects Children and Adolescents* (American Psychological Association, 2002).

[43] Beth A. Le Poire, "Inconsistent Nurturing as Control Theory: Implications for Communication-based Research and Treatment Programs," *Journal of Applied Communication Research* 23, no. 1 (1995): 60–74; Michelle Miller-Day, "Necessary Convergence Communication Theory: Submission and Power in the Family," in *Engaging Theories in Family Communication: Multiple Perspectives*, 2nd ed., eds. Dawn O. Braithwaite, Elizabeth A. Suter, and Kory Floyd (New York: Routledge, 2018), 221–231.

[44] Norah E. Dunbar, "A Review of Theoretical Approaches to Interpersonal Power," *Review of Communication* 15, no. 1 (2015): 1–18.

[45] Miller-Day, "Necessary Convergence Communication Theory."

[46] Ibid., 222.

[47] Miller-Day, *Communication among Grandmothers*.

[48] John Gottman with Joan DeClaire, *The Heart of Parenting: Raising an Emotionally Intelligent Child* (New York: Simon & Schuster, 1997).

[49] Jessica Newman and Linda Dusenbury, "Social and Emotional Learning (SEL): A Framework for Academic, Social, and Emotional Success," in *Prevention Science in School Settings*, ed. Kris Bosworth (New York: Springer, 2015), 287–306.

[50] "Fundamentals of SEL," CASEL, para. 1, https://casel.org/fundamentals-of-sel/

[51] Gottman, *The Heart of Parenting*.

[52] See Douglas L. Kelley, *Intimate Spaces: A Conversation about Discovery and Connection* (San Diego: Cognella, 2020).

[53] Philip A. Cowan and Carolyn Pape Cowan, "Interventions as Tests of Family Systems Theories: Marital and Family Relationships in Children's Development and Psychopathology," *Development and Psychopathology* 14, no. 4 (2002): 731–759.

[54] Anthony Biglan, "The Ultimate Goal of Prevention and the Larger Context for Translation," *Preventive Science* 19, no. 3 (2018): 328–336.

[55] Chris Bruno, *Man Maker Project: Boys are Born. Men are Made* (Searcy, AZ: Resource Publications, 2015).

[56] Jeffrey Jenson Arnett, *Emerging Adulthood: The Winding Road from Late Teens through the Twenties* (Oxford University Press, 2004).

[57] Ibid., 8.

[58] Alan Booth, David R. Johnson, Douglas A. Granger, Ann C. Crouter, and Susan McHale, "Testosterone and Child and Adolescent Adjustment: The Moderating Role of Parent-Child Relationships," *Developmental Psychology* 39, no. 1 (2003): 85–98.

[59] Cline and Fay, *Parenting with Love and Logic.*

[60] Paul Watzlawick, Janet Beavin Bavelas, and Don D. Jackson, *Pragmatics of Human Communication* (New York: Norton, 1967).

[61] Ibid.

[62] James Strong, *Strong's Greek Dictionary of the Bible* (Miklal Software Solutions, Inc., 2011).

[63] Hebrews 12 uses three distinct yet related words: discipline, rebuke, and chasten. See Henry George Liddell and Robert Scott, *A Greek-English Lexicon* (Oxford, Claredon Press, 1996), 1286, 1083, 1308.

[64] The Passion Translation, *New Testament with Psalms, Proverbs, and Song of Songs, Second Edition* (BroadStreet Publishing Group, LLC., 2018), 650.

Chapter 15: Family Legacy: Material, Spiritual, and Relational Inheritance

[1] Mathew Baldwin, Ludwin E. Molina, and Pegah Naemi, "Family Ties: Exploring the Influence of Family Legacy on Self and Identity," *Sex and Identity* 19, no. 1 (2020), 64–65.

[2] Ibid.

[3] Erik H. Erikson, Joan M. Erikson, and Helen Q. Kivnick, *Vital Involvement in Old Age: The Experience of Old Age in Our Time* (New York: W. W. Norton, 1986).

[4] Liliana Sousa, Ana Raquel, Lilian Santos, and Marta Patrão, "The Family Inheritance Process: Motivations and Patterns of Interaction," *European Journal of Ageing* 7, no. 1 (2010), 5.

[5] Karen L. Fingerman, Meng Huo, and Kira S. Birditt, "A Decade of Research on Intergenerational Ties: Technology, Economic, Political, and Demographic Changes," *Journal of Marriage and Family* 82, no. 1 (2020): 383–403.

[6] Deirdre G. Drake and Jeanette A. Lawrence, "Equality and Distributions of Inheritance in Families," *Social Justice Research* 13 (2000): 271–290.

[7] Brian Dimmock, Joanna Bornat, Sheila Peace, and David Jones, "Intergenerational Relationships among Stepfamilies in the UK," in *Families in Ageing Societies: A Multi-Disciplinary Approach*, ed. Sarah Harper (Oxford: Oxford University Press, 2004), 82–94; Lawrence H. Ganong, Marilyn Coleman, Mark Fine, and Patricia Martin, "Stepparents' Affinity-Seeking and Affinity-Maintaining Strategies with Stepchildren," *Journal of Family Issues* 20, no. 3 (1999): 299–327.

[8] Drake and Lawrence, "Equality and Distribution of Inheritance in Families"; Sousa et al., "The Family Inheritance Process."

[9] Fingerman, Huo, and Birditt, "A Decade of Research on Intergenerational Ties."

[10] Lorna de Witt, Lori Campbell, Jenny Ploeg, Candace L. Kemp, and Carolyn Rosenthal, "You're Saying Something by Giving Things to Them," *European Journal of Ageing* 10 (2013), 183.

[11] Ibid., 181–189.

[12] Charles Collier, "How Do You Start a Family Conversation about Financial Inheritance," in *Wealth of Wisdom: The Top 50 Questions Wealthy Families Ask*, eds. Tom McCullough and Keith Whitaker (United Kingdom: John Wiley & Sons 2019), 161–164.

[13] Maureen P. Keely, "Family Communication at the End of Life," *Behavioral Sciences* 7, no. 6 (2017): 1–6; Maureen P. Keeley and Mark A. Generous, "Advice from Children and Adolescents on Final Conversations with Dying Loved Ones," *Death Studies* 38, no. 5 (2014): 308–314.

[14] Glen R. Horst, "Tips for Talking with Someone Who Is Dying," The Amateur's Guide to Death and Dying, August 17, 2020, https://theamateursguide.com/tips-for-talking-with-someone-who-is-dying/; Frank Davis, "Hospice Care: Essentials of Communication While Approaching the Patient," January 2, 2021, https://hospicevalley.com/hospice-care-essentials-of-communication-while-approaching-the-patient/

[15] Horst, "Tips for Talking with Someone Who is Dying."

[16] Michael Hebb, *Let's Talk about Death (Over Dinner): An Invitation and Guide to Life's Most Important Conversation* (New York: Da Capo Press, 2018).

[17] "Let's Have Dinner and Talk about Death," Death over Dinner, https://deathoverdinner.org/

[18] Jordan Eli Soliz and Mei-Chen Lin, "Communication in Grandparent-Grandchild Relationships," in *Widening the Family Circle: New Research on Family Communication*, 2nd ed., eds. Kory Floyd and Mark T. Morman (Los Angeles: Sage, 2014), 35–50.

[19] Angie Williams and Jon F. Nussbaum, *Intergenerational Communication across the Lifespan* (Mahwah, NJ: Lawrence Erlbaum Associates, 2001).

[20] Soliz and Lin, "Communication in Grandparent-Grandchild Relationships."

[21] Ibid.

[22] Ibid.

[23] Matthew D. Deprez, "The Role of Grandparents in Shaping Faith Formation of Grandchildren: A Case Study," *Christian Education Journal* 14, no. 1 (2017): 109–127.

[24] Ibid., 122.

[25] Kara Powell, *The Sticky Faith Guide for Your Family: Over 100 Practical and Tested Ideas to Build Lasting Faith in Kids* (Grand Rapids, MI: Zondervan, 2014).

[26] Robert M. Milardo, "Family Communication among Uncles and Nephews," in *Widening the Family Circle: New Research on Family Communication*, 2nd ed., eds. Kory Floyd and Mark T. Morman (Los Angeles: Sage, 2014), 69–84; Patricia J Sotirin and Laura L Ellingson, "The 'Other' Women in Family Life: Recognizing the Significance of Aunt/Niece/Nephew Communication," in *Widening the Family Circle: New Research on Family Communication*, 2nd ed., eds. Kory Floyd and Mark T. Morman (Los Angeles: Sage, 2014), 51–68.

[27] Milardo, "Family Communication among Uncles and Nephews."

[28] See, for example, Aaron Earls, "Most Teenagers Drop Out of Church When They Become Young Adults," Lifeway Research, https://research.lifeway.com/2019/01/15/most-teenagers-drop-out-of-church-as-young-adults/; Sharion Otey, "Resolving the Shortage of Youth at Mount Moriah Baptist Church," (thesis, Liberty University, John W. Rawlings School of Divinity, 2021): 20–23, https://digitalcommons.liberty.edu/cgi/viewcontent.cgi?article=3947&context=doctoral

[29] Fuller Youth Institute, https://fulleryouthinstitute.org/

[30] Christian Smith and Melina Lundquist Denton, *Soul Searching: The Religious and Spiritual Lives of American Teenagers* (New York: Oxford University Press, 2005).

[31] Cultural Research Center, "Counterfeit Christianity: 'Moralistic Therapeutic

Deism' Most Popular Worldview in U.S. Culture," Arizona Christian University, April 27, 2021, https://www.arizonachristian.edu/2021/04/27/counterfeit-christianity-moralistic-therapeutic-deism-most-popular-worldview-in-u-s-culture/

[32] "Sticky Faith Parents: Building Lifelong Faith," Fuller Youth Institute, https://fulleryouthinstitute.org/stickyfaith/parents

[33] Richard J. Foster, *Celebration of Discipline: The Path to Spiritual Growth, Special 20th Anniversary Edition* (San Francisco: Harper, 2000).

[34] Quentin J. Schultze, "The 'God Problem' in Communication Studies," *Journal of Communication and Religion* 28, no. 1 (2005), 1.

[35] Dallas Willard, *The Spirit of the Disciplines: Understanding How God Changes Lives* (San Francisco: HarperOne, 1998).

[36] Ibid., 114.

[37] Ibid., 115.

[38] A. E. Winship, *Jukes-Edwards: A Study in Education and Heredity* (Harrisburg, PA: R. L. Myers & Co., 1900), https://www.gutenberg.org/files/15623/15623-h/15623-h.htm

[39] Ibid., chapter 1, para. 8.

[40] Ibid.

[41] Ibid.

[42] Larry Ballard, "Multigenerational Legacies—The Story of Jonathan Edwards," *Family Ministries*, July 1, 2017, https://www.ywam-fmi.org/news/multigenerational-legacies-the-story-of-jonathan-edwards/

[43] Dutch Sheets, *An Appeal to Heaven: What Would Happen If We Did It Again* (Dallas, TX: Dutch Sheets Ministries, 2015).

[44] Ibid., 8.

[45] Ibid., 6.

[46] Neil T. Anderson, *The Bondage Breaker: Overcoming *Negative Thoughts *Irrational Feelings *Habitual Sins* (Eugene, OR: Harvest House Publishers, 2019).

[47] Francis MacNutt, *Deliverance from Evil Spirits: A Practical Manual* (Grand Rapids, MI: Chosen Books, 2009).

[48] Robert Henderson, *Operating In the Courts of Heaven: Granting God the Legal Rights to Fulfill His Passion and Answer Our Prayers* (Shippensburg, PA: Destiny Image Publishers, 2021).

[49] Sylvia Gunter and Arthur A. Burk, *Blessing Your Spirit: With the Blessings of Your Father and the Names of God* (Columbus, MS: Father's Business Publishing, 2006).

[50] Anna C. Muriel, Cynthia W. Moore, Marguerite Beiser, Elyse R. Park, Christopher T. Lim, and Paula Rauch, "What Do Surviving Children Wish for from A Dying Parent?: A Qualitative Exploration," *Death Studies* 44, no. 5 (2020): 319–327.

[51] Ibid., 322.

[52] Ibid., 324.

Scripture Index

Subject Index

conflict resolution strategies, helping
navigate solvable conflict, 81
conflicts, types of, 212
conformity orientation, 233, 234
confrontative control, 234
congenial siblings, 223
connection
creating meaningful, 73
establishing points of, 255
experiencing within family through
Christ, 41
intimacy requiring, 213
listening as a lifestyle for, 63–65
needed with God himself, 177
push toward holistic, 214
rituals, 59–73, 213
consensual (high conformity, high
conversation) family type, 233
consensual and pluralistic families,
benefiting children the most, 234
consequences, 260
consistency, providing stability and
predictability, 260
constraint commitment, 173
consummate love, 189
consummation, of marriage, 15
contemplation, as a strategy for
resilience-building, 123
contempt, 83, 84
content level, of conflict, 81–82
continuous improvement, disposition
of, 229
contractualism, 170
contradictions, 51
control
decreasing as children and youth age,
247
as a hidden issue, 79
as a social need, 152
conventionality-uniqueness, external
contradiction, 51
convergence communication pattern, 254
conversation orientation, 233, 234
conversations
categories of for couples, 165
establishing parameters for hard,
75–93
serving as teachable moments, 122

Coontz, Stephanie, 33–34
cooperative colleagues, associated with a
"good divorce," 206
coordination, of household chores,
132–33
co-parenting behaviors, parents engaging
in cooperative, 205–6
corporal punishment, 248, 251
corporate spiritual disciplines, 276
correction, framing in the affirmative,
261
cosmic accidents, humanity as the result
of for atheists, 26
cost-benefit analysis, of maintenance
behaviors, 66
countries, legalizing gay marriages, 31
couple date night, 63
couples
different views of marriage, 162
diverging from "happily ever after," 202
engaging in honest self-reflection, 165
with enough money for daily demands,
138
gradually growing apart, 203
courtship, 150, 151, 160, 168
covenant, marriage as, 168, 169–71
covenantal relationships, principles of,
210
covenantalism, 170
CPA. See Character, Performance, and
Appearance (CPA)
CPM (Communication Privacy
Management Theory), 141–42
creation, 8
act of the biblical grand narrative, 41
creativity, 229
critical paradigm, 44, 45
critical perspective, for individuals or
groups, 44
critical theorists, 44
criticism, 83
cross of Jesus Christ, 7, 8
cross-cultural applicability, of the
triangular theory of love, 188
Crouch, Andy, 142
cultural context, socializing children
within, 60

discovery, intimacy requiring, 213
discussion forgiveness-granting strategy, 107
discussion-based mediations, 141
disgust, contempt conveying, 84
Disillusionment Model, 202
disorganized attachment style, 230
dissatisfied couples, 196
dissolved duos, not associated with "good divorce," 206
distributive communication, as verbally aggressive responses, 99
diversion, 248
diversity, families and, 38
diversity and pluralism, occurring throughout life, 53–54
Divine forgiveness, 102
Divine intervention, family discussions on, 123
Divine love, as basis for all Christian love, 190
Divine Trinity, as a system, 48
division of labor, 134
divorce, 199–209
  biblically based reasons for, 208
  Christian perspective on remarriage and, 207–9
  economic disadvantage perspective of, 205
  effects of, 203–5
  never intended by God, 6
  predicting, 201–3
  presenting legal grounds for, 200
  rates of, 35–36, 171–72, 199–201
  statistics on, 199–200
  time frame for early, 203
  widespread practice of, 209
Divorce and Remarriage: Four Christian Views (Gigy and Kelly), 207
divorced adults, characteristics of, 203–4
divorced couples, types of, 203
"doing life together," 129, 139, 143
domestic abuse victims, wanting to see the best in their abuser, 198
domestic or intimate partner violence, free services for, 199
Double ABC-X Model, 114–15

"doubling up," as a living arrangement for children, 221
dread, deep-rooted sense of, 88
"dream detectives," becoming, 212
dreams, 88, 140
"drug talks," 236, 237
duality of nature, in sexes, 175
duty sex, 180
dynamic equilibrium, sustaining in a given relationship, 66

eating, nutrition as the purpose of, 177
economic disadvantage perspective, of divorce, 205
economic exchange metaphor, 158–59
economic well-being, divorce associated with declines in, 203
economics, decline in marriage rates and, 35
economists, explaining marriage in terms of free market forces, 157–58
education
  attainment affecting marriage rates, 35
  prominent in the Edwards family line, 278
  same level of predicting partnering, 162
  women with more having lower fertility rates, 36
Edwards, Jonathan, family line of, 278–79
Edwards, Sarah, 278
egalitarian versus non-egalitarian partners, 134
Egbert, Nichole, 70
Elijah, 124
emergencies, impacting the budget, 140
emerging adulthood, characteristics of, 258
Emerging Stress Model, 202
emotional coaching, 254–56
emotional connection, intimacy as, 187
"emotional currency," families having, 120
emotional forgiveness, 106
emotional or verbal abuse, signs of, 198
emotional reserve, building, 120
emotions, 255–56
empathy, 82, 255

parental modeling, across spiritual practical domains, 241–63

parent-child conversations, important, 236–38

parent-child interaction theories, 229–35

parent-child power structure, 246

parent-child relationships, 15, 224

parenting

  associated with lower levels of marital happiness, 222

  basic skills, 257

  classifying practices, 256

  interventions, 257

  modeling for communication with children, 228

  versus mothering and fathering, 243–45

  post-divorce styles, 206

  styles of, 234–35

  variety of specific tactics, 248

  in ways that reflect and honor God, 219–39

Parenting with Love and Logic (Cline and Fay), 260

parents

  in an arranged marriage, 161

  children with, 222–23

  continuing to talk about deceased, 283

  in control of their own emotions when spanking, 252

  disciplining their children, 242

  exerting dominance over children, 253

  having authority in an open relationship, 235

  helping children with decisions on drug use, 236

  influence on their grandchildren and subsequent generations, 283

  as an influence throughout childhood and early adolescence, 236

  instructed regarding children in the Shema of Deuteronomy, 235

  interactions with firstborn children as different, 226

  of Jesus dedicated him to the Lord, 219

  mediating children's smartphone use, 141

  modeling behaviors and setting expectations for their children, 253

  modeling routines supporting individual disciplines of study and prayer, 277

  near absolute authority over infants, 246

  needing to be involved in their children's lives, 255

  positive, overlapping qualities of, 235

  putting their children's needs above their own, 152

  responsible for children, 28–29

  sharing expressive and warm relationships, 236

  subcontracting aspects of education but are ultimately responsible, 29

  treating subsequent children differently, 226

  wielding influence and control with strategies or parenting practices, 248

parent-teacher associations, participating in, 29

partners

  forgiveness of, 102–3

  multiple creating an attachment to multiple people, 179

  withdrawing from social networks, 164

passion, 186–87

passive responses, to hurtful messages, 98

Passover Seder, as a ritual, 60

pastor in Seattle, conversion to Christianity, 273

pathology, sexual attacking God's design for marriage, 179

pathways, to marriage, 149–68

patterned interactions, as family rituals, 62

patterns, as a characteristic of systems theory, 46–47

Patterson, Joan, 114

Patton, Paul, 140

Paul

  on Abraham's sons, 16

  on Athens's Mars Hill, 44–45

  on being adopted into God's family, 18

www.ingramcontent.com/pod-product-compliance
Lightning Source LLC
Chambersburg PA
CBHW021700120626
46545CB00004B/1327